Garden Plants
for Everyone

Garden Plants for Everyone

Adrian Bloom · Alan Bloom

Jack Harkness · Royton E. Heath

Arthur Hellyer · Frances Perry

Percy Thrower

Dennis Woodland

Hamlyn

London · New York · Sydney · Toronto

Published by The Hamlyn Publishing Group Limited
London . New York . Sydney . Toronto
Astronaut House, Feltham, Middlesex, England

First published in 1975 under the title
"The Collingridge Guide to Garden Plants in Colour"
by The Hamlyn Publishing Group Limited.

Phototypeset in England by Tameside Filmsetting Ltd in 9 on 11 Times

Printed in Italy

ISBN 0 600 30562 7

Acknowledgements

Line and tone illustrations by The Hayward Art Group.
Line drawings on pages 14, 117, 119, 210, 211, 213, 188 (left) by Colin Gray.

Photographs
Pat Brindley 22 (top), 33, 36, 63, 68, 104, 135, 138, 158, 161, 168, 173, 179, 182, 197,
226, 235, 238.
The Hamlyn Publishing Group 182.
Jack Harkness 55.
Royton E. Heath 208, 218, 223.
Robert Pearson 196.
The Harry Smith Horticultural Photographic Collection title page, 6, 10, 18, 22
(below), 27, 30, 31, 44, 65, 92, 101, 122, 131, 186, 200, 214, 230, 239, 243.
Michael Warren 50–1, 88, 96, 112, 126, 143, 150, 154, 204.
Dennis Woodland 84.

The editor would like to acknowledge the Forestry Commission's Arboriculture
Research Note 40/82 which was used as reference for the illustrations on page 71.

Contents

Introduction

To walk into a well-stocked nursery or garden centre these days, as an enthusiastic gardener, is perhaps to be put in the position of a small boy given a handful of money and let loose in a sweet shop to help himself. The choice is wide, so wide it may become bewildering.

A similar sense of bewilderment may also be felt when the nurserymen's and seedsmen's catalogues drop through the letterbox during the months of winter. Then, the keen gardener settles down in an armchair to plan his future planting or new additions to his garden only to be overwhelmed yet again by the sheer number of plants available.

Such an enormous range has taken time to accumulate; many plants, in fact, have been lost to cultivation over past decades, either because they may have been superceded by improved cultivars with showier blooms or a hardier constitution, or have simply gone out of fashion. For gardening has, over the centuries, been as much subject to whim and fancy as anything else; just think of the mania for tulips during the middle of the 17th century and the amazingly high prices at which the bulbs changed hands.

However the enthusiasms of previous generations of garden owners have also been important factors in determining the range of plants we now enjoy. This is mainly because the ever-increasing demand for new plants for the garden was met by generations of plant hunters who have, often at risk of life and limb, bought back exotic species from all over the world.

At first, plant hunting was usually incidental to the purpose of foreign travel. The Crusaders were some of the earliest people to bring back small plants and seeds from strange blooms they found in the lands of the infidel. Later in the 15th and 16th centuries, diplomats and explorers discovered plant curiosities and sent them home to their native lands. These aroused the interest of botanists and wealthy men of taste, and so it was that the true plant hunters set out expressly in search of new material.

Many of the names of these intrepid travellers have since become famous and have been commemorated by the plant they discovered. For example, John Tradescant, gardener to Charles I, visited Russia and brought back a number of plants he found growing wild. His son was also a plant collector and gardener and was responsible for introducing such plants as the Occidental Plane and the Tulip Tree. That swashbuckling character William Dampier, seaman and buccaneer, travelled round the world, visiting South America, New Guinea and Australia. He had a keen interest in natural history and brought back a number of plants from his voyages.

From then onwards the number of plant-hunting missions steadily increased, sponsored by wealthy aristocrats, nurseries and the Royal Botanic Gardens at Kew.

Until his death in 1820, the premier driving force at Kew was Sir Joseph Banks. Then, after a lull of twenty-one years, Sir William Hooker was appointed the first Director of the Royal Botanic Gardens. It was under the

OPPOSITE: A mixed border in July with *Genista cinerea.* *Eremurus bungei* and *Origanum vulgare* 'Aureum', the Golden-leaved Oregano

direction of Hooker and his son Joseph, who followed in his father's footsteps, that many more expeditions were organised. It was these three men that established the formidable reputation Kew has continued to have up to this day as a repository for plant material which is second to none in the world.

However it was The Royal Horticultural Society, established in 1804, which sponsored David Douglas, one of the most famous and certainly one of the most adventurous of plant hunters. Douglas went to the New World from where he sent back numerous plants of all types including many species of handsome conifers, mostly from North America, that have now become very much a part of our landscape.

One of the problems of the plant collector was the high mortality rate of plants in transit. Until the advent of Dr Nathaniel Ward's case in 1833, only a very small proportion of the plants loaded were still alive when anxious nurserymen awaited the unloading at the home port. Dr Ward discovered that small ferns growing in a sealed glass container continued to flourish without additional water for several years. He had some special glazed cases built and in these he transported plants across the world. He found that with only an occasional watering, most tender plants successfully survived long and hazardous journeys in the way.

At this point the plant hunter was relieved of responsibility; those plants still alive and the seed that had been collected were given over to the nurserymen and to the botanic and physic gardens who took on the rather daunting task of raising these new discoveries.

The production of plants from seed and by grafting, or by other forms of vegetative propagation used in commerce, has a long history. But the establishment of commercial nurseries really began to flourish during the 17th century. Seedsmen, too, began to produce catalogues and plant lists at about this time.

The most famous of these early nurseries was the Brompton Nursery in Kensington. This reached the height of its reputation under George London and Henry Wise during the reign of Queen Anne. As more nurseries sprang up, so competition increased. In order to offer a wider range of plants to customers, experiments in hybridization increased and any attractive sport was eagerly taken note of and increased by vegetative propagation. The demand and the quest for something new seemed insatiable.

So it was that the enthusiastic gentlemen gardeners and plantsmen were able to obtain and cultivate this ever-increasing range of plant material. Stove houses, conservatories and orangeries were built and it was in these buildings that many of the new introductions were nurtured by their gardening staff. A number of, what we know today as quite hardy plants, were originally cossetted in stove conditions.

Another influence that the nurserymen had on the buying public – aristocratic though it was during the 18th century – was the launching of a number of magazines. The popular gardening press had made its beginnings and duly increased in strength during the 19th century. William Curtis launched his *Botanical Magazine* in 1787 which is still being published today and from then on followed a number of periodicals. J. C. Loudon started *The Gardener's Magazine* in 1826. This journal and his many books were aimed at the increasingly affluent middle classes, whose interest in gardening and plants was constantly growing. The catalogues of the seed firms also became more alluring in appearance and the names we know so well today – Sutton, Thompson and Morgan, and Carters – became established.

The search for new plants continues today, increasingly by the work of the seedsman, nurseryman and plant breeder rather than the plant hunter. Competition is still rife as each year, in the catalogues and at the horticultural shows, new plants are featured. Although nowadays we may feel the world holds few secrets, plant gathering expeditions continue to take place. New forms are still being discovered in remote regions and accounts of these trips make exciting reading and enthralling television documentaries.

This extremely brief account of how the range and diversity of garden plants has increased over the centuries expresses in some small way our obligation to generations of enterprising men, many of them exceedingly brave, who have been involved in their production and continued existence.

What we would like to think is that *Garden Plants for Everyone* will become your passport to garden enjoyment, that it will be a book you will turn to without hesitation every time you are making up an order for a nursery or are treating yourself to a spending spree at your local garden centre. A book, too, which you will get down off the shelf whenever some new decorative garden feature is planned – for inspiration and a comforting helping hand.

For it is a helping hand which we all need in gardening. The subject's so vast that nobody can claim to be an absolute master of all its highways and byways. Therein lies its fascination. You can garden for pleasure for a lifetime, and still, in all humility, recognize that you don't know the half of it.

As a reference book this has everything to commend it – it is a survey of plants from the four corners of the world, as well as from the plant breeders' skilful hands and from gardens, for it should not be forgotten that many a good plant has arisen naturally in this way. All the plants described can bring to your garden increased beauty and interest. And that, after all, is what decorative gardening is all about.

Shrubs and Climbers

ARTHUR HELLYER

American gardeners, who are very good at inventing names that are highly descriptive, often refer to the trees and shrubs used in gardens as foundation planting. This expresses perfectly one of the major roles which these plants perform in providing the permanent framework into which other plants with a shorter life or a greater need for renewal can be fitted. Because they are the foundation of the whole planting scheme, one grasps immediately why they must be considered with the greatest care and why also, as a rule, this must be done at the beginning of every new planting scheme or, if this is quite impossible, a very clear picture of where these foundation plants are to go must be in mind before anything else is put in.

However, though this foundation role is immensely important, it is not the only part that shrubs have to play in the garden. They provide some of the shade and shelter that can be so much appreciated by other plants, they assist in preserving privacy and they can also cut out much of the noise of the outside world. Their roots can be very valuable in binding the soil on steep slopes or in other places subject to erosion, though it must not be overlooked that the roots of some species can be so numerous, so near to the surface and so hungry that they can make life difficult for close neighbours.

Some shrubs are so beautiful or striking in shape that they are best planted individually so that they can be seen from all sides. They may then become important focal points or accents in the garden design.

Shrubs can be divided into evergreen and deciduous kinds, the former retaining leaf cover throughout the year, the latter dropping all their leaves each autumn and producing a new flush of growth the following spring. Both types have their value and the proportions in which they are used need to be considered carefully.

Evergreens tend to dominate in winter when their solid shapes stand out conspicuously amid the tracery of bare branches of deciduous trees and shrubs, and at this season they provide much of the shelter, which can be very important for plants growing close to them. However, deciduous shrubs offer the advantages of constantly changing patterns, textures and colours which can be entrancing. It is broadly true to say that a garden with too many evergreens can be heavy and dull and that a garden with too many deciduous trees and shrubs can seem bare and bleak for five or six months each year. The ideal is one in which there are constantly changing patterns with new combinations of colour and form emerging all the time and never a dull moment from January to December.

Into this scheme of permanent planting, perennial or shrubby climbers fit perfectly. They too may be evergreen or deciduous, and they too are there all the time, though it is fair to observe that deciduous climbers in general have considerably less to offer in winter than deciduous trees and shrubs since most of them are then reduced to a more or less meaningless tangle of growth and may even, in some cases, need to be cut back almost to ground level. Yet by summer-time these same plants can have shot up to 4.6 or 6 m (15 or 20 ft) and be draping over walls, screens, buildings and even trees and shrubs with their leaves and flowers.

If one thinks of garden planting in terms of interior decor (and for very small gardens it is by no means an inappropriate comparison), shrubs may be regarded as major objects of furniture and climbers as wall coverings, curtains

OPPOSITE: The glorious autumn colour of *Parthenocissus tricuspidata* 'Veitchii'

and other drapes. Where the comparison breaks down is that a room remains much the same at all seasons, whereas a garden is in a state of constant change which is one reason why making a garden and then living with it can be so very exciting and satisfying.

This raises another point that must be carefully considered. Shrubs may continue to increase in size for many years. If they are planted sufficiently close to give a well-furnished appearance almost from the start, they are certain to be over-crowded after a few years, yet if they are spaced at the outset to accommodate their ultimate proportions, the garden may well appear thin and poorly balanced for a long time.

There are several ways in which these difficulties may be overcome. One is deliberately to overplant at the beginning in such a way that there can be a progressive thinning out of plants over the years without materially upsetting the balance. Another is to use some swift-growing shrubs to give a quick effect with the knowledge that they will be too big, and so will have to be removed, after a few years, and at the same time to plant slower-growing kinds which will be ready to take over when that time arrives. Yet a third way is to plant the trees and shrubs thinly and to fill in during the early years with herbaceous and bedding plants which by their nature must be renewed frequently. All three methods have their merits and drawbacks and which is chosen must depend upon personal preference and circumstances.

Preparation of the soil

Shrubs and climbers are always planted for years and often for permanency so the preparation of the ground should be thorough. In particular, difficult weeds such as nettle, docks, ground elder, couch grass and bindweed should be removed, for though it is possible to deal with these later on with herbicides, it is much more time consuming and expensive then than making a clean sweep at the outset. If the sites for the shrubs are dug about 45 cm (18 in) deep, it will be possible to pick out most of the weed roots, but to make doubly sure the weeds can be treated with

a suitable herbicide a few weeks before digging commences, so that they are already more or less dead when cultivation starts. If you do choose this course, be sure to use a herbicide with a wide spectrum of effectiveness, since some kinds only kill weeds of a particular type, and also one that leaves no harmful residues in the soil. Paraquat and glyphosate are both very suitable for this purpose, but since they operate through the leaves they are most effective in fairly warm, sunny weather when growth is active.

If well-rotted manure or garden compost is available, this can be mixed with the soil while it is being prepared at the rate of 2.7 to 3.3 kg per m^2 (5 to 6 lb per sq yd). Peat at 1 to 2 kg per m^2 (2 to 4 lb per sq yd) will improve the texture of both heavy and light soils, and bonemeal (applied while wearing gloves) at 136 g per m^2 (4 oz per sq yd) will provide a steady source of plant food for the first few months.

Selection of plants

Plants may be sold as "bare root", "balled" or "container grown". Bare root means that they are lifted from a nursery bed and that all, or most, of the soil adhering to the roots is shaken off so that the plants are as light as possible to transport. Transplanting bare root can be done only in autumn and winter when plants are dormant or nearly so. It is the cheapest way of buying plants, but many kinds, particularly evergreens, cannot be transplanted safely in this way, even at the most favourable periods.

Balled plants are also lifted from nursery beds but with as much soil as practicable and this soil is then held around the roots with hessian or polythene so that it does not fall off during transplantation. Balled plants weigh a great deal more than bare root plants and so cost more to transport, but provided the work of balling and replanting is well done they have a better chance of survival. The planting season is a little more extended, balled evergreens often being moved in early spring or early autumn.

Container-grown plants are those that

are really well established in pots, polythene bags or anything else which will ensure that all the roots and the soil around them can be transported and planted with the minimum of disturbance. Well-grown container plants can be put in at any time of the year when the soil is in good working condition, but they weigh more and usually cost more than comparable bare-root or balled plants. Most of the shrubs and climbers offered for sale in garden centres are container grown and this is an ideal method for the cash-and-carry trade. Even for mail order many climbing plants are pot grown since some do not transplant well in any other way, and it is a method used for many other plants that resent root breakage, such as brooms, romneya and perowskia.

Some plants refuse to grow in alkaline soils unless regularly fed with iron and manganese in specially prepared (chelated or sequestrated) forms. Rhododendrons and azaleas are two of the most important groups of plants in this category and unless one is prepared to make special acid soil beds for them it is really unwise to attempt to grow them on soils containing much chalk or limestone. Other lime-hating plants are mentioned in the individual notes on plants.

Planting

If container-grown or balled plants are obtained, it is only necessary to prepare a hole just a little larger than the container and slip the plant into this with as little root disturbance as possible, any space remaining being filled with a mixture of peat and well broken down soil. Pot-grown plants can usually be tapped out quite safely by turning them upside down and rapping the rim of the pot sharply on something firm, such as the handle of a spade thrust well into the soil. Of course the plant itself must be carefully held while this is done so that it does not fall to the ground and possibly snap off. In the case of balled plants and those grown in polythene bags, the covering material can usually be cut and then stripped off with the plant on the edge of, or actually in, the hole it is to occupy. But whatever the precise method used, the covering must

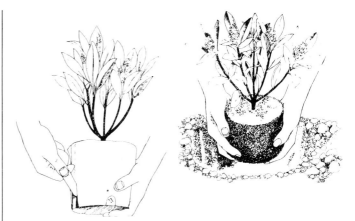

come off unless it is only of paper or compressed peat or some other substance that will rot away in the soil.

With bare-root plants a little more thought and care are necessary. The hole made must be large enough to ensure that there is space for all the roots to be naturally disposed, with room at the top for a covering of 2.5 or 5 cm (1 or 2 in) of soil over the uppermost roots. Another way to determine depth is to look for the dark soil mark on the stem or stems, indicating where the soil came to in the nursery bed, and to replant so that this is just beneath the surface. With bare-root plants it is also necessary to work soil around and between the roots and to make this easy it often pays to prepare in advance a planting mixture of well-broken soil mixed with about a third its bulk of peat and containing a sprinkling of bonemeal.

Whatever type of plant is being used, once the soil has been returned around and over the roots it should be made thoroughly firm by pressing all round with the foot, after which a little loose soil or peat can be scattered over the soil to leave everything tidy.

Shelter

Some shrubs, particularly evergreens, may require some shelter from wind or sun for a few months after planting until they are well established and able to look after themselves. Large plastic bags of the type used for fertilizers, composts and peat make excellent shelters if slit top and bottom and then slipped over the shrub and held open with three or four canes.

Remove the container and position the plant in the previously-prepared hole. This should be slightly larger than the rootball. Ensure that the soil in the container is moist and that the plant is well firmed

Shrubs can be heeled in a shallow trench until conditions are suitable for planting

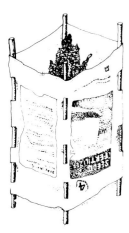

A plastic fertilizer bag supported by canes will provide shelter for a newly planted shrub

Screens of hessian or fine mesh nylon netting can be made by wrapping the material around stakes and fastening it securely. Alternatively quite effective temporary shelter can be given by thrusting evergreen boughs into the soil around the newly planted shrubs.

Pruning

Not many shrubs require pruning immediately after planting, though it always pays to cut out damaged stems or any that appear so badly placed as to upset the balance of the specimen. Some hedge shrubs, notably privet and lonicera, will repay immediate shortening to ensure that they branch freely right from the base, but it is not until later years that pruning becomes a serious problem.

Basically pruning has four aims: the first to prevent plants from growing too large; the second to get rid of diseased or decrepit growth; the third to improve the natural appearance of the plant by removing badly placed or overcrowded stems and the fourth to improve the quality of the flowers or leaves.

Often the steps taken to achieve one of these ends also look after some of the others as well. Thus it is always wise to start by removing obviously diseased, damaged or weak growth, because when this has been done the specimen may look very different and require little further pruning. If it does appear that something more is needed, thinning out over-crowded, crossing branches may put things right.

A few shrubs, particularly those that flower in summer such as the purple buddleia, the cultivars of *Hydrangea paniculata*, fuchsias and caryopteris, can be cut hard back each spring with considerable benefit to the quality of their flowers and without destroying their natural habit. Some spring and early summer-flowering kinds, such as for-sythia, weigela, philadelphus and cytisus, can have most of their flowering growth removed immediately the flowers fade, and this can be a convenient way of restricting their size and improving the quality of their flowers at one and the same time. Details are given in the list which follows.

Selected Shrubs and Climbers

Acer

Most species are trees but some cultivars of *Acer palmatum*, the Japanese Maple, are shrubby and very useful for planting as isolated specimens because of their usually picturesque shape and attractive foliage. Specially recommended are the 'Dissectum' cultivars with deeply divided almost fernlike leaves, green in 'Dissectum' itself, beetroot red in 'Dissectum Atropurpureum', yellowish in 'Dissectum Flavescens' and bronzy in 'Dissectum Ornatum'. These all grow 1.5 or 1.8 m (5 or 6 ft) high and maybe more in diameter. All forms of *A. palmatum* like soil that is fairly moist in spring and summer but not wet in winter when the bushes are leafless. Pruning is undesirable, except to remove any badly placed stems, which can be done in winter.

Actinidia

Two kinds are grown, both twiners but very different in appearance. *Actinidia chinensis* is very vigorous, capable of covering a whole outbuilding or a large wall with its red-haired stems and large heart-shaped leaves. Its clusters of creamy flowers are followed by edible, gooseberry-like fruits, and since it comes from China it is sometimes called the Chinese Gooseberry. It is as a tropical looking, yet quite hardy, foliage plant that it is most valued. *A. kolomikta* is much less vigorous and more fussy, needing good soil and a sheltered place and it is valued for its green, cream and pink leaves. These colours are best developed when the plant is grown against a warm sunny wall. Both kinds lose their leaves in winter, and both can be pruned by shortening side growths to about 15 cm (6 in) in summer and taking out the tips of any stems that threaten to grow too far.

Aucuba

The kind cultivated is *Aucuba japonica*, a vigorous evergreen with large, shining green, laurel-like leaves. It is often used as a hedge or screen plant because of its dense growth in almost any soil and place. But there are several handsome forms which can be used in more decorative ways, notably 'Crotonifolia', 1.8 to 2.4 m (6 to 8 ft) high, with leaves heavily splashed with yellow, and 'Nana Rotundifolia', only 60 to 90 cm (2 to 3 ft) high, a female plant which will produce good crops of scarlet berries if planted near a male such as 'Crassifolia'; a cultivar with extra large green leaves, 'Sulphurea' has green leaves with a broad margin of yellow. All aucubas can be pruned hard in spring or can be trimmed more lightly at any time during the summer, though with fruiting bushes it is best to leave this until after the berries are set when care can be taken not to cut them off.

Azalea

From a botanical standpoint all azaleas are rhododendrons, but in nursery catalogues they are usually listed separately. Some cultivars are evergreen and some deciduous, and these differ greatly in appearance. The evergreens mostly have small leaves and a rather twiggy, densely-branched habit and small- to medium-sized flowers in shades of pink and lavender to scarlet and crimson, plus white, whereas the deciduous azaleas have larger leaves, often turning crimson in autumn, a more open habit and larger flowers in shades of yellow, orange, coppery red, crimson, pink and white. The flowers of some deciduous kinds, particularly the common yellow, are spicily scented.

All flower in spring or early summer and grow best in lime-free, moderately acid soils and half-shaded places, but the deciduous kinds will also grow well in full sun provided the soil is not dry. It pays to work in plenty of peat of leafmould before planting and to topdress with either or both each spring. Pruning is usually undesirable, but badly placed branches can be cut out in spring, immediately after flowering.

Berberis

This is one of the big families of shrubs, containing both deciduous and evergreen species, the former grown mainly for their heavy crops of small scarlet or crimson berries, the latter for their yellow flowers and attractive foliage. Most are very spiny, which makes them suitable for use as outer protective hedges or screens, and most are also very hardy and easy to grow in almost any soil.

Specially recommended deciduous kinds are 'Buccaneer', 1.2 to 1.8 m (4 to 6 ft), red berries; *B. thunbergii* 'Atropurpurea' 1.5 to 2.1 m (5 to 7 ft), beetroot-purple leaves; *B.t.* 'Rose Glow' with pink and purple leaves; and if there is room for a really big bush, *B. jamesiana* 2.4 to 3 m (8 to 10 ft), with arching, stems and berries which change from coral red to crimson.

Fine evergreen kinds are *Berberis darwinii*, 2.4 to 3 m (8 to 10 ft), with small holly-like leaves and orange flowers in spring, followed by grape-purple berries; *B. × stenophylla*, 2.4 to 3 m (8 to 10 ft), with arching stems wreathed in spring in sweet-scented, yellow flowers, and *B. verruculosa*, which has much the effect of *darwinii* reduced to half its size. There are also dwarf forms of *Berberis × stenophylla*, such as 'Corallina Compacta', red buds opening to yellow flowers, and 'Gracilis', yellow, which can be very useful in small gardens.

The dense growth of most barberries tends to kill the stems beneath and so dead wood needs to be cut out in winter, and at the same time unwanted or overgrown stems of deciduous kinds can be removed. Pruning of evergreen kinds is best done after flowering.

Buddleia

Most familiar are the numerous cultivars of *Buddleia davidii*, a normally rather tall, shuttlecock-shaped shrub with small, honey-scented flowers packed into conical spikes in late summer. Of this fine shrub there are lavender, purple, deep blue and white cultivars. There are also other good species that are quite different in appearance, such as *B. alternifolia*, a big shrub with long, slender, arching stems wreathed in early summer with lavender-blue flowers, and *B. globosa*, open and rather gaunt in habit, with orange flowers in globose clusters which suggested its common name, Orange Ball

Berberis darwinii has blue-black fruits

Prune *Buddleia davidii* in spring

Tree. There is a hybrid between this and *B. davidii*, named *B. × weyeriana*, but this is variable in colour, basically orange suffused with purple but becoming dirty mauve in some plants. So it should be selected when in bloom.

All buddleias thrive on chalk and limestone soils and grow well wherever the soil is well drained and the situation warm and sunny. All cultivers of *B. davidii* can be cut back hard early each spring if desired, which somewhat reduces their size, though they can still reach 2.4 m (8 ft) in a season, and this improves the size of the flower spikes. *B. alternifolia* is best pruned in summer immediately after flowering, when the old flowering stems can be cut back to side shoots. With *B. globosa* it is usually sufficient to cut out weak and dead growth in early spring, but if bushes are too big they can be cut back, though with loss of flower that year.

Buxus

This is the Common Box or Boxwood, an evergreen that is much used for making topiary specimens and also for forming small hedges and the elaborate clipped patterns in knots and parterres. Its little rounded leaves have a pungent scent which some people like and others find disagreeable. There are numerous forms of *Buxus sempervirens*, of which the most

useful are 'Gold Tip', young leaves yellowish; 'Handsworthensis', a sturdy cultivar specially recommended for hedges; 'Elegantissima', small leaves edged with white and 'Suffruticosa', the Edging Box, a dwarf form that has become scarce, but is particularly good for clipping to a maximum height of 45 cm (18 in).

All varieties grow well in most soils, including chalk. They can be clipped at any time in summer, but any hard pruning necessary is best done in spring.

Callicarpa

Not many shrubs have violet or lilac-blue berries, but callicarpas have, and this is their special contribution to the garden. They are not the hardiest of plants and should be given a warm, sunny place in good fertile soil. The best kind is *Callicarpa bodinieri*, or the form of it know as *giraldii*, both of which usually grow 1.5 or 1.8 m (5 or 6 ft) high, though in favourable places they can be taller. As plants age some of the older or less well-placed stems can be cut out annually in early spring.

Camellia

Handsome evergreen foliage and abundant flowers make the camellia a valuable garden shrub wherever conditions are suitable. It requires an acid or neutral soil, unless it is regularly fed with specially prepared iron and manganese, and, although fairly hardy, its flowers are produced so early in the year that these are subject to severe damage by frost unless planted in fairly sheltered places. They succeed well in thin woodland, especially in the south and west, and also do well in many town gardens since they do not mind shade and benefit from the slight extra warmth that comes from many closely packed buildings.

Two races are of major importance, one composed of the almost innumerable cultivars of *Camellia japonica*, the other of hybrids between this species and *C. saluenensis*. The colour range is similar in both races from white and palest pink to scarlet and crimson, and flowers may be single, semi-double or fully double.

Camellias transplant easily and it is

best to buy them in flower so that the colours and flower shapes that appeal most to the purchaser can be selected. Most will make big bushes in time, but are fairly slow growing. Regular pruning is undesirable, but bushes can be cut hard back in spring after flowering, though with loss of flower the following year. A few misplaced or overlong branches can be removed without this danger and if this is done while the bushes are in bloom these branches may be useful for decoration indoors.

Campsis

This is the botanical name of the trumpet vines, rambling or self-clinging climbers with clusters of trumpet-shaped flowers in late summer or early autumn. In warm, sunny, sheltered places they can be spectacular, but they are unsuitable for cold gardens, partly because much growth may be killed by frost, but even more because flower buds may form so late in the season that they have no chance to open. The best place for them is against a wall facing south or west. Each spring most of the old stems should be cut out or shortened as the best flowers are borne on young growth.

The hardiest and most self-clinging kind is *Campsis radicans*, with orange-scarlet flowers. *C. grandiflora* has larger orange and red flowers but is only partially self-clinging and this is also true of 'Madame Galen', the fine salmon-red hybrid between these two species.

Carpenteria

There is only one species, *Carpenteria californica*, a lovely but slightly tender evergreen for a warm, sunny, sheltered place in fertile, well-drained soil. It grows 1.5 or 1.8 m (5 or 6 ft) high and produces its white flowers, each with a golden boss of anthers in the centre, in July. Little pruning is necessary, but worn-out stems that are producing little new growth can be cut out in spring.

Caryopteris

This sun-loving shrub is often killed almost to ground level in winter, but sprouts up again strongly in the spring to produce 60-cm (2-ft) stems set with small

greyish leaves and producing, in late summer and early autumn, rather fluffy-looking clusters of lavender-blue flowers. The best kind to plant is a hybrid named *Caryopteris × clandonensis*, and of this there are several forms with extra deep blue flowers, such as 'Ferndown' and 'Kew Blue'. All can be pruned to within a few centimetres of ground level early each spring and do best in well-drained soils.

Ceanothus

There are both deciduous and evergreen species and they require different treatment in the garden. Most of the evergreen kinds flower in spring and many are best grown against sunny walls as they are not fully hardy. If they are pruned at all it should be immediately after flowering when unwanted stems can be cut out and side shoots shortened a little. By contrast the most useful deciduous types flower in late summer and early autumn and can, with advantage, be pruned hard each spring when they will make long stems terminated by sprays of the typical thimble-shaped clusters of small flowers. All like good, well-drained soil and a warm, sunny position.

Ceanothus impressus, 1.8 m (6 ft) high and wide, with deep blue flowers and a densely branched habit, and *C. thyrsiflorus*, with light blue flowers, are two of the hardiest evergreen kinds. *C. thysiflorus* is variable in habit, tall with arching growths in the cultivar 'Cascade', but making low, wide-spreading mounds of growth in the variety *C.t. repens*. Typical deciduous cultivars are 'Gloire de Versailles', light blue; 'Topaz', deep blue, and 'Perle Rose', rose pink.

Chaenomeles

These shrubs are closely related to quince (cydonia), and gardeners often refer to them as Japanese quinces or japonicas. They are deciduous with apple-like blossom, scarlet, crimson, pink or white, according to cultivar, produced in late winter or early spring, usually followed by large, hard, fragrant fruits which can be used to flavour apple pies and make quince preserves. Grown naturally the various cultivars of chaenomeles make densely branched, spiny bushes, but they

Genista hispanica (left) and *Ceanothus thyrsiflorus repens* (right)

are often trained against walls, when they should be pruned after flowering to get rid of any stems that cannot conveniently be tied in and to shorten forward-pointing side growths to a few centimetres so that everything is tidy. Bushes in the open need not be pruned unless they need to be reduced in size or density.

All kinds are very hardy and easy to grow in almost any soil, in sun or semi-shade. There are two good species, *Chaenomeles japonica*, 60 to 90 cm (2 to 3 ft) high, and *C. speciosa*, 1.8 to 3 m (6 to 10 ft) high, and a hybrid between them named *C. × superba*, 1.2 to 2.4 m (4 to 8 ft) high. Good cultivars of *C. speciosa* are 'Cardinalis', scarlet; 'Moerloosii' ('Apple Blossom'), pink; 'Nivalis', white; and 'Simonii', crimson. Recommended cultivars of *C. × superba* are 'Knap Hill Scarlet', 'Crimson and Gold', 'Pink Lady' and 'Rowallane' which is crimson.

Chimonanthus

This is the Wintersweet, a name which perfectly describes its chief attraction, that of scenting the air in winter for many metres around. There is only one species,

Chimonanthus praecox (also sometimes called *C. fragrans*) and its pale yellow, purple-centred flowers are not in the least spectacular, but they make up in perfume what they lack in colour. It is deciduous, makes a large, rather open-branched bush which is best left unpruned, though this may not be possible if it is trained against a sunny wall, as it often is. Then forward-growing stems that cannot readily be trained in can be cut out or be shortened in late winter. The Wintersweet thrives in most well-drained soils, including chalk.

Choisya

The popular name of *Choisya ternata*, Mexican Orange Blossom, describes both the appearance and the scent of its white flowers, most freely produced in late spring, though usually there are some more to follow in summer. The leaves are evergreen, divided and bright shining green, making this a very decorative shrub even in winter. Unfortunately, though it will withstand quite a lot of frost, it is not completely hardy, so it should be given a sunny place sheltered from north and east winds. It is not fussy about soil, does well in town gardens and can be pruned in early summer when the first blossoming is over, at which time stems can be shortened by up to 30 cm (1 ft).

Cistus

No doubt these would be much more widely planted if they were just a little more reliably hardy, for they have many good qualities including evergreen foliage and tremendous flowering capacity in early and mid-summer. There are no better shrubs for hot, dry places in reasonably good soil, but they are not really suitable for cold districts or poorly drained soils. The hardiest kinds are *Cistus × corbariensis*, white 60 to 90 cm (2 to 3 ft); *C. crispus*, magenta, 60 cm (2 ft); *C. × cyprius*, white blotched crimson, 1.8 m (6 ft); *C. ladaniferus*, very large white flowers blotched with maroon in most forms but sometimes pure white 1.2 to 1.5 m (4 to 5 ft); *C. laurifolius*, white 1.8 to 2.1 m (6 to 7 ft); *C. × pulverulentus* and its cultivar 'Sunset', magenta, 60 to 90 cm (2 to 3 ft); and 'Silver Pink', light pink, 60 cm (2 ft). One of the most beautiful kinds is *C. × purpureus*, deep rose, maroon blotched, 90 cm to 1.2 m (3 to 4 ft), but it is less hardy than those just listed.

Cistus do not transplant easily and so are best purchased in containers. They need little pruning, but frost-damaged stems should be cut out in spring. As a rule bushes are not long lived so replacements must be made from time to time. Cuttings can be rooted in a propagating case in summer and species can be raised from seed.

Clematis

There are herbaceous species of clematis, but the kinds we are concerned with here are all climbers with slender stems and spiralling leaf stalks with which to cling to twigs, wires, trellises or other not-too-stout supports. There are a great many different kinds, ranging from plants of quite modest size which can be trained up pillars, to sturdy climbers that will ascend tall trees or cover large outbuildings. Some have small flowers, some large,

there are single, semi-double and fully double-flowered cultivars; the colour range is from white, pink and lavender to crimson and deep violet purple and there are cultivars to bloom from early spring until autumn. Small wonder that clematis is the most popular of all climbing plants.

Clematis will thrive in most fertile soils and are particularly happy on chalk and limestone provided they are well fed. They do not transplant particularly well and so are best purchased in containers. They enjoy having their roots in the shade and their leaves in the sun which can be achieved by planting small shrubs or herbaceous plants around or in front of them to shade the soil. Some cultivars particularly some of the large-flowered hybrids, suffer from wilt disease which causes whole stems or even complete plants to collapse suddenly. The best preventative is to spray every fortnight each April and mid-June with a copper fungicide.

Most kinds benefit from pruning and this may be essential if clematis have to be fitted to a particular area, but the pruning time and methods differ according to type. Those that have finished flowering by mid-June can be pruned immediately after that as there will still be time for them to make good new growth for the following year. All the shoots that have just flowered can be removed, also some of the older growth if there is too much.

Cultivars that do not start to bloom until mid-summer or later are pruned in February by removing much of the old growth or even cutting the whole plant down to within about 30 cm (1 ft) of ground level if available space is limited.

Good small-flowered species are *Clematis armandii*, white, early spring, one of the few evergreen kinds, to 6 m (20 ft); *C. flammula*, white, scented, August–September, to 4.5 m (15 ft); *C. montana*, white, and *C.m rubens*, purplish pink, both May flowering, to 9 m (30 ft); *C. tangutica*, yellow, July–October, to 4.5 m (15 ft).

Good large-flowered hybrids are 'Barbara Dibley', violet purple, May–August; 'Comtesse de Bouchard', pink, June–August; 'Countess of Lovelace', pale blue, double, June–September; 'Daniel

Deronda', purplish blue, semi-double in May–June, but single from July–September; 'Ernest Markham', petunia purple, July–September; 'Hagley Hybrid', pink, June–September; 'Henryi', white, May–June and again August–September; 'Jackmanii', violet purple, July–September; and 'Jackmanii Superba' similar but a more reddish purple and with wider sepals; 'Lasurstern', lavender blue, May–June and again August–September; 'Nelly Moser', mauve and carmine, May–June and again August–September; 'Perle d'Azur', blue, June–August and 'Ville de Lyon', carmine, July–October.

Colutea

These are the bladder sennas, deciduous shrubs with clusters of pea-type flowers followed by inflated seedpods which are distinctive and decorative. They will thrive in dry, hot places where many other plants would fail. *Colutea arborescens*, with yellow flower, will grow 3 or 3.6 m (10 to 12 ft) high if unrestricted, but can be kept to half that height by cutting back most or all the previous year's growth each February or March. *C. orientalis*, coppery is smaller and *C. × media* also coppery, is a hybrid between the two and intermediate in size.

Cornus

These are the dogwoods, some of which are grown primarily for their coloured stems, some for their flowers, or the showy, petal-like bracts that surround the true flowers. Since these different effects entail different treatment in the garden the groups need to be treated separately. All are deciduous.

The dogwoods with coloured stems or variegated leaves all thrive in most soils and places, including those that are very wet. The best bark effects are produced by cutting all stems back to within a few centimeters of the base in early spring and the same treatment can be given to the foliage varieties or they can simply be thinned out a little, some of the older stems being removed where overcrowded. *Cornus alba* 'Sibirica', the Westonbirt Dogwood, has crimson stems and *C. stonlonifera* 'Flaviramea' has

greenish-yellow stems. *C. alba* 'Elegantissima' has white-variegated leaves and *C. a.* 'Spaethii', yellow-variegated leaves.

Cornus alternifolia 'Variegata' ('Argentea') makes a large bush, 3 m (10 ft) or more high, with attractive leaves broadly edged with creamy-white. It likes a warm, sunny place and does not usually require pruning, although it can be thinned in early spring.

The best dogwood to grow for true flowers is *Cornus mas*, the Cornelian Cherry, a tall, loosely branched shrub with clusters of small yellow flowers in February, but more spectacular are the bract-bearing kinds such as *C. kousa* with big white bracts in June, and *C. florida rubra* with pink bracts in May. Both make big bushes or small, widely branched trees and do best in good, loamy soil, preferably moderately acid and without lime or chalk. They need no pruning. *C. mas* is similar in height, up to 6 m (20 ft), but more erect in habit. It will grow in any reasonably fertile soil and can be thinned, if necessary, after flowering is over. However this will reduce the crops of small edible cherry-like fruits.

Corylopsis

Some kinds make small trees, but *Corylopsis pauciflora* is a shrub 1.2 to 1.8 m (4 to 6 ft) high, with clusters of primrose-yellow, pleasantly scented flowers in March. It does best on lime-free soils and as a rule requires no pruning. Larger kinds are *C. glabrescens*, *C. sinensis*, *C. spicata* and *C. willmottiae*, all with primrose-yellow flowers produced in little dangling chains along the bare stems in early spring.

Cotinus

This is the correct name for a handsome shrub which gardeners may know as *Rhus cotinus*, the Smoke Tree or Wig Tree. The popular names refer to the tangle of hair-like filaments which carry the small flowers and which turn smoky grey in late summer. The rounded leaves become coppery red in autumn before they fall and in some varieties such as *purpureus* and the cultivar 'Royal Purple' are reddish purple all the summer. *Cotinus coggygria* is a big shrub, often 3 m (10 ft) high and considerably more in diameter, but if grown for foliage effect only it can be pruned annually in early spring, each stem made the previous year being shortened to a few centimetres. Plants thrive best in a warm sunny place and well-drained soil.

Cotoneaster

All the cotoneasters are capable of producing showy crops of berries, usually scarlet or crimson, but many are also first-rate foliage shrubs with an interesting diversity of habit and leaf shape. *Cotoneaster dammeri* is completely prostrate, making a carpet of evergreen leaves ideal as covering for a bank or under other shrubs. *C. horizontalis* has a curious fishbone habit of branching and will make a wide low bush in the open or spread itself flat like a climber against a wall or fence. Its small leaves turn orange and scarlet before they fall in autumn.

Cotoneaster microphyllus has small, dark green, evergreen leaves and its branches will mould themselves to any solid object or mound themselves into low, wide bushes. *C. conspicuus* 'Decorus', makes a bigger, domeshaped bush, is also evergreen and notably free fruiting. *C. franchetii sternianus* is semi-evergreen, of open shuttlecock habit *F. magellancia* 'Variegata', leaves green edged with cream. *C. salicifolius* is fully evergreen and has a number of forms, some spreading, some erect. Finally there are large, almost tree-like kinds, such as *C. frigidus*, which is deciduous and has a yellow-fruited cultivar named 'Fructuluteo', and scarlet-fruited hybrids such as *C.* 'Cornubia' and *C. × watereri* which can reach 4.5 m (15 ft) or more.

All are very adaptable as to soil and position and, though pruning is not essential, stems or branches can be shortened or removed in spring if bushes occupy too much room, and when used as hedges they can, in addition, be trimmed lightly in summer.

Cytisus

This is one genus (the other two being *Genista* and *Spartium*) of the trio collectively known as brooms. Nearly all species of cytisus have the small pea-type flowers typical of the family, but in other respects they differ widely. There are prostrate kinds with creeping underground stems such as pale purple flowered *Cytisus purpureus*; low wide-spreading kinds such as cream-coloured *C. × kewensis*, 30- to 45-cm (12- to 18-in) small bushes such as bright yellow *C. × beanii*; medium-sized bushes such as 90 cm (3 ft) sulphur-yellow *C. × praecox*, and tall bushes such as 1.8- to 2.4-m (6- to 8-ft) *C. multiflorus*, better known as the White Spanish Broom. All these are April or May flowering as are the numerous varieties and hybrids of the Common Broom, *C. scoparius*, available in yellow, yellow and crimson, cream, pink, cerise and crimson cultivars and all making bushes 1.5 to 1.8 m (5 to 6 ft) high. By contrast *C. battandieri*, 1.8 m (6 ft) or more, does not commence to produce its erect spikes of yellow, pineapple-scented flowers until June and its silky grey leaves are quite large. All the foregoing are deciduous.

Cytisus monspessulanus and *C.* 'Porlock' are evergreen 1.8 to 2.4 m (6 to 8 ft) high with yellow flowers in spring and early summer, sweet scented in 'Porlock'. Unfortunately they are less hardy and therefore most suitable for southern, western and maritime gardens.

All brooms succeed best in sunny places and well-drained, moderately acid or neutral soils. Most can be pruned moderately immediately after flowering and *Cytisus battandieri* can have old stems cut back to young side growth in spring.

Danae

There is only one species, *Danae racemosa*, the Alexandrian Laurel, grown for its slender stems closely set with narrow evergreen "leaves" which are in fact flattened branches or phylloclades. It will grow in most soils and places, even in dense shade, and is excellent for cut foliage at any time of the year as well as making an attractive 90 cm (3 ft) high bush.

Daphne

Many kinds have richly scented flowers but by no means all are easy to grow and

Cornus alba
'Westonbirt'

Cotoneaster 'Cornubia'

some have a tendency to die suddenly without obvious cause. Most do not transplant well and so are best purchased in containers from which they can be moved with a minimum of root disturbance. All succeed best in open, sunny places and in soils that remain moist in summer but do not become waterlogged in winter.

Daphne mezereum, which is deciduous and produces its purple or white flowers on leafless stems in February and March, likes limestone or chalk soils. It has scarlet berries containing seeds and if the berries are sown outdoors as soon as ripe some seeds will germinate the following spring and probably even more the second spring. Other good kinds are *D. blagayana*, creamy white, March–April, prostrate; *D. × burkwoodii*, pink, May–June, 90 cm (3 ft), deciduous; *D. cneorum*, rose pink, May–June, evergreen, prostrate; *D. collina*, reddish purple, May, evergreen, 60 to 90 cm (2 to 3 ft); *D. odora*; reddish purple, February–March, evergreen 90 cm to 1.8 m (3 to 6 ft); and 'Aureo-marginata', hardier and with yellow-edged leaves. None of these require regular pruning.

Deutzia

These are most attractive deciduous shrubs with small flowers freely produced in spring and early summer. They succeed in all reasonably fertile soils, prefer sunny positions and can have most of the flowering stems removed immediately the flowers fade, provided there is plenty of young growth coming along to flower the following year.

Good kinds are *Deutzia × elegantissima*, rose pink, June, 1.2 m (4 ft); *D. gracilis*, white, April–May, 90 cm to 1.5 m (3 to 5 ft), needs sheltered place as flowers are liable to be injured by spring frosts; *D. × magnifica*, white, double June–July 1.8 to 2.4 m (6 to 8 ft); 'Mont Rose', purplish pink, May–June, 90 cm (3 ft); *D. scabra* 'Plena', white and purple, double, June–July 2.4 to 3 m (8 to 10 ft).

Elaeagnus

Sturdy evergreen and deciduous shrubs of which the former, grown mainly for their foliage, are the most useful.

Elaeagnus pungens 'Maculata', with dark green leaves heavily splashed with yellow, is one of the brightest of all golden variegated shrubs and a good bush catching the sun is a heartwarming sight in winter. It will make a bush 3 m (10 ft) or more high and the same across, but can be kept much smaller by annual pruning in May. Its small silvery-white flowers, produced in autumn, often pass unnoticed but are delightfully scented. *E. macrophylla* has similar flowers, makes a wide-spreading bush 2.4 m (8 ft) or more high and has large leaves, silvery all over at first but becoming green on the upper surface as they age. It can be pruned in the same way as *E. pungens*.

Both kinds prefer neutral or moderately acid and fairly fertile soils, can be grown in sun or shade and make useful windbreaks near the sea. There is also a quick growing hybrid between the two species named *Elaeagnus × ebbingei*, a useful shrub where shelter is required.

Enkianthus

The best kind, *Enkianthus campanulatus*, is grown for its little bell-like flowers in spring, buff or reddish bronze in colour and freely produced, and also for its fine autumn colour before the leaves fall. It makes a bush 1.8 to 2.7 m (6 to 9 ft) high and succeeds best in a lightly shaded place in lime-free, moderately acid soil – the same conditions as those which suit azaleas and rhododendrons, to which it is related.

Escallonia

There are deciduous escallonias but the most useful cultivars are all evergreen or semi-evergreen with rather small shining green leaves and small bell-shaped flowers freely produced in summer. They have a reputation for tenderness but there are plenty of good kinds that will stand a lot of frost, notably *Escallonia* 'Langleyensis' with arching stems and rose-pink flowers and the numerous cultivars associated with it. These include 'Apple Blossom', pink and white; 'Donard Radiance', rose red; and 'Edinensis', red buds, pale pink flowers. All will make big bushes up to 2.4 m (8 ft) high.

Escallonia rubra can grow even taller

and is frequently used as a hedge or screen plant near the sea, but it not so reliable inland. 'Crimson Spire' is a fast-growing erect form of it with crimson flowers. All these will grow in any reasonably fertile soil, but *E. virgata*, which is deciduous, white flowered and notably hardy, dislikes lime and chalk and needs an acid soil. All can be thinned in spring or even cut back severly at the sacrifice of a season's flowering. When grown as hedges they should be trimmed in summer after flowering.

Euonymus

There are evergreen and deciduous kinds and they serve quite different purposes in the garden; the evergreens being grown for their ornamental foliage and as hedges and screens, particularly in maritime districts, since they withstand salt spray; the deciduous kinds (known as spindle trees) for their highly ornamental fruits and autumn leaf colour. All grow freely in most soils including chalk and limestone, and they will also succeed in sun or shade, though the deciduous kinds colour and fruit best in light places. Evergreen kinds can be pruned in spring as necessary to keep them in bounds and can be clipped in summer if this seems desirable. Deciduous kinds are best pruned in March when old stems can be cut out or shortened to younger replacement stems.

Euonymus fortunei is an evergreen, trailing or climbing according to situation and able to cling to tree trunks or walls with aerial roots. It has several cultivars and varieties such as 'Coloratus', green leaved in summer, purple in winter; *E.f. radicans*, with small green leaves; 'Silver Queen', bushy in habit, with a wide cream edge to every leaf, and 'Variegatus' leaves grey green, edged with white and often splashed with pink.

Euonymus japonicus is the kind commonly used for hedges and screens, a bushy evergreen which can reach 6 m (20 ft) but can be kept to a quarter of that height by pruning. Typically dark shining green, it also has variegated cultivars such as 'Aureopictus' sometimes called 'Aureus' with a splash of gold in the centre of each leaf, 'Ovatus Aurcus' also

called 'Aureo-variegatus' has a cream margin to each leaf; 'Microphyllus' (also known as 'Myrtifolius') is very slow growing, compact and has small green leaves.

Good deciduous kinds are *Euonymus europaeus* and *E. latifolius*, both with scarlet fruits, and *E. yedoensis* with rose-pink fruits. Most have orange seeds which show prominently as the fruits ripen, and all can grow to 3 m (10 ft) or more. *E. alatus* has the most brilliantly coloured autumn foliage and will reach 2.4 m (8 ft).

Fatsia

There is only one species, *Fatsia japonica*, an evergreen 1.8 to 2.4 m (6 to 8 ft) high, with large deeply lobed, rather thick-textured leaves which have a fine architectural look enhanced by the cream-coloured flowers produced in globular heads on stiffly branched sprays in autumn. It grows in most soils, in sun or shade, and is first rate both in city gardens and near the sea. It is related to ivy, though it does not climb, and there is an interesting hybrid between it and ivy named × *Fatshedera lizei*, which has long lax (not climbing) stems and leaves intermediate in size and shape.

Forsythia

These are among the first shrubs to make a massive display in early spring when covered in their yellow blossom, provided the buds have not been picked out in winter by birds. This can be a serious difficulty in country gardens, but in towns and near roads there is usually little trouble. All will grow in any reasonably fertile soil in sun or partial shade. They can be pruned immediately after flowering when the old flower stems can be cut out but strong young stems, particularly those from near the base, should be retained to flower the following year.

Recommended kinds are *Forsythia* × *intermedia* and its cultivars 'Lynwood' and 'Spectabilis', deep yellow 1.8 to 2.4 m (6 to 8 ft), and *F. suspensa* with paler flowers and long arching stems which can be trained against a wall or fence. There is an attractive variety of this, *atrocaulis*, with purplish black young stems.

Fuchsia

Even the hardiest fuchsias are liable to be killed to ground level in very cold winters, but they usually shoot up again strongly from the roots in spring. Since the flowers of fuchsias are highly attractive and are produced more or less continuously all summer and well on into the autumn, until stopped by frost, they must be considered valuable garden plants despite this risk of winter damage.

To reduce losses to a minimum the following precautions should be observed. Choice of cultivar should be restricted to those proved to be suitable for growing out of doors. Young plants should be obtained in containers in mid- or late spring and planted in saucer-like hollows, the lowest point about 5 cm (2 in) below soil level. These hollows will serve to hold water when the plants are watered in summer, which they should be whenever the soil is dry, and then in autumn they can be filled in with a mixture of equal parts soil, peat and sand and a little more mounded on top to protect the basal buds in winter. In February or March all dead, weak or unwanted growth should be cut off 2.5 cm (1 in) or so above soil level. Further pruning can be done when the new shoots are 10 cm (4 in) or more long and it can be seen where the best growth is.

Recommended cultivars are 'Alice Hoffman', rose and white 45 cm (18 in); 'Chillerton Beauty', pink and violet 60 cm (2 ft); 'Corallina', scarlet and purple, wide-spreading habit, 45 cm (18 in); 'Howlett's Hardy', scarlet and violet, 90 cm (3 ft); 'Lady Thumb', carmine and white, 30 cm (1 ft); 'Lena', pink and purple 60 cm (2 ft); F. magellanica gracilis, scarlet and violet 90 cm (3 ft); F.m. 'Variegata', leaves green edged with cream, 90 cm (3 ft); F. m. 'Versicolor', scarlet and violet, leaves grey green, pink and white, 90 cm (3 ft); 'Margaret', scarlet and violet purple, 90 cm (3 ft); 'Margaret Brown', carmine and rose, 60 cm (2 ft); 'Mme Cornelissen', scarlet and white 60 cm (2 ft); 'Mrs Popple', scarlet and violet purple, 90 cm (3 ft); 'Mrs W. P. Wood', pale pink 90 cm (3 ft); 'Ricartonii', scarlet and purple, 1.2 to 1.8 m (4 to 6 ft); 'Tennessee Waltz', rose and mauve 76 cm (2½ ft), and 'Tom Thumb', scarlet and mauve, 30 cm (1 ft).

Garrya

The best kind is Garrya elliptica, a vigorous evergreen with long narrow grey-green catkins freely produced in winter. Male and female catkins are produced on separate bushes and though the males are most handsome in flower, the females will produce pendant clusters of small purple fruits if there is a male nearby to effect pollination. Garrya is a little tender and should be given a sunny sheltered place or may be trained against a wall, in which case forward-growing stems can be shortened in spring.

Genista

This is the second of the genera which are commonly known as brooms (see also cytisus and spartium). Like the other two genistas enjoy sunny, warm places and prefer neutral or acid soils, though they will grow where there is lime or chalk. They can also be cut back lightly after flowering, but not into hard, old wood, which usually refuses to produce new growth.

There are many different kinds varying greatly in size and habit. Genista aethnensis, the Mount Etna Broom, is almost a tree, often 4.5 cm (15 ft) or more high with slender, whip-like hanging stems covered with small yellow flowers in summer. It needs secure staking as it is very easily blown over.

By contrast Genista hispanica is a dwarf plant, like a 60 cm (2 ft) gorse bush, spiny and stiff and spreading gradually to cover quite a lot of ground. Its light yellow flowers appear in May–June. G. lydia is also a small plant but quite smooth and spineless with arching stems and yellow flowers in May–June. It looks well on a rock garden or terrace wall.

Genista tinctoria, the Dyer's Greenweed, creeps and is best planted in its double-flowered form 'Plena', with showy yellow blooms from June to September. G. virgata (also known as G. tenera) and G. cinerea are both vigorous, erect-growing shrubs, 2.4 m (8 ft) or more high, with yellow flowers in June and July.

The flowers of
Hamamelis mollis

Hamamelis

These are the witch hazels, valuable because they flower in mid-winter. They look rather like nut bushes until the spidery flowers begin to unfurl their narrow petals along the bare branches in December and January. By far the best for general planting are *Hamamelis mollis*, daffodil yellow, and its primrose-yellow cultivar 'Pallida'. Both can make big bushes, 3 m (10 ft) high and wide, but overlong branches can be removed or shortened either for forcing into flower from bud or after flowering. All kinds thrive best in good, loamy, lime-free soil.

Hebe

These used to be known as veronica, a name which now applies only to the herbaceous species. Hebes are all evergreen shrubs, mostly rather tender though they usually thrive well by the sea and can be grown in many gardens that are sunny, warm and sheltered. They are not at all fussy about soil and transplant safely even when quite large. They can be pruned in spring or be trimmed in summer if used as hedges, though some loss of flower that year will result. The hardiest species are *Hebe brachysiphon* (often wrongly called *H. traversii*) and *H. salicifolia*. The first is 1.5 to 1.8 m (5 to 6 ft) high with neat, box-like leaves and white flowers in small spikes in July, the second 1.8 to 3.6 m (6 to 12 ft) high with narrow leaves and white flowers in slender trails from June to August.

Hebe hulkeana is one of the most graceful kinds, normally 60 cm (2 ft) high but twice as much if trained against a wall, with rather loose stems bearing sprays of lavender-blue flowers in May–June, but it is distinctly tender.

Hebe pinguifolia 'Pagei' has grey leaves, white flowers in June, is semi-prostrate and makes excellent ground cover, and *H. ochracea*, often wrongly called *H. armstrongii* is grown for its foliage, the whole 60 cm (2 ft) plant looking rather like a windswept coppery-bronze cypress.

There are also a great many garden hybrids since hebes cross freely and seed germinates readily. The most handsome but also the most tender are the *H. speciosa* hybrids with stout leaves and showy spikes of flowers in late summer such as 'Alicia Amherst', violet purple; 'La Seduisante', carmine, 'Simon Delaux', crimson, and *H. andersonii* 'Variegata', purplish blue, leaves heavily variegated with cream. All are about 90 cm (3 ft) high.

A little hardier is 'Midsummer Beauty', with long lavender trails from July to November and growing to 1.8 m (6 ft). Still hardier are 'Autumn Glory', 60 cm (2 ft), purplish blue, July to November; 'Carl Teschner', sprawling, violet, July; 'Carnea' and 'Great Orme', both 90 cm (3 ft), white and pink, flowering from May to September; *H. × franciscana*, often sold as *H. elliptica* which seems to be scarce in cultivation, a neat bush with violet-purple flowers and its form 'Variegata' with cream-edged leaves; 'Margery Fish', 60 to 90 cm (2 to 3 ft), violet blue and white, July to September; and 'Majorie', 60 to 90 cm (2 to 3 ft), light blue, July to September.

Hedera

These are the ivies which many people fear in gardens because they believe that they will damage the masonry of their houses or kill their trees. In fact it is only old-fashioned lime mortar that may be shrunk and dragged out by ivy and only very old trees that are already dying that are likely to be overrun by it. Ivy can actually protect walls and keep them dry, but it can be a nuisance if it is allowed to fill gutters or grow beneath roofing tiles. There is, however, no reason why ivy should not be cut back drastically in spring or be clipped or pruned at any time of the year. It will grow in any soil and situation, in sun or shade, and all forms of the Common Ivy are completely hardy, though this is not true of all the other species.

There are also, in addition to the normal climbing ivies which support themselves by aerial roots, bush ivies with no ability to climb and the habit of flowering freely and producing abundant crops of black berries. These are produced by rooting cuttings from the flowering stems of ordinary ivies and they resemble their parents in every respect

ABOVE: *Hibiscus syriacus* 'Woodbridge'

BELOW: *Hydrangea macrophylla* 'Westfalen'

except habit.

The Common Ivy, *Hedera helix*, has a great many cultivars differing in leaf size, leaf colour and habit. Representative examples are 'Arborescens', green leaved, non-climbing; 'Buttercup', leaves yellow; 'Cavendishii', leaves edged cream and pink; 'Conglomerata', dwarf, non-climbing, with crowded wavy-edged leaves; 'Cristata', leaves round, crimped at the edge; 'Glacier', leaves grey, white edged; 'Gold Heart' (also known as 'Golden Jubilee'), leaves dark green with central yellow blotch; 'Hibernica', the Irish Ivy, leaves to 15 cm (6 in) across; 'Marginata' ('Silver Queen' and 'Tri-color' are the same or very similar), leaves edged white and with some pink as well in winter; 'Sagittifolia' leaf arrow shaped, lobes very narrow.

Hedera colchica has much larger leaves up to 18 cm (7 in) across, and in cultivar 'Dentata Variegata' they are dark green, grey green and cream. This is one of the most handsome of all variegated climbing plants. There is also a fine green, grey and cream-variegated form of *H. canariensis*, the Canary Island Ivy, named 'Variegata' or 'Gloire de Marengo', but this is a little less hardy.

Hibiscus

Many kinds of hibiscus are so tender that they can only be grown in warm greenhouses, but *Hibiscus syriacus* is hardy in all but the coldest parts of Britain. It is a handsome deciduous shrub which can reach 3 m (10 ft) but is more usually about 1.8 m (6 ft), with showy, mallow-type flowers in late summer and early autumn. It likes a warm sunny place, will thrive in all reasonably fertile, well-drained soils, including those containing lime, and can be pruned in late winter if it grows too large. It transplants badly so should be purchased in containers while still small and plants should also be staked securely for the first few years to prevent roots being damaged by wind rocking. There are numerous cultivars such as 'Caeruleus Plenus' and 'Ardens', both with double purple flowers; 'Coelestis', single blue shading to purplish red; 'Hamabo', single pale pink and crimson; 'Monstrosus Plenus',

double white and maroon; 'Snowdrift', single white, 'Violet Clair', double red-purple flowers, and 'Woodbridge', single rose and deep carmine.

Hydrangea

This is one of the big and important families from the garden standpoint and one which contains climbing as well as bushy plants. All are deciduous and all thrive best in fairly fertile soil that does not dry out severely in summer. All will grow in sun or shade.

Hydrangea macrophylla is the species that has produced the greatest number of cultivars and these bear variously coloured flowers in summer and early autumn. In some all the flowers are sterile and have large sepals so that the flower head is ball shaped. These are often known as Hortensias. In other cultivars the flowers are arranged in a flat, more or less circular cluster with small fertile flowers in the centre and sterile flowers with showy sepals forming a ring outside. These are often known as Lacecaps. In both types, if the sepals are coloured, the colour will be changed by the character of the soil, tending towards pink, red and crimson in alkaline soil and to blue or violet purple in acid soil. White sepals remain the same whatever the soil.

All forms of *Hydrangea macrophylla* are a little tender, some more so than others. They do best in warm, sheltered gardens, particularly in towns, near the sea and in thin woodland which provides some protection from frost. Old flower heads should be removed in winter or early spring and at the same time weak stems can be removed. As a rule this is all the pruning required, but if bushes get too large stems can be cut back in early spring but with loss of flower that year.

Hydrangea paniculata and *H. arborescens* 'Grandiflora' can be hard pruned each March without loss of flower since they bloom on strong young stems. Both are fully hardy. *H. paniculata* has white flowers fading reddish, in large conical heads in August–September. *H.p.* 'Praecox' starts to flower in July, *H. arborescens* 'Grandiflora' has white flowers in clusters from July to September.

Hydrangea petiolaris climbs by aerial

roots and can reach the tops of tall trees. Its white flowers are produced in June in flat, lacecap trusses. It can be pruned in spring, but only with some loss of flower that summer.

Hypericum

Easily grown shrubs thriving in most soils, including those overlying chalk and limestone. All have yellow flowers, some have evergreen leaves, some are semi-evergreen and some are fully deciduous. Most do best in sunny or at any rate fairly light places, but *Hypericum calycinum*, the Rose of Sharon, will grow equally well on hot, sunny banks and under trees. It is prostrate, fast spreading, has large flowers from July to September and makes excellent ground cover where there is room for its invasive growth. It can be cut back or sheared off a few centimeters above soil level in April.

Hypericum 'Hidcote', semi-evergreen 1.2 to 1.5 m (4 to 5 ft) high, flowering in summer and autumn, is one of the best kinds for general planting. *H. forrestii* (also known as *H. patulum forrestii*) is similar but deciduous and has a shorter flowering season, but can give pleasant autumn colour of leaf and bronze-red fruits. Even better in this respect is *H. × inodorum* 'Elstead', with abundant small yellow flowers followed by shining orange-red fruits.

Jasminum

There are shrubby jasmines, most notably *Jasminum humile* 'Revolutum', 1.5 to 1.8 m (5 to 6 ft) high, with more or less evergreen leaves and good yellow flowers in summer. But it is the climbing or rambling jasmines that are most popular with gardeners, such as *J. officinale*, the Common Jasmine, a vigorous deciduous twiner with white, sweetly scented flowers in summer and early autumn, and *J. nudiflorum*, the Winter Jasmine, with long green stems and yellow flowers from November until February.

Jasminum officinale simply wants a trellis, wires or something similar to climb over; *J. nudiflorum* has no means of holding itself up and so must be tied to whatever support is provided or allowed to spread. The Common Jasmine likes a warm sunny place, does not need any regular pruning, and can be cut back or thinned out in late winter if overcrowded. The Winter Jasmine will grow in sun or shade and is improved in habit if each old flowering stem is shortened to 2.5 cm (1 in) or so after flowering. All jasmines will thrive in any reasonably fertile soil.

Kalmia

These beautiful evergreen shrubs thrive in acid, lime-free soils in similar conditions to rhododendrons. The highly distinctive flowers, produced in May or June, look like little Chinese lanterns. The most showy species is *Kalmia latifolia*, the Calico Bush, with pink flowers. It grows slowly but can eventually make a big rounded bush 2.4 to 3 m (8 to 10 ft) high. *K. angustifolia* seldom exceeds 90 cm (3 ft) and has smaller deep rose or red flowers.

Kalmia latifolia

Kerria

It is a curious fact that the double-flowered form of *Kerria japonica* is markedly different in habit from the single form. It has much longer stems which can readily be trained against a wall or over a screen, whereas the single-flowered kind forms a 1.2 to 1.5 m (4 to 5 ft) high thicket of growth, constantly spreading by suckers. Both are useful but it is the double form, 'Pleniflora' or 'Flore Pleno', which is most popular. Its little, buttercup-yellow, pompon flowers are freely produced in late spring. Both kinds will grow well in any reasonably good, not too dry soil and can be pruned after flowering, when some of the older stems can be cut out and those that are too long can be shortened.

Hypericum calycinum

Kolkwitzia

American gardeners call *Kolkwitzia amabilis* the Beauty Bush, and a good specimen in full bloom in June is certainly a lovely sight. The flowers are similar in shape to those of weigela, but smaller, downy, very freely produced and clear pink with a splash of yellow. It is deciduous and will make a big bush growing to 2.4 m (8 ft) high with arching stems. It is quite hardy, will grow in all reasonably fertile soils and flowers best in sunny places. Old and weak branches can be cut out immediately after flowering, but care should be taken not to spoil the naturally graceful habit of the bush.

Lavandula

This is the botanical name for lavender, a genus of small shrubs which succeed best in warm sunny places and on well-drained soils, particularly those that are neutral or alkaline. All are improved by moderate clipping after flowering.

The most popular kind is the Common or Old English Lavender, which has narrow grey leaves and flowers in spikes in June–July. It is usually known as *Lavandula spica* though it is probably a hybrid between *L. angustifolia* and *L. latifolia*. There are numerous cultivars such as 'Alba', white slightly flushed with pink, 60 cm (2 ft); 'Grappenhall', lavender blue, 60 to 90 cm (2 to 3 ft); 'Hidcote', violet purple, 45 to 60 cm (18 to 24 in); 'Munstead', bluish purple, 45 to 60 cm (18 to 24 in); 'Rosea' lilac pink 45 to 60 cm (18 to 24 in); and 'Twickel Purple', purple 45 to 60 cm (18 to 24 in).

Lavandula stoechas, the French Lavender, has its purple flowers crowded into cylindrical heads with a few purple bracts on top. It grows about 45 cm (18 in) high and is in flower for a long time in summer and early autumn, but it is far less hardy than the Common Lavender.

Lavatera

The best shrubby species, *Lavatera olbia*, makes a loosely branched bush 1.8 to

2.1 m (6 to 7 ft) high with rounded leaves and funnel-shaped rose-pink flowers, freely produced all summer. It likes warm sunny places and well-drained soils and is first class near the sea. The rather soft stems often die back in winter and should be pruned in early spring to good live wood near the main branches or the base of the bush. It is seldom long-lived but can be readily renewed by seed or from cuttings taken in summer.

Leycesteria

The kind commonly grown, *Leycesteria formosa*, makes long, green, cane-like growths carrying, in summer, drooping sprays of white flowers enclosed in maroon bracts. These are followed by quite large and decorative deep reddish-purple berries which contain seeds that are distributed by birds. In severe winters the rather soft stems can be damaged by frost but new growth generally comes freely from the roots in spring. Leycesteria succeeds best in fairly good soil and a sunny place, though it will grow in shade. Dead, damaged or weak stems should be cut out each spring.

Ligustrum

This is the botanical name of privet, an invaluable shrub for screens and hedges, but there are also other species, some more decorative. *Ligustrum lucidum* is one of the best of these, a big evergreen shrub or even a small tree in favourable places, with shining green leaves and sprays of flowers, rather like a small white lilac, in August and September.

The best hedge-making kind is *Ligustrum ovalifolium*, which is semi-evergreen and can reach 4.5 m (15 ft), but can be pruned to 90 cm (3 ft) without harm. Its yellow-leaved cultivar 'Aureum', is the popular Golden Privet and it also has an attractive cultivar named 'Argenteum' with a creamy-white border to each leaf.

All privets grow best in fairly fertile soil and the variegated cultivars colour best in the sun, but there are few soils or places in which privet cannot be grown. When planted as hedges the tops should be cut out immediately to ensure branching from the base. Privet can be pruned hard in spring, and at any time in summer.

Lonicera

These are the honeysuckles of which there are shrubby as well as climbing species. One of the bushy kinds, *Lonicera nitida*, is a popular hedge-making shrub with little rounded evergreen leaves giving somewhat the appearance of box. It stands clipping well, but because of its rather thin, flexible stems is not suitable for hedges above 1.5 m (5 ft) in height. There is also an excellent yellow-leaved cultivar named 'Baggessen's Gold'.

Also useful are the winter-flowering shrubby honeysuckles, such as *Lonicera fragrantissima*, *L. standishii* and the hybrid between them, *L. × purpusii*, all of which make medium-sized open branched shrubs with small, sweetly-scented, white or cream flowers in winter.

The climbing honeysuckles are all vigorous twiners, suitable for growing over arches, pergolas and screens. All like fairly rich soils that do not dry out seriously in summer, and most will grow in sun or shade, but the Scarlet Trumpet Honeysuckle, *Lonicera sempervirens*, is

Lonicera periclymenum

The fruits of *Mahonia japonica*

best in a sunny, warm place. Its orange-scarlet flowers are very showy but not scented, and it is semi-evergreen. So is *L. japonica*, usually planted in one or other of two forms; *L.j. halliana*, with creamy, intensely scented flowers in summer, and 'Aureo-reticulata', grown primarily for its gold-netted leaves.

The most popular climbing honeysuckle is the Woodbine, *Lonicera periclymenum*, though again it is one of its cultivars or hybrids rather than the true species that is usually planted. The two best are 'Belgica', known as Early Dutch Honeysuckle, and 'Serotina', known as Late Dutch Honeysuckle. Both have handsome, reddish-purple and yellow flowers in summer, but 'Serotina' is to be preferred because of its longer flowering season. Growth of the climbing honeysuckles is usually so intertwined that pruning is difficult, but growth can be clipped after flowering or some of the older stems can be cut out.

Magnolia
Most magnolias are trees, but *Magnolia stellata* is a shrub growing slowly to about 2.7 m (9 ft). It is an exceptionally beautiful plant, with rather narrow-petalled white flowers, very freely produced in March and April. There are also pink cultivars, one very pale in colour named 'Rosea', another, a little deeper named 'Rubra'. All succeed best in neutral or moderately acid soil and a rather sheltered position as the flowers are apt to be spoiled by frost or cold winds. Pruning is undesirable. It is advisable to purchase young plants in containers as, like most magnolias, it resents root injury.

Mahonia
Handsome evergreen shrubs with holly-like leaflets often arranged in long, compound leaves that are very distinctive and decorative. All mahonias will grow in any reasonably good, well-drained soil and in sun or shade, but the winter-flowering kinds should be given a fairly sheltered position, and a few kinds are distinctively tender. *Mahonia aquifolium*, with clusters of yellow flowers in March–April, followed by grape-purple berries, is one of the easiest and hardiest, thriving in sun or shade, usually 90 cm to 1.2 m (3 to 4 ft) high.

Mahonia japonica makes a much larger bush, has long leaves composed of numerous leaflets and has pale yellow, sweetly scented flowers in slender spikes arranged like the spokes of a wheel. *M. lomariifolia* is taller and more stiffly erect and carries its scentless yellow flowers in slender, upward pointing spikes. A hybrid between these two is called *M. × media* and in habit it more closely resembles *M. lomariifolia* but is hardier. The best known hybrid 'Charity' is scentless but 'Lionel Fortescue' has some perfume. Both these handsome shrubs need a warm, sheltered but not necessarily sunny position. Neither is improved by pruning, but *M. aquifolium* can be cut back after flowering or trimmed lightly in summer.

Olearia
These are the daisy bushes, so called because of their numerous, daisy-like flowers. All are evergreen and all will grow in most adequately drained soils, including those overlying chalk and limestone. They will withstand salt-laden wind, which makes them good shrubs for seaside gardens, and *Olearia × haastii* is also an excellent town shrub. But not all are fully hardy so selection must be

determined by the kind of temperatures likely to be experienced in winter.

Olearia × haastii, 1.5 to 1.8 m (5 to 6 ft) high, with small, rounded leaves and a dense habit which makes it suitable for use as a screen or hedge, is probably the hardiest but its flowers in July–August are not so pure a white as those of *O. scilloniensis*, 90 cm to 1.2 m (3 to 4 ft) high, with small grey leaves and flowering in May–June. *O. gunniana*, now renamed *O. phlogopappa*, and *O. stellulata* are similar to the last named, but the latter also has blue and pink-flowered forms, distinguished as cultivar 'Slendens', but these appear to be even more tender. *O. macrodonta* has the largest leaves, resembling those of a holly. It has big flattish clusters of scented white flowers in June, can reach 3 m (10 ft) and is a very handsome shrub often used as a windbreak in maritime gardens.

Most kinds prefer warm sunny places, but *Olearia × haastii* will grow in semi-shade. All can be cut back in spring, if necessary, but with some loss of flower that summer.

Osmanthus

The most popular kind is *Osmanthus delavayi*, a densely branched evergreen, eventually 1.8 m (6 ft) high and more through, with small rounded leaves and scented white flowers in April–May.

Osmanthus heterophyllus (also known as *ilicifolius*) is a fine foliage shrub. It grows slowly to 3 m (10 ft) or more, could easily be mistaken for a holly and has small white scented flowers in October. It is best planted in one of its variegated forms, such as 'Aureomarginatus', leaves edged with yellow, and 'Variegatus', leaves edged with white. *O. burkwoodii*, often known as *× Osmarea* 'Burkwoodii', is a hybrid between *O. delavayi* and *O. decorus* (*Phillyrea decora*). It is rather like the former in appearance with similar flowers, but it is stiffer in growth and hardier which makes it suitable for use as a hedge or screen and it also makes an attractive specimen bush, eventually 2.1 or 2.4 m (7 or 8 ft) high.

All kinds thrive in any reasonably fertile soil, in sun or partial shade, but *Osmanthus delavayi* is a little tender and

Paeonia lutea 'L'Esperance'

may need to be grown against a sunny sheltered wall in cold districts. All can be pruned in spring, *O. delavayi* immediately after flowering.

Paeonia

This is the botanical name for peony and in addition to the familiar herbaceous kinds it covers several useful shrubs. Easiest to grow are *Paeonia delavayi* with single deep crimson flowers and *P. lutea* with single yellow flowers which are larger and better displayed in variety *ludlowii*.

All make quite large bushes 1.5 or 1.8 m (5 or 6 ft) high and flower in May, and all will grow freely in any reasonably fertile soil and sunny place. But they are not so spectacular as the cultivars of *P. suffruticosa* which are usually only 90 cm or 1.2 m (3 or 4 ft) high and have much bigger, often fully double flowers in a range of colours including pink, scarlet and crimson. These are also hybrids between *P. suffruticosa* and *P. lutea*, collectively known as *P. × lemoinei*, with double yellow or yellow and red flowers.

All these need a rather sheltered position, not subject to severe spring frosts as they start to grow early and the young shoots are rather tender. They enjoy rather rich soil, not liable to dry out badly in summer but never waterlogged in winter.

Parthenocissus

These are the climbers that gardeners often call ampelopsis or Virginia creepers, though the latter name properly belongs to one kind only, *Parthenocissus quinquifolia*, which has extra large vine-like leaves that colour brilliantly before they fall in autumn. It is partially self clinging and excellent for covering sheds, screens or fences, or for running up into old, not very valuable trees.

Better as a wall covering, because it is entirely self-clinging by little adhesive pads, is *Parthenocissus tricuspidata*, popularly known as Boston Ivy. It also colours well but is more variable in leaf than the Virginia Creeper, one of the most popular forms being 'Veitchii' with relatively small leaves.

Parthenocissus henryana has deeply

lobed leaves that combine dark green and bronzy purple with white veins. It is exceptionally decorative since the colour is there all summer and it is completely self-clinging but it needs a sheltered wall as it is a little tender.

All kinds will grow well in most soils, in sun or shade, though autumn colour is best in a light place. No regular pruning is necessary but shoots that grow too far can be cut back in the autumn.

Passiflora

All the passion flowers are more or less tender, but *Passiflora caerulea* is near enough hardy to be worth planting out of doors in sunny, sheltered places. It is a very vigorous climber which is capable of growing 4.5 m (15 ft) even after it has been cut to ground level by winter frost. The white flowers look a little like those of a clematis, but with a central corona of filaments which are in three concentric zones of blue, white and purple in the species but are all white in the cultivar 'Constance Elliott'. Both plants climb by

Passiflora caerulea

tendrils so require wires, trellises or something similar to which to cling. They succeed best in fertile, well-drained soils. Frost-damaged growth should be cut out in spring at which time any stems that threaten to grow too far can also be shortened.

Pernettya

Evergreen shrubs grown primarily for their marble-like berries which may be scarlet, crimson, purple, pink, lilac, mauve or white according to cultivar. *Pernettya mucronata* is the best species, usually about 90 cm (3 ft) high, spreading into a dense thicket by means of suckers, and with small, white, heather-like flowers in May–June. Sometimes the flowers on a bush are all of one sex, and since only the female flowers can produce berries and then only if fertilized with pollen from male flowers, it may be necessary to plant several bushes to be certain of a display. But there are also hermaphrodite cultivars (these producing both male and female sex organs) which will both produce berries on their own and fertilize purely female bushes. 'Bell's Seedling', with deep red berries, is such an hermaphrodite form and 'Thymifolia' has all male flowers so is useful for pollinating females.

All cultivars require acid soil, dislike chalk and limestone, and fruit freely in sunny places though they grow quite well in shade. Pruning in the ordinary sense is not usually necessary or desirable, but if plants threaten to spread too far they can be chopped back with a sharp spade in spring. Many of the rooted pieces dug out in this way can be grown on into good bushes if desired.

Perovskia

The best kind, *Perovskia atriplicifolia*, looks rather like a tall unusually spiky lavender, with grey leaves and stems and lavender-blue flowers in late summer. It grows well in warm, sunny places and well-drained soils, but is only semi-shrubby and the 90 cm (3 ft) stems are usually partly killed each winter. This matters little as the best results are obtained by shortening all stems to a few centimeters each spring.

Perovskia (sometimes spelled perowskia) transplants badly and plants should always be purchased in containers from which they should be planted with a minimum of root disturbance.

Philadelphus

The correct popular name for these easily grown shrubs is mock orange from the resemblance in appearance and scent of the flowers of some species and cultivars to orange blossom. It is a pity that they are sometimes called syringa, the botanical name of lilac, a totally unrelated shrub.

All the popular cultivars of philadelphus are completely hardy and will grow in all reasonably fertile soils preferably in a sunny, or at least light and open position where they flower most freely. All flower in June and nearly all are white, though often with some suffusion of purple and with yellow stamens which show clearly in the single-flowered cultivars. Cultivars differ greatly in size and habit, a few reaching a height of 3 to 3.6 m (10 to 12 ft), but all can be reduced in size by cutting out the old flowering stems as soon as the flowers fade. The young, non-flowering stems should be retained to flower the following year.

Good forms are 'Beauclerk', white and purple 2.1 m (7 ft); 'Belle Étoile', white and purple 1.8 m (6 ft); *P. coronarius*, creamy white, 1.8 m (6 ft), and its cultivar 'Aureus', not very free flowering but with yellow foliage; *P. delavayi*, white and purple, 3 m (10 ft); *P. erectus*, small white flowers, 1.5 m (5 ft) high; 'Manteau d'Hermine', creamy white, double, 90 cm (3 ft); *P. microphyllus*, white, small flowers and leaves, 90 cm (3 ft); *P. intectus* (*P. pubescens intectus*), white 3.6 to 4.5 m (12 to 15 ft); 'Sybille', white and purple, 1.2 m (4 ft); 'Virginal', white, double 2.4 m (8 ft).

Phlomis

The kind most commonly planted is *Phlomis fruticosa*, the Jerusalem Sage, which grows about 90 cm (3 ft) high, has downy grey sage-like leaves and whorls of large yellow hooded flowers in summer. It is handsome in foliage and flower but also worthy of attention is another less familiar species, *P. chrysophylla*, which is similar in habit and appearance, but has yellowish-grey leaves. Both are shrubs for warm places and well-drained, even rather dry soils, just the plants in fact for a difficult sun-baked situation. Sometimes their rather soft stems are damaged by

Pieris formosa forrestii

frost in which case they should be cut back to live growth in spring.

Pieris

These evergreens are sometimes called lily-of-the-valley bushes because of the slight resemblance of their sprays of white, urn-shaped flowers, produced in spring, to those of the Lily-of-the-valley. All like rather acid soils such as those suitable for rhododendrons and will grow in full sun or light shade.

The young growth of *Pieris formosa forrestii* is bright red and it is often grown primarily as a foliage shrub, especially in forms selected for this leaf colour, such as 'Wakehurst'. However, it is less hardy than some of the others and so in cold gardens or exposed places it would be better to plant 'Forest Flame', a hybrid between it and the hardier, green-leaved *P. japonica*. All these will eventually grow to 2.1 or 2.4 m (7 or 8 ft) high, but *P. taiwanensis* is a little shorter and *P. floribunda* grows even more slowly and may take years to reach 1.8 m (6 ft). Pruning is as a rule unnecessary, but if plants get too big they can be cut back in

spring after flowering.

Pileostegia

Another of the climbing hydrangeas, this time an evergreen one with dense clusters of small ivory-white flowers in autumn. *Pileostegia viburnoides* is a vigorous climber adhering by roots on the stems, like ivy, and can be grown over a tree stump or up a wall. It likes fertile soil and will grow in sun or shade. It can be cut back in spring as necessary to keep it in bounds or the tips of straying stems can be pinched out in summer.

Polygonum

Most polygonums are herbaceous plants but one, *Polygonum baldschuanicum*, the Russian Vine, is a very vigorous climber capable of ascending to the top of a tall tree or completely covering a sizeable outbuilding with its twining stems which erupt into foaming cascades of creamy-white or pinkish-white blossom in late summer and early autumn. It will grow in most soils in sun or semi-shade and is very useful for quick cover of an unsightly building, though it loses its effectiveness as a screen in winter as it is deciduous. If it strays too far, as it often does, it can be cut back in winter.

Potentilla

The shrubby potentillas are particularly valuable because of their long flowering season, often from May to October. They are mostly small shrubs with dense twiggy growth, small divided leaves and yellow, orange, pink, red or white flowers. All will grow in semi-shade, but flower most freely in sunny, rather warm places and they thrive in all reasonably well-drained soils. The naturally rather dense habit can be improved if some of the older stems are cut out each March and the previous year's growth is shortened by a third or even more.

Good kinds are *Potentilla arbuscula*, yellow, 60 cm (2 ft); 'Abbotswood', white, 90 cm (3 ft); 'Elizabeth', light yellow, 90 cm (3 ft); and cultivars of *P. fruticosa* such as 'Daydawn', peach pink; 'Katherine Dykes', light yellow, 1.8 m (6 ft); *P.f. grandiflora* (or 'Jackman's Variety'), canary yellow, 1.2 m (4 ft); *P.f. mandschurica*, white 30 cm 'Princess', pink; 'Royal Flush', rose-pink, 90 cm (3 ft); 'Red Ace', orange-red, 60 cm (2 ft); 'Tangerine', orange yellow 60 cm (2 ft); and 'Vilmoriniana' silvery leaves, cream flowers, 1.2 to 1.8 m (4 to 6 ft).

Prunus

This is the great genus to which the cherries, plums, almonds and peaches belong, most of which are trees, but there are valuable shrubby kinds as well. Among the best known of them are the Cherry Laurel or Common Laurel, *Prunus laurocerasus*, and the Portugal Laurel, *P. lusitanica*, both of which are vigorous evergreens capable of reaching 4.5 m (15 ft) or more and much planted as hedges or screens. Both will grow in any reasonably fertile, not too dry soil, in sun or shade, the Common Laurel being particularly well able to survive in very shady places and in cities, though grime does spoil the appearance of its large glossy green leaves. Both plants have spikes of white flowers, those of the Common Laurel appearing in April, those of the Portugal Laurel in June. Both

also have useful forms, *P.l. azorica* being a particularly large-leaved, handsome-flowered variety of Portugal Laurel, and 'Otto Luyken', a short 1.2 m (4 ft) free-flowering cultivar of the Common Laurel. Others are 'Schipkaensis' and 'Zabeliana', both with narrow leaves and a wide but low habit. All can be pruned in May as necessary to keep them in bounds, or can be lightly trimmed any time in summer.

Prunus glandulosa 'Alba Plena' is a small bushy cherry 1.2 m (4 ft) high, with double white flowers in April. *P.* 'Cistena' looks like a dwarf version of the Purple-leaved Plum, has similar white flowers in spring and reddish-purple leaves and makes an excellent 90 cm to 1.5 m (3 to 5 ft) hedge. *P. incisa* can also be used as a hedge and covers itself in March with small white flowers as freely as a Sloe. *P. tenella* 'Fire Hill' is a dwarf almond with small deep rose flowers in March. *P. triloba multiplex* needs a warm sunny place to ripen its wood and produce its very beautiful double pink flowers in spring. All these are deciduous and succeed best in good, fertile, netural or alkaline soil and a sunny place.

Pyracantha

The firethorns are often planted against walls and they can be trained in such places very effectively, but they are not climbers, they will make big bushes in the open and are perfectly hardy. They have clusters of white flowers in early summer followed by red, orange or yellow berries in autumn and winter and all are evergreen. They are not fussy about soil and do especially well on chalk or limestone. All can be pruned in spring or summer, the most convenient time for doing this usually being immediately after flowering when it can be seen where the berries are forming and care be taken not to cut them off.

Good kinds are *Pyracantha atalantioides*, scarlet berries; *P. coccinea* 'Lalandei', orange-red berries; 'Orange Glow', orange berries; *P. rogersiana* 'Flava', yellow berries; and 'Watereri', red berries.

Rhododendron

There are so many different rhododendrons, varying in height from ground cover plants to trees, some with minute leaves and some with very large leaves, with an equally wide range in flower sizes, forms and colours and a flowering season from January to July, that it would be possible to stock a garden with this remarkable genus alone and still have plenty of variety. All kinds thrive best in rather acid soils and are not happy on chalk or limestone unless regularly fed with specially formulated iron and manganese. Most succeed best in soil that contains plenty of peat or leafmould so that it retains moisture well in summer without becoming waterlogged in winter, and most also like to grow in the dappled shade provided by fairly widely spaced trees. However, the cultivars collectively known as Hardy Hybrids, all of which make fairly large evergreen bushes carrying flowers in May and June in dome-shaped clusters, are extremely adaptable and will succeed quite well in full sun. They are also the best rhododendrons for town gardens since they put up with a chemically-polluted atmosphere better than most of the species and pedigree hybrids.

Rhododendrons transplant well and can be moved in autumn or late winter, even when quite large, which makes them specially useful where quick results are essential. They will submit to quite hard pruning in spring, but this results in the loss of at least one year's flowering.

Cultivars are so numerous that it is impossible to do justice to them in any short list. Because they transplant so readily and are usually available either balled or in containers, there is much to be said for purchasing them in flower, but since most start to flower while still very young, the size of nursery plants does not give any indication of ultimate dimensions which should therefore be ascertained.

Ribes

The currants and gooseberries that are grown in the fruit garden are species of ribes, but there are also purely ornamental kinds, none more useful in the garden than the Flowering Currant, *Ribes sanguineum*. This quickly makes a big bush up to 2.4 m (8 ft) high, with currant-like leaves and short trails of rose-pink flowers in April. There are several cultivars including two with much deeper coloured flowers, 'King Edward VII', crimson, and 'Pulborough Scarlet', magenta red; and one named 'Brocklebankii' with yellow leaves. All forms flower on year-old stems and the quality of the flowers can be improved and the bushes reduced in size by cutting out the old stems immediately after flowering. They will grow in all soils, in sun or shade.

Other useful species are *Ribes odoratum*, sometimes wrongly called *R. aureum*, rather shorter than the Flowering Currant with richly scented, yellow flowers in April and *R. speciosum*, often called the Fuchsia-flowered Gooseberry because of the resemblance of its crimson flowers to very small fuchsias. It flowers in April and May, grows about 1.5 m (5 ft) high and, should be given a warm sunny place.

Rosmarinus

Charming evergreen shrubs with narrow, aromatic leaves and small blue flowers, freely produced in spring or even earlier in warm, sheltered places. They grow best in well-drained soils and will withstand a good deal of heat and drought. All are a little tender, some more so than others, but the Common Rosemary, *Rosmarinus officinalis*, can be grown successfully in all but the coldest parts of the British Isles. Typically bushy, 90 cm or 1.2 m (3 or 4 ft) high, it has numerous cultivars including white flowered, pink flowered, deeper blue flowered and narrowly erect forms.

Rosmarinus lavandulaceus (also known as *R. officinalis prostratus*) is prostrate or semi-weeping, a lovely shrub for the top of a sunny terrace wall, but decidedly more tender than the Common Rosemary. All kinds can be pruned in spring, immediately after flowering, but frost-damaged growth should be removed as soon as noted.

Rubus

These are the brambles, the genus to which the Blackberry and the Loganberry belong, but there are also several decorative species well worth planting where there is room for them. They will grow in almost any soil, in sun or partial shade. Those grown for their white stems (often known as whitewash brambles) can be pruned almost to ground level early each spring just before they re-start into growth; those grown for their flowers are best pruned immediately after flowering when the old flowering stems can be cut out.

Rubus deliciosus, *R. trilobus* and the beautiful hybrid between them, Tridel, all make long arching stems bearing big white flowers rather like single roses in May and June. *R. spectabilis* is shorter 1.2 to 1.5 m (4 to 5 ft), spreading by suckers and with magenta flowers in April. *R. ulmifolius* 'Bellidiflorus' is semi-climbing or rambling with little double pink, pompon flowers in summer. One of the best whitewash brambles is *R. cockburnianus* (also known as *R. giraldianus*) making a wide spreading bush 1.8 or 2.1 m (6 to 7 ft) high and even more across.

Sambucus

This is the genus to which the Common Elder or Elderberry belongs, and although the handsome British species, *Sambucus nigra*, is only worth planting in the wilder parts of the garden, it has several useful cultivars, the most popular of which are 'Aurea', the Golden Elder, with yellow leaves, and 'Laciniata', with finely divided leaves. It thrives in most soils, including those overlying chalk or limestone, colours best in light places and can be pruned to within a few centimeters of the main stems every spring. *S. racemosa*, the Red-berried Elder, has a handsome cultivar named 'Plumosa Aurea', in which the leaves are both yellow and deeply divided. For flowers the best kind is *S. canadensis*, the Canadian Elderberry, which has very large flat heads of small white flowers in summer followed by black berries.

Santolina

These small evergreen shrubs, collectively known as lavender cotton, are ideal for edging borders or for grouping in hot,

rather dry places where they grow especially well. They have narrow, finely divided leaves, grey in *Santolina chamaecyparissus* and its shorter variety *corsica* (also known 'Nana'), bright green in *S. virens*; often known as *S. viridis*. All forms have small button-shaped yellow flowers like the central disc of a daisy. They succeed best in well-drained soils and can be made even more bushy and compact by being trimmed with shears in summer as soon as the flowers fade or before if the flowers are not regarded as attractive.

Sarcococca

These are useful evergreen shrubs for shady places and though their white flowers are small and partly hidden by the leaves they are very welcome because they are so sweetly scented and come in late winter or early spring. The best kinds are *Sarcococca confusa* and *S. hookeriana digyna*, both about 90 cm (3 ft) high and both excellent for cutting as foliage.

Schizophragma

This is yet another genus of self-clinging climbing hydrangeas. Soil, aspect and pruning are exactly the same as for *Hydrangea petiolaris* which these plants resemble except that the sterile flowers have one large showy sepal. The most spectacular kind is *Schizophragma integrifolia* with a large creamy-white bracts. *S. hydrangeoides* is similar but the sepals are a little smaller and are tinged with pink in 'Roseum'.

Senecio

The best-known shrubby member of this very large and varied genus has long been known as *Senecio greyii*, a grey-leaved evergreen about 90 cm (3 ft) high and becoming considerably broader than this with age, but is usually a hybrid of this species which should be known as 'Sunshine'. It is hardier than the species and in summer it produces similar showy clusters of yellow daisy flowers. It is a fine plant for a warm sunny place, though like most shrubby senecios it is not completely hardy. If it does get damaged by winter frost, it can be pruned back to live wood in spring. *S. laxifolius* is similar and

The fruits of the Elderberry, *Sambucus niger*

much confused with *S. greyii* but has narrower, less rounded leaves.

Senecio rotundifolius (also known as *S. reinoldii*) is useful near the sea since it will withstand salty gales better than most shrubs. It has large round leathery leaves, green above and grey beneath, and it can reach 2.4 m (8 ft) or so but is usually considerably less. It will not survive much frost.

Skimmia

These useful shrubs are attractive in leaf, flower and fruit and will grow well in all reasonably fertile soils, in sun or in shade. The most popular kind, *Skimmia japonica*, grows 90 cm to 1.5 m (3 to 5 ft) high, has small white flowers in spike-like clusters and segregates male and female flowers on separate bushes. Only the females produce crops of berries and then only if fertilized with pollen from a male so it is wise to plant both sexes. However, this is no hardship since the males are most effective in flower, especially such cultivars as 'Fragrans' in which the flowers are scented, or 'Rubella', in which the flower buds are red. 'Foremanii' is a good female cultivar and usually the berries remain so long that they are still there the following spring when the plants start to flower again or even when the next crop of berries has set.

Skimmia reevesiana (also known as *S. fortunei*) has flowers of both sexes on the same bush so if there is only room for one plant this is the kind to choose provided the soil does not contain chalk, to which it objects. It is shorter than *S. japonica* and has narrower leaves, but otherwise the effect is similar.

Solanum

The two most useful shrubby kinds, both deciduous, are *Solanum jasminoides* and *S. crispum*. The first is a true climber supporting itself by twining around branches, posts, trellis work or wires. In the common form the flowers, produced in late summer and autumn, are a rather slaty blue, but it is usually the pure white cultivar 'Album', that is planted and this is very attractive. Both blue and white forms are distinctly tender and require a warm sunny place where winter frosts are

not likely to be severe, though even if stems are damaged new growth is usually produced in spring from lower down.

The other popular kind, *Solanum crispum*, is usually grown as a climber but is really a sprawling shrub and if used to cover a wall or fence its long flexible stems need to be tied to some kind of support. The flowers, are produced in summer and autumn, are larger than those of *S. jasminoides* and a good violet blue with raised yellow centre. This species is a little hardier but still in need of a warm, sunny, sheltered place. It can be hard pruned in spring if desired and frost-damaged growth should certainly be removed then.

Sorbaria

These handsome, suckering shrubs are closely allied to spiraea and their large plumy clusters of small white or cream flowers, produced freely in summer, closely resemble those of some of the herbaceous astilbes. *Sorbaria aitchisonii*, 2.4 to 3 m (8 to 10 ft) high, is one of the best. *S. arborea* and *S. tomentosa* will easily reach 4.5 m (15 ft) and *S. sorbifolia* is the shortest at 1.2 or 1.5 m (4 or 5 ft). They succeed best in fairly fertile, rather moist soils, but are not really fussy and provided there is room for them, there are few places in which they could not be grown. Left unpruned vigorous kinds will reach 3 or 3.6 m (10 or 12 ft) and be as much or more through, but suckers and the oldest stems can be removed in winter and young ones shortened by a third or more.

Spartium

The Spanish Broom, *Spartium junceum*, is invaluable in the garden because it continues to produce its bright yellow, sweetly scented flowers throughout the latter half of summer and even into the autumn when they are a splendid foil for purple buddleia and blue or red hydrangeas. Though deciduous, spartium has an evergreen look because of its bright green, rush-like stems and though in good soil and sheltered places it may grow too tall for convenience it can be kept to 1.5 or 1.8 m (5 or 6 ft) by shortening each spring all or most of the previous year's growth. In rather poor sandy soils or in windswept places near the sea, conditions for which it is well suited, it remains naturally compact. Its flowers last well in water.

Spiraea

From a garden standpoint there are two very distinct groups of spiraea, one which makes a thicket of erect stems the other spreading ever wider by suckers. The latter, though excellent in semi-wild places where there is plenty of room, can be a nuisance in small gardens or more formal situations where they must be constantly kept in place by chopping through their tough stolons in winter. All these suckering spiraeas produce their flowers in fluffy bottle-brush spikes in late summer, and the least overpowering and most beautiful of them is *Spiraea × billiardii* 'Triumphans' (also known as *S. menziesii* 'Triumphans') 1.8 to 2.4 m (6 to 8 ft), with rose-pink flowers, but it is not suitable for markedly alkaline chalk or limestone soils.

In the other group there are numerous fine garden shrubs. *Spiraea × arguta*, popularly known as Bridal Wreath, crowds its thin, twiggy stems with snowy bloom in April and May. It is 1.5 to 1.8 m (5 to 6 ft) high. *S. thunbergii* is similar, 90 cm to 1.2 m (3 to 4 ft) high, and a week or so earlier. *S. japonica* grows 90 cm (3 ft) high and has flattish heads of rose-pink flowers all summer; 'Anthony Waterer' is 90 cm (3 ft) high with crimson flowers; and 'Goldflame', 90 cm (3 ft) high, has leaves which are coppery yellow when young but become green with age. *S. prunifolia* is 1.5 or 1.8 m (5 or 6 ft) high with arching stems loaded with double white flowers in April and May. *S. × vanhouttei* is similar in habit but has clusters of single flowers in June. *S. veitchii* is a larger shrub, 2.4 or 2.7 m (8 to 9 ft) high, with white flowers all along the arching stems in June and July. There are many more.

Symphoricarpos

The Snowberry is the most popular species of this genus, a twiggy bush 1.2 or 1.5 m (4 or 5 ft) high with small pink flowers followed by white, marble-like berries. There is considerable confusion regarding its name and it may appear in catalogues as *Symphoricarpos albus*, *S. laevigatus*, *S. racemosus* or *S. rivularis*, but the first appears to be correct. It will grow in all soils, in sun or shade, can be used as a hedge or as game cover and its berries are very useful for winter decorations. There are several other useful kinds, equally easy to grow, including the Coral Berry, *S. orbiculatus*, similar in appearance but with rose-pink berries, and numerous hybrids such as 'Magic Berry', purple; 'Mother of Pearl', pink, and 'White Hedge', white. All kinds can be pruned in spring as necessary to keep them in shape.

Syringa

These are the lilacs, some of which will grow almost to tree size in time. They are beautiful shrubs thriving in all reasonably fertile soils and succeeding particularly well on chalk and limestone. They will grow in shade but flower most freely in warm, sunny places. Pruning is not essential but, if bushes must be restricted in size, old flowering stems can be cut back to young growths immediately after flowering. When lilacs are cut for flower decoration they automatically receive this kind of pruning.

The Common Lilac, *Syringa vulgaris*, is available in numerous cultivars, both single and double flowered. Typical single cultivars are 'Blue Hyacinth', mauve and blue; 'Charles X', purple; 'Clark's Giant', lavender and mauve; 'Congo', deep reddish purple; 'Maud Notcutt', white; 'Primrose', pale primrose yellow, and 'Souvenir de Louis Spaeth', wine red.

Typical double forms are 'Charles Joly', purplish red; 'Kathleen Havemeyer', purple and lilac pink; 'Madame Antoine Buchner', rosy mauve; 'Madame Lemoine', white; 'Michael Buchner', lilac; and 'Mrs Edward Harding', wine red. All these cultivars are scented and all flower in May or early June.

A little later are the Canadian hybrids (*Syringa × josiflexa* and *S. × prestoniae*) such as 'Bellicent', rose pink, and 'Elinor', a purplish red.

The Persian Lilac, *Syringa × persica*, is a smaller bush, to 2.1 m (7 ft) high, with sweetly-scented pink flowers (white in 'Alba') in May. The Rouen Lilac, *S. × chinensis*, is a hybrid between the Persian and the Common Lilac, similar in size to the former and with white, pink or reddish-purple flowered cultivars.

Tamarix

The tamarisks are splendid shrubs to plant as a windbreak in exposed gardens near the sea and some kinds, such as *Tamarix pentandra*, with plumes of pink flowers in August and September, and *T. parviflora* often sold as *T. tetrandra*, with small pink flowers wreathing the long slender branches in May, make beautiful specimen bushes. All grow best in open sunny places and well-drained, preferably acid or neutral soils. The spring-flowering types are best if cut back moderately immediately after flowering and the late summer-flowering types in early spring.

Viburnum

There are a great many useful species of viburnum and from a decorative point of view they can be divided into kinds grown primarily for their flowers, or for their fruits, or for their foliage. Some are evergreen and some deciduous, and though most will grow well in any fairly fertile soil and are hardy in all parts of the British Isles, a few have special requirements or are just a little tender.

A few species have flowers of two kinds, as in hydrangea, small fertile flowers gathered into a flattish cluster and showy sterile flowers surrounding them. The British native Guelder Rose, *Viburnum opulus*, is of this kind and the fertile flowers are followed by shining currant-red fruits (yellow in 'Fructuluteo'). Normally 2.4 or 2.7 m (8 or 9 ft) high, it has a shorter cultivar, 'Compactum', only 1.2 to 1.5 m (4 to 5 ft) high. It also has a cultivar, 'Sterile', in which all the flowers are sterile, forming large white balls, hence it is known as the Snowball Tree. All forms flower in June as does the Japanese Snowball, *V. plicatum*, which has smaller but equally effective flower clusters. A form of this with some sterile, some fertile flowers is known as *V. plicatum tomentosum*. The flat flower clusters are carried all along more or less

horizontal branches and it is a notably decorative shrub but one which needs a fair amount of space to do itself justice.

Other kinds with the ball-like type of flower head are *V. macrocephalum*, which is just a little tender and needs a warm, sunny place, and its hybrid with *V. carlesii*, *V. × carlcephalum*, quite hardy with scented flowers.

Then there are numerous species with flower clusters entirely composed of fertile flowers. Most of these are sweetly scented and they include *Viburnum fragrans* (also known as *V. farreri*), white, to 2.4 m (8 ft), flowering in winter; *V. × bodnantense*, pink, to 2.7 m (9 ft), also flowering in winter; *V. × burkwoodii*, white, evergreen, 1.5 m (5 ft), flowering in late winter and spring; *V. carlesii*, similar to the last but deciduous and spring flowering; *V. × juddii*, yet another in the same style, also deciduous, and by many considered easier to grow than *V. carlesii*, and *V. utile*, white, evergreen, flowering in May.

Viburnum betulifolium and *V. lantana*, the British Wayfaring Tree, are grown primarily for their berries, small and currant red in the first which makes a big big bush with arching stems, red becoming black in *V. lantana* which is stiffer in habit and thrives on chalk.

Viburnum tinus, the Laurustinus, is a big bushy evergreen, to 2.4 m (8 ft) high with clusters of white flowers in winter and spring. It will thrive in sun or shade and can be used as a hedge or windbreak. It does well in town gardens and by the sea.

Viburnum rhytidophyllum has the largest leaves, evergreen, wrinkled and dark green above, covered with rusty coloured down beneath. It can reach 3 m (10 ft) and is a very handsome foliage shrub. In the common form the flower clusters, which come in May, are a rather dull white, but there is a cultivar 'Roseum' with rose-tinted flowers which are more decorative. Another evergreen species, *V. davidii*, is also grown primarily for its foliage, but it is very different in appearance, only 60 to 90 cm (2 to 3 ft) high, wide spreading with ribbed dark green leaves. The small white flowers are sometimes followed by good crops of small turquoise berries.

Vitis

The Grape Vine belongs here, its name being *Vitis vinifera*, and a few cultivars are worth planting for ornament. Particularly recommended are 'Brandt', with blackish-purple fruits and leaves which turn crimson before they fall in the autumn, and 'Purpurea', similar in fruit and with leaves that are purple throughout the summer. Both are vigorous climbers clinging by tendrils and capable of covering a fairly large house front, but the tips of the shoots can be pinched out at any time in summer and all the year's growth can be cut to within 2.5 cm (1 in) or so of the main stems in winter if it needs to be restricted. Vines succeed best in warm sunny places and fertile, neutral or alkaline soils.

Even more rampant in growth is *Vitis coignetiae* which is grown solely for its very large rounded leaves which colour brilliantly in the autumn. This is a handsome climber to run up into an old tree or to cover an outhouse or large wall. Treatment is the same as for the cultivars of the grape vine.

Weigela

Sometimes these easily grown shrubs are known as diervilla. They grow well in almost all soils and reasonably open places and produce their funnel-shaped flowers freely in May and June. Most kinds grow 1.5 or 1.8 m (5 or 6 ft) high and can spread fairly widely, but they can be kept smaller by cutting out most of the old flowering stems as soon as the flowers fade. Most of the cultivars grown are garden hybrids such as 'Abel Carriere', rose; 'Bristol Rugby', ruby red, and 'Newport Red', bright red, but there is a very good cultivar of a species, *Weigela florida*, named 'Variegata', with pale pink flowers and cream-variegated leaves.

Wisteria

There are two species of particular value in the garden, both twiners with trails of scented, pea-type flowers in spring, but differing in vigour and flower character. The Chinese Wisteria, *Wisteria sinensis*, is the kind usually seen covering house fronts or climbing high into trees. It is a very vigorous plant capable of reaching 15 m (50 ft) or even more and its flowers, blue mauve in the common form, are in trails 23 to 30 cm (9 to 12 in) long. There are also white and double-flowered cultivars. The Japanese Wisteria, *W. floribunda*, is less vigorous, usually about 3.6 m (12 ft) high and often trained as a kind of small weeping "tree". In general the flower trails are a little shorter, but the remarkable *W. multijuga*, also known as *W. floribunda*, 'Macrobotrys', has trails up to 90 cm (3 ft) long. This is the blue purple of the species, but there are also white, pink and violet-blue cultivars.

All wisterieas grow best in warm, sunny places and fertile, well-drained soils. They transplant badly and should be purchased young in containers, moved from these without root breakage and watered and syringed frequently in hot dry weather until established. They can be pruned in summer when all young growths not required for extension can be shortened to five leaves and again, if desired, in winter when the same growths can be cut back to two dormant buds. When the plants have filled their allotted space all surplus growth can be cut out each winter.

Yucca

These are shrubs that give the garden a really exotic, sub-tropical appearance, yet several of them are surprisingly hardy and all succeed well in a wide variety of places from seaside to city gardens. They make large rosettes of stiff, sword-shaped leaves and the large bell-shaped flowers are carried in broad, upstanding spikes. Some kinds, such as *Yucca gloriosa*, the Adam's Needle, and *Y. recurvifolia*, gradually form a stout trunk about a metre high, but the hardiest and most easily grown kinds, *Y. filamentosa* and *Y. flaccida* sit more closely to the soil and only produce short basal stems. All flower in summer or early autumn. There flower in summer or early autumn. There are also cultivars of *Y. gloriosa* and *Y. filamentosa* with yellow-striped leaves. All grow best in full sun and well-drained soil. No pruning is desirable.

Roses

JACK HARKNESS

Roses are deciduous shrubs and climbers of great diversity in habit, foliage, fruit and flower. These differences arise from their far flung natural distribution, all around the temperate zones of the northern hemisphere.

Popular practice puts the Queen of Flowers in a bed. Whether so used, or as a flowering shrub, hedging plant, climber or standard, she is valued by many as the most desirable of garden plants.

Roses are normally grown in the open, being so hardy as to render winter protection uncustomary in Britain, but they also grow well in greenhouses, and in pots. Their great advantages are beauty, ease of cultivation, cheapness and long life.

Conditions

Roses require a soil which retains moisture but permits drainage. The more fertile the soil the better, because roses grow readily in response to fertility. Tolerant of alkalinity or acidity, they are unhappy only at the further ends of the scale, more particularly at the acid extreme. They are not shade plants; they prefer to grow in the sun. Roses usually endure exposed places well, with some inhibition of growth.

Soil preparation

The three objects are to feed the plants, to give them anchorage and to drain the soil. Deep digging attains all three, preferably by trenching; at the same time one can mix organic substances with the soil. But preparation must be adapted to the soil, of which here follow four instances.

A soil impervious to water (which may be tested by filling a hole with water to see if it drains in 48 hours) demands the lower spits be broken, and if necessary a soakaway provided, to prevent the bed becoming a sump for the surrounding area. Render heavy clay more porous with gypsum (calcium sulphate) at about 1.6 kg per m² (3 lb to the sq yd) in the bottom of the trench.

A soil with a high water table will only grow roses if the beds are raised.

A shallow soil which drains well needs to be dug only for the purpose of adding food, particularly substances to hold moisture. The lower spit may be replaced with better soil. Beds must not be raised on such soil because in the summer they dry out.

A fertile, well-drained soil need only be cleaned, levelled and planted.

If the soil is dug deeply, then each stratum must be returned to its proper place, the bottom to the bottom, the top to the top. After such disturbance, it must be given a long time to settle before roses are planted in it.

Planting

Buy good strong plants, and be suspicious of cheap offers. Plant October to April when the soil is crumbly. The ground is the place for roses, but if they cannot enter it at once, keep them in a cool place, not in a heated room, for the briefest possible time. If the soil is not crumbly, plant them temporarily elsewhere, close together and firmly, with the roots wet. Do not plant in prepared ground until it has re-settled.

The average planting distances to create a close array are: miniatures 30 cm (12 in); dwarf floribundas 40 cm (15 in); floribundas and hybrid teas 53 cm (21 in); shrub roses 1 m (3½ ft); climbers at least 3 m (10 ft) apart, and standards 1.2 m (4 ft). But all may be grown individually at optional distances, and standards in particular do not really need to be closely set.

Use a good seed and potting medium as

OPPOSITE: The climbing rose 'Mme Grégoire Staechelin'

Staking a standard rose

a planting mixture; or enthusiasts can make their own by mixing two handfuls of sterilized bonemeal (use gloves) and one of hoof and horn to a large bucketful of peat. Do not let other fertilizers or manure touch the roots.

Trim off snags, suckers and damaged or immature growth before planting, and wet the roots. Dig a shallow hole, and place the plant to one side of it, with the roots spread out on the bottom, towards the horizontal. Place at soil level the point where thorny stems and smooth rootstock join. If the plant does not sit comfortably, deepen the hole – 15 or 18 cm (6 or 7 in) is usually deep enough. Cover the roots first with planting mixture, then half fill the hole with soil, and tread very firmly, for rose roots must be tight to the ground. Fill the hole, tread lightly and level off. The plant should resist a firm tug. When filling up, take the soil from the next planting position, then the next hole is ready dug.

Put the stake in before the standard, the top of it just below the lowest graft.

When the soil is dry in April to June, tread again, especially any slow starters, which will also benefit from a bucketful of water, after treading.

Roses grown in containers must be planted, after removing the container, with the soil closely firmed to the sides and bottom of the container soil, which should be moist. Planting time, obviously, is optional for container plants.

Pruning

A rose shoot normally grows to its terminal point in one season. It exists in the future by means of side shoots, which are usually incapable of girth greater than the parent shoot. By pruning, only the strongest wood is left, and new growth is therefore obliged to arise from it.

Such, in a nutshell, are the reasons and methods, to which we add one fact; after a few years, rose stems resist sap flow, which is forced into new growth elsewhere on the plant, whereupon the old growth system can be cut away.

Efficient secateurs and a narrow-bladed saw (or long-handled secateurs) are the tools. The time is winter or spring, before growth is far advanced, but it is well to shorten the plants in November or December to reduce wind damage. Cuts are made just above an eye, without injuring it, and on a slant of which the eye side is the higher. Unless the plant's development demands otherwise, an outward-facing eye is chosen. All weak, unripe, damaged or dead wood is removed.

Prune new plants hard: bedding roses being left about finger length out of the ground; flowering shrubs up to 30 cm (1 ft); climbers 60 to 90 cm (2 to 3 ft), and standards about 15 cm (6 in) from the grafts. When the plants are mature, strong growths can be retained to any length; they will develop into a considerable system, which may be encouraged and retained, with suitable shortening of the side shoots, or of a part of the system if the top of it is becoming unproductive.

Exceptions are many belonging to the group known as the old garden roses, which grow one year, and flower the next. Unless adequate length is retained, the flowers will have been pruned away. Wild roses look more graceful if the long

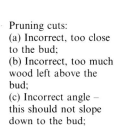

Pruning cuts:
(a) Incorrect, too close to the bud;
(b) Incorrect, too much wood left above the bud;
(c) Incorrect angle – this should not slope down to the bud;
(d) Correct pruning cut

Dead, diseased and a certain amount of old wood is removed from large-flowered bush roses (hybrid teas) to leave an open framework about one third the height of the original bush

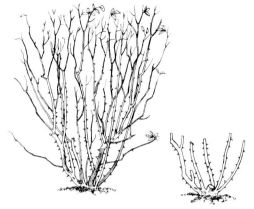

shoots are not shortened. Standard roses do not replace growth as easily as the others, and caution is needed in removing large parts of them.

The long growths of climbers are trained to fit their position, and in future years their side shoots shortened; or the best may be trained. The main stem is kept until it is not satisfactorily productive, when it may be removed entirely, or shortened to a point where it is productive.

Cultivation

After pruning, shallow cultivation by spade or fork will tidy the beds; but only 2.5 to 5 cm (1 to 2 in) deep – the roots hate being disturbed. Weeds may be controlled by the hoe, or by weedkillers or suppressants, first ensuring the herbicide may safely be used among roses.

Fertility is increased by the proper use of mulches, soil fertilizers or foliar feeding; it is better not to use fertilizers in the first year after planting.

The best mulch is good farmyard manure, spread shortly after pruning, when the plants do not have many young growths obtruding. It should be chipped into the top 5 cm (2 in) of soil with a sharp spade; not deeper, for fear of disturbing the roots; and not with a fork, which will catch and loosen roots, whereas a spade will chop, and in effect prune them. Mulches are more usually applied when the soil is warmer, in May. They are

spread on the surface, without being chipped in, and thus help to feed, to conserve moisture, and to smother weeds. Compost, leafmould or peat may be used. Grass mowings, if used, should not be from lawns recently treated with hormone weed killers; and they should be followed by herbicides to destroy the seeds that may germinate from them.

Fertilizers for roses are so carefully prepared by the leading manufacturers that most people can safely buy them, and apply first after pruning. They go down more quickly if spread on a frosty morning. A second dressing can be applied in June when the buds have formed, preferably in a rainy spell. Ideally, fertilizers should answer the needs of the soil, which can only be discovered by expert analysis, and in cases of difficulty this is a sensible procedure.

Nitro-chalk is unsuitable for chalky soils; sulphate of magnesium should be a constituent of a good rose fertilizer, for magnesium in a small amount is an essential rose food; Kieserite is a good source. Lime must be used with caution, only on a soil proved to be too acid without it, and preferably in the form of calcium carbonate.

Foliar feeding is especially useful if the soil is alkaline or chalky.

Suckers should be pulled or cut off, as soon as noticed. They are recognized by their different leaves and by their point of origin being below the grafting union. It is not true that they can be detected by counting their leaflets.

Fading flowers should be dead-headed before they set seed, to induce new flowering shoots; ideally, trim them down to the next sound eye, but failing that, trim them off quickly.

Suckers which arise from the stock on to which the rose was budded should be pulled or cut off as close to the plant as possible as soon as they are noticed

Black spot can be controlled by removing all infected foliage and by spraying with a fungicide such as Benlate, Saprol, Nimrod-T or Tumbleblite

Pests and diseases

Be prepared with efficient sprayers and remedies because troubles spread very swiftly. The chief enemies are greenfly, mildew, blackspot and rust. The leading companies have good remedies for each, and regularly introduce new products.

Greenfly killers should be applied when the greenfly become obvious.

Mildew is a light greyish mould; look just under the flower buds for early warning, and spray when seen. Current remedies include Benlate, Saprol, Nimrod-T, Mildothane and Tumbleblite. Always observe safety precautions notified on any sprays used.

Blackspot and rust are the most damaging diseases. Blackspot shows as irregular black spots on the leaf, and rust as orange (later black) pustules underneath it. Current remedies are Benlate, Saprol, Nimrod-T and Tumbleblite for blackspot; Plantvax, Calirus and Maneb for rust. These two diseases need preventive spraying, from pruning time until flower buds form, if there has been any sign of them in the previous year; and remedial spraying after flowering should the diseases appear. Prevention is more effective than cure, and the undersides of the leaves must be sprayed as well as the tops.

The choice of cultivars resistant to fungal diseases is also a sensible precaution.

Lesser pests are thunderflies (thrips) and leafhoppers, which are controlled by greenfly killer; caterpillars and sawflies, which make the leaves curl up, for which trichlorphon is effective, and red spider mites, like miniature spiders, slightly mobile, on the undersides of the leaves. Red spider mites are difficult to kill, but they dislike regular jets of water, white oil and paraffin emulsion (equal parts liquid medicinal paraffin and water, with a dash of washing-up liquid; then diluted 1 part to 25 parts water).

Classification

In 1971, The Royal National Rose Society produced a framework of classification, which we simplify here as follows:

MODERN GARDEN ROSES
Large-flowered bush roses (Hybrid Tea)
Cluster-flowered bush roses (Floribunda)
Shrub roses
Miniature roses
Climbing roses
OLD GARDEN ROSES
Shrubs and climbers
WILD ROSES
Shrubs and climbers, either wild, or hybrids resembling wild roses.

With which preamble, we can now explore the best and most beautiful roses which cover the whole range of the genus at this present time. The more unusual and diverse types have received the longer descriptions.

Selected Roses

Large-flowered bush roses (Hybrid Teas)

Average height is 76 to 90 cm (2½ to 3 ft), or as varied by conditions and cultivation.

Alec's Red Crimson to cherry red. A large flower with strong sweet scent, it has collected four international awards for fragrance. Average height. Raised by Cocker (Scotland) 1970.

Alexander Vermilion. A breath-catching colour, especially vibrant in the sunlight. Good form, moderately full, but plenty of flowers on long stems. Above average height. Raised by Harkness (England) 1972.

Alpine Sunset Light peach yellow. Great, wide bloom, very full, on rather short plants. The flowers are held upright, and are very handsome, with quite a good scent. Below average height. Raised by Cants (England) 1974.

Benson & Hedges Gold Bright yellow, a very fine colour. The blooms are large, very well formed, and if not so freely produced as they might be, at least have superior quality. Moderately scented. Average height. Raised by McGredy (New Zealand) 1979.

Blessings Rose pink, slightly salmon. An excellent bedding rose, very free flowering, of even growth. Medium-sized flowers, well formed. Average height. Raised by Gregory (England) 1968.

Blue Moon Lilac pink. The best of the hopefully blue roses, and very fragrant. Handsome flowers (better still under glass) but watch it for blackspot. Average height. Raised by Tantau (Germany) 1964.

Can Can Orange red, a lovely warm roseate colour. The large blooms are well scented, and of good form. The plants are not over robust, but are worth putting in good soil for the pleasure they can produce. Below average height. Raised by LeGrice (England) 1982.

Chicago Peace Phlox pink and yellow. Excepting colour, it has the characteristics of 'Peace', large flowers and all. Above average height. Raised by Johnston (U.S.A.) 1962.

Congratulations Rose pink. A remarkable plant, tall and vigorous, producing a great number of flowering shoots. The blooms are fairly large, of excellent form, very good indeed for cutting. A rewarding rose to grow, except that there is not much scent. Above average height. Raised by Kordes (Germany) 1978.

Double Delight Creamy white, edged red. This photogenic rose can produce marvellous blooms, full and richly scented. The plant, however, has a sulky, dingy aspect, pale in leaf and apt to wither in parts. Average height. Raised by Swim and Ellis (U.S.A.) 1977.

Duke of Windsor Vermilion. A bright colour, a rich scent, a popular rose; but not a large flower, and not a very healthy plant. One authority calls it Duke of Mildew, but this may be less of a problem in your area. Average height. Raised by Tantau (Germany) 1968.

Dutch Gold Clear yellow. A strong growing rose with large yellow blooms, which when open are apt to reveal their tendency to split. It is however a good performer. Average height. Raised by Wisbech Plant Co. (England) 1978.

Elizabeth Harkness Ivory shaded buff or pink. Most handsome and consistent in

flower form. Free flowering, fragrant; and beautiful beyond words. Average height. Raised by Harkness (England) 1969.

Ena Harkness Bright crimson. The most famous red rose. The form of flowers and rich colour have made it a household name. Does not like dry conditions in which it hangs its head. Average height. Raised by Norman (England) 1946.

Ernest H. Morse Deep crimson. Has an excellent habit of growth for a bed, and produces well-formed flowers without a great many petals. Average height. Raised by Kordes (Germany) 1964.

Eroica Dark crimson. Large flowers, perhaps a little dull in colour, but richly scented. Average height. Raised by Tantau (Germany) 1968.

Fragrant Cloud Dusky scarlet. Wonderful scent has made it a best seller, but the colour fades. Good habit for a bed. Some risk of blackspot. Average height. Raised by Tantau (Germany) 1963.

Fragrant Gold Clear yellow. A well shaped flower, with excellent scent and good, but not over full form. The flowers are carried on good stems, fine for cutting. Average height. Raised by Tantau (Germany) 1980.

Grandpa Dickson Lemon yellow; takes some red flushes especially on later blooms. An excellent rose, from which flowers of supreme quality in size and form can be obtained. Average height. Raised by Dickson (Ireland) 1966.

Harry Wheatcroft Scarlet with yellow stripes and flecks; this is a flamboyant sport from 'Piccadilly', which it resembles except for the colour. Average height or less. Raised by Wheatcroft (England) 1973.

John Waterer Deep crimson. The colour is deep and bright, set off well against lustrous foliage. Not much scent, unfortunately, but a very handsome rose for a bed. Average height. Raised by McGredy (Ireland) 1970.

Josephine Bruce Dark crimson. The darkest of them all, stunning on its first

flower, a bit ragged later, and apt to mildew. Below average height. Raised by Bees (England) 1949.

Julia's Rose A kind of tan colour, with pink in it. A rose of unusual colour, named for Julia Clements the flower arranger. Not very robust. Below average height. Raised by Wisbech Plant Co. (England) 1976.

Just Joey Buff and coppery pink. No ordinary colour, it sometimes looks between fawn and orange, and invites pleased notice. Below average height. Raised by Cants (England) 1973.

King's Ransom Deep yellow. The clear yellow colour agrees well with the glossy green of the foliage. Average height. Raised by Morey (U.S.A.) 1961.

Lolita Light orange. The blooms are large and fairly full, the growth upright, apt to be on the leggy side. But the colour is good. Average height or more. Raised by Kordes (Germany) 1972.

L'Oréal Trophy Orange, in a shade all its own so far as roses go. A sport from 'Alexander', similar to that rose except for colour. Above average height. Raised by Harkness (England) 1982.

Mischief Salmon pink; the September flowers have a hint of orange. Popular, fragrant, well formed and free flowering, but it may get rust. Average height. Raised by McGredy (Ireland) 1961.

Miss Harp Yellow, the flowers large and very full. The growth is upright and the scent moderate. Known abroad as 'Oregold', 'Anneliese Rothenburger' and 'Silhouette'. Average height. Raised by Tantau (Germany) 1970.

National Trust Bright crimson. The flowers are smaller than most, not fragrant, but for a blaze of red in the garden it is superb. Below average height. Raised by McGredy (Ireland) 1970.

Papa Meilland Dark crimson, strongly scented, the flowers large. Would be everyone's favourite rose if it would grow better and renounce mildew. Most people cannot make it behave, but a few are lucky. Below average height. Raised by Meilland (France) 1963.

OPPOSITE: The large-flowered bush rose 'Double Delight'

51

Pascali White. The best white hybrid tea, and one of the best of all garden roses for cutting. A most satisfactory rose to grow. Average height. Raised by Lens (Belgium) 1963.

Peace Yellow flushed pink. One of the easiest to grow, provided blackspot is controlled. Famous for the beauty, size and delicate colouring of its flowers. Above average height. Raised by Meilland (France) 1942.

Peer Gynt Bright yellow flushed red. One of the boldest yellow colours, capable of producing blooms both exquisite and substantial. May need mildew control. Average height. Raised by Kordes (Germany) 1968.

Piccadilly Scarlet and yellow. A brilliant bedding rose, not only in flower, but in glistening dark foliage too. Keep an eye on it for blackspot. Average height or less. Raised by McGredy (Ireland) 1959.

Pink Favorite Bright pink. Wonderful foliage, very resistant to disease. The flowers grow large and shapely. Good habit for a bed. Average height. Raised by Von Abrams (U.S.A.) 1956.

Pot o' Gold Clear yellow. The flowers open wide, with many rather short petals, and look beautiful against the dense, bright green leaves. A most attractive plant, with moderate scent. Average height. Raised by Dickson (Ireland) 1980.

Precious Platinum Bright red. A fine, strong bush, with big colourful flowers, perhaps the most showy red rose there is. Not much scent. Above average height. Raised by Dickson (Ireland) 1974.

Prima Ballerina Deep rose pink. The fragrance is delightful, the colour kind, and the flowers handsome without many petals. Strong growth, some chance of mildew. Above average height. Raised by Tantau (Germany) 1957.

Pristine Ivory, with flushes of pink. A large bloom, with fewer petals than one would expect, because they are so firm they hold the shape of a much fuller flower. Very beautiful. Average height. Raised by Warriner (U.S.A.) 1978.

Red Devil Light crimson. Famous for the enormous size its flowers can grow to, this is the best cultivar to put its owner in the exhibitor's class without really trying. Fragrant, and a handsome plant. Above average height. Raised by Dickson (Ireland) 1967.

Red Planet Deep bright crimson. Health and colour are superb, but fragrance is lacking. The autumn flowers are usually the best. Average height. Raised by Dickson (Ireland) 1970.

Rose Gaujard Carmine rose and white. Usually proves one of the easiest to grow, with attractive slim buds, opening to show a twisted centre. Average height. Raised by Gaujard (France) 1959.

Rosy Cheeks Carmine, with yellow reverse. The flowers are large, fairly full and freely produced. A reliable bicolour, with moderate scent. Average height. Raised by Anderson (Scotland) 1976.

Silver Jubilee Peach pink, rose pink and cream, a regular confection of colour. Long, large flowers on a bush dense with leaves. It has little scent, but all the same became a national favourite very quickly. Average height. Raised by Cocker (Scotland) 1978.

Simba Yellow. Produces very fine flowers notable for purity of colour. One might question its robustness, so give it good treatment. Average height. Raised by Kordes (Germany) 1981.

Sunblest Yellow. An upright grower, with neat flowers, not large for a hybrid tea, on straight, slim stems. Useful bedding rose, but with little scent. Average height. Raised by Tantau (Germany) 1970.

Super Star Light vermilion. A famous rose, with beautifully formed flowers, in attractive colour. Apt to mildew. Above average height. Raised by Tantau (Germany) 1960.

Sutter's Gold Yellow flushed pink. Ruddy gold buds open to well-formed flowers, without many petals. Elegant, fragrant, free flowering. Average height. Raised by Swim (U.S.A.) 1950.

Troika Orange and red. Attractive in colour and form when young, but discolours with age. The orange colour is one of the best in roses. Average height. Raised by Poulsen (Denmark) 1972.

Wendy Cussons Deep pink, near to light red. A splendid English rose, easy to grow, usually well behaved and fragrant. Above average height. Raised by Gregory (England) 1959.

Whisky Mac Amber yellow. One of the most beautiful colours in roses, with elegant, fragrant flowers to set it off. But watch out for mildew. Average height. Raised by Tantau (Germany) 1967.

Cluster-flowered bush roses (Floribundas)

Average height is 76 to 90 cm ($2\frac{1}{2}$ to 3 ft), or as varied by conditions and cultivation.

Allgold Bright yellow. Clusters of well-formed buds open to clear yellow blooms, holding the colour well. Deep green, shiny foliage provides a lovely backing. Below average height. Raised by LeGrice (England) 1956.

Amber Queen Amber yellow. Full, double flowers, upon a tidy bush that grows fairly wide but holds its blooms upright. The dark foliage suits the amber flowers very well. Below average height. Raised by Harkness (England) 1984.

Anna Ford Deep orange. Small leaves (this is half miniature by parentage) and single flowers in great profusion on a short bush with many stems. A fine, healthy edging plant. Colour fades eventually. Well below average height. Raised by Harkness (England) 1980.

Anne Cocker Glowing vermilion. Flowers the size of overcoat buttons, double, long lasting, one to a stem in mighty inflorescences. May need anti-mildew precautions. Above average height. Raised by Cocker (Scotland) 1971.

Anne Harkness Apricot yellow. An unusual rose, growing tall and flowering late, thus apt to be blooming when the others are over. The petal bases are shadowed. Above average height. Raised by Harkness (England) 1980.

Apricot Nectar Light apricot. Wide, semi-double flowers, charming pale colour, with fragrance. Average height. Raised by Boerner (U.S.A.) 1965.

Arthur Bell Bright yellow, fading cream. Grows upright, with handsome bright green leaves, and is one of the most fragrant of its class. Above average height. Raised by McGredy (Ireland) 1965.

Beautiful Britain Orange scarlet. Double flowers, with a particularly intense colour. Upright habit. Average height. Raised by Dickson (Ireland) 1983.

Bonfire Night Brilliant orange red with a touch of yellow. The crowded semi-double flowers and dark sparkling foliage provide a deep glow of colour. Average height or more. Raised by McGredy (Ireland) 1971.

Bright Smile Clear yellow. A compact plant with everything bright about it, the semi-double flowers fairly glistening against the fresh green foliage. Below average height. Raised by Dickson (Ireland) 1980.

Chorus Bright red. The flowers are fairly large and full, and make a brave show of red on top of the plants. Average height. Raised by Paolino (France) 1975.

City of Belfast Bright scarlet. An aggressive display of colour from quite a modest plant. Colour is held very well. Below average height. Raised by McGredy (Ireland) 1968.

City of Leeds Salmon pink. Rather a plain colour but a splendid performer, giving quantities of well-formed flowers. Makes an excellent bed. Average height. Raised by McGredy (Ireland) 1966.

Dearest Soft rose pink. Gains a subtle touch of salmon, especially as a cut flower. Fragrant and well loved, although it gets in a mess in rain, and needs a watch for disease. Average height. Raised by Dickson (Ireland) 1960.

Elizabeth of Glamis Salmon shaded apricot. Included here for the supreme beauty of elegant flowers in glorious colour – and with fragrance too. But watch it like a hawk for rust. Average height. Raised by McGredy (Ireland) 1964.

Escapade Rosy violet, white centre. Has about nine petals, which it opens to show its stamens, and to diffuse its perfume. Unconventional, very charming, and a gem to cut – take it when the buds show colour. Above average height. Raised by Harkness (England) 1967.

Esther Ofarim Orange red, touched yellow. A wonderful, glowing colour in a perfect button-hole bud; but the plant is not robust. Below average height. Raised by Kordes (Germany) 1971.

Europeana Very dark crimson. The flowers are double, very full of petals, in a flat, rosette shape. Superb where it prospers, but apt to mildew. Very bushy. Average height. Raised by De Ruiter (Holland) 1963.

Evelyn Fison Bright deep scarlet. One of the most generally used modern cultivars for bedding. A good, satisfying red colour. Average height. Raised by McGredy (Ireland) 1962.

Evening Star White. A very fine rose, almost a hybrid tea by its shape and size. Upright growth. Average height or more. Raised by Warriner (U.S.A.) 1974.

Fragrant Delight Light orange pink. Large clusters of semi-double flowers; individually one might pass them by, but they come in masses to command admiration. Scented. Average height. Raised by Wisbech Plant Co. (England) 1978.

Frensham Crimson. Having been relegated because of mildew, this rose seems to be making a comeback. Vigorous, tall, wide and thorny, at its best no red can match it. Above average height. Raised by Norman (England) 1946.

Geraldine Orange. Neat, double flowers of a most attractive colour on a reliable, bushy plant. Average height or a little more. Raised by Pearce (England) 1984.

Glenfiddich Amber yellow. The pleasing colour, attractive flower form and good dark foliage have made this cultivar popular. Average height. Raised by Cocker (Scotland) 1976.

Iceberg White. The flowers are of lovely formation, and borne abundantly on a plant which lends itself both to bedding and to being grown as a shrub. The supreme white rose; it can get mildew and blackspot, but is responsive to a helping spray. Average height or more. Raised by Kordes (Germany) 1958.

Iced Ginger Light coppery pink, a pale but subtle colour. The flowers are double and well formed. Good for cutting. Upright growth. Average height. Raised by Dickson (Ireland) 1971.

Intrigue Darkest red. As near as one would wish to black. Rather small blooms of many petals open to rosette style. Bushy growth. Average height. Raised by Kordes (Germany) 1979.

Kim Yellow flushed red. One of the dwarf floribundas, making cushion plants 38 cm (15 in) or so high. The flowers are full and well formed. Well below average height. Raised by Harkness (England) 1973.

Korbell Salmon. Also known as 'Anabell', this has delightful flowers in colour and form, good for cutting. Average height. Raised by Kordes (Germany) 1972.

Korp Vermilion. A brilliant colour. Its blooms are good for cutting, but the pale foliage detracts from its beauty in the garden. Also known as 'Prominent'. Average height or more. Raised by Kordes (Germany) 1970.

Korresia Bright yellow. Generally considered the best lasting yellow colour since 'Allgold'. The flowers are double and the foliage glossy. Average height or less. Raised by Kordes (Germany) 1974.

Lilli Marlene Bright crimson. A workmanlike producer of brilliant red by the yard. A good bedding rose, semi-double, to be found in most parks. Average height. Raised by Kordes (Germany) 1959.

Living Fire Orange red. Grows upright, with a mantle of fairly large semi-double flowers to justify the name. Above average height. Raised by Gregory (England) 1973.

Lovers Meeting Orange red. The flowers are double, fairly large, and of a vivid colour which makes this cultivar prominent. Upright growth. Average height or more. Raised by Gandy (England) 1980.

Margaret Merril White to blush. The flowers are beautifully formed and delightfully fragrant, just a few to a cluster but nearly perfect. It can get blackspot. Bushy growth. Average height. Raised by Harkness (England) 1978.

Marlena Deep crimson. The best dwarf floribunda, making extremely neat rounded plants 30 cm (1 ft) or so high. Very good looking and free flowering. Well below average height. Raised by Kordes (Germany) 1964.

Masquerade Yellow, turning pink and finally red. The rose which showed the world at large the chameleon ability in the genus. Semi-double flowers. Generally infected with rose mosaic virus. Average height. Raised by Boerner (U.S.A.) 1949.

The cluster-flowered bush rose 'Southampton'

Matangi Red and white. One of the best "hand-painted" roses, orange red with white eye and white reverse. Very free flowering. Bushy, excellent bedder. Average height. Raised by McGredy (New Zealand) 1974.

Memento Salmon, with red and pink. A good bedding rose, producing many blooms in large clusters. Bushy growth. Average height. Raised by Dickson (Ireland) 1978.

Mountbatten Yellow. The flowers are full and noticeable, being borne on an upright, rather tall plant. Makes a good shrub. Scented. Above average height. Raised by Harkness (England) 1982.

News Reddish purple. A bold beetroot kind of colour, which goes well with cream roses, and shows the interesting range of rose hues available. Average height. Raised by LeGrice (England) 1968.

Paul Shirville Pink. This has large flowers for a floribunda, in a lively, pleasing kind of pink. A vigorous, bushy grower, with a very fine scent. Average height or more. Raised by Harkness (England) 1983.

Peek a Boo Light apricot to pink. As a result of floribunda × miniature parentage, this has small leaves and flowers, and dense bushy growth to about 46 cm (1½ ft). Charming and interesting. Below average height. Raised by Dickson (Ireland) 1981.

Pink Parfait Pink with creamy shading. Elegant and free flowering, with long flowers of much beauty. Average height. Raised by Swim (U.S.A.) 1960.

Priscilla Burton Red and light carmine. A "hand painted" rose with fairly large flowers, showing variable but striking patterns of its colours. Paler at the base. Average height. Raised by McGredy (New Zealand) 1978.

Queen Elizabeth Rose pink. Tall and easy growing, the best rose for a hedge, and also one of the best for cutting; its clusters of well-formed pink flowers are compact, on pleasant straight stems. Well above average height. Raised by Lammerts (U.S.A.) 1955.

Redgold Yellow marked red. The blooms are shapely, of good size, and the colours bright and pleasing. Average height. Raised by Dickson (Ireland) 1967.

Rob Roy Brilliant crimson. About as fine a shade of red as one could wish to see. The flowers are large, the foliage abundant. Average height. Raised by Cocker (Scotland) 1971.

Sarabande Bright red. Not so easy to procure as it should be; the flowers have five petals, and fairly cover the spreading plants in red. Below average height. Raised by Meilland (France) 1957.

Southampton Apricot orange. Those who want a good orange floribunda cannot do better than plant this healthy rose. Fragrant. Above average height. Raised by Harkness (England) 1972.

Sue Lawley Carmine and blush white. The wide open flowers show a pattern as definite and dramatic as any of the "hand-painted" roses. Average height. Raised by McGredy (New Zealand) 1980.

Topsi Vermilion. A dwarf floribunda, with clusters of closely set flowers borne not only in profusion, but in quick succession. Well below average height. Raised by Tantau (Germany) 1972.

Trumpeter Orange red. An effective bedding rose of good clear colour and bushy, free flowering habit. Double flowers well spaced in the clusters. Average height. Raised by McGredy (New Zealand) 1978.

Warrior Bright red. A good, low growing floribunda, with a fine colour. The bushes stay trim and neat. Below average height. Raised by LeGrice (England) 1978.

Woburn Abbey Orange-yellow and red. This well known rose makes a splendid show of colour, but does not have a good health record. Upright growth. Average height. Raised by Sidey and Cobley (England) 1962.

Yvonne Rabier White. Sweetly-scented, small double flowers on neat bush plants. Not widely grown unfortunately. Average height or less. Raised by Turbat (France) 1910.

Modern Shrub Roses

Some of these are to be found as floribundas in the rose catalogues, and they may be grown in beds, or as shrubs, or as hedges. Average height is 1.2 m (4 ft) or as varied by conditions and cultivation.

The origin and old classes are shown at the end of each. Except where stated, they flower in summer and autumn.

Ballerina Light pink, white eye. Tiny single flowers crammed dozens together in mop heads. Impression of a solid square plant nothing will harm. Easy to grow, and rewarding. Average height. Raised by Bentall (England) 1937. Polyantha.

Buff Beauty Creamy buff. Double flowers, apt to nod; nothing special but somehow the charm is there. Fragrant. Average height. Origin unsure, introduced 1939. Hybrid musk.

Chinatown Bright yellow. Such lush green foliage and rich yellow flowers, there is no chance of overlooking this one. Fragrant into the bargain. Average height or more, grows fairly wide. Raised by Poulsen (Denmark) 1963. Floribunda.

Cornelia Light pink, touch of strawberry pink. Semi-double, small flowers in large clusters; the stems usually grow up and outwards, and have attractive dark bark. Fragrant. Average height or more, grows fairly wide. Raised by Pemberton (England) 1925. Hybrid musk.

Dorothy Wheatcroft Scarlet. Large heads of closely set semi-double flowers, very bright. Apt to grow tall and thin. Above average height. Raised by Tantau (Germany) 1960. Floribunda.

Felicia Light pink, touch of yellow. Small flowers, well formed and fragrant; unobtrusive. Average height. Raised by Pemberton (England) 1928. Hybrid musk.

Fountain Bright crimson. A multitude of wide-petalled flowers wave their glorious red colour for all to see. Growth is quick, foliage ample, and 'Fountain' wastes no time before flowering again. Average height. Raised by Tantau (Germany) 1970. Floribunda.

Fred Loads Vermilion. An upright plant, with large heads of vivid semi-double flowers, showing stamens; the colour is bright and pure. Very effective. Above average height. Raised by Holmes (England) 1967. Floribunda.

Fritz Nobis Rich, beautiful pink. One of the few roses in this section which is summer flowering only (in June usually). Also one of the most glorious shrubs in existence. The flowers are fairly large, with firm petals and a form that invites close inspection. They are carried evenly on the plant. Grows fairly wide. Well above average height. Raised by Kordes (Germany) 1940. Has sweet-briar breeding.

Frühlingsgold Creamy yellow. Summer flowering only in May usually. Very fragrant, semi-double flowers. A large shrub, very spectacular in its two or three weeks of glory. About twice average height. Raised by Kordes (Germany) 1937. Has *spinosissima* breeding.

Frühlingsmorgen Pink with yellow centre and maroon stamens showing against the yellow. Large single flowers, worth a long look for their simple and lovely construction. Strong scent, rather mealy. Mainly early summer flowering, but some appear in autumn too. Above average height. Raised by Kordes (Germany) 1941. Has *spinosissima* breeding.

Golden Wings Light primrose. Wide single flowers, each an essay on how to be fragile and beautiful. Average height. Raised by Shepherd (U.S.A.) 1956. Has *spinossissima* breeding.

Joseph's Coat Yellow and various shades of red. A brilliant and versatile rose, may be grown in a bed, as a shrub or persuaded to climb. Semi-double flowers; the name conveys the effect very well. Average height. Raised by Swim (U.S.A.) 1964. Floribunda.

Kordes' Robusta Scarlet. Large, single blooms are carried in clusters on a grand, stalwart bush, with dense foliage of *rugosa* type. Growth is very bushy, quite wide. Average height. Raised by Kordes (Germany) 1979. Has *rugosa* breeding.

Marguerite Hilling Rosy pink, looks as if brushed on a white base. Large single flowers. Branches tend to arch, have soft dull leaves, and are festooned with flowers coming on very short stems direct from the branch. A most agreeable sight. Above average height. Raised by Hilling (England) 1959. Sport of 'Nevada'.

Marjorie Fair Red with white eye. After the style of 'Ballerina', with small single flowers in large clusters. Makes a fairly wide bush of striking colour. Average height. Raised by Harkness (England) 1978. Polyantha.

Nevada White. Apart from the colour, all the agreeable features of 'Marguerite Hilling' are repeated in this splendid shrub. Both are much more showy in summer than in autumn. Above average height. Raised by Dot (Spain) 1927. Has *moyesii* breeding according to the records, but more likely *spinosissima*.

Pearl Drift Blush. A marvellous mantle of soft pearl blossom covers the plants, which are bushy, fairly short, and wide spreading. The flowers have about 15 petals. Below average height. Raised by LeGrice (England) 1980. Has *bracteata* breeding.

Penelope Blush. Semi-double flowers, small and fragrant. Not much in themselves, but there is something satisfying in their abundant appearance. Average height, may be less. Raised by Pemberton (England) 1924. Hybrid musk.

Pink Grootendorst Rose pink. This is the one with small double flowers frilled at the edges. Interesting, although one may feel bush and flowers are out of scale. Above average height. Raised by Grootendorst (Holland) 1923. Has *rugosa* breeding.

Sally Holmes Ivory. A unique rose shrub, at a distance one might take it for a rhododendron for the shape of the bush and carriage of the flowers. They are large, single, in close, big clusters. Average height. Raised by Holmes (England) 1976. Hybrid musk type.

Schneezwerg White. Very hardy and trouble free, with smallish foliage, and a long succession of flat, well-formed, semi-double blooms. Average height. Raised by Lambert (Germany) 1912. Has *rugosa* breeding.

The Fairy Pink. Masses of little double flowers, like those of the old ramblers, from July onwards; the smother of blooms is soft against the small dark shiny leaves. Apt to stay short; below average height. Raised by Bentall (England) 1932. Has *wichuraiana* origin.

Yesterday Rose to lilac pink. Very small flowers and leaves. Blooms in large heads, opening on a programme that ensures long continuity. The flowers are semi-double, open from rose red to pink with a touch of lilac, beautiful in conjunction. Sweetly fragrant. Has power to exert a very strong charm. Average height or less. Raised by Harkness (England) 1974. Polyantha.

Miniature Roses
Average height 38 cm (15 in).

Angela Rippon Coral pink. Fully double flowers are carried close together, making very colourful little bushes. Good for cutting. Average height. Raised by De Ruiter (Holland) 1978.

Baby Masquerade Yellow marked pink. The easiest miniature to grow, with plenty of shoots, tiny leaves and narrow-petalled flowers similar in effect to 'Masquerade'. Average height. Raised by Tantau (Germany) 1956.

Colibri 79 Light orange pink, with some yellow. The miniature buds are beautifully formed, and the open flowers measure about 4 cm ($1\frac{1}{2}$ in) across. Good for cutting. Average height. Raised by Meilland (France) 1979.

Darling Flame Vermilion and yellow, making a fine "flame" effect. The plant, having fewer stems than most miniatures, tends to look rather open. It can get blackspot. Average height. Raised by Meilland (France) 1971.

Easter Morning Cream. Well-shaped buds, true miniature roses. Average height. Raised by Moore (U.S.A.) 1960.

Lavender Jewel Pink with lavender cast. The flowers are very double and freely borne, the little bushes spread quite wide for their size. Average height. Raised by Moore (U.S.A.) 1978.

Magic Carrousel White, with pink at the petal tips. A bigger bush than many miniatures, with plenty of flowers, which are good for cutting. Average height or more. Raised by Moore (U.S.A.) 1972.

New Penny Light coral pink. Flowers, growth and leaves are all that one expects a miniature should be. Glossy foliage. Average height. Raised by Moore (U.S.A.) 1962.

Pour Toi White touched yellow at base. Small neat flowers and leaves on a bushy little plant. Average height. Raised by Dot (Spain) 1946.

Rise 'n' Shine Yellow. The flowers are a little larger than average, but very good for cutting. Bushy growth. Also known as 'Golden Sunblaze'. Average height. Raised by Moore (U.S.A.) 1977.

Sheri Anne Orange red. A very good cultivar, especially for cutting, due to its highly attractive buds. Average height or more. Raised by Moore (U.S.A.) 1973.

Starina Orange red. This very popular variety covers itself with blooms, and is good for cutting. A fine performer, its main fault is fading with age. Average height. Raised by Meilland (France) 1965.

Modern Climbing Roses

Height of climbing roses is extremely variable, according to the conditions and cultivation.

Albéric Barbier Cream. Small flowers open semi-double from elegant buds. Glossy leaves stay on late in winter. One of the best to grow on a north or east wall, or in other difficult positions. Flowers in summer with a fair scattering again in autumn. Well above average height. Raised by Barbier (France) 1900.

Albertine Salmon and light rose. Attractive buds, the flowers pale as they open. A rose famous for its fantastic abundance of summer flower. Does not repeat in autumn. Some liability to mildew. Best allowed some freedom, that is by a tree stump, or over a shed or shelter, not tied to walls or posts. Well above average height. Raised by Barbier (France) 1921.

Aloha Rosy salmon. Double flowers, full of petals, looking rich and confident. Occupies quite a small space, and if it has a disappointed owner, I have not yet met him or her. Repeat flowering. Below average height. Raised by Boerner (U.S.A.) 1949.

Altissimo Bright crimson. Handbreadth single flowers, spectacular. Repeat flowering, and adaptable for most uses. Above average height. Raised by Delbard-Chabert (France) 1966.

Compassion Light salmon pink shaded apricot. Double flowers, well formed and very fragrant. Abundant dark foliage. Repeats well and is adaptable for most uses. Average height or more. Raised by Harkness (England) 1973.

Crimson Shower Deep crimson. A rambler, that is to say the shoots would be more or less prostrate unless tied up. Consequently ideal to tie to a post for a waterfall effect of bloom. Small flowers in close clusters, mid-July and August. Average height. Raised by Norman (England) 1951.

Danse du Feu Scarlet. Double flowers, well formed and very spectacular until the colour fades, at which stage it can scarcely be termed pleasing. Repeats its bloom exceptionally well, and is suitable for most uses. Average height. Raised by Mallerin (France) 1954.

Dublin Bay Bright crimson. The flowers are fairly large, but not very full, and provide an expanse of rich red colour. Repeats very well. Below average height. Raised by McGredy (New Zealand) 1976.

Ena Harkness, Climbing Bright crimson. Best grown on a wall or fence; the large red flowers are likely to be even better than on the bush form. Some scattered repeat bloom. Average height. Raised by Murrell (England) 1954.

Etoile de Hollande, Climbing Deep crimson. Very fragrant; a fine red climber for

Miniature rose 'Pour Toi'

the wall, but flowers early and is not very generous in repeating. Above average height, often after a slow start. Raised by Leenders (Holland) 1931.

Golden Showers Bright yellow. Attractive buds open semi-double, at times with very attractive spread of petals around stamens. Extremely free flowering, repeats like a bush, has good foliage. Can be grown as a shrub or trained on a smallish area of fence or wall. Below average height. Raised by Germain (U.S.A.) 1957.

Handel Cream flushed rose particularly at petal edges. Handsome flowers. Very free flowering, repeats well, and could be regarded as the finest climber of all, but for some risk of blackspot. Average height. Raised by McGredy (Ireland) 1965.

Iceberg, Climbing White. The climbing form of this famous rose blooms both in summer and autumn. The flowers are sometimes slightly pink. Average height. Raised by Cants (England) 1968.

Leverkusen Yellow. This excellent rose has a clear colour, fine healthy foliage, and a long period in flower in summer. There is a lesser offering in autumn. Average height. Raised by Kordes (Germany) 1955.

Maigold Bronzy yellow. Rich colour, mealy scent, beautiful leaves; the stems are handsome, closely set with bristles. Quite an individual character, its rather untidily formed semi-double flowers are a riot in early summer, sparse later. Adaptable, easy to grow. Average height, but variable. Raised by Kordes (Germany) 1953.

Mermaid Light primrose. Great moon-like single flowers, with handsome amber stamens. Very continuous in bloom and holds its smooth cut foliage late in winter. Awkward to train because the shoots are brittle and thorns viciously hooked, nevertheless a wall is the place for it. May be killed in hardest winter. Above average height, after a slow start usually. Raised by Paul (England) 1918.

Mme Alfred Carrière White. A Noisette rose, with rather soft petals and light green leaves; but nevertheless a very good performer summer and autumn. The flower form, although slightly rounded is attractive. Average height. Raised by J. Schwartz (France) 1879.

Mme Grégoire Staechelin Pink. Although it flowers only once, around midsummer, it is worth every penny you pay for it. Wide, crinkled flowers, sweetly scented, come in great profusion. Fat hips follow. Also known as 'Spanish Beauty'. Average height or more. Raised by Dot (Spain) 1927.

Morning Jewel Bright pink. The semi-double flowers and bright foliage make a delightful glowing plant. Repeats well and adaptable for most uses. Below average height. Raised by Cocker (Scotland) 1968.

New Dawn Pearl pink. Very light colour; small flowers of admirable form and fragrant. Adaptable to most uses, can also be grown as a large shrub, and is best not too strictly confined. Useful cut flower for mixed arrangements. Repeats, but not generously. Average height. Raised by Somerset Nurseries (U.S.A.) 1930.

Nozomi White to pearl. This is a climbing miniature. Its flowers are only single, and it flowers only in summer, but it has beauty and charm to survive those handicaps. May be used as ground cover, and as a shrub. Below average height. Raised by Onodera (Japan) 1968.

Pink Perpetue Pink, with deeper reverse. Well-formed flowers, and plenty of them both in summer and autumn. Reliable and adaptable to most uses. Average height. Raised by Gregory (England) 1965.

Sander's White Rambler White. Cascades of small double flowers, sweetly scented, shown well against small dark leaves. See 'Crimson Shower' (p. 59) for comments on ramblers. This flowers for several weeks in summer, and it is a beauty. Average height or more. Raised by Sander (Belgium) 1912.

Schoolgirl Apricot pink, towards orange. Large double flowers, well formed. Useful as the only climber in this colour. Flowering is usually intermittent through the season rather than in a spectacular flush. Adaptable to most uses. Average height, or more. Raised by McGredy (Ireland) 1964.

Swan Lake White. The flowers are large and full, of good form. A popular white climber, despite the threat of blackspot. Repeats well. Below average height. Raised by McGredy (Ireland) 1968.

Veilchenblau Greyish lilac pink. Perhaps the best of the climbers showing a touch of violet colour; small semi-double flowers, abundantly produced in summer only. Adaptable to most uses, but preferably not a wall. Above average height. Raised by Schmidt (Germany) 1909.

White Cockade White. Well-formed double flowers, small to medium size. Repeats very well, adaptable to most uses. Can also be grown as a shrub. Below average height. Raised by Cocker (Scotland) 1968.

Old Garden Roses

Some of the old roses are charming, and others are mildewy old wrecks. This list of the choicest rejects sentiment in favour of performance. The average height is around 1.2 m (4 ft) and the traditional class follows each description.

Blanche Moreau Creamy white. Calyx has brown mossy covering, flowers are double, confused, appear summer only. Upright grower, likely to mildew; flower stems arise from last year's wood so do not prune it all off. Above average height. Raised by Moreau-Robert (France) 1880. Moss.

Camaieux Purple pink with white marks, fades grey and white, the white marks prominent. Double flowers in summer only, arising from previous year's wood. Fragrant. Some mildew. Below average height. Raised by Vibert (France) 1830. *Gallica.*

Capitaine John Ingram Dark crimson. Only slightly mossed calyx. Flowers small, very double, with button eye which is paler. Blooms summer only, from previous year's wood. Some mildew likely. Average height. Raised by Laffay (France) 1856. Moss.

Cardinal de Richelieu Purple. Double flowers, small, colour nicely varied in flower. Blooms in summer only, from previous year's wood. Average height. Raised by Laffay (France) 1840. *Gallica.*

Cécile Brunner Light pink. Clusters of miniature rose buds; a young flower would go in a thimble, most appealing; flowers summer to autumn, either from old or current season's wood. About half average height. Raised by Ducher (France) 1881. China.

Cécile Brunner, Climbing Light pink. Vigorous climbing form of the foregoing, good to cover 6 m (20 ft) or so once it gets going. Some repeat bloom, abundant foliage. Raised by Hosp (U.S.A.) 1894. China.

Celestial Soft pale rose. The flowers are fairly large, of delicately lovely form, and set a perfect picture against grey-green leaves. Fragrant. Flowers in summer only, from previous year's wood. Average height or more. Origin unknown, probably France 1780–1836. *Alba.*

Charles de Mills Crimson purple. The buds look as if their tops were cut off, but open to full, fragrant blooms, in red, purple and maroon shades. Flowers in summer only, from previous year's wood. Mildew likely. Average height or more. Origin unknown, probably France 1820–1840. *Gallica.*

Commandant Beaurepaire Pink with red and purple stripes, all splashed together and marbled white. Large double flowers in summer, and perhaps a few later, mainly from wood of previous years; fragrant. Keep an eye on it for rust. Fairly spreading habit. Average height. Raised by Moreau-Robert (France) 1874. Bourbon.

Common Moss Pink. Calyx bears green mossy covering. Smallish double pink flowers, fragrant, in summer only, from previous year's wood. Upright habit, liable to mildew. Average height. Origin unknown, possibly Holland early 1700s. Moss.

Crested Moss Pink. Calyx has a wavy frill, hence its popular name 'Chapeau de Napoleon'. Double pink flowers, summer only, from previous year's wood. Average height. Found growing in a convent in Fribourg, introduced in France 1827. *Centifolia.*

Félicité et Perpétue Creamy white. An old climber, with pink buds, opening to white pompon flowers, small, but perfectly formed by many tiny petals. Foliage stays on late in winter. Flowers in summer, may be a few later; good wall plant, better still if it can be given its head. Vigorous climber, averages 4.5 m (15 ft). Raised by Jacques (France) 1827. *Sempervirens.*

Gallica Versicolor Red striped blush white. The semi-double flowers open wide and flat, thus showing the stripes clearly. The traditional name is 'Rosa Mundi'. May revert to its all-red original. Flowers summer only, on wood of previous years. Usually gets mildew after flowering. Compact growth. Below average height. Origin unknown. *Gallica.*

Lady Penzance Coppery pink, yellow centre. The flowers are small and fleeting; the sweet briar scent from the foliage is the object of growing this, and the small dark leaves provide it beautifully on a still summer evening. Some blackspot risk, however. Above average height. Raised by Lord Penzance (England) 1894. Sweet briar.

Laneii Purple. Large flowers, flat, with many petals and a remarkable rich colour. Flowers summer only, from wood of previous years. Although called a moss rose, there is next to no moss to be seen. Average height. Raised by Laffay (France) 1846. Moss. (Alleged to be 'William Lobb' which came from the same raiser in 1855. But 'Laneii' appears to be more compact in growth and richer in colour).

Little White Pet White. Rare and difficult to obtain. Double flowers, just like those of 'Félicité et Perpétue', except that on this little bush they keep flowering into the autumn. Half average size. Raised by Henderson (U.S.A.) 1879. *Sempervirens.*

Lord Penzance Fawn yellow; apart from which all that is said for 'Lady Penzance' applies.

Maiden's Blush Light blush. A handsome shrub, with grey-green leaves, and lovely unsophisticated flowers which are pale yet colourful, and very fragrant. Blooms in summer only, from wood of previous years. Above average height. The only difference between the great and small forms of this rose is a relatively minor one of growth. The origin of the former is unknown, and the latter is attributed to Kew Gardens (England) 1797. *Alba.*

Mme Hardy White. Pale green leaves, untidy sort of plant, but the flowers are marvellous. They open wide and flat, with what appear to be hundreds of small petals in meticulous array, with old-fashioned quartering and green centre. Flowers in summer only, from wood of previous years. Fragrant. Above average height. Raised by Hardy (France) 1832. Damask.

Mme Pierre Oger Cream, heavily shaded rose pink. Has the same fascinating bowl shape as 'Reine Victoria', and the colour is perhaps more interesting. The description of 'Reine Victoria' otherwise fits this. Raised by Oger (France) 1878. Bourbon.

Nuits de Young Dark purplish red. Small, flat flowers, double, but showing golden stamens. Not much mossy growth. Flowers in summer only, from wood of previous years. Average height. Raised by Laffay (France) 1854. Moss.

Old Blush Cheerful pink. This is the old Monthly Rose, with small, bright pink, semi-double flowers on an open bush. Flowers from new and old wood, summer to late autumn intermittently. Small bright leaves. Below average height. Originated in China, recorded in Europe in 18th century. China.

Petite de Hollande Pink. Small double flowers, of attractive pompon form. Flowers in summer only, from wood of

The popular old garden rose *Rosa gallica* 'Versicolor'

previous years. Likely to get mildew. Average height. Origin unknown, said to be Holland before 1800. *Centifolia.*

Pompon de Paris, Climbing Pink. This is in effect a climbing miniature rose, with small bright pink flowers and tiny leaves. Very charming, but not easy to find. Flowers in summer, with a few odd blooms later. Growth pliable, about 3.6 m (12 ft), ideal for a terrace wall. Origin unknown. China.

Président de Sèze Purple red with tinted white areas mostly at the petal tips. Double, quartered flowers in summer only, from wood of the previous years. Apt to get mildew. Average height. Origin unknown; was grown in France in 1836. *Gallica.*

Reine Victoria Pink. The petals open out into the shape of a bowl. Fragrant. Upright grower, flowering in summer, with some in autumn, mainly from wood

of previous years. May get blackspot. Average height or a little over. Raised by Schwartz (France) 1872. Bourbon.

Rose de Meaux Rose pink. Small flat flowers, ring upon ring of little petals. Fragrant. Flowers in summer only, from previous year's wood. Blackspot likely. Below average height. Raised by Sweet (England) 1814. *Centifolia.*

Souvenir de la Malmaison Blush. Has something of the delicacy of the *alba* roses about its large, pale, quartered flowers. Blooms in summer, with a few later, mainly from wood of previous years. Fragrant. Average height. Raised by Béluze (France) 1843. Bourbon.

Spong Pink. Small pompon flowers in generous clusters on a compact plant. Attractive neat flower form, pleasant scent. Blooms from wood of previous years, and in summer only. Apt to get mildew. Below average height. Origin unknown, introduced 1805. *Centifolia.*

Stanwell Perpetual White shaded blush. Double, fragrant flowers in early summer, and intermittently afterwards. Useful in floral arrangements to give an informal, old-fashioned effect. Growth rather lax, plants thorny, leaves small. Below average height usually. Raised by Lee (England) 1838. Scotch.

Tuscany Superb Dark crimson purple. Double flowers, opening flat, a telling deep colour. (The original 'Tuscany' has fewer petals, and therefore shows more of its stamens). Flowers in summer only, from wood of previous years. Growth upright, rather a narrow plant, with large leaves. Average height. Origin unknown, before 1848. *Gallica.*

Zéphirine Drouhin Deep pink. Flowers of medium size, quartered, fragrant; produced in summer and quite a few later, from both new and old wood. Usually grown as a climber, but suitable also as a shrub or hedge. Some mildew susceptibility. Well known as the thornless rose, which it is – almost. Above average height. Raised by Bizot (France) 1868. Bourbon.

Wild Roses

The wild roses and their hybrids teach us that the genus has beauties to offer unseen by those who know only the conventional bedding roses. Height is variable according to conditions and cultivation, but may be taken as 1.2 m (6 ft), except for the climbers. The common names are used, with proper botanical name or source in brackets. Note that many flower on short stems along the branches made in previous years.

Altaica (*R. spinosissima altaica*) Ivory white. Single flowers, borne along the branches, in early summer. Flowers are large in relation to the thin stems. Looks very fresh and pure. Has round, black hips, small leaves. Below average height. Introduced from northern Asia, about 1820.

Austrian Copper (*R. foetida bicolor*) Brilliant orange red with yellow reverse.

Single flowers on the small side fairly set the bushes ablaze in early summer. Rarely, it may revert to its yellow progenitor. Likely to get blackspot. Below average height. Introduced from Asia Minor, prior to 1590.

Banksian Yellow (*R. banksiae lutea*) Yellow climber. Small flowers of unusual formation for a rose – more like double primroses. They grow closely in clusters, are fragrant, and the foliage behind them is smooth cut and handsome. Flowers best from sub-laterals, so prune very cautiously. Only hardy enough for favoured localities. Can grow 7.6 m (25 ft) easily. Introduced from China 1824.

Blanc Double de Coubert (cultivar of *R. rugosa*) White. Large, semi-double flowers, with petals like thin paper, sweetly fragrant; blooms summer to autumn, from both old and new growths. Large, thick leaves, rather open growth. Below average height. Raised by Cochet-Cochet (France) 1892.

Californica Pink, with suggestion of lilac. Small single flowers with bright yellow stamens are produced in large untidy inflorescences. Flowers intermittently summer to autumn, and has small bright red hips. Foliage is dull, small, and looks rough cut, but it makes a good thicket. There is also a double form. Average height. Introduced from North America 1878.

Canary Bird (*R. xanthina* 'Canary Bird') Yellow. Single flowers with numerous stamens are borne along and very close to the branches, causing them to bow under the beautiful load. The blooms are medium size, fragrant, and appear in early summer. The leaves are small, divided (fern-like) on the average into eleven little leaflets. Amazingly beautiful. A little below average height usually. Introduced from China, probably about 1907, but its history is unclear.

Dupontii (Hybrid possibly from a *gallica* and *R. moschata*) White tinted blush. Fragrant single flowers, showing yellow stamens agreeably, cover the bush in summer. Foliage light greyish green, fairly large. Average height or less. Origin

ABOVE: 'Banksian Yellow', a beautiful wild rose

LEFT: The fruits of the wild rose *Rosa moyesii*

unknown, was before 1817.

Farreri persetosa Bright pink. Although the bush is quite lusty, the flowers are just about the smallest of any rose, single, with pretty yellow stamens. They appear in early summer. Hair-like thorns bristle the stems; the leaves are subdivided into tiny leaflets. Average height. Introduced from China 1914.

Frau Dagmar Hartopp (Hybrid of a *rugosa* rose; also known as 'Fru Dagmar Hastrup') Light rose pink. Large and luminous single flowers with creamy stamens and sweet scent. Blooms in summer and repeats into autumn from new and old wood. Large thick leaves, and big round red seedpods. Compact growth, below average height. Raised by Hastrup (Denmark) 1914.

Golden Chersonese (Hybrid of *R. ecae* × 'Canary Bird') Bright yellow. Single flowers are borne along and close to the branches in early summer; fragrant and very richly coloured. This lovely plant holds its flowering branches reaching handsomely upwards. Dark bark, small leaves subdivided into many leaflets. Average height or a little more. Raised by Allen (England) 1967.

Hispida (*R. spinosissima hispida*) Ivory. This spreading shrub has handsome single flowers in May or June, followed by round, purple black hips in autumn. It is a fine, commanding plant, easily grown. Average height. Introduced from Siberia before 1781.

Kiftsgate (*R. filipes* 'Kiftsgate') Creamy white. A mighty climber, used for scrambling into trees. Single flowers after midsummer, very fragrant and profuse in enormous clusters. Handsome foliage. Can grow to 9 m (30 ft) easily. Found in Gloucestershire (it is a form of the Chinese species, *R. filipes*) and introduced 1954.

Longicuspis White. A vigorous climber, with large clusters of fragrant single flowers after midsummer; has particularly handsome shiny leaves. Used for growing through trees, or on spacious pergolas. Can easily grow 6 m (20 ft). Introduced from China before 1904.

Mirifica (*R. stellata mirifica*) Bright pink. A rare and interesting rose, whose leaves are like those of gooseberries; the flowers are single, with bright stamens, appearing intermittently for a long period in summer. Likes a hot sunny spot. Below half average height. Introduced from New Mexico about 1910.

Moyesii Geranium Crimson. The *moyesii* crimson has its own distinct character. The flowers are single, with effective light stamens. Blooms in summer only, but that is only half the story, because long seedpods of gorgeous red hang like lanterns on the plants in the autumn. Above average height. A form of *moyesii* found by The Royal Horticultural Society 1938. *Moyesii* itself is a Chinese species.

Multibracteata Pink. Very small, single flowers in summer only. The leaves are subdivided into tiny leaflets, and are a regular work of art in themselves. It is quite a big shrub, hung with a cloud of fairy scale foliage and bloom. Average height. Introduced from China 1910.

Mutabilis (*R. chinensis mutabilis*) Quickly changing its colours from buff yellow to pink to salmon red to crimson. A rare plant, not perfectly hardy, with large single flowers produced early summer to late autumn. Half average height, unless you are lucky. Origin doubtful; came from China, who knows when?

Paulii rosea Silky pink. Large single blooms, fragrant and very beautiful, in summer only. The habit of growth is to trail a metre or so along the ground in all directions, the plant itself 90 cm (3 ft) or less high. Therefore advocated for ground cover, but is so prickly that weeding will be painful. Sport from *paulii*, which is a white *rugosa* hybrid. Before 1903.

Roseraie de l'Hay Purple red. A blatant nobility guides this outrageous colour into favour. The touch of purple is royal, on strong plants with thick bright green leaves, and in flowers which are fairly full, with the petals worn carelessly. Fragrant; flowers freely in summer and repeats generously. Makes a splendid hedge. Average height. Raised by Cochet-

Cochet (France) 1902.

Roxburghii (*R. roxburghii normalis*) Pink. A spreading shrub, with single pink flowers in early summer. They are succeeded by prickly green hips, for which it is known as the 'Chestnut Rose'. It has the strange habit of shedding its bark. The leaves too are unusual, having 15 or more leaflets quite frequently. There is a double form. Below average height. Introduced from China 1908.

Rubrifolia Pink. The flowers are small and fleeting; the foliage is the joy – soft grey with a sheen of reddish purple over it. The smooth stems are purplish when young, maturing red brown. Generous supply of round red hips in autumn. A lovely garden plant. Average height. Introduced from Central Europe, long ago.

Rugosa alba White. Single white flowers, fairly large, fragrant, and suitable as purity's emblem. Blooms summer, and repeats later. Orange-red hips, thick *rugosa* foliage. Below average height. A sport from *R. rugosa*, which is a Japanese species; origin uncertain.

Rugosa scabrosa Mauve pink. Very large single blooms, the colour fortified by dusty yellow stamens. Blooms early summer to autumn, commendably con-tinuous. Bright red seedpods, round and big; thick *rugosa* foliage. Average height or less. Origin obscure, but close to *R. rugosa*.

Sericea pteracantha (Name has recently been changed from *R. omeiensis pteracantha*) White. The flowers are small and fleeting. This is grown for its extraordinary thorns, whose juncture with the stem can be 2.5 cm (1 in) long; on the young growths, they are red and translucent. They narrow to an extremely sharp point. Average height or a bit more. Introduced from China 1890.

Virginiana Bright pink flowers in summer, followed by scarlet hips. A fine species, covered with leaves to the ground, it is surprising this has not been used more frequently as a hedge. Grows fairly wide. A specialist in autumn tints, when the weather lets its leaves turn yellow and red at leisure. Below average height. Introduced from North America before 1760.

Viridiflora (*R. chinensis viridiflora*) Green. A sterile oddity, in which the flower parts are imperfectly modified leaves. Quite a small plant, blooming (if that is the right word) summer and autumn. Less than half average height. Origin obscure; 1855 or earlier.

Trees

DENNIS WOODLAND

I think most would agree that the garden scene is incomplete without the inclusion of a tree or, if space permits, a number of trees. Perhaps the most noble of all nature's creations, trees add stature and grace to the garden as well as remarkable interest and variation of both colour and form in foliage and flower and often berry. Furthermore, trees are indispensable to frame and balance the garden; to provide permanent and satisfying focal points of interest; to cast shade where required and often, at the same time, to perform some necessary screening function.

A number of notable garden trees give two seasons of spectacular effect. Spring flower is often followed by a grand display of berry or autumn tint; others are noted for their unique winter bark as well as for autumn colour of leaf. Striking effects can be produced in the garden by the use of trees with brightly coloured foliage, a feature often retained throughout the growing season. Leaves may be red, purple, grey, yellow and there are many examples of attractive variegation; such colours effectively contrasting with the many shades of green of the other trees and shrubs.

A considerable variety of shape, form and size is to be found among trees suitable for planting even in the smallest of gardens. They may be of narrow, upright growth (columnar or fastigiate), and therefore ideal for confined areas even near buildings; or their shape may be pyramidal, broadly pyramidal, ball headed, mushroom headed, wide spreading, upright spreading or weeping.

With the great range of small or medium-sized trees available today, I feel it is a mistake to plant forest trees, ultimately of large size, in small gardens. While recognizing the noble stature of oak, beech, lime or ash, I consider such trees are best suited to parkland or more spacious circumstances and should be used where there is room for them to grow unrestricted to their full height and spread.

However, owners of small new gardens in recent building developments often inherit large forest trees perhaps planted a hundred years ago or more. Although such trees are valued for their undoubted beauty and for the exclusive air of grandeur and maturity they add to the scene, they can be rather a mixed blessing. Their large canopies cast deep shade and darken windows; it is usually difficult, if not impossible, to grow other trees, shrubs and plants satisfactorily under the overhanging branches and in competition with the hungry feeding roots of such large trees which invariably invade the entire area of a small garden. This situation usually has to be accepted and a compromise reached by careful heading back or removing branches or thinning the head of the tree – work which in these days should be carried out only by a skilled tree surgeon or reliable tree surgery company. However, I feel that the lesson to be drawn from this state of affairs is the advisability of planting, wherever possible, only small trees (ultimate height 3.6 to 9 m [12 to 30 ft]) or, at the most, medium-sized trees (ultimate height 9 to 15 m [30 to 50 ft]) in small gardens and particularly near buildings.

It is worth a study of the ultimate height, spread and shape of the trees you choose and to bear this knowledge carefully in mind when considering their sites. Where there is room for a number of garden trees, sensible spacing, again with due regard for mature growth, is equally vital. It is better to remove every other tree in later years where initial spacing has been too close rather than to indulge in heavy pruning or "lopping" – a

OPPOSITE: *Acer griseum* has decorative peeling bark

practice despised by the skilled tree surgeon – thus ruining the natural form and beauty of the individual tree. Most garden trees – Japanese cherries (prunus), ornamental crabs (malus), mountain ashes and whitebeams (sorbus) and thorns (crataegus) – allowing for mature growth, should be initially spaced at least 5.4 to 7.6 m (18 to 25 ft) apart – some varieties considerably more – unless it is proposed to remove every other tree after six or eight years. However, it is becoming the custom today to treat the small garden as one might a room, refurnishing it after eight or ten years – a task often carried out anyway if the property changes hands.

I appreciate also that closely planted trees may perform a necessary screening function. Nevertheless, it is important that thinning is attended to before too densely sited trees ruin or suppress one another. As an efficient evergreen screen it is better to plant cypresses (Lawson's or Leyland) or *Thuja plicata* (Western Red Cedar) or one of their forms or tall-growing evergreen *Cotoneaster* or *Stranvaesia* perhaps along the appropriate boundary of your garden. Your deciduous garden trees are best sited as lawn specimens with their heads well clear of other plantings and where their natural beauty and form can be enjoyed to the full.

Soils vary widely from district to district: some people are blessed with a good, rich loam; others have the doubtful blessing of heavy clay; some have to contend with a poor thin soil overlying chalk, gravel or rock, while others must garden in very acid, peaty and often boggy conditions. With a few exceptions most garden trees will grow reasonably well on most of these soils although their ultimate sizes may vary according to the poverty of the ground. Some leading nurserymen give details of anticipated ultimate growths in their catalogues and in the alphabetical list which follows this introduction, I shall be describing a wide range of trees for small gardens and giving details of their size and shape under average conditions.

I think it will be helpful to detail here the various forms of tree usually available from nurserymen.

A bush form tree may branch into a number of stems a little above ground level; such trees are useful for their multi-stemmed bark effects.

A feathered tree (or "whip") is a young specimen, usually 1.2 to 1.8 m (4 to 6 ft) high, without a formed head of branches. Lateral growths may still be retained from near the ground upwards. A standard or half standard may be formed from a feathered specimen by correctly stopping the leading shoot and pruning or thinning the lateral branches formed as a result to form a head; ultimately lateral twigs are removed flush to the stem below the head to form the standard or half standard. Alternatively, a feathered tree may be allowed to develop naturally if a specimen is required "furnished to the ground" whereupon most side branches are retained.

A half standard usually has a 1- to 1.3-m ($3\frac{1}{2}$- to $4\frac{1}{2}$-ft) and a standard tree a 1.5- to 1.8-m (5- to 6-ft) clear stem before branching commences; varying somewhat according to species, the overall height of a standard may be between 2.1 and 3 m (7 and 10 ft).

In recent years, primarily to counter vandalism to trees planted in public places, select standards and extra heavy standards have appeared. These forms may be 3.6 to 4.5 m (12 to 15 ft) with a 2.1- to 2.7-m (7- to 9-ft) clear stem and a good head of branches. Trees of this size are also useful in providing more immediate effects in gardens and particularly where screening is required. They are likely to be less successful if planted in exposed circumstances. Trees of this dimension are now becoming available especially grown in containers – they have an excellent chance of good establishment and should be looked upon, generally speaking, as the largest size tree in a wide variety of sorts that can be safely transplanted.

Although confined advisedly to a restricted variety of trees which transplant easily, finally there is the semi-mature or instant tree which should be especially prepared for lifting by the vendor in order to ensure an adequate ball of fibrous roots. A crane or specialized lifting gear may be necessary to lift and transport such trees which may vary in height from 4.5 to 10.6 m (15 to 35 ft) or more and weigh one or two tonnes. The value of semi-mature trees

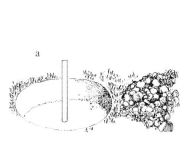
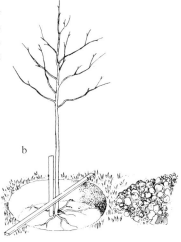
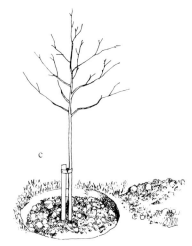

for immediate effects in gardens (or elsewhere) is considerable but I stress that such specimens must be adequately prepared and competently lifted, handled and replanted to be successful. They are not suitable for exposed sites where "whips" or young feathered trees establish more readily. Before ordering ensure there is adequate access to the proposed site for both tree and handling gear.

Nurserymen lift and despatch deciduous trees in open weather between the end of October and about mid-March. Occasionally, dry conditions in early autumn may delay commencement of lifting. Evergreens may be moved from early October until about mid-April. Where available, pot or container-grown specimens may be planted at any time.

Preparation of sites and planting
To ensure rapid establishment and satisfactory growth it is essential to prepare each site by taking out a hole for each tree (of normal nursery size) at least 90 cm (3 ft) in diameter and 45 cm (1½ ft) deep. If in the course of this preparation, chalk, gravel, sand, clay or poor subsoil is encountered, this should be excavated and replaced by good topsoil imported if necessary for the purpose. On poor soils a bucketful of well-rotted farmyard manure dug into the bottom of the hole is a worthwhile addition. Ideally this work should be done well in advance of planting, the holes being temporarily filled back. At planting time remove the

Planting a tree:
(a) The hole should be large enough to accommodate all the roots and deep enough to plant the tree to the correct level. The stake is inserted before planting.
(b) The tree is inserted and the hole checked for size. The stick laid over the hole should align with the soil mark on the stem of the tree.
(c) The soil, which may be mixed with peat and slow-release fertilizer or well-rotted manure, is replaced; shake the tree gently to ensure fine soil gets around the root fibres. Firm the soil well with the heel as planting progresses. Finally, the tree is fastened to the stake with a purpose-made tree tie, nailed to the post to prevent slipping

loose soil to the depth of about 30 cm (1 ft) and thoroughly firm the soil remaining in the hole. Before attempting to plant, position a stout stake about 5- to 8-cm (2- to 3-in) in diameter, driving the pointed and preserved end 45 to 60 cm (1½ to 2 ft) into the ground. Position the tree against the stake, well spreading the root system. Fill back with a mixture of topsoil and moist peat, shaking the tree gently to work the soil among the root fibres, leaving no air spaces. A handful of Growmore or a slow-release fertilizer mixed with the peat is a worthwhile addition to assist establishment and rapid growth. It is most important to firm the tree very thoroughly using the full weight of the body behind the heel. Ensure that the finished level of planting corresponds with the previous soil mark near the base of the stem.

Finally, secure the tree to the stake using purpose-made tree ties, one at the very top of the stake where it should terminate immediately below the head and one half way down the stem, in the case of standard trees. Shorter stakes and one tie may be sufficient for smaller feathered or young trees while extra heavy standards may require a stake either side of the trunk, the tree being secured between them with a wooden cross-piece and/or rubber or plastic spacers and belting. Large-headed, semi-mature trees need guying, using galvanized wire hawsers and wooden plugs driven into the ground. Rubber hose should be used to prevent chafing from the metal hawser.

Maintenance and aftercare

Intelligent maintenance and attention to watering is very necessary and need not be arduous and time consuming.

If there is a drought in the spring or early summer, when a newly moved tree is in greatest need of moisture at the roots, then it is certainly worth the application of at least two bucketfuls of water per standard tree per week. Those trees set in grass are at greater risk as they have to compete with the grass for all available food and moisture. A cultivation area at least 90 cm (3 ft) in diameter should be maintained free of grass or weeds for the first three years following planting. A mulch of peat, strawy manure, well-rotted leaves or pulverized bark-fibre, applied to moist ground, is a useful means of both conserving essential moisture and maintaining the cultivation area in a clean condition.

Once the tree is fully established, bulbs – winter aconites (*Eranthis*), grape hyacinths (*Muscari*), snowdrops (*Galanthus*) – may be added or one of the many ground-cover plants – Lesser Periwinkle (*Vinca minor*), green and variegated forms of ivy (hedera), hardy geranium or Ladies' Mantle (*Alchemilla*) – may be installed in the cultivated area. Not only is this an additional attraction, but such a planting helps to ensure that the base of the tree which is set in mown grass, is not subjected to repeated wounding by the lawn mower – a distressing complaint I see all too often in both private gardens and public plantings.

Trees benefit from a mulch of peat, strawy manure, well-rotted leaves or bark. This will conserve moisture as well as keeping the area weed-free

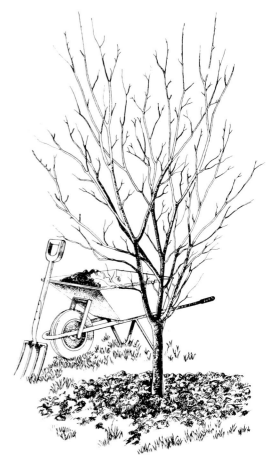

If the bottom 76 cm (2½ ft) of the stake has been stripped of bark and dipped in a preservative such as Green Cuprinol (not creosote please), the stake should last until the tree is firmly anchored and is growing well; but the tree ties will require annual adjustment as the stem expands. This amounts to the loosening of a buckle or the refixing of rubber belting at the end of each winter to allow the stem to grow without restriction. Neglect of this may result in strangulation and lasting damage to the tree.

Pruning

As the newly planted tree develops, some pruning is usually necessary to maintain a balanced and well-spaced head of branches with the leading shoot carefully preserved. This generally involves the removal or shortening back of badly placed or crossing branches and the removal of thin superfluous growth. When the trunk has developed to reasonable proportions, the tree should begin to assume the shape and outline characteristic of its species or variety. In later years, some further thinning of superfluous growth from the head may be necessary periodically.

The trees described are considered suitable for a wide range of conditions in European and North American gardens. Most are also appropriate for South African and Australasian conditions. Attention is drawn in the text to those subjects succeeding only in mild or maritime conditions, otherwise most can be considered hardy in all but the most extreme climates involving cold and exposure.

Ultimate sizes

The mature height of a tree will vary according to the soil, degree of shading, amount of rainfall etc. However, in the British Isles and in countries with similar climates, the following measurements may serve as a guide to the range of anticipated eventual growth of trees growing under average garden conditions: small trees, 3.6 to 9 m (12 to 30 ft); medium trees, 9 to 15 m (30 to 50 ft); large trees, over 18 m (60 ft). Some indication is given in the following descriptions of expected shape or spread of head of the trees listed which should assist in the selection of a tree for a particular site.

Selected Trees

Acacia

The acacias, also commonly known as the wattles or mimosas, comprise a large genus of Australasian trees and shrubs. There are a few species which in mild coastal areas of the northern hemisphere will make small garden trees, interesting in their variable evergreen foliage and often spectacular in their early spring flower. The hardiest species are successful in warm sheltered coastal districts especially when grown against south or west-facing walls. In their native Australia and in the Mediterranean countries, they may make bushy-headed trees

of medium or large size. The acacias grow well in most well-drained soils but will be short lived with yellowing foliage on shallow chalky soils.

The best-known and most widely planted species is *Acacia dealbata*, the Silver Wattle, with its finely divided fern-like leaves and young shoots, both covered with a silvery down against which are seen in early myriads of ball-like, fragrant, yellow flowers – a perfect association. Forms of this species are the popular florists' mimosa.

The Sydney Golden Wattle, *Acacia longifolia*, is quite distinct with its long lance-like leaves or phyllodes. Cylindrical spikes of bright yellow flowers are produced in the axils of the leaves. This is one of the hardiest and also one of the most lime-tolerant species.

Acer

The maples provide us with a wide range of mostly hardy deciduous and easily cultivated trees. Many are notable for their elegance and for the spectacular effect of their autumn foliage. The tree-like forms of *Acer japonicum* and *A. palmatum* are particularly significant in this respect. Garden forms of Sycamore (*A. pseudoplatanus*), Norway Maple (*A. platanoides*) and the Box Maple (*A. negundo*) can be useful for screening and for garden effect, while several other species are grown as much for their unusual bark effects as for the autumn colour of their leaves.

Acer campestre, the Common, Field or Hedge Maple, is often grown and clipped as a hedge plant but this hardy European species if unpruned will make a picturesque, round-headed, small or medium-sized tree. It is notable for the clear, bright yellow of its attractively lobed autumn leaves and will show up well as a hedgerow tree or as a specimen near the perimeter of a larger garden. There is also a cultivar 'Schwerinii' with leaves which are purple tinted in the spring.

Acer cappadocicum is a medium to large-sized hardy tree from the Caucasus, having large five or seven-lobed leaves which colour well in the autumn. It is usually represented in cultivation by its cultivars which are both vigorous, fast-growing trees as useful for screening as for foliage effect in the garden. In the cultivar 'Aureum' the young leaves unfold red tinted, turn golden yellow for several weeks, then change to green, finally reverting to yellow again in the autumn. In 'Rubrum' the leaves of the new shoots on young trees are blood red, while on older trees the unfolding leaves are deep purple red. Striking and unusual effects are created by associating these two cultivars together.

The Snake-bark Maple, *Acer davidii*, is a small Chinese tree of open spreading habit. This is one of the group of maples notable for the attractive, white, snakeskin-like striations on the bark of the trunk and branches. The leaves colour a rich red in the autumn when the winged fruits or "keys", also suffused red, hang thick clustered along the branches. The form usually available is called 'George Forrest' (syn. 'Horizontalis'), in honour of the great plant collector who introduced it to western gardens in 1922. There are several allied species exhibiting similar snake-bark qualities as well as autumn colour of leaf. Among these are *A. capillipes*; *A. grosseri*; *A. hersii*; *A. pensylvanicum*, and *A. rufinerve*. All make attractive small or medium-sized garden trees and are of Asiatic origin with the exception of the North American *A. pensylvanicum*.

The choice Chinese species *Acer griseum*, the Paperbark Maple, is generally regarded as one of the most striking and beautiful of all garden trees. The peeling from the trunk and main branches of its mahogany-brown outer bark to reveal orange or cinnamon-coloured underbark is its most outstanding feature. Delightful soft red and orange autumn colouring of leaf, unfailingly produced, is a further attribute. An ideal specimen tree for the small garden, it usually assumes a neat vase or wine-glass shape in outline, slowly attaining 3 to 3.6 m (10 or 12 ft) in about fifteen years. *Acer griseum* grows well on most soils including chalky ones; it may make as much as 13.7 m (45 ft) on rich loamy soils.

Acer japonicum is one of the group known as the Japanese maples. It is a slow-growing, small, bushy-headed tree,

usually represented in cultivation by the following cultivars. 'Aureum' is a choice, rather slow-growing but very beautiful form effective throughout the growing season by reason of its handsome soft yellow leaves. For the best effect plant in a sheltered, semi-shaded position preferably facing west in order that the late afternoon sunlight is projected most tellingly through the yellow leaves. Care in siting is important as the leaves will scorch in full sunshine. With leaves up to 15 cm (6 in) across, 'Vitifolium' is the largest-leaved Japanese maple and one which contributes a vivid kaleidoscope of colour to the autumn scene. Yellow, orange, scarlet, crimson, purple and green are usually represented particularly on neutral or acid soils. It is a more vigorous small tree than 'Aureum' and often as wide as it is high.

The Box Elder, *Acer negundo*, a North American maple, is usually seen in cultivation as a medium-sized tree with a wide-spreading head. The bright green young shoots are a notable feature; the pinnate leaves have a variable number of leaflets, bright green with paler undersides. A useful screening tree, the Box Elder, requires plenty of room if allowed to develop its full spread and is perhaps better represented in small gardens by its several variegated forms which are generally more modest in ultimate growth and more striking in garden effect. 'Auratum' is one of the few garden trees retaining its bright golden-yellow leaves throughout the growing season. It is a striking small tree. 'Elegans' (syn. 'Elegantissimum') is a form with its leaves broadly margined bright yellow. 'Variegatum' ('Argenteovariegatum') is the most commonly planted cultivar and is most effective with its leaves irregularly bordered with white, some leaflets may be completely white. These three cultivars are very worthy garden trees but have a tendency to produce branches where the leaves have reverted to the more vigorous green of *A. negundo*. Such branches should be carefully pruned out as soon as they are noticed; if neglected they will tend to dominate, eventually suppressing the variegated form.

Acer nikoense, the Nikko Maple, a

small to medium-sized, round-headed tree from Japan and central China, is related to *A. griseum*. The large leaves, consisting of 8- to 13-cm (3- to 5-in) long leaflets with grey undersides, colour magnificently a combination of scarlet, flame and yellow unfailingly each autumn. Suitable for all soils, this is one of the most beautiful, hardy, autumn-colouring trees that we can grow.

In cultivation *Acer palmatum*, the Japanese Maple, is seen as a small multi-stemmed tree, up to 6 m (20 ft) high and as much through. The five or seven-lobed bright green leaves assume rich autumn tints of red, orange and yellow. This and the more robust of its many forms will grow in a moist but reasonably well-drained situation on most soils including alkaline or chalky ones. A sheltered semi-shaded site is desirable as these maples will resent exposure to full sunshine and to cold winds. The following are among the most worthwhile of those cultivars which will reach proportions of small trees. 'Atropurpureum' is often seen as a small vase-shaped tree up to 3 to 3.6 m (10 or 12 ft) high. Good forms have rich crimson leaves consistently throughout the growing season; this is justifiably the most popular Japanese maple. Equally 'Heptalobum Osakazuki' is generally regarded as the finest Japanese maple for autumn colour. The seven-lobed green leaves, larger than in the type species, turn brilliant shades of scarlet and orange. It is a small tree of similar dimensions to 'Atropurpureum'. Although the soft yellow or orange autumn colour of 'Senkaki', the Coral Bark Maple, is not to be despised, this cultivar is most notable for its coral-red young twigs and branches which are most conspicuous in winter. It makes a small tree of erect habit.

A large, fast-growing, broad-headed, hardy tree, the Norway Maple, *Acer platanoides*, is now much planted as a landscape tree. Like the Sycamore, it transplants readily even at semi-mature size and is often used in gardens where immediate screening is required. The leaves resemble those of the Sycamore but are thinner in texture and a brighter green turning clear yellow in the autumn.

If need be it may be pruned to keep it within bounds. There are a number of cultivars usually slower growing and less large in ultimate growth. Of French origin 'Columnare' makes a large tree of erect habit. The form 'Crimson King' is much valued for its dark crimson-purple leaves which retain their colour throughout summer. 'Goldsworth Purple' and 'Faasen's Black' are very similar. 'Globosum' is perhaps the most suitable form for the small garden as it makes a small mop-headed picturesque tree. The leaves of the compact-headed cultivar 'Drummondii' are reguarly bordered with white.

Although invaluable in extreme exposure the Sycamore, *Acer pseudoplatanus*, a large vigorous tree, is best represented in gardens by its slower-growing forms notable for the brilliance of their young leaves in spring. These include 'Brilliantissimum', a small slow-growing tree with a neat, compact head. The unfolding leaves in spring are for three or four weeks a delightful tawny pink, changing to pale yellow green and finally mid-green. Another slow-growing cultivar is 'Prinz Handjery' which makes a small shrubby tree; the young foliage is tinted with yellow on the upper surfaces and with purple beneath. 'Simon-Louis Frères' is similar, often with pink tinting in the leaves.

Aesculus
Commonly cultivated species and cultivars of the well-known Horse Chestnut are among the most beautiful of spring and summer-flowering trees and make magnificent large round-headed specimens for a parkland setting. The American buck-eyes, less spectacular in flower and variable in their garden value, make small shrubby trees. The following are particularly useful in smaller gardens.

Aesculus × carnea 'Briotii' is a compact medium-sized cultivar of the Red Horse Chestnut having deeper coloured, larger flower panicles. *A. pavia* 'Atrosanguinea', the best-coloured form of the Red Buckeye, is an unusual small round-headed tree producing its deep red flowers in June. All the chestnuts and buckeyes are trouble free, at least in their youth, and thrive in all well-drained soils.

Platanus orientalis (yellow) and *Acer palmatum* (red)

Amelanchier

Several members of this genus assume the dimensions of small trees and provide us with two seasons of effect – a dense canopy of small white fragrant flowers in the spring, often with the developing young leaves, followed by rich colouring of the foliage in the autumn. The snowy mespiluses are more successful on moist but well-drained lime-free soils. Their nomenclature is confused but the following species are usually available in tree forms. However, avoid specimens grafted on thorn (*Crataegus*).

The true species under the name *Amelanchier canadensis* (syn. *A. oblongifolia*) forms an erect-growing shrubby tree, native of swampy land in eastern North America. The leaves are oblong in shape and the flowers produced in compact erect racemes. Another North American species is *A. laevis*; here the bronzy-pink young leaves appearing with the fragrant white flowers are an added feature. It is often wrongly grown under the name of *A. canadensis*.

Amelanchier lamarckii (syn. *A. grandiflora*) is the best species for general

Amelanchier lamarckii

garden planting; it will form a small specimen of rather spreading habit. A striking tree in flower and autumn colour, it is now naturalized in several areas of Europe including England. *A. lamarckii* 'Rubescens' (syn. *A. × grandiflora* 'Rubescens') is a cultivar with flowers purple pink in bud and tinted pink when open.

Arbutus

Arbutus andrachnoides (syn. *A. hybrida*, *A. andrachnae × unedo*) is a small evergreen tree, grown mainly for the glorious cinnamon-red shaggy bark on trunk and branches. Racemes of parchment-coloured, pitcher-shaped flowers appear on the ends of twigs in the late autumn or winter. It is a hybrid between the Grecian and Killarney Strawberry Trees.

The Killarney Strawberry Tree. *Abutus unedo*, is a handsome small tree, gnarled with age; this species produces white or pale pink flowers, together with the hanging strawberry-like red and yellow fruits in the autumn of the year. It is a native of the Mediterranean and south and west Ireland. Its cultivar 'Rubra' has deeper pink flowers and a compact habit.

Both the above-mentioned strawberry trees are remarkably successful in chalky or limy soils.

Betula

The birches are a well-loved genus of hardy medium-sized trees, much valued for their elegance of habit and for the striking effects created by the silvery-white or orange-brown bark of trunk and branches. Those species or cultivars with light, narrow heads are often planted quite closely in groups to give a multi-stemmed effect. Soft golden autumn colour of leaf is a further feature of many species.

Although ultimately a tall tree, *Betula ermanii*, a handsome species from north eastern Asia, is, with careful siting, truly magnificent in the garden from quite an early age. The trunk has cream or pink-tinted peeling bark while the upright-spreading branches are a glistening orange brown. Species with similar qualities of effectively peeling bark, making fine specimen trees, are *B. costata* with cream-white bark and *B. jacquemontii*, a west Himalayan species with vivid white trunk and branches.

The Common Silver Birch or Lady of the Woods, *Betula pendula*, is one of the most attractive of the European native species but trees raised from seed can be variable in the quality of their silver-white trunks and in the size and spread of head. In small gardens, the species is perhaps best represented by its selected forms though the type tree is excellent for small copses or where multi-stemmed effects are required. *B.p.* 'Dalecarlica', the Swedish Birch, is remarkable as much for its slender, graceful, drooping habit and finely cut leaves as for its silvery-white trunk. *B.p.* 'Tristis' makes a fine, narrow-headed, white-trunked, tall tree with pendulous branches and is of more robust constitution than the Swedish Birch. *B.p.* 'Youngii', Young's Weeping Birch, forms a small, mushroom-headed garden tree with branches weeping to the ground.

Carpinus

The hornbeams are handsome, hardy trees of medium to large size suitable for all soils. Their hop-like seed clusters are unusual and attractive. The Common Hornbeam is *Carpinus betulus*, a British and European native tree often with a rounded picturesque head and grey fluted trunk. The foliage, superficially resembling that of the beech, is markedly ribbed and toothed, turning yellow in autumn. The following forms, which are of architectural interest, are particularly useful in gardens. 'Columnaris' is a slow-growing, dense-habited, small tree of narrow upright growth. Although quite narrow when young, 'Fastigiata' ('Pyramidalis') matures to a medium-sized tree

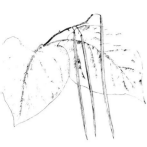

Seedpods of *Catalpa bignonioides*

of broadly pyramidal, almost onion-like shape.

Catalpa

Catalpa bignonioides, the most usually planted Indian Bean Tree, forms a small to medium-sized tree of wide-spreading habit. The large, handsome leaves may grow up to 25 cm (10 in) long and 20 cm (8 in) wide while the conspicuous panicles of foxglove-like flowers, white with yellow and purple spots, appear towards late summer. After hot summers, the long cylindrical seedpods are quite effective and remarkable. The catalpa thrives in any well-drained soil but should not be sited in an exposed position. A native of the eastern U.S.A., this is one of the most beautiful and desirable of all flowering trees. It has a striking cultivar 'Aurea', whose soft golden leaves maintain their colour throughout the summer and autumn. A fine lawn specimen.

Cercis

The redbuds or Judas trees are a small genus of late spring-flowering trees or large shrubs suitable for warm sunny sites on any well-drained soil. *Cercis siliquastrum* is the Judas Tree. Although often grown as a shrub, it is best seen as a small picturesque tree; the bright rose-purple, pea-shaped flowers are produced in clusters along the bare branches as the round leaves begin to unfold, bronze tinted in the late spring. In late summer and autumn, the purple-tinted seedpods are a conspicuous feature. There is also a white-flowered cultivar 'Alba' and a fine deep purple form, 'Bodnant'. The Judas tree from the eastern Mediterranean is the most satisfactory species in European gardens while the North American Redbud, *C. canadensis*, is popular in the U.S.A. and Canada. Recently introduced to Great Britain, *C.c.* 'Forest Pansy', a form notable for its deep red-tinted, purple foliage, is striking throughout the growing season.

Cordyline

Cordyline (Dracaena) australis, the Cabbage Tree of New Zealand, is a small tree of exotic aspect for mild or maritime areas, slowly forming one or more cylindrical stems crowned by dense heads of arching sword-like leaves up to 90 cm (3 ft) long. Panicles of small fragrant white flowers are produced early in the summer. There is also a form 'Atropurpurea' with purple-tinted leaves.

Cornus

Those members of this genus which reach the proportion of small or medium-sized trees are most desirable and ornamental, contributing both striking floral and autumn-colouring effects. The flowers are conspicuous by reason of white or coloured bracts or modified leaves which surround the true flower clusters. The cornels or dogwoods will grow on most soils but several species make poor growth in shallow chalky conditions.

Cornus capitata (syn. *Benthamia fragifera*) is an evergreen Himalayan species making a small bushy tree often wider than high. Its leaves are up to 13 cm (5 in) long, grey-green and downy making a pleasing background for the mid-summer "flowers" which comprise four to six large pale yellow bracts surrounding the remaining flower parts. Equally conspicuous in the autumn are the large, strawberry-shaped, crimson fruits. Regrettably this handsome tree is only successful in the mildest coastal districts of south and west England and similar climates.

A fine and architecturally significant Japanese species, *Cornus contraversa* eventually makes a medium-sized tree with tiers of horizontal branches. These are arrayed at mid-summer with clusters of cream-coloured bracts. On most soils the leaves turn purple in the autumn. 'Variegata' is a fine form of smaller size with conspicuous white-margined leaves.

The Flowering Dogwood, *C. florida*, forms a small tree, often with a wide-spreading head conspicuous in late spring when it displays masses of white petal-like bracts. This is also one of the trees responsible for the spectacular fall colour of the eastern U.S.A. where it is native. After a hot summer, the leaves colour well in the British Isles but it is generally less happy here thriving best in east or south-east England in sites free from spring or early autumn frosts. This species is rather intolerant of chalk soils. There are a number of varieties and cultivars selected on account of the exceptional colour of their flower bracts. The variety *rubra* is rose red; 'Cherokee Chief' is a deeper rose red, an American selection, and 'White Cloud', another American selected form, has brilliant white bracts freely borne.

Cornus kousa chinensis is a geographical form of the Japanese *C. kousa* and a most beautiful hardy small flowering tree. It produces its large long-lasting white bracts at mid-summer followed by round red edible fruits. The leaves, also larger ·than in the type, colour well for a long period in autumn. It is less successful on chalky soils.

The Pacific Dogwood, *Cornus nuttallii*, is the doyen of the cornels, a native of western North America where it attains a height of 15 m (50 ft) or more. The large white bracts open in late spring. Regrettably it tends to be short lived in Great Britain but it is often seen as an upright shrubby small tree spectacular in flower from the ground to its summit. It is not suitable for chalk soils.

Crataegus

The thorns are very useful and ornamental small, hardy trees mostly with wide-spreading and dense twiggy heads; spring flower, mainly white, is followed in the autumn by attractive haws. Equally at home in city street or exposed coastal or moorland garden, and on all soils, they are deserving of wider planting.

Crataegus crus-galli, the Cockspur Thorn, is a particularly worthwhile species from eastern North America making a flat-topped picturesque tree. It is a copious flowerer, notable for both brilliant red autumn leaf colour and for the crimson haws which often persist until spring. The hybrid *C. lavallei* (syn. *C. carrierei*) makes a splendid small garden tree; both glossy green leaves and orange-red fruits persist until the New Year making an attractive and unusual winter feature.

A form of the Common Hawthorn, *C. monogyna* 'Stricta' ('Fastigiata') with a narrow, erect-growing branch system, is particularly useful in cold windswept sites. *C. oxyacantha* is the European and British native Hawthorn or May, and it has given rise to a number of cultivars or hybrids some with double and coloured flowers which form excellent small garden trees with compact heads. 'Paul's Scarlet' is a double red; 'Plena', double white, and 'Rosea Flore Pleno', a lovely double pink.

Crataegus phaenopyrum, the Washington Thorn, is one of the most outstanding of the American thorns; a handsome round-headed tree with shining maple-like leaves which colour well in autumn and masses of scarlet haws often persisting until spring.

Crataegus pinnatifida major from northern China is perhaps the most effective of all thorns in respect of its rich autumn leaf colour and hanging clusters of large glossy deep red berries.

Davidia

Davidia involucrata, the Handkerchief or Ghost Tree, is a most ornamental hardy Chinese tree ultimately of medium. size with a broad, spreading habit. The large handsome leaves are reminiscent of those of the lime (*Tilia*). The tree receives its popular names by reason of the two large and conspicuous white bracts which surround each small flower cluster appearing in late spring and early summer. This imposing tree, which is happy on all soils of reasonable depth, is ideal as a lawn specimen particularly in the larger garden. Flowering usually commences about ten years after planting and is well worth waiting for. The subspecies *D.i. vilmoriniana* is of equal garden merit and differs only in minor botanical details.

Eucalyptus

Although widely planted in coastal areas of tropical and sub-tropical countries, there are a number of species of this large Australasian genus suitable for milder areas of Great Britain and countries with similar climates. The evergreen foliage often differs greatly even within a species – juvenile leaves on young specimens being quite distinct from the adult foliage found on older trees. In mild districts many species will make medium-sized or large trees and are frequently in danger of blowing over if exposed to strong winds. In such circumstances and indeed in small gardens generally, the gum trees are best grown as multi-stemmed bushy plants when their attractive foliage can be enjoyed at eye level. Such bushes also provide quantities of excellent and easily accessible foliage for floral arranging. Although less successful on chalk, most species will grow on a considerable range of soils. Spring planting of small pot-grown plants is to be recommended. Once established and growing vigorously, cut back to about 45 cm (18 in) to strengthen anchorage. Then select the best newly formed stem to make a tree, or grow as a multi-stemmed bush if desired.

One of the hardiest species is *Eucalyptus dalrympleana* which makes a medium-sized tree with silvery-white patchwork trunk and branches; the adult foliage, 10 to 18 cm (4 to 7 in) long, is scimitar shaped. *E. gunnii*, the Cider Gum, a hardy Tasmanian species, is now much planted in the British Isles. The juvenile leaves are round, stem clasping and bright glaucous blue while adult foliage is sickel shaped and sage green. It is most striking if grown as a bush.

The Snow Gum, *Eucalyptus niphophila*, is a remarkably hardy species from Australia's Snowy Mountains. It is a small attractive tree which is very garden worthy with its grey and cream-coloured peeling trunk and branches and long, lance-shaped, blue-grey adult leaves. Young branches and twigs are covered with blue-white bloom and new leaves open mahogany red. A very hardy species, *E. parvifolia*, makes a medium-sized tree and is successful on chalk soils. The juvenile leaves are usually dark green, ovate-lanceolate and pointed while adult foliage is narrower (linear-lanceolate), blue green, about 6 cm (2½ in) long.

Eucryphia
The evergreen *Eucryphia × nymansensis* 'Nymansay' is a magnificent small or medium-sized tree of upright habit. Maturing specimens are spectacular in late summer or early autumn when increasing quantities of large white flowers with prominent stamens are produced. It is a hybrid between two South American species and very worthy of a sheltered site in most gardens having deep moist lime-free loam.

Fagus
The Common Beech, *Fagus sylvatica*, is a European species, also indigenous to the British Isles. It is without doubt Britain's most impressive large landscape tree, admired equally for its fresh green young leaves, for its handsome smooth grey trunk and winter-branch tracery and for the rich golden brown of its autumn foliage. It thrives on all well-drained soils and is particularly at home where the subsoil is chalk. There are many forms in cultivation, some of which are restricted enough in ultimate growth for use in small gardens. *F.s.* 'Aurea Pendula' is a remarkable form of tall slender habit, with branches which hang down almost perpendicularly. The foliage is golden yellow. It should be sited in semi-shade. *F.s.* 'Dawyck' (syn. 'Fastigiata'), the Dawyck Beech, becomes a handsome tall tree of conical habit; a deep purple-leaved form of the same upright habit 'Dawyck Purple' has recently been introduced. *F.s.* 'Heterophylla', the Fern-leaved Beech, is one of the most beautiful and unusual forms making a large tree. The fern-like leaves are variable in shape but usually deeply cut and lobed. There is also a beautiful variant of the Fern-leaved Beech, 'Rohanii', with purple leaves.

'Purpurea', the Purple or Copper Beech, is a popular large tree but it is often variable in foliage colour if raised from seed. The best cultivar 'Riversii', which nurserymen supply as a grafted young tree, has large, deep purple, lustrous leaves.

'Purpurea Pendula', the Weeping Purple Beech, makes a magnificent small weeping tree and is perhaps the best form of purple-leaved beech for the small garden.

Fraxinus
The ashes are a large genus of hardy, fast-growing deciduous trees, mainly native of the temperate regions of the northern hemisphere countries. Many of the large-growing species make stately parkland

Winged fruits of the ash

trees, noted for their elegant, large, pinnate leaves, while the flowering ashes form interesting and attractive summer-flowering specimens of more moderate growth. They are generally happy in any fertile soil, and are tolerant equally of town conditions, seaside and exposed localities and moist situations.

Fraxinus excelsior, the Common Ash, is a familiar large and handsome tree for parkland or similar circumstances, with typical long pinnate leaves and distinct black winter buds. Some of its forms are suitable for gardens. 'Jaspidea' (syn. 'Aurea'), the Golden-barked Ash, makes a compact tree, notable for its yellow young shoots and yellowish winter bark. The leaves turn clear yellow in the autumn. 'Pendula', the Weeping Ash, is a vigorous weeping tree, usually forming a wide-spreading mound of stiffly pendulous branches. It is excellent as a lawn specimen where there is ample room for its development.

Fraxinus mariesii is perhaps the most ornamental of the flowering ashes bearing quantities of cream-white flowers at mid-summer, followed by unusual fruits which quickly turn purple. It is a small tree with a rounded head, ideal for many gardens. The Manna Ash, *F. ornus*, forms a medium-sized, round-headed tree and is the most commonly planted of the flowering ashes. White flowers are abundantly produced in late spring.

Fraxinus oxycarpa 'Raywood' is a selected form of an elegant eastern European species, making a fine specimen tree of medium height, but compact and upright habit. The blue-green summer foliage turns purple in the autumn.

A striking and unusual Japanese Flowering Ash, *Fraxinus spaethiana*, forms a small to medium-sized tree, remarkable for its very large leaves and leaflets with distinctive swollen bases to the leaf stalks.

Gleditsia

Gleditsia triacanthos is a handsome large central North American tree, allied to the False Acacia (*Robinia*). The beautiful frond-like glossy dark green leaves turn clear yellow in autumn. In warm and sunny climates formidable spines of 8 to 30 cm (3 to 12 in) develop on the trunk and branches, a feature less marked in cooler climates or shaded areas. In autumn, glossy brown pods 30 to 45 cm (1 to $1\frac{1}{2}$ ft) long hang effectively along the branches. The Honey Locust is happy in all soils and is tolerant of industrial air pollution. In small gardens it is best represented by either of the following forms. 'Bujoti' (syn. 'Pendula') makes an elegant small weeping tree. The leaflets are narrower than in the type. 'Sunburst' (syn. 'Inermis Aurea') is a thornless cultivar forming a small or medium-sized tree of somewhat spreading habit. Bright yellow young leaves at the ends of the branches appear effectively among the older emerald-green leaves. This is a striking garden tree for foliage effect.

Halesia

The snowdrop trees are beautiful North American flowering trees, suitable for well-drained (lime free) soils in sunny, sheltered gardens. The hardiest species is *Halesia monticola*, the Mountain Snowdrop Tree, from the mountains of the south eastern United States. In gardens it makes an imposing small spreading tree, its branches hung in late spring with multitudes of pure white bell-like flowers. These are followed by unusual four-winged fruits. It is a tree worthy of wider planting; the variety *vestita* has larger flowers often tinted pink.

Juglans

The walnuts are medium-sized to large stately trees traditionally planted in gardens for many centuries, as much for their noble appearance as for their fruit and timber value. They have large and imposing pinnate leaves which are reminiscent of ash. Walnuts are happy in most well-drained soils.

The Black Walnut, *Juglans nigra*, is a native of east and central U.S.A., forming a large wide-spreading tree with deeply channelled bark and magnificent leaves, 60 cm (2 ft) long, which are aromatic when crushed.

The Common Walnut, *Juglans regia*, is a slower-growing, less imposing, south eastern European and Asiatic species forming a medium to large-sized round-headed tree. There are a number of varieties of French origin grown only for their nuts and making large bushes or small compact trees.

Koelreuteria

Koelreuteria paniculata is a very handsome Chinese summer-flowering tree, ultimately broad headed and of medium size. Long fern-like leaves emerge pink tinted and colour yellow in the autumn. Large upright panicles of golden-yellow flowers are followed by unusual bronze-tinted bladder-like seed vessels. To flower freely, the Golden-rain Tree or Pride of India requires a sheltered but sunny situation in any well-drained soil. There is also an interesting, though rare, narrow upright form, 'Fastigiata', ultimately growing about 7.6 m (25 ft) high and 90 cm (3 ft) wide which is ideal for small gardens and for confined areas.

Laburnum

These spectacular, early summer-flowering, small, hardy trees have the descriptive common name of golden rain and are much planted in gardens, thriving on any soil. Large crops of unattractive seedpods, containing poisonous seeds, if left on the trees, tend to sap the vigour and decrease the life span of an already rather short-lived tree. *Laburnum anagyroides* 'Pendulum' is a dwarf form with long drooping branches while *L. × watereri* 'Vossii' is the best laburnum for general planting in gardens. The long racemes of bright yellow pea flowers are produced freely.

Ligustrum

The Chinese Tree Privet, *Ligustrum*

Liriodendron tulipifera

lucidum, becomes a fine evergreen small or medium-sized tree of upright-growing habit, forming ultimately a dense rounded head. The large deep green leaves, 8 to 15 cm (3 to 6 in) long, are an excellent foil for the erect panicles of white flowers, 15 to 20 cm (6 to 8 in) high, produced in late summer. 'Excelsum Superbum' is a striking variant of similar ultimate size with its large leaves effectively variegated with yellow and white.

Liquidambar

Liquidambar styraciflua, the Sweet Gum, is a handsome hardy large tree from the eastern U.S.A., ultimately forming a narrow pyramidal head. The lustrous maple-like leaves are alternately produced and colour magnificently deep red or crimson in the autumn; corky protrusions on the older branchlets are a winter feature. Several selected forms are now available, notably 'Lane Roberts' with deep crimson autumn leaves. This tree is conspicuous from an early age but it is not successful on chalky or alkaline soils.

Liriodendron

Liriodendron tulipifera, the Tulip Tree, a noble large tree from North America, is much valued for its stately appearance and remarkable blunt-ended leaves which turn golden yellow in autumn, and for the unique tulip-like flowers, yellow green with orange basal markings, appearing on older trees at mid-summer. It is successful in most deep loamy soils.

The cultivar 'Aureomarginatum' has leaves conspicuously bordered with yellow and is a striking and unusual variegated tree for the smaller garden while 'Fastigiatum' (syn. 'Pyramidale') is a narrow upright-growing form, ultimately of medium size.

Magnolia

The large members of this exotic genus are perhaps the most distinguished and magnificent of early-flowering trees that can be grown in gardens. They transplant more successfully from the open ground in the spring and grow well on good, well-drained loams and clays. A number of species are lime tolerant. Regrettably, some of the most magnificent tree species do not flower for many years after planting.

Perhaps the most remarkable and spectacular of the magnolias, *Magnolia campbellii* is a giant tree in its native Himalaya and it reaches considerable proportions in favoured gardens. The immense tulip-shaped flowers, in varying shades of pink, are produced early in the year on maturing trees. The flowers open like water lilies before falling. A number of varieties have now appeared which, unlike the type tree, may flower within ten or fifteen years of planting. In particular these are *mollicomata*, 'Charles Raffill' and 'Princess Margaret'. All have pink or rose-purple flowers and show signs of greater hardiness than the type. Lime-free soil is necessary.

One of the best small magnolias for general planting is *M. kobus*, producing quantities of white early spring flowers usually within fifteen years of planting. It is a very hardy Japanese species which is happy on all soils and particularly successful on chalk.

The fine hybrid *Magnolia × loebneri* (*kobus × stellata*) makes a handsome small shrubby tree producing its fragrant white strap-like flowers at a very early age. Like its parents, it succeeds on all soils. There are several cultivars now available from this cross, particularly noteworthy are 'Leonard Messel', lilac pink; 'Merrill', an American selection with larger fragrant white flowers, and 'Neil McEacharn', white pink-flushed flowers. *M. salicifolia*, an elegant Japanese species, forms a small broadly pyramidal tree with narrow willow-like leaves, usually glaucous on the undersides. Fragrant white flowers are produced in early spring, even on young trees.

Although often grown as a wall specimen in cooler localities, the magnificent *Magnolia grandiflora*, from the southern U.S.A., can perhaps claim to be the finest of flowering evergreens, reaching the proportions of a small to medium-sized tree in southern European and similar favoured localities. The handsome, leathery, glossy, dark green leaves, 15 to 25 cm (6 to 10 in) long, have attractive red-brown felt on the undersides and form a perfect background to the immense cream-coloured, globular, fragrant flowers which are produced continuously in late summer and autumn. The cultivar 'Exmouth' flowers at an early age. Fortunately, this species is tolerant of all soils of reasonable depth.

Malus

The flowering crabs or rosyblooms are an invaluable group of hardy, small, occasionally medium-sized garden trees providing a variety of shapes and attractive spring bloom in a range of colour from white to deep wine red. Some have purple or red-tinted foliage and many give attractive autumn fruits which are also useful for crab apple jelly. A few provide autumn-tinted leaves. All the following species and cultivars thrive on any reasonably fertile soil and make a short list of the best of the numerous varieties available today which combine beauty with vigour and reliability.

'Almey' is a Canadian-raised small tree, ultimately of rounded habit with reddish young leaves, and large red flowers with white centres, followed by orange-red persistent fruits. *Malus coronaria* 'Charlottae' (syn. 'Flore Pleno'), a form of an eastern North American species, makes a small tree of spreading habit. The large, semi-double, violet-scented, shell-pink flowers are produced in late spring and early summer. The large leaves colour richly in autumn.

Malus floribunda is the Japanese Crab. It forms a small free-flowering tree of graceful habit, semi-pendulous, broadening with age. This handsome species is truly spectacular when in bloom in the early spring, its arching branches densely wreathed in apple-blossom pink flowers which are crimson in bud.

'Golden Hornet' makes a small round-headed tree with erect-growing branches. The white spring flowers are followed by heavy crops of persistent bright yellow fruits. This is a fine fruiting crab. A small tree of somewhat pendulous habit in maturity, 'John Downie' is generally regarded as the best fruiting crab for both appearance and preserve making. The attractive conical scarlet and orange

Malus floribunda

fruits are reliably produced each autumn.

'Katherine' is a small round-headed tree of American raising. It has very large semi-double pink flowers which slowly fade to white and these are followed by bright red, yellow-tinted fruits. 'Profusion' ('Lemoinei' × *sieboldii*) is the best of several cultivars with red young leaves and wine-red flowers. A small tree of good constitution, its large flowers are profusely borne in clusters of six or seven, and are followed by small red fruits.

Malus tschonoskii is a vigorous Japanese species of medium-sized erect pyramidal habit. It is notable for its silvery-white felted young shoots and in particular for its magnificent display of autumn leaf colour. The large pink-tinted flowers fade to white. Finally there is 'Van Eseltine' which is an ideal small garden tree of distinct narrow upright form. The large semi-double flowers, red in bud, open soft pink and are followed by yellow fruits.

Mespilus

Mespilus germanica, the Medlar, forms a picturesque small hardy tree of low spreading habit. The large distinctive hairy leaves turn russet brown in autumn. In the spring, five-petalled large white flowers are produced singly and are followed in the autumn by the typical brown edible fruits. Cultivated for centuries, the Medlar rivals the Black Mulberry for architectural effect.

Metrosideros

This is a small genus of Australasian evergreens related to the myrtles. Two or three species make spectacular small or medium-sized flowering trees for gardens in the mildest maritime districts preferably on neutral or acid soils.

Metrosideros excelsa (syn. *M. tomentosa*) is a native of North Island, New Zealand, where it is known as the Christmas Tree. In summer, this species appears as a solid crimson mass of large bottle-brush flowers. *M. robusta* with thick rounded leaves and scarlet autumn flowers produces a similar effect.

Michelia

Michelia doltsopa is a most desirable small semi-evergreen Himalayan tree related to the magnolias but it is suitable only for lime-free soils in mild or sheltered districts. The handsome leathery leaves, 15 to 18 cm (6 to 7 in) long, are glaucous beneath. White fragrant magnolia-like flowers, opening in the spring, are borne in the axils of the leaves.

Morus

Planted for centuries for their picturesque form and for their edible fruits, the mulberries make small or medium-sized hardy trees on most well-drained soils. *Morus alba* is an economically important Chinese species, long cultivated for its handsome large, heart-shaped leaves upon which silk worms are fed. The sweet fruits are white, changing to deep pink. Its cultivar 'Pendula' makes an outstanding small weeping tree, suitable as a focal point in the garden.

The Black Mulberry, *Morus nigra*, is a well-known, small, wide-spreading tree renowned for its longevity. The large, heart-shaped, rough-textured leaves are down covered beneath; the deep red fruits are produced in increasing quantities from an early age.

Myrtus

In mild and maritime localities the very beautiful Chilean Myrtle, *Myrtus apiculata* (syn. *M. luma*), makes a small aromatic evergreen tree, covered in the late summer with white myrtle flowers, often followed by edible sweet red and black fruits. In addition, the peeling cinnamon brown of trunk and branches is a striking feature. Best sited in a sunny position in any well-drained soil.

Nyssa

There are two species of the tupelo especially worthy of mention. *Nyssa sylvatica* is a broadly pyramidal medium-sized North American tree for moist lime-free soils. It is one of the most spectacular autumn-colouring trees for the large shining, usually oval, green leaves turn red, orange and yellow. *N. sinensis* is a Chinese species attaining small tree size and of equal merit in the autumn. In addition its young growths appear red throughout the growing season. Both species are excellent by the side of water.

Ostrya

Ostrya carpinifolia, the Hop Hornbeam, forms a medium-sized, round-headed south European tree, usually grown on any fertile soil and worthy of wider planting. In the spring, the long male catkins are attractive, while later in the year the branches are hung with decorative, hop-like fruits. The double-toothed, hornbeam-like leaves turn yellow in autumn.

Paulownia

This genus contains small to medium-sized Chinese trees grown for their large handsome leaves and unusual foxglove-like flowers, opening in erect panicles in the spring. On pruned trees the leaves often attain 60 cm (2 ft) or more across. *Paulownia fargesii* makes a medium-sized tree producing at a relatively early age fragrant heliotrope flowers liberally speckled with purple. The best-known species, *P. tomentosa* (syn. *P. imperialis*), forms a smaller round-headed tree with deep heliotrope-coloured flowers.

Platanus

Although a magnificent large broad-headed tree for parkland, I must mention the well-known hybrid *Platanus × hispanica* (syn. *P. × acerifolia*), the London Plane, for its handsome large maple-like leaves and mottled flaking bark. No tree is more tolerant of city conditions and if necessary, may be restricted by severe pruning. The hanging burr-like fruit clusters are effective for much of the year.

The Oriental Plane or Chennar, *Platanus orientalis*, is again a magnificent large long-lived south eastern European tree, much planted in Mediterranean lands as a shade tree. The deeply lobed leaves are particularly attractive when newly opened in the spring, appearing with the hanging fruit clusters.

Populus

This is an extensive genus of fast-growing, medium-sized or large deciduous trees, very useful as specimens or as a tall summer screen where circumstances allow. However, the majority, by reason of their vigour, surface-rooting habits and thirst for moisture, are quite unsuitable for small gardens and for planting near buildings. We will therefore not consider them in detail in this work beyond an honourable mention for *Populus tremula* 'Pendula', the Weeping Aspen, a very effective small weeping tree particularly conspicuous in early spring when the branches are hung with long purple-grey male catkins and *P. tremuloides* 'Pendula', Parasol de St Julien, which makes a charming small pendulous specimen tree of French origin.

Although a large tree *Populus* 'Serotina Aurea', the Golden Poplar, with its effective golden foliage, may be restricted by pruning to control the size of the head and to encourage brightly coloured young foliage. The large heart-shaped leaves are bright yellow in the spring and early summer, and again in the autumn.

Prunus

A large family of beautiful flowering trees (and shrubs) of small or medium size, many of which are ideal for the small garden. In addition to spectacular spring or winter flower, many give a second display in their autumn leaf colour. Although some species and hybrids are not long lived, all succeed in any well-drained soil in a sunny position. Under this heading we will consider a selection of the best flowering ornamental species and hybrids of Almond (*Prunus dulcis*), Japanese Apricot (*Prunus mume*), Jap-

anese and other cherries, peach (*P. persica*) and plums (*P. cerasifera*).

Flowering Almonds These are extensively cultivated and naturalized throughout the Mediterranean lands for their edible almonds and universally grown in gardens as an early spring-flowering small tree. They are generally trees of upright, but often ungainly, habit and like peaches subject to peach leaf curl in country districts. They are good trees for town conditions. There are a number of cultivars and in particular: *Prunus dulcis* 'Macrocarpa', with very large pale pink or white flowers and large almonds; *P.d.* 'Praecox', a very early-flowering form with pale pink flowers; *P. × amygdalopersica* (*dulcis × persica*) 'Pollardii', a hybrid between the Almond and the Peach which makes a very beautiful small tree, the deep rich pink flowers are particularly striking when seen against a dark evergreen background.

Flowering Apricots The Japanese Apricot, *Prunus mume*, forms a charming small garden tree, producing almond-scented pink flowers opening over an extended period in late winter and spring. A sheltered sunny site is desirable. Particularly good forms are: 'Alboplena', with semi-double white flowers; 'Alphandii' ('Flore Pleno'), semi-double, pink, and 'Beni-shi-don', fragrant flowers which are an unusual shade of rich deep pink.

Japanese and other Flowering Cherries *Prunus* 'Accolade' (*sargentii × subhirtella*) is an early April-flowering cultivar of upright spreading habit, slightly pendulous with age. Semi-double, pale pink flowers are produced in clusters of three.

'Amanogawa' (*Prunus serrulata erecta*) is a well-known cultivar which forms a slender pillar up to about 4.5 m (15 ft) high by 60 to 90 cm (2 to 3 ft) in width and is ideal for small gardens or restricted places, and for architectural planting. The flowers are fragrant, pale pink opening in mid-May.

A handsome species native of the woods of Europe (including the British Isles) and western Asia, *Prunus avium*, the Gean or Wild Cherry, forms a medium sized tree conspicuous in spring with its clusters of large cup-shaped white flowers, and again in autumn, when the leaves colour red. The Double Gean, *P.a.* 'Plena' ('Grandiflora') is a tree of pyramidal habit and one of the best double white cherries for garden planting.

Prunus × hillieri (*incisa × sargentii*) is a prolific early-flowering hybrid of rather broad-headed habit. Masses of pale, soft pink, spring flowers are followed in the autumn by fiery-red leaf colour. A selection of narrow upright habit, *P. × hillieri* 'Spire', forming a tree about 7.6 m (25 ft) high and about 2.4 m (8 ft) through at the widest part, is much in demand as a street tree, and is ideal for restricted circumstances in gardens.

'Kanzan' ('Sekiyama') is a popular, perhaps overplanted cultivar forming a vigorous medium-sized tree with stiffly ascending branches, assuming a typical funnel-shaped head in maturity. The rather harsh purplish-pink large double flowers are freely produced. For those who prefer a less garish pink, and require a tree of similar ultimate size and habit, 'Pink Perfection' ('Shimidsu Sakura' × 'Kanzan') is ideal. Its large double bright pink flowers, often two toned in effect, are produced on long drooping clusters with the bronzy young leaves.

'Kiku-shidare Sakura' makes an attractive weeping tree with arching branches, ideal as a focal point specimen for the small garden. The deep pink, very double flowers are like miniature chrysanthemum blooms.

'Kursar' (*kurilensis × sargentii*) is a very desirable early spring-flowering hybrid of upright-spreading habit. The flowers are an unusual shade of deep cerise pink. Autumn leaf colour is rich orange. 'Okame' (*campanulata × incisa*) is very similar in flower and autumn colour. Both these cultivars were introduced by the renowned authority on ornamental cherries, the late Captain Collingwood Ingram.

Prunus padus, Bird Cherry, makes a small or medium-sized hardy tree of wide distribution. The buddleia-like flower spikes are produced in late spring after the Japanese cherries have faded. *P.p.*

'Watereri' ('Grandiflora') is considered the best form, making a tree of broadly pyramidal shape, festooned with exceptionally long racemes of slightly fragrant white flowers.

Prunus sargentii, Sargent's Cherry, is a small to medium-sized, round-headed tree, often considered to be the most desirable of all cherries; it displays its large deep pink flowers in early spring before the foliage opens; in the autumn it is one of the earliest trees to colour in rich tones of orange, scarlet and crimson.

Prunus serrula (*serrula tibetica*) is a Chinese species, forming a small round-headed tree, remarkable for the beautiful shining mahogany-coloured bark of its trunk. The white spring flowers are not conspicuous, but nurserymen are now top grafting large-flowered kinds of Japanese cherries, such as *P. × hillieri*, 'Shirofugen' or 'Ukon' on to 1.8-m (6-ft) stems of this species, in order to make a more garden worthy combination.

'Shimidsu Sakura' (*Prunus longipes*), a cultivar of considerable distinction and beauty, forms a small mushroom-headed tree, ideal as a lawn specimen in the small garden. The large hanging flower clusters are a delightful shell pink in bud, opening to pure white semi-double blooms, each reminiscent of a ballet dancer's skirt.

'Shirofugen' forms a small flat-headed tree with wide-spreading branches. Its flowers, pale pink in bud, opening pure white and fading again to purplish pink, are produced with the young coppery-bronze leaves, making a particularly beautiful combination. The flowering period is later and more long lasting than most other Japanese cherries.

'Shirotae' ('Mount Fuji') is an outstanding cherry most distinct in its flat-topped, horizontal-branching habit, the branches extending sometimes to a width of 9 m (30 ft) in favourable circumstances. It is best planted in isolation where there is adequate room for its development. The large snow-white single or semi-double flowers festoon the branches in early spring. One of the most effective cultivars.

Prunus subhirtella, Spring Cherry, is a notable but very variable species, cultivated for centuries in its native Japan,

Prunus 'Kiku-shidare Sakura'

where specimens of great size may be seen. It is usually represented in cultivation today by a number of distinct cultivars which are among the finest of all spring-flowering trees. The cultivar 'Rosea' ('Ascendens Rosea'), Pink Spring Cherry, forms a small tree with upright-ascending branches. The flowers are an exquisite shell pink and are enhanced by red-purple calyces. The foliage colours red and yellow in autumn. *P.s.* 'Autumnalis', the Autumn Cherry, is a popular cultivar forming a small tree of open wide-spreading habit. The white, pink-tinted flowers are intermittently produced from autumn to spring as weather allows. 'Autumnalis Rosea' is identical apart from its deep shell-pink flowers. The Weeping Spring Cherry, *P. s.* 'Pendula' ('Pendula Rosea'), makes a small weeping tree, ultimately about 3 m (10 ft) high and 6 m (20 ft) wide, with a dense pattern of thread-like branches weeping to the ground and arrayed in early spring with pale pink flowers. 'Pendula Rubra' has deeper pink flowers.

'Tai-haku', the Great White Cherry, forms a small tree of robust upright-spreading habit, remarkable for its very large single pure white blooms, produced most tellingly with the bronzy young leaves. It has the largest flowers of any cherry.

'Ukon' (*serrulata luteovirens*) makes a strong-growing, wide-spreading tree, of good constitution, distinct in its green or yellow-green flowers. It is very effective when planted in association with 'Pink Perfection' or 'Kanzan', whose blooms are produced at the same time.

'Umineko' (*incisa × speciosa*) is a welcome addition to the few forms of narrow upright habit. It is a tree of vigorous growth with single pure white early spring flowers. The leaves colour well in autumn.

Prunus × yedoensis (*speciosa × subhirtella rosea*), the Tokyo Cherry or Yoshino, becomes a vigorous small to medium-sized tree; its arching branches and graceful habit are typical of Japan, where it is widely planted in the Tokyo district. The single blush-white, almond-scented flowers are produced early in the spring. 'Perpendens' is a smaller form of the tree which has branches weeping to the ground.

Flowering Peaches There are a number of varieties of peach, *Prunus persica*, grown for the beauty of their flowers in spring. Most make small bushy-headed trees, some with pendulous habit. As with the fruiting peaches, it is necessary to maintain these trees in good health by spraying, against peach leaf curl, with a copper fungicide, twice in early spring as the flower buds swell, and again in early autumn.

The following cultivars are particularly recommended: 'Crimson Cascade', a weeping cultivar with double carmine-red flowers; 'Iceberg', semi-double, snow-white flowers, freely produced; 'Klara Mayer' ('Clara Meyer'), the best pink double-flowered peach; 'Russell's Red', the best double red-flowered cultivar.

Flowering Plums *Prunus cerasifera*, Myrobalan or Cherry Plum, a long cultivated western Asiatic species, is usually represented in ornamental plantings by several purple-leaved cultivars or hybrids which make round-headed small trees of dense branching habit. *P.c.* 'Pissardii' ('Atropurpurea'), the Purple-leaved Plum, a popular if somewhat over-planted form, makes an attractive combination when associated with laburnum or one of the silver-leaved pears (*Pyrus*). The early spring flowers are single, pink in bud opening to white. *P. c.* 'Nigra' is an even darker-leaved form in which both stems and leaves are black purple and the flowers single and pale pink.

Prunus × blireana (syn. *P. cerasifera* 'Pissardii' × *mume* 'Alphandii') I consider the most beautiful of this group, both in foliage and flower, the leaves are coppery purple and the large double flowers rose pink.

Pyrus

The pears are a genus of small trees mainly from south eastern Europe. Those with silver or white woolly leaves are most ornamental hardy garden trees, tolerant equally of town conditions and of seaside exposure.

Pyrus nivalis becomes a conspicuous tree in early spring when masses of snow-white flowers appear with the white woolly young leaves. It makes a pleasing contrast when planted with the purple-leaved plum. *P. canescens* (*nivalis × salicifolia*) provides a similar effect.

Pyrus salicifolia 'Pendula', the Weeping Willow-leaved Pear, is a very effective tree, suitable for most gardens. The branches of this elegant and picturesque small tree usually weep to the ground. The narrow silvery leaves are effective throughout the growing season while the cream-white flowers with red stamens are an added attraction in the spring. A first-class weeping garden tree.

Quercus

Surprisingly there are several hundreds of species of oak widely distributed throughout the temperate and tropical regions of the world. Both evergreen and deciduous, they vary from small dense shrubs to large noble trees of great ornamental and timber value. With a few exceptions, most species succeed in any deep rich soil, whether alkaline or acid.

While the majority of *Quercus* species must be looked upon as collectors' pieces, the following selection is very worthy of a place in gardens large enough to contain them.

Quercus cerris, the Turkey Oak, is notable for its elegance and rapidity of growth, and for its tolerance of chalk soils and seaside exposure. The variegated form, 'Variegata', with leaves boldly margined creamy white, makes a striking variegated tree, ultimately of medium or large size.

The Scarlet Oak, *Quercus coccinea*, is a large broad-headed tree from eastern North America, magnificent for six or eight weeks in autumn, when its glossy green leaves turn brilliant red. Its cultivar 'Splendens' is a fine form selected for the brilliance and reliability of its autumn colour.

Allied eastern North American species exhibiting similar, though less spectacular, qualities of autumnal leaf colour are *Quercus palustris*, Pin Oak, a more elegant large tree with smaller, five or seven-lobed leaves, and *Q. rubra*, the Red Oak, a vigorous, large, broad-headed species, its leaves are matt green turning russet red in the autumn and are larger than those of either *Q. coccinea* or *Q. palustris*. All three species are not successful on chalky or alkaline soils.

Quercus frainetto (syn. *Q. conferta*), the Hungarian Oak, is a stately and handsome species worthy of wider planting, making a fine hardy specimen tree of large size. The deeply lobed obovate leaves are exceptionally large. It is successful on all soils. *Q. ilex*, the Holm Oak or Evergreen Oak, is a Mediterranean species and perhaps the most majestic of all large hardy evergreen trees; its leaves are dark glossy green with grey downy undersides. In early summer the woolly young shoots and yellow catkins are a striking feature. At home in any well-drained fertile soil, the Holm Oak is excellent in maritime exposures. In small gardens its growth may be restricted by clipping – indeed it makes an excellent evergreen hedge.

Quercus phellos is the Willow Oak, a handsome species for lime-free soils from the eastern United States of America.

Usually forming a large round-headed tree, the willow-like leaves colour yellow and orange in autumn. A much renowned large, broad-headed tree, *Q. robur* (syn. *Q. pedunculata*), the Common or English Oak with its rugged bark, is notable for its longevity and for its timber value. Several cultivars are particularly appropriate in gardens including 'Concordia', the Golden Oak, a small, very slow-growing form with bright golden-yellow leaves throughout spring and summer. This is a rare form which is difficult to obtain but it is well worth the effort. *Q. r.* 'Fastigiata', the Cypress Oak, forms a large tree of dense, narrow, upright habit and 'Fastigiata Purpurea' makes a smaller tree of similar shape, but with young shoots and leaves red purple throughout the spring and summer.

Rhus

The Stag's-horn Sumach, *Rhus typhina*, is commonly seen in gardens as a small shrubby tree with a familiar widespreading, antler-like branch system. A native of eastern U.S.A., this small suckering tree is most spectacular in autumn when its large pinnate leaves turn vivid shades of red, orange and yellow. Conical hairy clusters of crimson fruits are attractive particularly after the fall of leaf. There is also an equally worthy cultivar 'Laciniata' with more deeply divided leaves.

Robinia

Hardy North American trees which are most ornamental in their elegant habit and attractive pinnate leaves. Pink or white pea-shaped flowers are produced in summer. They thrive on all soils and are particularly valuable in dry, sunny positions, sheltered from wind. If grown in lush or exposed circumstances, their brittle branches are liable to break in gales. Many of the smaller forms are successful in town gardens.

Robinia × ambigua 'Decaisneana' (*R. pseudoacacia* 'Decaisneana') becomes a handsome, medium-sized tree; the large racemes of pale pink flowers are very conspicuous. *R. fertilis* 'Monument' is a small tree of narrow upright growth also bearing pale pink flowers.

A graceful and elegant tree for the small garden, *Robinia × hillieri* (*kelseyi × pseudoacacia*) has lilac-pink flowers which are produced at mid-summer. The Common or False Acacia, *R. pseudoacacia*, makes a large picturesque suckering tree with spiny twigs, naturalized in parts of Europe; its white flowers are produced in early or mid-summer. It is best represented in gardens by one of its cultivars which are generally small or medium-sized trees of more compact habit. The best of these includes 'Frisia', a small or medium-sized tree of recent introduction and one of the most striking of foliage trees available today. Its bright golden-yellow leaves maintain their colour from spring to autumn. It is most effective when associated with purple-leaved trees or shrubs. The cultivar 'Inermis', the Mop-head Acacia, is a small, round-headed tree, formed by a dense mass of spineless branches and deep green pinnate leaves. It is a popular tree for street or public planting, particularly in France.

Salix

The large members of this family are usually seen as graceful waterside trees in gardens or landscape planting. Many are also conspicuous in their coloured winter bark which is more attractive if the trees concerned are pollarded or heavily pruned in spring every other year. In many species, the spring catkins are an additional feature. Most succeed in any deep, moist soil.

One of the most beautiful of large trees for landscape planting is the White Willow, *Salix alba*, but the silvery colour of its silky hairy leaves and shoots varies from tree to tree. It is very successful in maritime conditions if planted in moist soil. In small gardens, several of its cultivars are good value. *S. a.* 'Chermesina' ('Britzensis', 'Chrysostella'), the Red or Scarlet Willow, is particularly conspicuous in winter when the bark of twigs and young stems appears bright scarlet. Pollard every other year in spring to maintain this feature at its best.

Salix alba 'Sericea' ('Argentea'), the Silver Willow, makes a small round-headed tree with consistently shining silvery leaves. It is considerably less vigorous than the type, and ideal for the small garden. The golden willow, *S. a.* 'Vitellina', has brilliant yellow winter shoots which make it the perfect companion for *S. a.* 'Chermesina'. It should be similarly pruned every other spring.

Salix × chrysocoma (*S. alba* 'Tristis', *S. a.* 'Vitellina Pendula', *S. babylonica* 'Ramulis Aureis') is a handsome, fast-growing, medium-sized weeping tree with a wide-spreading habit, extensively planted for its grace and beauty and particularly for its long golden-yellow weeping branchlets. Although ideal for public planting, it will quickly become too large for small gardens. Regrettably, in country districts, this hybrid is also particularly prone to willow scab or canker (anthracnose) which is difficult to control on large trees. It is, however, worth spraying young trees two or three times during spring and summer with a liquid copper fungicide to reduce the incidence of this disfiguring disease.

The Violet Willow, *Salix daphnoides*, makes a vigorous, upright-growing small tree, conspicuous in winter when its violet-tinted shoots appear over-laid with a white waxy bloom. The bright yellow catkins of male trees ('Aglaia') are a striking feature each spring.

The Purple Osier, *Salix purpurea*, is rarely more than a tall shrub of loose open habit with attractive oblong leaves with blue-white undersides. However, its variety *eugenei* forms an upright-growing small tree with unusual grey-pink male catkins; in particular its cultivar, 'Pendula', the Purple Weeping Willow, makes an effective small weeping tree and is particularly suitable for small gardens and for sites where *S. × chrysocoma* would be too large.

The Purple Osier and its forms are very worthy of garden space, and succeed even in dryish positions if need be.

Sophora

Though widely planted in Japan, *Sophora japonica*, the Japanese Pagoda Tree, a hardy medium-sized to large round-headed tree, is a native of China. The handsome, long, pinnate leaves consist of up to fifteen leaflets; the creamy-white,

pea-shaped flowers are produced in late summer and autumn on maturing trees, and particularly in the hot dry summers of the Mediterranean countries. It is successful in all fertile well-drained soils. The cultivar 'Pendula' is a very desirable picturesque tree for the small garden, with its stiffly pendulous branches forming a low natural arbour.

Sorbus

A large family of hardy, small or medium-sized trees indispensable in the garden for their flower, attractive foliage, berry and autumn-colouring leaf. In the main, they have an elegant and compact habit of growth. For our purposes the sorbus may be conveniently divided into two groups – the whitebeams (*Aria* group) and the mountain ashes or rowans (*Aucuparia* group).

All species and cultivars will thrive in any fertile soil, but the whitebeams are notably successful on chalk and limestone and the rowans happiest and longest lived on light neutral or acid soils. The following species and cultivars are among the best of the many available today.

Sorbus aria, Whitebeam, a small to medium-sized round-headed European tree, with oval or obovate dentated leaves, green above and vivid white beneath. The spring flowers, although dull white, are heavily scented. In autumn, bright red fruits are produced in quantity; it is tolerant of wind and maritime exposure and is best represented in small gardens by one of its cultivars 'Decaisneana' ('Majestica') is the largest-leaved whitebeam with elliptical leaves up to 15 cm (6 in) long and 10 cm (4 in) wide and with larger fruits than in the type. The best whitebeam is 'Lutescens', a cultivar which is particularly effective in spring and early summer, when its new leaves are downy white on both surfaces.

Sorbus aucuparia, the Rowan or Mountain Ash, is a familiar European species forming a small or medium-sized tree, usually of erect habit. In marked contrast to those of the Whitebeam, the leaves are pinnate, 13 to 23 cm (5 to 9 in) long, and composed of up to nineteen leaflets. The flat terminal white flower heads 8 to 13 cm (3 to 5 in) across, which open in late spring, are followed by quantities of scarlet berries. There are a number of equally worthy cultivars; 'Sheerwater Seedling', a recent introduction of narrow, upright and compact habit, is ideal as a street tree or for a restricted site in the small garden. The foliage is an attractive blue green and the fruits orange scarlet in large clusters 'Xanthocarpa' ('Fructuluteo') develops golden-yellow fruits which are less attractive to birds.

Sorbus commixta (*Aucuparia* group), a Japanese species, also of upright habit, is notable for the brilliant flame or scarlet autumn colouring of its leaves and for the freely produced orange-red fruits. *S. hupehensis* (*Aucuparia* group) is a distinct and beautiful Chinese species, forming a compact head of ascending branches. The foliage is of an unusual blue-green hue, acting as a perfect foil for the white or pink-tinted fruits, which are produced in drooping clusters, and persist well into winter. The varieties *obtusa* and *rosea* are equally worthy variants with pink fruits.

The Swedish Whitebeam, *Sorbus intermedia* (*Aria* group), is a very hardy small or medium-sized tree useful in exposed or bleak situations. The distinct leaves are lobed towards the base, green above and grey felted beneath. The large orange-red fruits are conspicuous in autumn.

'Joseph Rock' (*Aucuparia* group) is an outstanding introduction from China and an ideal small garden tree of dense narrow habit. The pinnate leaves assume rich autumn tints of red, orange, bronze and purple, making an excellent background for the amber-yellow fruits, which persist well after leaf fall.

Sorbus pohuashanensis (*S. conradinae*) (*Aucuparia* group), the Chinese Rowan, is a hardy and robust small or medium-sized tree, spectacular in autumn when laden with heavy bunches of large orange-red fruits. A choice Chinese species, *S. sargentiana* (*Aucuparia* group) slowly attains about 7.6 m (25 ft). The sticky winter buds are reminiscent of those of the Horse Chestnut (aesculus). The handsome pinnate leaves, among the largest of the genus, colour magnificently

OPPOSITE: *Robinia pseudoacacia* 'Frisia'

a rich red in the autumn.

A small tree from western China, *Sorbus scalaris* (*Aucuparia* group) is distinct in its wide-spreading head, and in its unusual dark glossy green fern-like leaves with grey downy undersides. The orange fruits are freely produced and the foliage turns crimson and purple in autumn.

Sorbus vilmorinii (*Aucuparia* group) is an elegant and delightful small tree from western China. In late summer and autumn the branches are hung with clusters of rosy-red fruits which turn pink and finally fade to white, tinted pink. This is an excellent tree for the smallest garden.

Styrax

Styrax japonica fargesii, the Snowbell, is handsome both in leaf and flower. This distinguished, small, broad-headed Chinese tree is worthy of wider planting. The magnolia-like leaves are obovate or broadly elliptic and the white bell-shaped flowers, about 2 cm ($\frac{3}{4}$ in) across, hang all along the branches at mid-summer. Fertile lime-free soil is necessary and although quite hardy, a sheltered west-facing site is desirable, particularly where there is danger of late spring frosts.

Tilia

The limes are stately, medium-sized or large trees with handsome leaves and producing great quantities of cream-yellow flowers during the summer. They are successful in any fertile soil, and are magnificent in parkland or in public places, but they are in the main too large for the small garden. However, several species are tolerant of pollarding or hard pruning, and are often used for street plantings or in gardens as pleached lime screens.

Pleaching consists of planting standard, half-standard or feathered specimens, 2.4 or 3 m (8 or 10 ft) apart, and training the side branches to link together to form a curtain-like screen; any shoots growing forward or backwards are pruned back to the main stem.

In parkland, for municipal planting, or in the larger garden the following readily available species and varieties are parti-

cularly worthy of consideration.

Tilia americana, the American Lime, forms a medium-sized tree with rugged bark on older trees. It is remarkable for its exceptionally large leaves. The cultivar 'Redmond' is an interesting selection of dense, narrow habit.

Tilia cordata, the Small-leaved Lime, is a medium to large-sized European tree of neat rounded habit, bearing comparatively small heart-shaped leaves. The fragrant flowers appear somewhat later than those of other species.

A very graceful, medium-sized tree, *Tilia × euchlora* (*cordata × dasystyla*) has lower branches which are pendulous on older specimens while immature trees have arching branches and bright glossy green leaves. This hybrid is free from aphid (greenfly) attack – a troublesome complaint of many limes.

The Weeping Silver Lime, *Tilia petiolaris* (*americana* 'Pendula'), forms a most graceful and beautiful tall weeping tree, with a rounded head and downward-sweeping branches. The long-stalked leaves are white felted beneath, and in a breeze add considerably to the attraction of this fine tree. The heavily scented flowers produced in late summer are regrettably narcotic to bees.

Tilia platyphyllos, the Broad-leaved Lime, becomes a large and rapid-growing tree of rounded habit, now much planted in parkland or public places instead of *T. europaea*, the Common Lime, which has a densely suckering habit. Its cultivar *T. p.* 'Rubra', the Red-twigged Lime, has the additional attraction of red-brown winter shoots, and a more upright habit.

Trachycarpus

Trachycarpus fortunei (*Chamaerops excelsa*), the Chusan Palm, is the only tree palm species reasonably hardy in the warmer counties of the British Isles and in similar favoured or maritime areas in the northern hemisphere. It slowly forms an unusual and picturesque tree, its trunk clothed with dark brown fibrous bases of old leaf stalks, and its head an umbrella of great fan-like leaves. On maturing trees, the conspicuous panicles of yellow flowers are produced among the leaves in summer.

Ulmus

The elms are a genus of fine stately landscape trees, growing well in any fertile soil, and tolerant of seaside and other exposed positions. There are several picturesque lower-growing forms, some with coloured leaves, which are particularly suitable for small gardens. Regrettably, most species and forms must be considered to a lesser or greater extent vulnerable to the dreaded Dutch Elm Disease (a fungus disease spread by elm bark beetles) which in recent years has killed large quantities of the English Elm (*Ulmus procera*) and the Dutch Elm (*U. hollandica major*) in Europe, the British Isles and elsewhere.

In the early 1970s, a new aggressive strain of the disease was first identified in Britain, and then in other European countries. This strain of the disease has been devastating in its effect and elms have now largely disappeared from the British countryside. Cultivars bred in Holland in the 1930s and resistant to the earlier, milder strain of the fungus have not proved resistant to the newer aggressive strain of the disease. However, breeding continues in Holland, the U.S.A. and elsewhere. A new cultivar bred from the Japanese Elm (*Ulmus japonica*) and named *U.* 'Sapporo Autumn Gold' is now becoming commercially available and shows tolerance of the aggressive strain of the disease. This tree has excellent golden autumn leaf colour but in shape is not typical of the elms of our landscape.

It is hoped that public authorities and owners of private gardens will be encouraged to replant disease tolerant or disease-resistant elms as they become available. Other species and cultivars not resistant to Dutch Elm Disease are discussed below and are suitable for unaffected areas.

Ulmus angustifolia cornubiensis (*U. stricta, carpinifolia* 'Cornubiensis'), the Cornish Elm, is an excellent street tree, ultimately of large size and distinct in its conical head of upright-growing branches. It is a native of Devon and Cornwall in England and of Brittany in France.

Ulmus glabra, the Wych or Scotch Elm, makes a large tree with a dome-like head of wide-spreading branches. The large coarse-toothed leaves are very rough to the touch. The fruits densely wreathing the branches in spring are particularly attractive. Unlike most other species, the Wych Elm does not produce sucker growth. There are two weeping forms, both suitable as lawn specimens for gardens. These are 'Camperdownii', the Camperdown Elm, a small or medium-sized tree with an umbrella-like head of weeping branches and branchlets, and 'Pendula' ('Horizontalis'), the Weeping Wych Elm, which makes a flat-topped head of stiffly pendulous spreading branches. It may also be used to form a natural arbour.

Ulmus × hollandica is a natural hybrid of wide-spreading distribution throughout Europe. A form of this hybrid, 'Major', is the Dutch Elm, a large suckering tree, very vulnerable to Dutch Elm Disease.

Ulmus × sarniensis (*angustifolia × hollandica*), the Jersey or Wheatley Elm, is a large tree which develops a dense head of upright branches, narrower than those of the Cornish Elm. It is excellent in seaside exposure. 'Dicksonii' (*wheatleyi* 'Aurea'), Dickson's Golden Elm, becomes a compact-headed specimen with golden-yellow leaves. A most effective small tree for the garden. *U. × vegeta* (*carpinifolia × glabra*), the Huntingdon or Chichester Elm, is a hybrid found in the Midland counties of England. It forms a handsome, vigorous, large tree, with elliptical long pointed leaves of large size. Two interesting disease-resistant cultivars were introduced from Holland in the 1960s. 'Commelin' is a moderately resistant variety of Dutch origin, with smaller leaves than those of the type and a narrower habit of growth, and 'Groeneveld' is a slow-growing, small or medium-sized tree of columnar habit and possibly the most appropriate of the new forms for the small garden or for street planting due to its slow rate of growth. Regrettably neither of these cultivars is resistant to the newer aggressive strain of Dutch Elm Disease.

Conifers and Heathers

ADRIAN BLOOM

It may seem strange to put together in one section two unrelated families of plants, but I have chosen to do this because I believe the combination of conifers and heathers in the garden makes an unbeatable formula. Given the right treatment initially, a garden should be provided with year round – and I mean in the depths of winter too – colour, contrast and ground cover. If this is the sort of garden which appeals to you, then I hope I can begin to give you some further ideas as to how to achieve it, however small it may be.

Conifers in the garden

Before rushing out to buy a conifer to fill an odd corner in the garden, assess, if you know, what you require.

The conifers you obtain from any source will in all probability be quite small initially. This you must be prepared for but it is most important to find out the name of the tree and how large it might become because some conifers will grow only 60 cm (2 ft) in twenty-five years whilst others may reach 21 m (70 ft) during the same length of time. It depends upon the species and the form.

So what are the uses of conifers? All but a few are evergreen but such is the tremendous variety that one can choose from almost any form, shape, colour and eventual height. They can serve as a backcloth to a garden, as a windbreak or a hedge, as ground-cover plants or purely as ornamental specimens in their own right.

Cultural requirements
Few gardens would be complete, in my opinion, without conifers and few are too inhospitable to grow most types successfully.

However, conifers require a reasonable amount of moisture especially in the first year or two after planting when root systems are becoming established. Although not essential, moist peat incorporated with the soil prior to planting will help the plant get away to a good start, whether it be a specimen from the open ground or a container plant. The ideal times for planting conifers are September, October, March and April, but with the advent of the container plant any time of the year will do though in summer constant watering is essential.

Some conifers will tolerate shade but very few will put up with dry shade, with the exception perhaps of the yews. The golden cultivars certainly need sun to obtain their best colours and you will find both green and blue types will appreciate it more if planted in sunny open situations.

Three cultural hints which particularly apply to conifers are: firstly, the importance of planting in soil that is free from

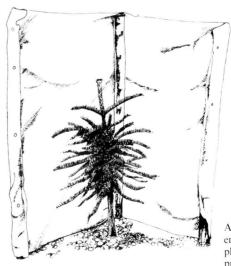

A hessian screen erected around a newly planted conifer will prevent wind rocking

perennial weeds; secondly, to allow a perimeter of soil around a specimen which is planted in grass. This should be at least to a width of 15 cm (6 in) from the base of the plant, and preferably 30 cm (12 in). I have seen more conifers spoilt this way than by any other.

Thirdly, I have found it always pays when planting a conifer to spray with an anti-dessicant such as S-600. This helps quite considerably in allowing the plant a breathing space to make fresh root without losing moisture through the foliage and thereby preventing much of the burning often seen on conifers in the late spring. The larger the plant the more important it is to spray it – conifers are valuable and worth a little extra effort.

Conifers for garden use

The majority of gardens these days could not accommodate the large forest trees and so the following list consists mainly of dwarf, slow-growing and medium-sized conifers. To make this more easily understood, approximate height, and spread where relative, of each plant is given at an age of ten years and at maturity. Of course this can be a guide only as rates of growth for the same plant can vary considerably from one side of the country to the other.

Snow should be shaken from the branches of conifers to prevent them being broken

Selected conifers

Abies
The silver firs consist of mostly large-growing forest trees but some attractive dwarf forms are well worth growing.

Abies balsamea 'Hudsonia' is a very hardy, very slow-growing shrub which is useful for the rock garden. It has dark green glossy leaves and is particularly attractive when making bright green fresh shoots in spring. At ten years it will be 20 to 30 cm (8 to 12 in) high and at maturity 60 to 90 cm (2 to 3 ft) high with a spread of 90 cm to 1.2 m (3 to 4 ft).

Abies koreana is a somewhat choice plant. Commonly known as the Korean Fir, it is slow growing but eventually forms a medium-sized tree. However, it is best known for its bright purple cones which appear quite early in its life. The habit is neat, and the leaves glossy green above, silvery white beneath. Not an easily obtainable plant but well worth searching for! After ten years it will be 1.5 to 1.8 m (5 to 6 ft) high; at maturity 12 to 15 m (40 to 50 ft).

Araucaria
Araucaria araucana is much better known as the Monkey Puzzle Tree and this species still seems to have a certain popularity. Although one sees some very scruffy specimens in gardens, it can make a very attractive tree – but it needs space. Its long tentacle-like branches have dark glossy green leaves, the points of which are very sharp. It prefers moist soils and will not usually succeed in industrial areas. It is a large tree attaining a height of 1.2 to 1.5 m (4 to 5 ft) after ten years and 21 to 27 m (70 to 90 ft) at maturity.

Calocedrus
The species most commonly associated with the genus is *Calocedrus decurrens* which can still be found under the genus *Libocedrus*. *C. decurrens* or *L. decurrens* is known as the Incense Cedar and whilst eventually making a large tree it is quite slow growing and being quite narrow in habit could be used more as a garden plant. It has rich green foliage throughout the year with fan-shaped flattened bran-

ches. Growing 2.4 to 3 m (8 to 10 ft) in ten years, it will under good conditions eventually grow to 24 to 30 m (80 to 100 ft) so be careful!

Cedrus

The cedars are some of the most useful and beautiful of conifers but once again must be planted with care, as most species grow extremely large in time. All have spirally arranged tufted leaves and, with age, large cones.

The Atlas or Blue Cedar, *Cedrus atlantica glauca*, is one of our most attractive conifers but it grows too large to be considered ideal for the average suburban garden. At ten years it will be 3 to 4.5 m (10 to 15 ft) high; at maturity 30 to 36 m (100 to 120 ft). Most plants on sale will be grafted and will need a cane or stake to train the leading shoot upwards. Once over 1.5 or 1.8 m (5 or 6 ft) it will find its own way upwards with no further assistance. This variety has striking blue foliage.

Cedrus deodara, the Himalayan or Deodar Cedar, is a graceful and imposing tree but I cannot stress too much that with such large-growing trees – at ten years it will reach 3 to 4.5 m (10 to 15 ft) and ultimately 39 to 46 m (130 to 150 ft) – it is sometimes better to avoid the temptation to try it in a small garden. Its branches, which are clothed in long green needles or leaves, droop at the tips and the leader is typically arched in its form of growth.

There are many dwarfer growing forms of cedars but one, of recent introduction is *C. deodara* 'Golden Horizon' which is semi-prostrate in habit and with bright golden leaves the year through. At ten years it can be expected to be 70 to 100 cm (27 to 39 in) in height with 76 to 120 cm (2½ to 4 ft) spread.

Chamaecyparis

This group, commonly known as the false cypresses, consists of a number of species and innumerable cultivars of plants and includes some of the most popular garden conifers in the United Kingdom.

However, none of the species is native to the United Kingdom or to Europe, as one might expect, but they mostly originate from North America and Japan.

Many are still referred to as *Cupressus* but this is in fact a separate group (see p. 103).

Most are easy to grow, preferring situations of good drainage but a reasonable amount of moisture.

Chamaecyparis lawsoniana, the Lawson Cypress, is perhaps the best-known conifer type planted in Britain, but was itself only introduced from western North America barely a hundred years ago. A great many cultivars have since been introduced and are often lumped under the general heading of Lawson's but such is the variety of colours, shapes and sizes in this group that this can be misleading. *C. lawsoniana* itself is often used as a hedging plant these days but seldom as a specimen, having been superseded by some of its cultivars for such purposes. Although varying somewhat in habit and rate of growth, most seedlings would grow 3 to 3.6 m (10 to 12 ft) in ten years and eventually anything from 23 to 30 m (75 to 100 ft) at maturity.

Chamaecyparis lawsoniana 'Allumii' is one of the most widely grown cultivars with bluish foliage and a narrow pyramidal habit. Of medium growth, it could be expected to grow 2.4 to 3 m (8 to 10 ft) in its first ten years and eventually 9 to 12 m (30 to 40 ft). In my opinion *C. l.* 'Columnaris' sometimes listed as 'Columnaris Glauca' is a more attractive cultivar, varying in its denser foliage and as the name suggests a more columnar habit. The blue is if anything more intense. Its rate of growth is a little slower than 'Allumii' and it would be likely to reach only 9 m (30 ft) at maturity.

There is little doubt that 'Ellwoodii' is the most popular garden conifer in Great Britain. It has close grey-green foliage and although often classed as a dwarf or rock garden conifer it grows quite vigorously in the first ten years to 1.8 m (6 ft) or so and eventually reaches 6 m (20 ft) or more. However, it is an attractive and valuable cultivar, the habit of which can vary but would normally be described as columnar.

Of fairly recent introduction is 'Ellwood's Gold', a copy in habit of

'Ellwoodii' if a bit slower in growth. Less a real gold than the name suggests, it is nonetheless a good garden plant and particularly pleasant in spring when the new yellow-tipped growths appear. 'Lanei' is one of the popular medium-growing, golden-yellow cultivars and still one of the best. Because there is so little else to see in the winter I feel it is important when choosing conifers to make a selection with this in mind. 'Lanei' suits this purpose admirably, being nearly as bright a yellow in winter as in summer. 'Lutea' is equally useful but lacks the bright winter colour. Both reach about 2.4 to 3 m (8 to 10 ft) after ten years and ultimately 9 to 12 m (30 to 40 ft).

'Minima Aurea' is, as one might suspect, a dwarf form but to my mind one of the most beautiful of all conifers. It has densely packed, bright yellow foliage the year round, ideal for a rock garden or at the front of a heather border. Growing about 30 cm (1 ft) in ten years and even after twenty or thirty years still likely to be under 1.8 m (6 ft), it could not be described as a plant that gets out of hand! Plants on sale are likely to be small as one might expect.

There is a green and more rounded cultivar in 'Minima Glauca' which has a similar rate of growth to 'Minima Aurea' and tends to grow on you with age! 'Pembury Blue' has probably the bluest colour of all the medium-growing cultivars especially in summer when its foliage attains a brilliant silvery hue. Broadly conical in habit, its leaves are coarser and more open than either 'Allumii' or 'Columnaris'. At ten years of age it can be expected to be about 3 m (10 ft) and eventually 9 to 12 m (30 to 40 ft) tall.

'Pymea Argentea' is another gem of a plant. A really slow-growing conifer which will even in maturity not exceed 90 cm (3 ft), reaching perhaps 30 cm (1 ft) after ten years. Compact and rounded in habit the bottom foliage is sea green but all the exposed growing tips are silvery white the year round. If planted in a sunny position against a contrasting background, a quite startling effect can be created.

'Stewartii' is one of the oldest of the golden cultivars but is still distinct and remains a useful plant for a medium to large garden. It is in fact more golden than yellow, but tends to lose its colour more in winter than either 'Lanei' or 'Lutea'. At ten years it will grow to about 3 to 3.6 m (10 to 12 ft) and ultimately 9 to 12 m (30 to 40 ft).

Although there are a great many other golden cultivars grown, many are not as proven as the three so far mentioned, although 'Stardust', a fairly recent introduction from Holland, looks distinct and seems to be an easy grower with good, year-round colour.

It is inevitable that many good cultivars cannot be mentioned because of space, but a last and distinctive *Chamaecyparis lawsoniana* form is of a completely different habit. 'Tamarisci-folia' is a spreading plant eventually forming a large bush much wider than high. It has bright green foliage winter and summer and this comes in overlapping sprays. It is sometimes listed in catalogues under the name of 'Know-fieldensis'. In ten years it will have attained a height of 90 cm (3 ft) and a spread of 1.5 m (5 ft), and at maturity possibly 2.4 to 3 m (8 to 10 ft) high by 3.6 to 4.5 m (12 to 15 ft) across, so it will eventually need considerable space.

Chamaecyparis nootkatensis originates from western America and is generally much hardier than *C. lawsoniana*, but certainly not so well known. It is perhaps better known as one of the parents to the hybrid × *Cupressocyparis leylandii*, although a useful tree in its own right. Reaching 3 to 4.5 m (10 to 15 ft) in its first ten years, it will eventually attain forest-tree proportions of 27 to 30 m (90 to 100 ft). There are one or two useful forms – 'Glauca', similar in habit but a more glaucous tinge to the foliage, and an attractive form 'Lutea' which deserves wider recognition. There is also a weeping form 'Pendula' which becomes an extremely beautiful plant with age but admittedly does not make much of a show in its first five to ten years. All are medium to large growers and not really suitable except for the larger garden.

Chamaecyparis obtusa originates from Japan and although the species known as

OPPOSITE:
Chamaecyparis pisifera 'Boulevard' planted with *Erica cinerea* 'Pink Ice' and a golden-foliaged calluna

Juniperus communis
'Depressa Aurea'

to grow but it is quite amenable as to soils and will even succeed in industrial areas.

Juniperus

The junipers are deservedly gaining in popularity as garden plants and a much wider range is being introduced to the British Isles from other parts of the world to give the gardener an even better choice. Most species are very hardy and grow successfully in even the poorest of soils, whether acid or alkaline. There is such a wide range of colours, shapes and forms in this genus that one would make quite an attractive garden growing only junipers. Unfortunately only a limited selection can be made here.

Juniperus chinensis 'Aurea' is an excel-lent cultivar of the Chinese Juniper. Although very slow growing initially, even to the point of finding it difficult to assert a leading shoot, it eventually makes a beautiful golden columnar-shaped specimen. What adds to the attraction is that the plant usually carries both adult and juvenile foliage giving it more variety in shade and texture. Perhaps growing only 90 cm (3 ft) in ten years, it eventually may get as high as 9 m (30 ft). One of the bluest junipers is 'Pyramidalis' which has a broadly conical habit and very prickly foliage. After ten years it will grow to 1.5 or 1.8 m (5 or 6 ft) and with age broaden and grow as high as 4.5 to 6 m (15 to 20 ft). Like many junipers it is better planted in an open position.

Juniperus communis is one of the three conifers native to the British Isles. It has given us several useful garden forms, some upright, some prostrate. *J. c.* 'Compressa' is quite a unique cultivar with its perfectly symmetrical outline, its slowness of growth and its usefulness as a sink or trough garden conifer. It is a must for the rock garden also and looks particularly attractive planted in groups of three or more. Bright green in summer, it turns a bluish-green hue in winter. Perhaps at ten years reaching 30 to 45 cm (12 to 18 in), it will be very rare to see a specimen over 90 to 1.2 m (3 to 4 ft).

'Depressa Aurea' is a golden prostrate form of great merit. It needs to be planted in an open position for best effect where its butter-yellow shoots in spring provide a beautiful effect. The foliage turns a bronzy hue in winter with the silver undersides of the leaves more prominent. One should expect a spread of 90 cm to 1.2 m (3 to 4 ft) in ten years and increasing after many more years to 3 to 3.6 m (10 to 12 ft).

'Hibernica', known as the Irish Juniper, is useful where an upright conifer is required. This will eventually reach 5.5 to 6 m (18 to 20 ft). One of the best ground-cover junipers is *J. c.* 'Repanda' which makes a very vigorous dark green carpet which turns a greeny brown during the winter months. It has a similar rate of growth to 'Depressa Aurea'.

Juniperus horizontalis is commonly known as the Creeping Juniper and this name describes the habit of the species and its many cultivars admirably. The species originates from North America where it and many cultivars are grown widely for garden and landscape use. The most popular form in Europe is 'Glauca', a carpet-forming plant which roots from runners as it spreads across the ground. The foliage is bright steel blue in summer, grey green in winter. To increase the density the runners can be pruned back occasionally. Similar forms occur in 'Douglasii', 'Bar Harbor' and 'Wiltonii'. All will spread quite rapidly covering a diameter of 1.8 to 2.4 m (6 to 8 ft) in ten years and ultimately considerably more. New and distinct cultivars are likely to be introduced to Europe from the United

States but one which is available and probably the best for ground cover is 'Plumosa', the Andorra Juniper. Where cultivars so far mentioned grow flat to the ground, this will reach 45 to 60 cm (1½ to 2 ft) in height providing a more effective smother to weeds. The foliage is softer and more feathery, the colour grey green turning a purple hue in winter. All *J. horizontalis* cultivars are hardy.

Juniperus × media includes some forms which may be listed under *J. chinensis* in books and catalogues. I think it is now generally accepted that they should belong in this grouping but the main thing from a gardener's point of view is that all those mentioned here are excellent garden plants. 'Hetzii' is an extremely vigorous semi-prostrate cultivar. It has grey-green foliage the year through and can be used as a specimen plant, as a low hedge or as a ground-cover plant. To increase density pruning will be necessary but in no way detrimental to the plant. Tolerant of alkaline soils it will grow better in sun than shade. An all-purpose plant but give it room as by the time it is ten years old it will be 1.5 (5 ft) high and 1.8 m (6 ft) across, eventually spreading 3.6 m (12 ft) across by 2.4 to 3 m (8 to 10 ft) in height. But also remember the pruning! 'Old Gold' is in my opinion better in a smaller garden than 'Pfitzeriana Aurea'. It is much more compact in growth with a better, year-round golden colour. It will probably reach 76 to 90 cm (2½ to 3 ft) in ten years and spread 90 cm to 1.2 m (3 to 4 ft) against 90 cm by 1.8 m (3 by 6 ft) for 'Pfitzeriana Aurea' over the same period. Ultimately it may be 1.8 m (6 ft) high and 2.4 m (8 ft) across whilst 'Pfitzeriana Aurea' might be 1.8 m (6 ft) high but 3.6 m (12 ft) or more in diameter. The green 'Pfitzeriana' is even more vigorous although like the garden form an excellent ground coverer. It is not for the small garden I suspect but hardy and adaptable succeeding well on chalk. Forms may vary from nearly prostrate to maybe 3 m (10 ft) or more in height. The growth rate for 'Pfitzeriana Aurea' applies but perhaps add 30 per cent on both the ten-year and ultimate figures.

Juniperus sabina, the Savin Juniper, has

given us many useful garden forms, mostly prostrate or semi-prostrate in habit. All have the pungent odour of the species when the foliage is crushed. The cultivar 'Blue Danube' doesn't really live up to its name as far as the blue is concerned but otherwise it is a very attractive garden plant, especially when used as a ground coverer. It will grow quite rapidly – in ten years about 90 cm (3 ft) high and a spread of 1.8 to 2.4 m (6 to 8 ft), eventually 1.2 m (4 ft) high and 4.5 m (15 ft) across.

Almost the most popular prostrate variety of Juniper is *J. s. tamariscifolia* which makes a beautiful specimen with age, building itself up in layers and covering a wide area. It is particularly attractive on a large rock garden or a bank where it moulds itself into the contours. The foliage colour is grey blue. After ten years it should grow about 30 cm (1 ft) high but spreading 90 cm (3 ft). However, as branches root along the ground, it can spread to 4.5 cm (15 ft) or more in time and attain a height of 45 to 60 cm (1½ to 2 ft).

Of recent introduction to Europe are forms of *Juniperus scopulorum*, the Rocky Mountain Juniper, which are very popular in the United States. They are mostly medium growers with conical or pyramidal habits. They would appear to be tolerant of most soil conditions but need to be placed in exposed or sunny situations for best results. Perhaps the best known is 'Skyrocket', a name which speaks for itself. This makes an extremely narrow column of blue grey, growing 2.1 to 2.4 m (7 to 8 ft) in ten years and ultimately 6 to 7.6 m (20 to 25 ft). It is extremely useful as an accent plant as are some of the others such as 'Blue Heaven' of similar growth rate but a more pyramidal habit. The colour of the foliage is an intense silver blue in summer but dulls somewhat in winter. 'Springbank' has bright silver-grey foliage but much thinner branches. It is somewhat slower in growth than the previous two mentioned.

Juniperus squamata has given us a few good forms and 'Blue Star', although only of recent introduction, promises to be one of the best for the smaller garden.

It is slow growing with dense steel blue foliage and a bushy habit. It is likely in ten years to be 30 to 45 cm (12 to 18 in) in height with a similar spread, and (taking a guess at it) probably at maturity 60 to 90 cm (2 to 3 ft) high by 90 cm to 1.2 m (3 to 4 ft) across. Probably the best-known form of the species is 'Meyeri' which was introduced from China early this century and is now grown all over the world. It is also steel blue in colour, making a somewhat irregular bush with nodding leading shoots which are typical of the species. It needs an open position and some trimming may be necessary from time to time – these precautions will help to prevent the browning of the foliage sometimes seen on older specimens. An excellent recent introduction is 'Blue Carpet', which makes quite a vigorous ground cover plant. Steel blue foliage is held on prostrate branches which are slightly raised at the tips, making a sheet of bright blue in summer, dulling somewhat in winter. In ten years it may be 30 to 40 cm (12 to 16 in) in height and as much as 1.5 to 2.1 m (5 to 7 ft) across, but it will benefit from regular pruning.

Juniperus virginiana is native to the eastern United States and Canada and there is known as the Pencil Cedar as the species generally has a narrowly columnar shape. It and the garden forms it has produced are all very hardy and amenable to most soil conditions. The cultivar 'Burkii' is known in the British Isles but not used widely which is a pity. It is a useful plant with a broadly conical habit, the dense foliage blue grey in summer, turning a purplish hue in winter. Growing 2.4 to 3 m (8 to 10 ft) high in ten years, it will ultimately reach 6 to 7.6 m (20 to 25 ft). One of the best of all the semi-prostrate junipers is 'Grey Owl' which has thin spreading branches of grey blue and is extremely vigorous in growth. A useful ground-cover plant it will, however, eventually need more space than is available in some gardens. After ten years it will probably reach 30 to 45 cm (12 to 18 in) in height and spread 2.4 to 3 m (8 to 10 ft) and after several more years 90 cm to 1.2 m (3 to 4 ft) in height with a spread of 4.6 to 5.4 m (15 to 18 ft).

Larix

The larches, whilst beautiful trees in any context, are generally unsuitable for all but the largest gardens. All species drop their leaves in the autumn many keeping in tune with deciduous trees by turning yellow and golden before doing so. Most have the distinctive tufted growth of the new leaves in the spring which is most attractive. Both species normally seen in the British Isles are used as forest trees and of course attain eventual heights of around about 30 m (100 ft). These are *Larix decidua*, the European Larch, and *L. leptolepis*, the Japanese Larch.

Metasequoia

Metasequoia is, as they say, "a tree with a story". There is only one species known and this is *Metasequoia glyptostroboides*, more easily remembered under the common name the Dawn Redwood. It was discovered in China as recently as 1941 and was before that time thought to be extinct and only to be found in fossilized form. Since that one plant was found it has now been distributed throughout the world and is generally available from many nurseries.

It has an open pyramidal habit with feathery bright green plumed leaves in summer turning bronze in autumn and dropping its leaves before the winter. This is not strictly a good garden plant on account of its size reaching 4.5 to 5.4 m (15 to 18 ft) after ten years and ultimately about 30 m (100 ft); it is nonetheless attractive with a very unusual and interesting history.

Picea

The spruces have given us a multitude of good garden varieties, although many are not generally available except from specialist nurseries. This is primarily because many cultivars have to be grafted which is a specialist propagation procedure. Many fine cultivars are likely to become widely known when supplies become more readily available, but in the meantime prices are likely to be high and some searching through specialist catalogues will be necessary to track down some of the most desirable forms.

Picea abies is known more commonly as the Norway Spruce or even more commonly as the Christmas Tree in the British Isles. The species is used only as a forest tree and is not recommended as a garden conifer even though it may look attractive in its early years.

Some confusion exists with the naming of many of the dwarf forms but here follows a selection of some of the most distinctive.

'Gregoryana' makes a very slow-growing hummock of tight dark green foliage which is prickly to the touch. Most of the *abies* cultivars have brownish resinous winter buds which add to their attractiveness. After ten years 'Gregoryana' will make a cushion-shaped plant about 15 to 20 cm (6 to 8 in) high and will ultimately only reach 45 to 50 cm (18 to 20 in) in height but spreading perhaps 90 cm to 1.2 m (3 to 4 ft).

'Nidiformis' is a most attractive dwarf form for any garden. It has a flat-topped and spreading habit, dark green with typical brown resinous winter buds which open in spring to produce the bright green shoots for the next season's growth. From 30 to 45 cm (12 to 15 in) high by perhaps 60 cm (2 ft) in width after ten years it will grow eventually as high as 90 cm to 1.8 m (3 to 6 ft) and spread 2.4 to 2.7 m (8 to 9 ft). A cultivar with a more upright habit is 'Ohlendorffii'. It has the same dark green foliage as the previous cultivar and dark orange-brown winter buds. Another gem of a plant is in fact *Picea abies* 'Little Gem', which makes a compact slow growing bush of mid green and bright fresh shoots in spring. It is ideal for the rock garden, in ten years only reaching 30 cm (1 ft) with a similar spread.

Picea breweriana must be classed as one of the most beautiful of all conifers – but it takes many years in most situations to attain this stature. Broadly conical in habit it has long pendulous branches with dark blue-green foliage. It prefers a situation of some shelter and even slight shade but enjoys plenty of moisture. Although eventually becoming a large tree it will probably only grow 1.2 to 1.5 m (4 to 5 ft) in its first ten years and after a great many more attain possibly 13.7 to 15 m (45 to 50 ft).

One of the most popular and widely grown spruces is *Picea glauca albertiana* 'Conica'. It is very hardy and not difficult to grow, a splendid garden plant, making a perfect cone-shaped specimen. The foliage is dark green except for the period in spring and early summer when its new growth gives it a bright emerald-green colour. This plant should in my opinion be in every garden although one has to admit it does seem to get attacked by its fair share of pests such as red spider mite. However, these can be controlled quite easily by spraying with a systemic insecticide once or twice through the summer months. After ten years it will grow to about 1.2 m (4 ft) and at maturity may be as much as 3 to 3.6 m (10 to 12 ft).

Picea omorika, the Serbian Spruce, is once again rather too large for all except the largest of gardens, but is one of the most trouble-free conifers and certainly one of the most attractive of spruces. With its narrow pyramidal habit and leaves of dark green, it associates well with silver birch and makes an excellent screening or accent plant with its stately bearing. Reaching 2.4 to 3 m (8 to 10 ft) at ten years of age, it will eventually grow to 18 to 22.8 m (60 to 75 ft).

Picea pungens has given us some of the most exciting silver and blue varieties of any genus – but all named forms need to be propagated by grafting – hence the scarcity of these in general circulation. Selections of seedlings from the species *P. pungens* are often made and these forms will generally be listed as *P. p. glauca* and can of course vary considerably. A selected dwarf form of great merit is *P. p.* 'Globosa' which makes a dense bush of silver blue. It is a beautiful foliage form and particularly useful for the small garden, growing in ten years perhaps 60 cm (2 ft) high and eventually 1.2 to 1.5 m (4 to 5 ft) with a similar spread.

Of the upright and larger-growing forms there is quite a wide selection but any of them could be considered worth having. Perhaps the most widely available is 'Koster'. This has a pyramidal shape but like all the grafted forms it may take a year or two of training the leading shoot in a vertical position before it decides to grow that way on its own

account. It is a silver blue the year round but the colour is particularly pronounced in the early summer when new shoots appear. Growing to 2.4 m (8 ft) in ten years, it will eventually reach 9 to 12 m (30 to 40 ft). Normally these forms of *P. pungens* have no particular fads or fancies but they prefer an open position. Other cultivars of merit are 'Spekii' and 'Moerheimii', 'Hoopsii' and 'Hoto'.

Pinus
The pines are some of our most picturesque trees, both in the landscape and in gardens whilst among the many species and varieties in this genus are some to fit every purpose. Once again many of the cultivars have to be propagated by grafting and so will not be so readily available as seedling raised plants or those which come from cuttings. They are also likely to be more expensive. Most are easy to grow, many succeeding on very poor dry soils where other conifers would fail. Some species are used for forestry purposes and among these is one of our three British native conifers, *Pinus sylvestris*, the Scots Pine. All pines have needle-like foliage and most species grow cones when well established which vary somewhat in size, shape and attractiveness.

Pinus cembra to my mind should be grown more widely than at present. Its common name is the Swiss Stone Pine and it makes a broad conical-shaped tree in time, retaining its bottom branches even as a mature specimen. The dark blue-green foliage only changes each spring when distinctive orange-brown shoots appear to herald another season's growth. Slow growing during its first few years, it may only be 1.8 to 2.1 m (6 to 7 ft) at the ten-year stage but eventually reaches 9 to 12 m (30 to 40 ft).

Pinus densiflora, the Japanese Red Pine, is somewhat similar to the Scots Pine, *P. sylvestris*, but although it is not often used in the British Isles it has given us a few useful dwarf forms, the most notable of which is *P. d.* 'Umbraculifera'. This unwieldy name when translated from latin means umbrella and this is indeed somewhat descriptive of the habit of a mature specimen of this plant. It has long dark green leaves which turn somewhat bronzed in winter. At ten years old it will be 90 cm to 1.2 m (3 to 4 ft) and ultimately perhaps 3 to 3.6 m (10 to 12 ft) high with almost a similar spread.

Although again perhaps too rapid growing for all but the largest gardens *Pinus griffithii*, or *P. wallichiana* as it should be now known, is such a beautiful tree that I feel it should be included in this section. It originated from the Himalayan Mountains and is commonly known as the Bhutan Pine. It has long bluish-green needles and a very graceful broadly conical habit. Reaching 4.5 cm (15 ft) in ten years, it will grow to well over 30 m (100 ft) at maturity.

Pinus mugo, the Mountain Pine, grows wild all over the mountains of central Europe, varying considerably in habit and rate of growth and as a garden plant can be expected to make a medium to large shrub. It is therefore somewhat difficult to give any more explicit indications as to rates of growth. Nonetheless it can make a most attractive garden plant but if a more regulated form is required the cultivar 'Mops' is worth looking for. This is of course grafted and can be expected to grow 60 to 90 cm (2 to 3 ft) high and spread about the same in its first ten years, eventually reaching a height and spread of 1.5 to 1.8 m (5 to 6 ft).

Pinus nigra, the Austrian Pine, offers an alternative to the Scots Pine for use as a windbreak and screen. It has dark green foliage, a colour held throughout the year, is hardy and adaptable to most soil conditions. It is conical when young but loses its bottom branches with age becoming more mop headed or flat topped. Eventually growing to 18 to 30 m (60 to 100 ft), it will at ten years reach 1.8 to 3 m (6 to 10 ft) so could not really be considered for the small garden. It has produced some useful dwarf forms.

Pinus parviflora, the Japanese White Pine, is an attractive species which is not grown widely in the British Isles at present. It has light bluish-green leaves and cones of greenish blue until they ripen. There is a selected form which is one of the most beautiful slow-growing pines, *P. p. glauca*. It has a narrower and

more ascending habit than the species with distinctively blue leaves. Both have similar rates of growth reaching 1.8 to 2.4 m (6 to 8 ft) in ten years and eventually 6 to 9 m (20 to 30 ft).

Pinus sylvestris is a familiar sight on the British landscape with its craggy appearance as a mature specimen. The Scots Pine varies as do most species in habit and rate of growth but it normally makes a medium to large tree. Conical when young it becomes mop headed or flat topped with age losing its lower branches in the process. The foliage is blue green, the bark reddish when it becomes exposed. At ten years it will grow 3 to 4.5 m (10 to 15 ft) and at maturity anything from 13.7 to 30 m (45 to 100 ft). It has given us some useful garden forms not least of which is the Golden Scots Pine, *P. s.* 'Aurea', which is similar to the species in all respects except that the leaves turn a wonderful yellow during the winter months – a real bonus! It will grow 1.2 to 1.5 m (4 to 5 ft) in ten years and eventually may be 6 to 9 m (20 to 30 ft). One of the dwarfest cultivars is 'Beuvronensis' which makes a dense blue-green bush wider than high. Like all plants and particularly dwarf conifers if grown on poor soil or with a restricted root run, it will be much dwarfer than if given extremely fertile conditions. With age it may become more vigorous than my growth estimates suggest, but at any rate it is a first-class garden plant. After ten years it may have made 60 to 90 cm (2 to 3 ft) in height and spread, ultimately 1.2 to 1.5 m (4 to 5 ft) in height and spreading as much as 2.4 to 3 m (8 to 10 ft).

Many other dwarf and slow-growing forms of pines are in existence and are well worth looking for in Garden Centres and specialist nurserymen's catalogues.

Podocarpus

Podocarpus is a genus which originates from the southern hemisphere and apart from a few species it is not hardy in our climate. The best known and to my mind most useful species is *Podocarpus nivalis* which is a native of New Zealand. It makes a compact bush with very dark green leaves reminiscent of a yew. Hardy and amenable to most soil conditions including those containing lime, it could be more widely known. Plants vary but at ten years it will grow perhaps only 15 to 20 cm (6 to 8 in) and after many years perhaps 45 to 60 cm (1½ to 2 ft) in height and 90 cm to 1.2 m (3 to 4 ft) across.

Pseudotsuga

The genus contains five species, the best known of which is *Pseudotsuga menziesii*, the Douglas Fir, a giant tree not at all suitable for gardens. However, this species in turn has produced a few dwarf forms, the best known of which is 'Fletcheri'. This makes an irregular flat-topped bush with blue-green foliage. It is quite different to any other dwarf conifer and extremely attractive at all stages of development and in my opinion needs to be better known. At ten years it will make a bush 60 to 76 cm (2 to 2½ ft) in height by 90 cm (3 ft) across and after many more years perhaps 90 cm to 1.8 m (3 to 6 ft) high by 2.4 to 3 m (8 to 10 ft) in width.

Sciadopitys

Sciadopitys, known as the Japanese Umbrella Pine, is a genus with only one species. *Sciadopitys verticillata* is a most distinctive tree looking rather like a pine which it is not. It has glossy green leaves or needles which are quite thick and rigid rather than grassy to the touch. It is an extremely slow grower for the first few years reaching perhaps 90 cm to 1.2 m (3 to 4 ft) in ten years but gaining strength and vigour with advancing years to eventually end up as a tree of some 9 to 10.6 m (30 to 35 ft).

Sequoia

Sequoia has also only one species attached to its name, this being *Sequoia sempervirens*, the Californian Redwood, which can in no way be considered a garden plant growing even in the British Isles over 46 m (150 ft). However, it has produced one interesting slow-growing or dwarf conifer in *S. s.* 'Adpressa'. This, if left to its own devices, would make a straggling bush or small tree of up to 9 m (30 ft). Trimmed reguarly to a bush of not more than 90 cm (3 ft) in height it will give a great amount of pleasure as a most beautiful artificial dwarf cultivar. The

tips of the foliage in the summer will turn creamy white so that the bush looks as though it is covered in snow. Worth a bit of trouble, this plant!

Sequoiadendron

Sequoiadendron again is represented by one species *Sequoiadendron giganteum*, more commonly known in the British Isles as a Wellingtonia. It is also called the Mammoth Tree on account of its ultimate size and whilst an attractive and spectacular tree it will eventually grow to 46 m (150 ft) or more so cannot be considered for the garden.

Taxodium

Taxodium is one of the few deciduous genera among the cone-bearing family which we call conifers and it originates from the south eastern United States and Mexico. The best-known species is *Taxodium distichum*, the Swamp Cypress. When grown in water or very close to the water it develops large roots which protrude well above ground. It will succeed in all soils where not too dry. Bright fresh green leaves in spring and summer turn bronze in autumn before dropping. A beautiful and stately tree it will get large in time. After ten years it will grow to about 4.5 m (15 ft) and eventually will attain 30 m (100 ft) or more.

Taxus

The yews are a very variable but useful group of plants which have somewhat dropped from favour in the public eye over the past few years. As commonly seen in the British landscape they are dark and sombre and associated somehow with cemeteries and graveyards – an association which needs dispelling as there is a very wide range of shapes, forms and colours available for garden use.

They are adaptable to most soil conditions, succeeding well on chalk and lime and tolerating quite dry shady conditions but all require good drainage. Some forms make excellent hedges and all withstand clipping well.

Taxus baccata, the Common or English Yew, is one of Britain's three native conifers and as such is so variable in shape and habit that no clear indication as to rates of growth can be given. There have been a great many cultivars produced from this species, one of the most widely used being 'Fastigiata', the Irish Yew. This makes a narrow column, broadening considerably with age with the typical dark, almost black-green foliage of the species. A far more attractive form for the garden is the golden 'Fastigiata Aurea' which has a similar habit but has deep yellow-green leaves turning a golden hue in winter, particularly when planted in an open sunny position. At ten years it will be 1.5 to 1.8 m (5 to 6 ft) in height and eventually may reach as much as 4.5 to 5.5 m (15 to 18 ft).

A useful ground-cover yew is 'Repandens' which is almost prostrate in habit with dark green leaves. It will grow well in shade which gives it particular importance as a landscaping specimen. Of similar habit though a little more prostrate and open is *T. b.* 'Repens Aurea' which is a golden-variegated cultivar and particularly attractive when the new season's growth begins each early summer. *T. b.* 'Summergold' is semi-prostrate and as the name suggests has foliage of a soft golden colour. Both can be expected to grow 30 to 45 cm (12 to 18 in) or so in height and spread 1.2 to 1.8 cm (4 to 5 ft) in ten years and eventually 60 to 90 cm (2 to 3 ft) in height and perhaps 3 to 3.6 m (10 to 12 ft) across after a great many years. The yews take well to pruning so prostrate forms need never be a nuisance.

Lastly one of the most attractive of the golden-foliaged yews is *Taxus baccata* 'Semperaurea' which is slow growing and makes a vase-shaped bush of golden yellow throughout the year. After ten years it will grow to perhaps 90 cm (3 ft) in height and eventually will reach a height of 2.4 to 3 m (8 to 10 ft) with a similar width.

Taxus cuspidata, the Japanese Yew, and its forms are not grown much in Europe but are widely used in the United States because of their superior hardiness to *T. baccata*. It makes a small to medium-sized tree in its native Japan but it is in its selected varieties that it is most useful. *T. c.* 'Nana' is the form most seen in Europe, making a dwarf, irregularly

shaped bush which will need pruning to keep it attractive. Not in my opinion a particularly desirable conifer.

Taxus × media is a hybrid between *T. baccata* and *T. cuspidata* and in truly American fashion has been dubbed the Anglo-Japanese yew. This hybrid makes a medium to large-sized spreading shrub and it and its cultivars are widely used in the United States. The most commonly seen cultivar in Europe is 'Hicksii' which makes a dense columnar bush of dark green and is probably the best form for hedging purposes. Growing 1.5 to 1.8 m (5 to 6 ft) in ten years, it will eventually reach 6 m (20 ft) or more with age.

Thuja
This genus has produced a great many good cultivars and in appearance they are very like some of the false cypresses. There are only three species and all except some forms of *Thuja orientalis* are hardy in the British Isles. Apart from a dislike of badly drained situations all are reliably easy to grow.

Thuja occidentalis, the White Cedar, originates from eastern North America and is the hardiest of the three species. The species itself is not used as a garden plant but it has given us many forms suitable for individual specimens and for hedging purposes. It has aromatic foliage particularly when crushed. *T. o.* 'Danica', as the name suggests, originated in Denmark. It is a very attractive dwarf cultivar forming a dense rounded bush somewhat like a cushion with erectly held flattened foliage sprays. Bright green in summer, it turns slightly bronze in winter. After ten years it can be expected to be about 30 cm (1 ft) high by the same width and eventually 60 to 90 cm (2 to 3 ft) high by a width of 90 to 1.2 m (3 to 4 ft). The cultivar 'Holmstrup' makes a dense narrowly conical bush of bright green, holding its colour well throughout the year. A first-class reliable plant which was introduced a few years ago in Denmark and worthy of wider recognition, it will grow perhaps 90 to 1.2 m (3 to 4 ft) in ten years and eventually 3.6 to 4.5 m (12 to 15 ft).

A similar form but faster growing and more open in habit is *T. o.* 'Lutea Nana'

which is golden yellow in summer, a colour which is almost intensified in winter – certainly a point to commend it for the garden. It is an extremely easy grower and will withstand exposed situations which cannot be said of some of the golden chamaecyparis cultivars. Growing 1.5 to 1.8 m (5 to 6 ft) in ten years, it will probably end up at the 4.5- to 6-m (15- to 20-ft) mark. A dwarfer form with equal attributes is *T. o.* 'Sunkist', this growing to 1 to 1.2 m ($3\frac{1}{4}$ to 4 ft) in ten years.

The best cultivar for hedging is probably *T. o.* 'Smaragd' which is also known as 'Emerald'. It has a narrow columnar habit and if used as a hedge would need to be planted at not more than 60-cm (2-ft) intervals. Tolerant of a wide range of conditions including some shade, this cultivar also makes an attractive specimen in its own right. It has densely held sprays of bright emerald green foliage in summer, retaining good colour in winter. It of course withstands

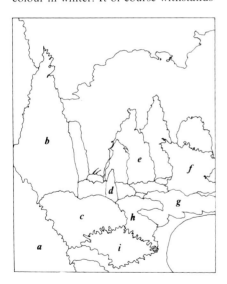

a. *Thuja occidentalis* 'Rheingold'
b. *Chamaecyparis lawsoniana* 'Lanei'
c. *Santolina chamaecyparissus*
d. *Chamaecyparis lawsoniana* 'Blue Nantais'
e. *Chamaecyparis lawsoniana* 'Lutea'
f. *Juniperus squamata* 'Meyeri'
g. *Calluna vulgaris* 'Golden Carpet'
h. *Erica cinerea* 'Atrosanguinea Smith's Variety'
i. *Abies koreana* 'Prostrate Beauty'

clipping well. At ten years it will grow 1.8 to 2.4 m (6 to 8 ft) and if allowed to grow to maturity probably 7.6 m (25 ft).

One of the best garden conifers is *T. o.* 'Rheingold', a slow-growing form which turns from golden yellow in summer to rich coppery gold in winter and in very hard winters almost reddish bronze. Quite often one will obtain plants with very soft feathery foliage which appear different to the more typical flattened sprays, or more often both types of foliage will appear on the same plant. 'Rheingold' is an excellent garden plant and associates well with winter-flowering heathers. Like all golden forms the best colour will be obtained by placing it in a sunny position. After ten years it will reach approximately 1.2 to 1.5 m (4 to 5 ft) and eventually will make a broad-based bush 3 to 3.6 m (10 to 12 ft) high and as much across.

Thuja orientalis is known as the Chinese Arbor-vitae or Tree of Life coming as it does from north and western China. The species makes a small tree mostly of conical habit which is not used much as a garden plant, although it has produced several useful dwarf and slow-growing garden varieties.

One of my favourite dwarf conifers is *T. o* 'Aurea Nana' which makes a densely foliaged bush of bright golden yellow in summer, turning yellow green in winter. The flattened foliage sprays are held erectly giving the plant a very neat attractive appearance. It will grow 60 to 76 cm (2 to $2\frac{1}{2}$ ft) in ten years and ultimately 1.5 to 2.4 m (5 to 8 ft). There appears to be more than one form in cultivation.

Thuja orientalis 'Conspicua' is a pyramidal cultivar of great attraction, a golden-yellow colour through most of the year but particularly bright in summer. It is a medium grower reaching 1.8 to 2.4 m (6 to 8 ft) in ten years and eventually as much as 5.5 to 7.6 m (18 to 25 ft). There is a similar but slower-growing cultivar in *T. o.* 'Elegantissima' which turns a deep bronze in winter.

Lastly a dwarf juvenile-foliaged form of some attraction is *T. o.* 'Juniperoides', a rounded bush turning from a summer colour of greyish green to a striking deep purple in winter. Unfortunately like a few other forms of similar foliage and habit, it is not reliably hardy and tends to open up with age. Reaching 60 cm (2 ft) in ten years, it is unlikely to exceed 90 cm (3 ft) at a somewhat young age of maturity!

Thuja plicata, the Western Red Cedar, as one might guess originates from western North America and is a very important timber tree. It is also an extremely useful tree for hedging although the selected form 'Atrovirens' is much better. *T. plicata* will grow too large as a garden specimen reaching well over 30 m (100 ft) at maturity. The foliage of this species is generally more rounded and glossy than the two so far mentioned and has a very pleasant odour when crushed. The species and all forms used for hedging withstand clipping very well and this is one of the few which will break new shoots from old wood if cut back hard – a definite advantage for this purpose.

Thuja plicata 'Rogersii' is an unusual but very useful conifer for the small garden. It has very dense foliage, dark green inside the plant and tips of golden yellow and bronze, particularly pronounced in winter, the whole effect giving a variegated look. Mostly globular in shape it will sometimes assume a leading shoot which alters its habit to conical. In ten years reaching 45 to 60 cm (1½ to 2 ft), it may ultimately grow to 1.5 to 1.8 m (5 to 6 ft) with a similar width. A quite choice form which is not generally known is 'Stoneham Gold', a slow-growing cultivar with foliage of a really old-gold colour. The habit is somewhat irregular particularly in the early stages of growth, but the plant develops into a broadly conical bush. The inside of the plant is dark green, accentuating the golden tips of the leaves which turn bright golden bronze in winter. After ten years perhaps reaching 60 to 76 m (2 to 2½ ft), it will eventually grow to 1.8 to 2.1 m (6 to 7 ft). If a more regular-shaped plant is required then a hard trim will not be resented.

Thujopsis

Thujopsis is a very similar genus to *Thuja*, but is only represented by one species *Thujopsis dolabrata*. This makes a medium-sized tree with a broadly pyramidal habit which has large flattened sprays of glossy green. Growing 1.8 to 2.4 m (6 to 8 ft) in ten years, it will eventually reach 9 to 10.6 m (30 to 35 ft) in the British Isles. There is a dwarf spreading form in 'Nana' of no great attraction.

Tsuga

This genus is usually known more commonly as the hemlock and has produced some very worthwhile garden forms which are not generally known to gardeners in the United Kingdom. This applies particularly to *Tsuga canadensis* and its cultivars which are very popular in the United States and likely in time to become so in Europe. The foliage is generally similar to the yews but with much thinner leaves and branches of a more arching habit. They are tolerant of most soil conditions succeeding particularly well in soils that are both moist and well drained.

Tsuga canadensis, the Eastern Hemlock, originates from the eastern United States and makes a large tree of pyramidal outline not really suitable for any but the largest gardens. It makes a tall graceful tree usually forked near the base, growing 3.6 to 4.5 m (12 to 15 ft) in ten years and ultimately between 22.8 to 30 m (75 to 100 ft). This species and its cultivars tolerate alkaline soil and in fact seem to prefer them to very acid conditions. There are several dwarf forms which will probably only be available from specialist nurseries at present.

'Bennett' makes an attractive flat-topped bush with graceful drooping branchlets. This and a very similar semi-prostrate cultivar 'Jeddeloh' are distinct in offering new forms and texture to the choice of conifers available to the gardener. Both have the mid- to light-green foliage typical of the species. Both have similar rates of growth making plants of 30 to 45 cm (12 to 18 in) high by a width of 90 cm to 1.2 m (3 to 4 ft) in ten years and eventually a height of 90 to 1.2 m (3 to 4 ft) and a width of up to 3 m (10 ft).

'Cole' is an extremely prostrate form which closely hugs the ground spreading slowly to a diameter of perhaps 60 to 90 cm (2 to 3 ft) in ten years and ultimately up to 3 m (10 ft) or so. Probably the most familiar cultivar in Great Britain is 'Pendula' which makes a spreading bush, slowly building up in height but always with a very pendulous branching habit. Although slow it will eventually make a large plant as high as 1.8 to 2.4 m (6 to 8 ft) and as broad as 6 m (20 ft) although at the ten-year stage perhaps only 45 to 60 cm (1½ to 2 ft) and 76 to 90 cm (2½ to 3 ft) across. It is particularly effective if placed on a bank or a wall where the branches can cascade down the slope or over the edge as the case may be.

Heaths and Heathers

Few types of plants have risen in popularity to such an extent in recent years as heaths and heathers and it is easy to see why.

They are relatively trouble free, look attractive the year round and provide excellent ground cover. Furthermore they associate well with other plants and to my mind none better than with conifers.

Heathers in the garden

Heathers is the term usually applied to both *Erica* and *Calluna*, although strictly speaking all ericas should be referred to as heaths and callunas as heathers. It should at the outset be stated that all the callunas and most of the summer-flowering ericas dislike alkaline soils. This problem can be overcome to some extent by the addition of quantities of peat, or, even better, by building a raised peat bed and with the help of a chemical called sequestrene. However, both remedies can be expensive so one should give it some thought before spending vast sums of money!

I hope this will serve as a warning but not a deterrent for there are a great many ericas that will grow well on alkaline soils, notably *Erica carnea*, *E. erigena* and *E. × darleyensis* and their cultivars. These types are in many ways the most useful to the gardener because they give flower throughout the winter and early spring, a time when most gardens are notable for the absence of colour.

Heathers have one definite requirement whether they succeed on acid or alkaline soil and that is to be placed in a sunny position. They will grow in some shade but they will not usually flower well and will tend to become straggly. As with conifers, golden-foliaged forms will turn dull without sun to brighten them.

Planning

We have ascertained what sort of soil we have and that we need a sunny position for best effect. The next stage, if a heather border is to give the most worthwhile result, is to decide on the amount of the space available and which cultivars to choose to give as much year-round colour as possible. This doesn't mean only selecting for colour of flower but colour of foliage, and of course the height the varieties will eventually grow to.

According to the space available one will need to decide how many plants of each variety can be used. Never plant less than three of a kind except for tree heaths where one will be ample. It will of course be more effective to use larger quantities than three but this will be entirely governed by the size of border you are able (or willing) to give.

Three plans are given on page 117 which will give an indication of what can be done with a small or larger border, together with appropriate conifers for such a situation. Plans A and B are similar but B is for alkaline soils.

Planting

The first step should of course be the preparation of the border which in the case of heathers can be considerable according to the type of soil you have in your garden. Most soils will benefit from the addition of peat but if your conditions are either sandy and well drained or to the other extreme, heavy clay and poorly drained, they may need a considerable amount. But like most plants, good soil preparation is a basic principle for success.

Dig the soil well, cleaning out perennial

weeds and mixing in moistened peat. If possible get some slight elevation to your border either in the middle, or rising from where it will be most often viewed. This always adds interest to a border and will be particularly useful if your soil is badly drained.

Having now ordered and received your plants of good quality and true to name we hope, you can start planting. This can be undertaken at almost any time of the year if the plants are in containers but spring and autumn if they are from the open ground. Correct spacing of plants is important as some heathers grow much more quickly than others. Generally most cultivars can be planted at a density of five to the square metre but for more vigorous types such as *Erica carnea* 'Springwood White' and *E. × darleyensis* 'Arthur Johnson' three plants to the square metre will be ample. It is a good idea to place your plants before planting in the positions you wish them to be planted – this ensures you have even spacing and don't end up with a gap at one end of the bed!

Remove the container – it is surprising how many people forget – and with a spade or a trowel dig a hole for the plant – mixing two handfuls of moist peat around the roots of each plant – which should of course also be moist. The plant can be inserted slightly deeper than the level of the soil in the pot so that the foliage of the heather rests on the soil. After planting the bed it is a good idea if you have any peat left, and even if you haven't, to mulch around each plant to a depth of about 4 cm (1½ in). This can of course be extended to the whole bed but it can become expensive. The mulch serves to prevent weeds and drying out of the roots – it also enables the heather to root along the stem, keeping it younger, more healthy and more vigorous.

Having finished the planting you will, I hope, find that your heathers will give you pleasure for many years to come.

Maintenance

All plants need some maintenance at some stage in their life in a garden situation and heathers are no exception. It should be unnecessary to mention that

A heather bed for year-round colour in neutral or acid soil. The heathers are planted 30 to 45 cm (1 to 1½ ft) apart so that they produce rapid ground cover. Where not otherwise indicated, groups are of five plants each. The bed is 4.5 m (15 ft) long and 2.7 m (9 ft) wide

(a) *Erica carnea* 'King George'
(b) *Calluna vulgaris* 'Gold Haze'
(c) *Erica cinerea* 'C. D. Eason'
(d) *Erica carnea* 'Springwood White'
(e) *Erica carnea* 'Vivellii'
(f) *Erica vagans* 'Mrs D. F. Maxwell'
(g) *Calluna vulgaris* 'Robert Chapman'
(h) *Erica cinerea* 'Purple Beauty'
(i) *Erica mediterranea* 'W. T. Rackliff' (3)
(j) *Calluna vulgaris* 'H. E. Beale'
(k) *Erica × darleyensis* 'Arthur Johnson'

Conifers

(l) *Picea albertiana* 'Conica'
(m) *Chamaecyparis pisifera* 'Boulevard'
(n) *Thuja occidentalis* 'Rheingold'

PLAN B

A heather bed for year-round colour in acid, neutral or alkaline soil. The dimensions of the bed are the same as those for Plan A

(a) *Erica carnea* 'Foxhollow'
(b) *Erica carnea* 'Praecox Rubra'
(c) *Erica carnea* 'Springwood White'
(d) *Erica × darleyensis* 'J. H. Brummage'
(e) *Erica vagans* 'Mrs D. F. Maxwell'
(f) *Erica carnea* 'Myretoun Ruby'
(g) *Erica mediterranea* 'W. T. Rackliff' (3)
(h) *Erica vagans* 'Lyonesse'
(i) *Erica × darleyensis* 'Arthur Johnson'

Conifers

(j) *Thuja occidentalis* 'Rheingold'
(k) *Picea albertiana* 'Conica'
(l) *Juniperus chinensis* 'Pyramidalis'

PLAN C

An island bed for year-round flower and foliage effect on neutral or acid soil. The heathers are planted in groups of ten, unless otherwise indicated. The bed is 6 m (20 ft) long and 4.5 m (15 ft) wide. The smaller bed is a mixed planting of dwarf conifers; in this bed the plants should be at least 45 cm (1½ ft) apart

(a) *Calluna vulgaris* 'Gold Haze'
(b) *Erica vagans* 'Mrs D. F. Maxwell'
(c) *Erica cinerea* 'Pink Ice' (5)
(d) *Calluna vulgaris* 'Darkness'
(e) *Erica carnea* 'Springwood White' (5)
(f) *Erica carnea* 'King George' (5)
(g) *Calluna vulgaris* 'Robert Chapman'
(h) *Erica × darleyensis* 'Arthur Johnson'
(i) *Erica cinerea* 'Purple Beauty'
(j) *Erica × darleyensis* 'Silberschmelze'
(k) *Erica carnea* 'Myretoun Ruby'

Conifers

(l) *Chamaecyparis lawsoniana* 'Elwoodii'
(m) *Thuja occidentalis* 'Rheingold'
(n) *Picea glauca albertiana* 'Conica'
(o) *Juniperus × media* 'Old Gold'
(p) *Cryptomeria japonica* 'Lobbi Nana'
(q) *Chamaecyparis pisifera* 'Boulevard'

Dwarf Conifer Bed

(a) *Abies balsamea* 'Hudsonia'
(b) *Chamaecyparis lawsoniana* 'Minima Aurea'
(c) *Chamaecyparis obtusa* 'Nana'
(d) *Juniperus squamata* 'Blue Star'
(e) *Chamaecyparis obtusa* 'Nana Lutea'
(f) *Thuja occidentalis* 'Danica'
(g) *Juniperus communis* 'Compressa'
(h) *Thuja plicata* 'Stoneham Gold'
(i) *Thuja occidentalis* 'Holmstrup'
(j) *Cryptomeria japonica* 'Vilmoriniana'
(k) *Chamaecyparis lawsoniana* 'Pygmaea Argentea'
(l) *Chamaecyparis pisifera* 'Nana'
(m) *Thuja plicata* 'Rogersii'
(n) *Chamaecyparis pisifera* 'Filifera Nana'
(o) *Thuja orientalis* 'Aurea Nana'
(p) *Juniperus horizontalis* 'Glauca'
(q) *Chamaecyparis obtusa* 'Nana Gracilis'

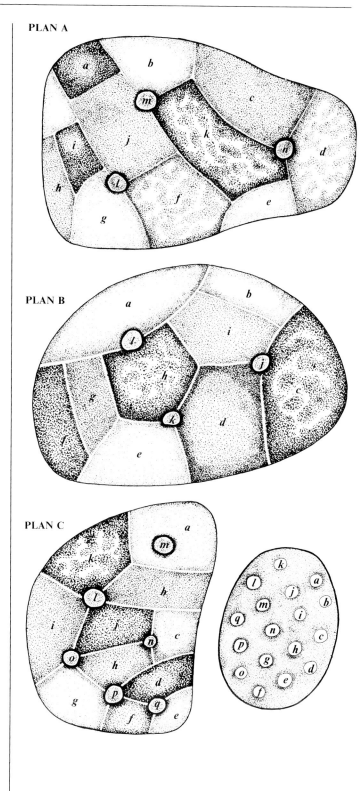

PLAN A

PLAN B

PLAN C

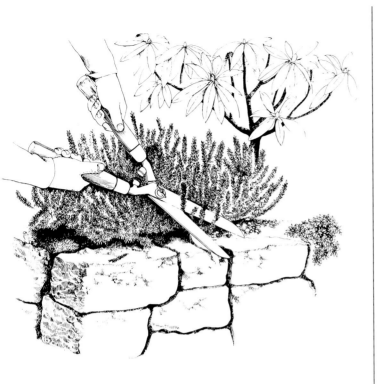

Trim off old flower heads of summer-flowering heathers in spring

only be available from specialists but all of those listed here have been selected because they have been tried under most conditions and for a number of years.

Selected Heathers

Calluna

Calluna vulgaris, the Common Heather or Ling, grows wild throughout many parts of Britain and Europe. It grows in a variety of places, from the Highlands of Scotland to the sandy Breckland of East Anglia but it will not grow where lime is present in the soil. Normally very hardy in the wild, on rich soils it will often grow soft and straggly and therefore more susceptible to winter damage. This is particularly true of some modern varieties and foliage forms. The Common Heather varies in height from 30 to 90 cm (1 to 3 ft), but some of the named cultivars will differ even more. The flowering period is normally from August until November.

'Beoley Gold' One of the best of the yellow-foliaged cultivars, it retains its colour throughout the year whilst producing attractive white flowers in August and September. It grows to 45 cm (1½ ft).

'Blazeway' Grown primarily for its startling foliage effect turning from golden orange in summer to a burnt red in winter. It grows 45 cm (½ ft) tall and has somewhat unattractive mauve flowers in August and September.

'County Wicklow' Growing only 23 to 30 cm (9 to 12 in), this is one of the best double pink-flowering heathers. The flowers are very freely produced in August and September.

'Darkness' Of fairly recent introduction, this is a valuable addition to the range, producing deep crimson flowers on 30-cm (1-ft) spikes in August and September. It is a vigorous grower but compact – further qualities to commend it to the gardener.

'Foxii Nana' A really miniature heather growing to a small mound of only 15 cm

any seedling weeds need to be kept under control – eventually most will be smothered by the spreading heathers. Summer-flowering types will always improve in appearance and flowering if the old flower heads are trimmed each spring, just as the next year's growth begins – this normally being in March. Also all callunas will benefit from a trim at the same time even if they do not normally flower – such as *Calluna vulgaris* 'Golden Feather'. The more vigorous the growth the more trimming or pruning is required. Winter-flowering heathers will seldom need any pruning as most are fairly compact in habit anyway, but taller cultivars such as *E. × darleyensis* 'Arthur Johnson' or the tree heaths should be pruned immediately after flowering.

In dry periods it is advisable to water your heathers, and particularly during the first season or two after planting until their roots systems are established.

There are only a few species of heathers but such is the choice of cultivars among those in cultivation some qualified selection has to be made. Many cultivars may

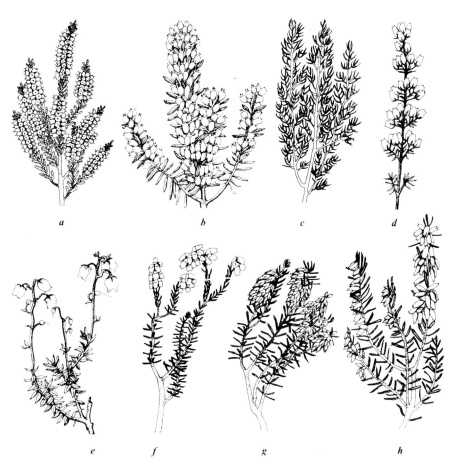

a   *b*   *c*   *d*

e   *f*   *g*   *h*

Good species of heaths and heathers which are readily available

(a) *Calluna vulgaris*
(b) *Erica vagans*
(c) *Erica arborea* 'Alpina'
(d) *Erica cinerea*
(e) *Daboecia cantabrica*
(f) *Erica tetralix*
(g) *Erica carnea*
(h) *Erica × darleyensis*

(6 in) high with rather sparse purple flowers. Ideal for the rock garden but not so much for a mixed heather border, as it is likely to look more than a little out of place!

'Golden Carpet' An apt description for one of the best foliage cultivars, this almost prostrate form is useful for the front of the border. Golden in summer, it becomes a more orange red in winter and is of interest the year round.

'Golden Feather' Rarely has a flower but in many ways this is an advantage. It has soft feathery golden-yellow foliage turning burnt orange in winter. Not always the easiest to grow or the longest-lived cultivar in my experience.

'Gold Haze' Has bright golden foliage the year round and, like 'Beoley Gold', white flowers. To my mind it neither flowers so well as the latter nor does it retain such a bright yellow foliage colour in winter

August and September flowering and growing to 60 cm (2 ft), it is still one of the most popular cultivars.

'H. E. Beale' Is probably one of the oldest cultivars but still one of the best. It has beautiful double pink flowers which last well through September and October on 60-cm (2-ft) spikes and is especially effective in a large grouping.

'J. H. Hamilton' Is also a double pink of a similar vintage to 'H. E. Beale'. However, it flowers earlier in August and September, is deeper in colour and only 23 cm (9 in) or so in height. These two cultivars have really proved themselves garden worthy.

'Mair's Variety' Grows vigorously to nearly 90 cm (3 ft) with long spikes of single white flowers in August and September. The bright green foliage is an attractive foil to the flowers which are useful for cutting.

'**Multicolor**' Is also known as 'Prairie Fire' and both names are descriptive of this excellent dwarf-growing form. It changes through the seasons but at most times has yellow, orange and red hues reflected in its foliage. The flowers are purplish during August and September and if anything detract from the pleasing foliage.

'**My Dream**' This cultivar arose as a "sport" on a plant of 'H. E. Beale' and is a first class double flowered white of similar habit to 'H. E. Beale'. Flowers well in September and October, the dead flower heads remaining attractive until the next spring.

'**Peter Sparkes**' Is of similar habit and flowering time to 'H. E. Beale', double but the flowers are a much deeper pink. An excellent form but there may not be room in most gardens for both.

'**Robert Chapman**' To my mind one of the most reliable foliage kinds, giving a range of colour the year round and only marred by its purple flowers in August and September. It is quite vigorous in habit growing to 45 cm ($1\frac{1}{2}$ ft) or so, the foliage colours turning from orange in summer to red in winter, particularly during frosty weather.

'**Silver Knight**' Has soft woolly foliage of silver grey and mauve-pink flowers in August and September. A good compact form growing to only 30 cm (1 ft); like 'Silver Queen' attractive used in association with golden-foliaged cultivars.

'**Silver Queen**' Also has silver-grey foliage which is a good deal tighter in habit, although the flowering spikes reach 45 cm ($1\frac{1}{2}$ ft) with purple flowers in August and September.

'**Sir John Charrington**' Arguably the best of the foliage cultivars. It has a bushy habit, the leaves in summer attaining a deep orange yellow turning in winter to the brightest red. Crimson flowers reach about 30 cm (1 ft) and make a good show in August and September.

'**Sister Anne**' Grows to a very compact 15 cm (6 in) with somewhat woolly foliage. It has pink flowers which are produced freely in August and September. Although very attractive in summer it looks somewhat dead and raggy in winter.

Daboecia

Daboecia cantabrica is commonly known as the Irish Bell Heather and as one might expect from a plant originating from western Ireland it likes moist conditions and is not considered fully hardy in some parts of the British Isles. The species and cultivars dislike lime. The flower heads should be trimmed back lightly after flowering, either in late autumn or early spring. Not every garden will be able to grow daboecias successfully but when well grown they offer a delightful contrast to other heathers.

'**Alba**' Has large white bells hanging on nearly foot-long spikes from July to October. The whole plant grows to nearly 60 cm (2 ft).

'**Donard Pink**' Is a strong grower to 60 cm (2 ft) with pale pink flowers from June until September.

'**Hookstone Purple**' Another vigorous grower to 60 cm (2 ft), it has bright purple bells, flowering from June to October.

'**William Buchanan**' A cross between *D. cantabrica* and *D. azorica*, the Azores Heath, this has a long flowering period from June until October with crimson flowers on compact 30-cm (1-ft) high bushes.

Erica arborea

As the latin name might suggest this is known as the Tree Heath and in fact it does grow in its native Mediterranean habitat to about 6 m (20 ft). However, the species is not hardy in the British Isles and the cultivar 'Alpina' is the one usually offered. This grows only 1.8 to 2.4 m (6 to 8 ft) and will withstand most British winters. It has pale green foliage and white flowers which make a much better show on alkaline than acid soils, covering the period from March until May. It makes a useful addition to the heather range but is more suited to the larger heather garden where it can be allowed to grow unrestricted.

Erica australis

This species originates from Portugal and western Spain and is generally hardy in Great Britain but can be easily damaged by snowfalls and strong winds. It grows from 1.2 to 1.8 m (4 to 6 ft) carrying purple flowers from April until June, extending the flowering season of heathers through what is generally a quiet period for colour. A cultivar called 'Riverslea' seems to be a definite improvement on the type with larger flowers of fuchsia purple. The species will withstand some lime.

Erica carnea

The Winter Heath or Mountain Heath is probably the most versatile and widely used heath in gardens. Originating from the European Alps, it is exceptionally hardy flowering even through a snow and ice cover. It grows successfully on alkaline as well as acid soils, flowering better if planted in an open position although it will grow quite well in shade if not too dry. Most cultivars grow less than 30 cm (1 ft) in height, but vary considerably in vigour and therefore spread. No trimming is required. There is a wide range of cultivars available but unfortunately many are very similar, but all flower within the November to April period. Here are some of the best and most distinct.

'Aurea' Has golden-yellow foliage which is particularly pronounced in spring and early summer when new growth begins. From February until April it is covered with pale pink flowers. It is a most useful and attractive cultivar reaching about 23 cm (9 in) and fairly compact in habit.

'Foxhollow' Is similar in having golden foliage but it is much more golden and more spreading in habit than 'Aurea' and with far fewer pink flowers. It seems to turn slightly bronzed in winter in exposed positions. Height similar to 'Aurea'.

'King George' Most heather enthusiasts I think would agree that this is probably the best of the *carnea* cultivars although first introduced over fifty years ago. It has a compact habit growing to 23 cm (9 in) or so with masses of rich pink flowers from January until April.

'Myretoun Ruby' Also goes under the more descriptive name of 'Winter Jewel' but whichever name is used it is an outstanding new cultivar. The habit is compact to 23 cm (9 in) high and against the dark green foliage are borne the most beautiful red flowers of any form of *carnea*. Flowering is from February until April.

'Pink Spangles' Is another recent introduction of great merit. Similar to the better known 'Springwood Pink' in habit and, like it, excellent for ground cover, the large flowers are bi-coloured pale lilac and deep rosy red, lasting from January until March.

'Praecox Rubra' An early-flowering form, as the name suggests, it has deep rosy-red flowers on 23-cm (9-in) bushes from December until March.

'Ruby Glow' Flowers in March and April and it is an attractive cultivar with a spreading habit. Rich ruby-red flowers give a colourful display although some seasons it seems a bit shy in flower.

'Springwood Pink' Like its white-flowered counterpart is one of the most popular cultivars and one of the best for ground-cover use. Dark green foliage, spreading rapidly but only to about 15 cm (6 in) high, is covered with masses of pale pink flowers which darken with age during February and March. Like all cultivars, of course, the length of flowering can be dependent upon the season.

'Springwood White' Must be the most vigorous *carnea* cultivar and is a real carpeting plant, rooting along the surface of the soil as it spreads. The foliage is a pleasant fresh green, particulaly in early summer and reaches to only about 23 cm (9 in). The flowers last from February until April with the real show coming in March when the foliage is made invisible by the pure white flowers.

'Vivellii' Really should be classed as a foliage plant, although its carmine flowers from January to March are distinct enough for it to be put in a collection on their own merit. The foliage is dark green in summer changing to bronze green in winter, a startling contrast to golden-

Daboecia cantabrica

foliaged heathers and conifers and to a cultivar such as 'Springwood White'.

Erica ciliaris

The Dorset Heath will not take lime soils at any price and prefers moisture so this immediately restricts its use in a great many gardens. Although in favourable conditions *Erica ciliaris* cultivars will give an excellent show of flowers from June until October, they can be most frustrating and difficult to grow for the average gardener, being intolerant of atmospheric pollution and inclined to be tender in hard winters.

'Aurea' Is the only golden-foliaged form of the species with pretty pink flowers from July until October. It is somewhat weak in growth reaching 30 cm (1 ft) but most attractive when grown well.

'Camla' Is useful for ground cover and is hardier than most cultivars. It is 30 cm (1 ft) high and has rosy-pink flowers from July to October.

'Corfe Castle' Has soft salmon-pink flowers from July to October on compact plants 23 to 30 cm (9 to 12 in) in height.

'David McClintock' Is of recent introduction with bi-coloured flowers which open white and turn to pink with age. Again flowering from June until October, it is taller than some at 38 to 45 cm (15 to 18 in).

'Stoborough' Grows vigorously to 60 cm (2 ft) and its pearl-white flowers over apple-green foliage from July until October make it one of the best *ciliaris* forms.

Erica cinerea

Erica cinera has a number of common names but is probably best known as the Scotch Heath or Bell Heath. It is found growing wild through most of western Europe and throughout the whole of the British Isles. It dislikes lime but withstands drier conditions better than many heaths and is often found on cliffs and growing among rocks in association with *Calluna vulgaris*. It prefers sun and good drainage so these two factors should be borne in mind when planting in the garden. There are a great many forms in cultivation and, as one might expect with such a free-seeding species, too many of a similar colour. Cultivars vary in height from 15 to 60 cm (6 in to 2 ft), but all benefit from trimming each March or early April just as new growth begins.

'Alba Minor' Has masses of white flowers from June until October on compact 23-cm (9-in) bushes. One of the best white cultivars.

'Atrosanguinea Smith's Variety' Flowers profusely from June until September. These are of an intense scarlet colour on 15 to 23 cm (6- to 9-in) spikes.

'C. D. Eason' Has dark green foliage which contrasts well with the bright red flowers appearing in June and lasting until September. A first-class plant which has proved its reliability over the years.

'C. G. Best' Like the preceding form, it is not likely to be popular by name alone! It has long stems with salmon-pink flowers from July until September. The flower heads remain, like most *E. cinerea* cultivars, attractive throughout the winter, but should be pruned fairly hard in March from 45 cm (18 in) to about 15 cm (6 in). This will improve both habit and flowering.

'Foxhollow Mahogany' Is of fairly recent introduction and has masses of rich mahogany-coloured flowers from July

until September to about 30 cm (1 ft) in height.

'Golden Drop' Can sometimes be difficult to establish but is well worth the effort as when growing well it is an outstanding foliage cultivar. The pink flowers are of little consequence but the foliage turns from copper orange in summer to red in winter and grows only 15 cm (6 in) high. It is particularly effective planted next to *E. carnea* 'Springwood White'.

'My Love' Has flowers of a bluish-mauve colour from July until September on erect 30-cm (1-ft) spikes. An extremely bright-flowered form which is somewhat similar to another called 'Vivienne Patricia'.

'Pink Ice' Is of recent introduction and a first-class plant with a distinct compact habit and beautiful pure pink flowers. The rounded dark green bushes reach only 23 cm (9 in) and are excellent at the front of a border. The short flower spikes give colour from June until September.

'Purple Beauty' Grows vigorously and flowers freely and to my mind is one of the best forms of *cinerea*. The foliage is very dark green and is covered with masses of bright purple flowers right from June through until October on plants reaching to 30 cm (1 ft) or so. A cultivar that should be in every heather garden!

'Velvet Night' Must be the darkest flowered of all having almost black-purple flowers on 30-cm (1-ft) stems from June until August. The foliage is also very dark, giving a slightly sombre appearance but once again if used as a contrast to golden foliage or white flowers extremely effective.

Many other good, distinct and worthwhile forms exist in this species, but obviously space does not allow more to be mentioned. The problem, of course, is more often what not to have than which ones to choose!

Erica × darleyensis

These hybrids all arose from a chance seedling between *Erica mediterranea* (*E. erigena*) and *E. carnea* producing what has been known for years as *E. × darleyensis*. As this was first raised at

Darley Dale Nurseries in Derbyshire, this is now known as $E. \times d.$ 'Darley Dale' and all other seedlings which arose from it are classed as cultivars of $E. \times darleyensis.$

One way and another the botanists have kept us all busy, but the plants are the main thing and these are very valuable to the heather garden. Most forms grow between 60 cm to 1.2 m (2 and 4 ft). All are vigorous, useful for ground cover and all grow successfully on alkaline soils.

'Arthur Johnson' To my mind this is one of the finest heathers introduced, flowering from December to April. Taller than most forms at 60 cm (2 ft) and with long spikes of deep pink blooms, it is vigorous, an easy grower and reliable in flower.

'Darley Dale' Formerly $E. \times darleyensis,$ it is more compact than 'Arthur Johnson' with much shorter spikes of a pinky-mauve colour which last from November until March. One of the best for ground cover growing between 45 to 60 cm ($1\frac{1}{2}$ to 2 ft) in height and quite amenable to a variety of soils and situations.

'Furzey' Is also listed in some catalogues as 'Cherry Stevens'. The dark green foliage is covered with masses of deep rose-pink flowers from January until April. A good form of fairly recent introduction.

'Jack H. Brummage' Has golden-yellow foliage which is more prominent in some gardens than others. It seems to prefer heavier, slightly alkaline soils to give its best in both foliage and flower. The latter are a pleasing shade of pink in February and March on 45-cm ($1\frac{1}{2}$-ft) bushes.

'J. W. Porter' Flowers from February to April on large rounded bushes of dark green which reach 45-cm ($1\frac{1}{2}$-ft) in height. The flowers are a direct contrast to the foliage, being a strong reddish purple but unfortunately are not always produced as freely as those of some other forms.

'Silberschmelze' Probably has been given more names than any other cultivar, mainly because of the Englishman's lack of knowledge of the German language where this plant was first raised! 'Alba' 'Molten Silver', 'Silver Beads' and 'Silver Bells' are just a few synonyms for what is really a white 'Darley Dale' and an excellent garden plant. It flowers from December until April on bushes 45 to 60 cm ($1\frac{1}{2}$ to 2 ft) high. Also a good ground cover with a vigorous habit, 'Silberschmelze' has single flowers of silvery white with distinct brownish stamens in the centre of each, creating a most pleasing effect.

Erica erigena

As might be imagined this species (syn. *Erica mediterranea*) is known as the Mediterranean Heath but what is not known so widely is that it is also native in western Ireland, northern Spain and south western France. Normally in the wild it makes a shrub varying in height from 1.2 to 2.4 m (4 to 8 ft) with small pink flowers from March until May. It grows well on lime soils but although withstanding some frost and snow is easily damaged by severe winter weather though seldom killed outright. Some forms are more adaptable to British gardens than others and most will benefit from sheltered positions – at the same time requiring full sun. They are useful in that they extend the flowering period in the heather garden from the *E. carnea* cultivars finishing in April almost to the *E. cinera* cultivars which begin in June.

'Alba' Reaches 90 cm to 1.2 m (3 to 4 ft) with rich green foliage covered with white flowers from March until May.

'Brightness' Has a compact bushy habit growing slowly to 60 cm (2 ft). The foliage is dark green, the flower buds turning bronze before opening in March into a purple-red colour and lasting until May. Flowers do not always appear freely all over the plant which seems to be typical of some other forms of this species.

'Irish Dusk' This is attractive for both its greyish bronze foliage and flowers, which are deep salmon in bud, opening to clear pink flowers. The flowering period spans from November until the following April. Good value indeed!

Superba Will under most conditions reach 1.8 m (6 ft) or so and has larger rosy-pink flowers more freely produced than the type which have an added bonus in being honey scented during the March to May flowering period.

'W. T. Rackliff' Grows in compact rounded bushes of rich green to 60 cm (2 ft) and is covered with pure white flowers in March and April. Like most *E. erigena* cultivars flowering can be spoilt by frost.

Erica tetralix

The Cross-leaved Heath is distributed in the wild through most of north western Europe where the moist airstreams flow in from the Atlantic. To thrive it must be in lime-free conditions and will undoubtedly succeed better in areas of high rainfall and where its roots can be assured of a constant supply of water. Grey foliage is a predominant feature of the species and most varieties, with flowers held in clusters mostly from June until October. Like *E. ciliaris*, *E. tetralix* cannot be expected to grow well in all gardens.

'Alba Mollis' Is quite a striking plant with silver-grey foliage and white flowers from June until September. Like most forms of the species it grows about 15 to 23 cm (6 to 9 in).

'Con Underwood' Has large crimson flowers on 23-cm (9-in) bushes from June until October and is one of the best and most reliable cultivars.

'Hookstone Pink' Flowering from June until October and growing to 30 cm (1 ft), it has terracotta flower buds opening to clear pink over grey foliage.

'Ken Underwood' Has very dark grey-green leaves and an upright habit to 30 cm (1 ft). The long flower spikes carry cerise flowers from June until August.

'Pink Star' Is of recent introduction but appears to be different to forms already in cultivation in having star-like flowers held upright rather than drooping as is the case with most. The contrast of bright pink against the grey foliage is most attractive.

Erica vagans

The Cornish Heath in the wild makes a low spreading shrub from 30 to 90 cm (1 to 3 ft) in height. Mostly found in Cornwall, it is also native to parts of western France and the Iberian peninsular. It will grow in acid, neutral or slightly alkaline soils and will occasionally get damaged in severe winters. There are several forms in cultivation but as white and pink are the two main colours many are very similar.

Although the dead flower heads remain attractive the whole winter, they should be trimmed fairly hard back in the spring when new growth begins to be assured of both compact plants and improved flowering during the next summer.

'Lyonesse' Flowers in August and September and is almost the purest white among the many white *vagans* cultivars and although introduced nearly fifty years ago has stood the test of time and still remains one of the most popular. It is quite compact in habit, reaching only 45 cm (1½ ft) with foliage of a fresh light green. When the spiky white flowers fade, they become an attractive golden brown, remaining so through the winter.

'Mrs D. F. Maxwell' Is often partnered by 'Lyonesse' because both were introduced about the same time and both have become old favourites. This is a very beautiful free-flowering deep rose cerise of compact habit. Like many *vagans* cultivars it will have an eventual spread of 1.2 to 1.8 m (4 to 6 ft) if space is given though only reaching 45 cm (1½ ft) in height. It flowers from August until October on dark green foliage.

'St Keverne' Received an Award of Merit from the Royal Horticultural Society as long ago as 1914, but still remains one of the best. Clear salmon-pink flowers are a distinctive feature on 45-cm (1½-ft) compact yet vigorous bushes.

'Valerie Proudley' Of recent introduction has golden-yellow and white flowers, an attractive combination even though the plant lacks the vigour of the green types. The gold remains summer and winter on compact 30-cm (1-ft) plants.

Perennials

ALAN BLOOM

Hardy perennials are no longer a neglected subject in the gardening scene. The time is happily past when they were relegated in so many gardens because the rewards they gave were disproportionate to the trouble entailed. The conventional herbaceous border was largely at fault because of its long narrow shape with a backing wall, hedge or fence. The plants it contained suffered from overcrowding, weakly growth and excessive competition for light and air. Quite often such borders were too narrow in relation to the height of the plants they contained. All this accentuated the main disabilities to which perennials are prone if not given a fair chance – difficulty of access to a border and the need for supports.

The factor of adaptability must be reckoned with. The majority of kinds grown and offered by nurseries are adaptable to ordinary garden conditions, but it would be as much as mistake to plant something which is by nature shade or moisture loving into a dry open situation as it would the other way round. It would also be a mistake to plant as neighbours something rank or invasive with what is by nature of slow or lowly growth. The need then is to have some foreknowledge of the habits of what one wishes to grow and to avoid indiscriminate planting.

The principle to apply is that of making a selection of plants best suited to the place in which they are to grow. The range of subjects existing in gardens and nurseries is sufficiently wide for this to be achieved, no matter how small the garden, or unkind the soil, so long as it is not completely hemmed in by tall buildings or overhung by large trees to exclude both light and air.

Overcrowding and overhanging by trees or other taller growth inevitably leads to stem weakness, and plants in close competition for light and air becomes excessively tall and spindly. In the majority of cases where border staking is necessary, it is not the fault of the plants but of the conditions under which they are grown. Light and air are vitally necessary to sturdy growth for all kinds of plants that prefer sunlight, or an open situation as most perennials do.

Bearing in mind the need to make a selection of plants best adapted to the site, the preparation for a bed or border of hardy plants should include drainage if the soil appears excessively wet or sticky in winter or hard baked in summer. Thorough digging will mostly suffice, since the surface may have been panned down by builders' vehicles or machines. Summer and autumn are of course the best times for deep digging on heavy soil, which will enable winter frosts to break down hard lumps and clots into quite fine tilth for spring planting.

On both light poor soils and heavy clays, humus, in the form of peat, compost or farmyard manure, are recommended. These will improve the texture, as well as the fertility of the soil, and give plants such as good start that nothing but occasional topdressings of fertilizer will be needed for years. Heavy soil can also be improved by digging in sharp or coarse sand.

There is not doubt whatever that island beds give the best reward in terms of value for money and effort in maintenance. An island bed can be sited anywhere so long as all-round access is possible, even if it is only a narrow path on one side or end. It is quite feasible to convert a backed border into an island bed so long as there is sufficient width for no matter what the backing consists of, rear access can be provided either by a narrow path of grass or paving used as stepping stones.

If the backing is of a wall, it can be used

OPPOSITE: Perennials planted in island beds at Bressingham Gardens

127

for climbers and a strip allowed along the foot for bulbs or any of the wide variety of dwarf plants or climbers that like such a spot. The rear part of the bed itself should have, as edging groups, dwarf early-flowering perennials such as bergenias, pulmonarias, epimediums, for even if the border has a sunny aspect, the taller kinds of perennials facing the adjoining groups will provide for summer shading. This strip at the rear will prove a source of delight in spring and if colour has gone by summer, one has at least easy access to the rest of the bed for maintenance work, and there will be far less staking anyway, because the weakening effect of the backing is greatly lessened.

Only one-sided beds which are on a small scale, where heights of plants grown are in keeping with the effective width of the border, are worthy of consideration. If a garden admits of no compromise, or has no site suitable for an island bed, fair enough, but a one-sided border will inevitably be more troublesome to maintain unless a very careful selection of plants is made.

Whatever type of border one decides to plan and plant, its success and potential interest will depend not only on a well-chosen site, well-prepared soil and the right selection of plants, but on its width. The narrower the bed, the more restrictive one should be on the height of subjects grown. Nothing looks more incongruous than to see plants flowering at 1.2 or 1.5 m (4 or 5 ft) high in a bed only 1.2 or 1.5 m (4 or 5 ft) wide. A safe guide in making a selection of plants is to measure the effective or plantable width of the border, and halve this figure to

arrive at the maximum height of plants it should contain. This would restrict a 1.2-m (4-ft) wide border to plants of no more than 60 cm (2 ft) tall, but a little latitude or discretion could be allowed for the very erect spiky plants – such as kniphofias – to exceed the limit.

This is a rule that can apply to any type of border – island or one-sided – bearing in mind that in the former, the tallest are in the centre parts, and at the rear in the latter.

Grouping is another factor worthy of careful consideration. Where space is very restricted and where there is a preference for variety, then a case could be made for having only one plant of each kind – but grouping of subjects or kinds should on the whole be practised from say three of a kind together for a small bed of about 30 m² (100 sq ft) in area, to ten or fifteen plants for the largest beds up to a 305 m² (1000 sq ft) or more.

The average spacing to be recommended if good quality nursery-grown plants are used is about five to the square metre. If, for example, groups are of five plants of a kind, this gives a planting distance of about 40 cm (16 in) from plant to plant within a group. But the space around it, up to the outer plants in adjoining groups, should be more, say 50 cm (20 in). Spacing required depends of course on the spread or robustness of the subject. It can vary all the way from a single plant occupying a square metre in a few cases, to nine plants of some dwarf slow-growing subjects.

If in the process of making a new bed or border, an error in placing occurs, it will show up during the first flowering season and can easily be rectified then.

BELOW: The tallest plants should be placed towards the back of a one-sided border
RIGHT: In an island bed the tallest plants should be positioned in the centre, their maximum height measuring no more than half the width of the bed

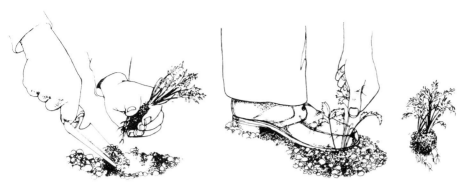

Planting a perennial:
FAR LEFT: Use a trowel to make a hole large enough to accommodate the rootball
LEFT: Firm the plant well

Selected Perennials

Acanthus

Acanthus are best placed in isolation in a sunny place rather than in a mixed border. *Acanthus longifolius*, *A. mollis* and *A. spinosus* will in time take up more than their allotted space as a group and then curbing becomes an annual task. Of the three *A. mollis* is the least satisfactory, flowering less freely than the other two. All have long classically jagged leaves, which die back in winter, of deep glossy green and from this welter of foliage arise spikes 90 cm to 1.2 m (3 to 4 ft) high of curiously hooded flowers of lavender lilac tinged with white. They prefer a well-drained soil, and a group can be very effective, especially as flowering lasts from early July onwards for many weeks.

Achillea

The yarrows or milfoils include a few good and very showy plants, but some of a weedy nature as well. All achilleas have serrated leaves which enhance the plant as a whole, and are flowers useful for cutting. They like a sunny position. *Achillea filipendulina*, with its plate-like heads of deep yellow on erect 2 m (4-ft) stems, is worthy of the popularity it holds. It is easy enough to grow in any well-drained soil, and needs the minimum of attention for years at a stretch. Usually offered under the name of 'Gold Plate', the stems, when cut at their best, can be dried for winter decoration. The cultivar 'Coronation Gold' is less tall than 'Gold Plate' and with smaller heads of deep yellow flowers. 'Moonshine' is much dwarfer and combines the best qualities of the species *clypeolata* and *taygetea*. It flowers from May to July, at about 45 cm (18 in), keeps its silvery backcloth for almost the whole year, and often throws a few late heads of glistening canary yellow in autumn.

A. millefolium is the Wild Milfoil of meadows and hedgerows. Deep pink and almost red cultivars, such as 'Cerise Queen', can make quite a brave show for a season or two before they need curbing or replanting back into position. Another disability is that the 90-cm (3-ft) heads become top heavy and often need supports. This applies also to the white achilleas, 'The Pearl' and 'Perry's White'. Both have double button-type flowers on loose heads, and grow up to 90 cm (3 ft). All achilleas should be divided in early autumn or spring.

Anaphalis

The anaphalis are no longer the neglected subjects they once were. This is because some have good ground-cover properties and will adapt themselves to rather harsh conditions. All are silvery grey and all have white or ivory flower heads of a crispy everlasting texture.

There is not much to choose between *Anaphalis margaritacea*, *A. nubigena* and *A. triplinervis* except in height. The first named is about 45 cm (18 in) high in flower and it carries a rather loose crop of branching heads. The other two are 23 to 30 cm (9 to 12 in) high, and all three have the virtue of surface spread unmarred either by unsightly fading or by an aggressive weedy nature in spite of fairly rapid growth.

Anaphalis yedoensis dies back in winter to a spreading root system but the new

Dividing perennial plants: some plants can just be pulled apart with the hands, but hard roots need to be cut through with a knife

shoots in spring are like silvery-white fingers. These run up to a good 60 cm (2 ft), making a solid bush of stems topped by papery white heads which are useful for cutting and drying.

Anchusa

Bright though anchusas are, I would not class them as good garden plants from a reliability standpoint, though quite well known under such names as 'Loddon Royalist', 'Morning Glory' and 'Opal'. The black fleshy roots send up large coarse abrasive leaves and spikes which carry a profusion of small but intensely blue flowers from late May to July on stems up to 1.2 m (4 ft) which mostly need supporting. After July there is a some-what blank space, and too often it is still largely blank next spring because plants have failed to survive the winter. The wetter or richer the soil, the more this is likely to happen.

Anemone

The anemones or windflowers are too diverse for any general remarks, and only one group will be mentioned covered by the name *hupehensis*, which was long known as *Anemone japonica*. No garden should be without these charming plants which can contribute so much to the late summer display. Though shades of pink and white are the only colours to be seen, it is the way their flowers are borne that makes for so much charm. Individual flowers ranging from 4 to 8 cm (1½ to 3 in) across remind one of the Dog Rose in shape, with yellow-stamened centres. From a base mass of vine-like leaves rise wiry, branching stems, tipped by nodding flowers and close set buds still to open. After a slow start in spring, most cultivars begin flowering in late July or early August and will continue until autumn has set in. Good drainage and a mainly sunny position are the only essentials to cultivation and they are especially good on chalky soil.

The tallest forms are white. 'White Giant' leads in both size of flower and height at 1 m (3½ ft), with 'Louise Uhink' very close. There is little to choose between some of the single pink cultivars such as 'Queen Charlotte', 'Max Vogel'

and 'Kriemhilde', which are about 76 cm (2½ ft) high. The semi-double 'Lady Gilmour' is much dwarfer, as are the deeper rose-pink 'Profusion' and 'Bressingham Glow'. These are only 50 cm (20 in) tall, which is the height of the single-flowered 'September Charm', a clear pink.

Anthemis

Most anthemis flower freely and for a long time, but their chief fault is that of a short life. The cultivars of *Anthemis tinctoria* are especially prone. The yellow daisy-type flowers come on somewhat twiggy and not very erect growth 60 to 76 cm (2 to 2½ ft) high from June to late August and, if the woody rootstock fails to produce new basal growth in autumn, there can be no survival.

'Grallagh Gold' is even trickier than the light yellow 'Wargrave' or 'Mrs Buxton', but the dwarfer species, *Anthemis sancti-johannis*, is, in my experience, much more reliable. It has the same deep green somewhat parsley-like leaves and the deep yellow flowers are carried quite neatly on 50-cm (20-in) bushes.

Armeria

The Common Thrift is *Armeria maritima* and it has produced some variations and hybrids of real garden value. 'Dusseldorf Pride' can be used as an effective edging for it will make a continuous evergreen row 30 cm (1 ft) wide within a year or two. The closely mounded deep green foliage is like sheep-grazed grass, and in May and June it is ablaze with 20-cm (8-in) drumstick heads of bright carmine pink.

The best clones of *Armeria maritima* 'Alba' serve a similar purpose, both for edging and grouping. The tallest, largest flowered and brightest is 'Bees Ruby' though the colour is in fact a deep carmine of lustred texture. Plants are mounded, much broader in the leaf than others, and the central root stem just below ground is so bare that division is seldom possible. Cuttings are not easy to strike, but some success comes from basal cuttings taken in early autumn or spring and inserted in a cold frame. Armerias need full sun and a very well-drained soil.

Artemisia

The wormwoods would not have any claims but for their foliage effect and the most brightly silvered, with the most finely cut leaves, are not very reliable in my experience, mostly because they dislike winter wet. *Artemisia nutans*, *A. discolor* and *A. splendens* run a little below ground and lose compactness after a year or two. They are best in a hot dry spot, and so is the semi-shrubby *A. nutans*. This is my preference amongst the silver-filigree species which have effective foliage up to about 30 cm (12 in) and very ineffective dirty white flowers above that height.

Another section, less silvery and less delicate of leaf, are decidedly more vigorous, so much so that curbing is necessary. These include *Artemisia ludoviciana*, *A. palmeri*, *A. pontica*, *A.* 'Silver Queen' and *A. villarsii* – useful amongst shrubs or on a dry bank but of little charm in a mixed border of perennials.

The only species I know that is worth growing as a border subject for its flowers is *Artemisia lactiflora*. This of course denotes milky white flowers, but the terminal heads of beady flowers are more of a creamy-ivory shade. These come on stiff-growing stems, reaching 1.2 m (4 ft) at least in the rich or dampish soil this splendid plant prefers and make a very effective, contrasting display in late summer and early autumn. It needs no staking.

Aster

The garden would be rather dull in autumn if no Michaelmas Daisies were to be seen. New cultivars have been produced over recent years and although decided advances have been made, enhancing the range of height and colour as well as the size of flower, it is purely a matter of personal preference when such a welter of choice exists. There is little point in my making recommendations, except to emphasize the need to keep to varieties which do not need staking, and to replant every three years, using only the outer healthier shoots.

There are many other asters in existence, apart from Michaelmas Daisies, which have been somewhat overlooked and which are virtually trouble free. *Aster acris*, for example, is a first-rate plant with myriads of starry, blue, yellow-centred flowers on bushy growth 76 cm (2½ ft) high in late summer.

Aster amellus, of which there are a number of cultivars, is long lived in well-drained soil. The cultivars grow erectly at heights varying from 45 to 76 cm (1½ to 2½ ft), with greyish leaves and woody stems from a compact rootstock. The best known is the violet-blue 'King George', but I like the deeper-coloured, very reliable 'Violet Queen'. Pink shades are not the easiest to grow, but 'Lady Hindlip' and 'Sonia' are amongst the best, whilst 'Nocturne', lavender lilac, and 'Lac de Geneve', light blue, more or less complete the colour range.

Aster × frikartii, a hybrid, grows taller at 90 cm (3 ft) than either of its parents (*A. amellus* and *A. thompsonii*). It has 5-cm (2-in) wide light lavender-blue flowers with the usual yellow centre on widely branching stems from July onwards for many weeks. *A. t.* 'Nana' is a splendid little plant which makes perfectly shaped greyish-leaved bushes up to 45 cm (18 in) or so, and set with 2.5-cm (1-in) lavender-blue flowers from July to October. It is slow growing, and quite reliable if grown in reasonably well-drained soil.

Aster ericoides is worth considering because it is neat and trouble free. The flowers are tiny, smothering the small-leaved and shapely bushes 76 cm (2½ ft) or so high in autumn. The colour range is limited; 'Brimstone' being a buff-yellow shade, 'Cinderella', lavender blue, and there is also 'White Heather'. *A. linosyris* is deep yellow, the flowers being carried on a terminal head like a bunch of little puffs. This species is August flowering, and a variant named 'Goldcrest' is a little later and a trifle more graceful. All asters are best divided in spring.

Astilbe

Astilbes grown in good soil with adequate moisture achieve perfection from every point of view as plants of incomparable beauty. Attractive wide-based foliage often mounds up to a shapely pyramid formation through which the plumed spikes appear of every imaginable shade from white through pink, salmon and cerise to fiery red and deep red. Some are erect, others arch and droop, and heights vary from 15 cm to 1.8 cm (6 in to 6 ft). None ever need staking and as plants they are completely hardy and can be left alone for years, trouble free and reliable, though they cannot stand hot, dry conditions. They respond heartily to mulching in spring, which of course conserves moisture, and all can safely be divided when dormant. In general, the tallest-growing astilbes are the strongest and least fussy about moisture, but these do not include the brightest colours.

One of the best of the taller kinds is *Astilbe taquetii* 'Superba', with imposing spikes, straight and strong, of an intense lilac-purple shade, about 1.2 m (4 ft) in height and at its best in July and August. *A. davidii* and the cultivars 'Tamarix', 'Salland', 'Venus' and 'Salmon Queen' are all quite tall and very robust with colours ranging from the pale pink of 'Venus' to the crimson magenta of *A. davidii*.

Given the right conditions, the more colourful range of dwarfer astilbes will provide a much longer flowering period. These are hybrids, growing from 45 to 90 cm (1½ to 3 ft) tall and flowering between late June and mid-August. 'Cologne', a deep carmine rose, and 'Dusseldorf', salmon pink, are about 60 cm (2 ft) high, as is 'Rheinland', early, clear pink, and 'Deutschland', a fine white. For reds of this height, 'Fire' is a very intense shade and 'Red Sentinel' is almost brick red. 'Glow', at 76 cm (2½ ft), is stronger and 'Spinell' is another fiery shade. The 76-cm (2½-ft) 'Federsee' is a rosy-red form and 'Bressingham Pink' has fine clear pink spikes. 'Fanal' is a deep red dwarf cultivar, barely 60 cm (2 ft) high, and another white cultivar of rare charm with dark green leaves is 'Irrlicht'. *A. simplicifolia* 'Sprite' has very dark foliage as background to the 30-cm (1-ft) spikelets carrying countless ivory-pink flowers like a cascade. This is a sturdy miniature of great charm.

The deeply divided foliage makes a big contribution to the beauty of astilbes and there is infinite variation in the shades of green to be found among them, including some of bronzy and purplish hue.

Bergenia

As space fillers for any but the hottest driest situations bergenias would take some beating. The large shiny leaves are almost evergreen – mostly dying off in late winter in readiness for the spring-flowering period of April and May, when the stubby spikes, from 23 to 60 cm (9 to 24 in) high, open to show a spray of little bell-shaped flowers. The usual colour is pink, rather washy in older species, but deeper, bordering on red, in such modern cultivars as the dwarf 'Abendglut' ('Evening Glow') and 'Ballawley', which is the largest of all. 'Bressingham White' is a free-flowering white form. Where flowering is less important, any *B. cordifolia* form or *B. × schmidtii* are cheaper to buy.

The value of bergenias is their bright foliage from May to March, and their ability to spread fairly quickly but unobtrusively in awkward places, almost regardless of soil, sun or shade and to smother most weeds.

Brunnera

The one species *Brunnera macrophylla* was formerly *Anchusa myosotidiflora*. It differs from most anchusas by being a good reliable perennial, with much less fleshy roots, forming clumps of rounded leaves, which have weed-smothering properties, all summer. In April, the sprays of tiny but brilliant blue forget-me-not flowers extend on low branching stems outward to make a pleasing display until June. In good or moist soil, plants become fairly massive.

A very bright-leaved form, 'Variegata', grows rather less robustly. The leaves are up to 15 cm (6 in) wide and more than half of each is a primrose shade. Flowering is similar to the green type, but for the sake of foliage effect it is best planted where hot sun does not scorch it.

Campanula

The bellflowers comprise a genus where a wide range of adaptability exists, as well as a range of height, from being prostrate to 1.5 or 1.8 m (5 or 6 ft) tall. With such diversity, recommendations will be easier to follow on the basis of height. Beginning with the dwarfest, the semi-prostrate hybrid *Campanula* 'Stella' can adorn not only a rock garden, a wall top, path edging or the front of a border, but makes a first-rate pot plant for an indoor or outdoor position. Its normal flowering time is June to August, but if cut back, divided when old, and re-vitalized it will flower again in autumn. Cultivation is easy in any reasonable soil, in sun or partial shade.

Almost any of the varieties of *Campanula carpatica* are valuable for frontal groups. They vary in height from 15 to 45 cm (6 to 12 in), having upward-facing, cup-shaped flowers 2.5 to 5 cm (1 to 2 in) across, are neat in habit and flower through June to August. Colours vary from white to violet blue and, though easy to raise from seed, one must obtain named varieties to avoid getting mixed shades.

Campanula burghaltii is distinctive for its near opaque smoky-blue bells, elongated in shape and dangling from 38 to 45 cm (15 to 18 in) stems. It flowers from June onwards from quite vigorous but not invasive plants. *C.* 'Van Houttei' is similar in habit with equally large bells of a pale blue shade.

Campanula glomerata has many forms. With all, the flowers grow in clusters, either as a terminal head or hugging the spike. The earliest is 'Joan Elliott' with fine deep violet-blue flowers on 38-cm (15-in) stems from May to July. Other dwarf forms exist, notably 'Nana' – both the white and mauve blue in this have flowers along the 30 to 45 cm (1 to 1½ ft) spikes for many weeks from early June, but the little 'Purple Pixie' does not begin until well into July. The best of the top-clustered group is 'Superba', which grows to 90 cm (3 ft), flowering June and July, with upturned violet flowers.

Campanula lactiflora is also variable. The deepest-coloured cultivar is 'Prichard's', growing leafily and erectly to 76 to 90 cm (2½ to 3 ft), with open clusters of bell-shaped flowers facing the sun. The pygmy of this long-flowering species is 'Pouffe', which grows outwards rather than upwards, making a green cushion for the light blue flowers from June to September. The tallest is 'Loddon Anna', reaching a rather precarious 1.8 m (6 ft), with heads of palest pink. The white

'Alba' is shorter, reaching 1.2 to 1.5 m (4 to 5 ft). All these, however, are reliable plants and will grow quite happily in shade as well as sun.

Campanula latifolia (syn. *C. macrantha*) is similarly adaptable and although its flowering season of June to July is briefer, it stands well, with strong spikes to 1.2 m (4 ft) or so carrying obliquely large pointed petalled bells. There is a good white 'Alba' and 'Brantwood' is deep violet blue, but the near opaque 'Gloaming' is of an entrancing pale sky-blue colour.

Campanula latiloba (formerly *C. grandis*) makes a surface mat of bright green rosettes and sends up 90-cm (3-ft) spikes on which saucer-shaped flowers are set for much of its length. The best form for colour and reliability is 'Percy Piper', with flowers of a deep china blue 8 cm (3 in) across. This type may need replanting every two or three years to ensure full flowering. But *C. persicifolia*, of somewhat similar habit, has greater faults.

It is prone to rust disease, and to die out sometimes from exhaustion. Stems are apt to topple over and self-sown seedlings to appear in wrong places. This is not to condemn it entirely, and it can be quite showy with large saucers for much of its 5- to 8-cm (2- to 3-ft) stems. Good cultivars are 'Snowdrift' and 'Telham Beauty', the latter a good blue.

The only double-flowered form that can be recommended appears to belong to the nettle-leaved campanula species *C. trachelium*. 'Bernice' is of obscure origin but it is reliably perennial, growing uprightly to 60 cm (2 ft) from a compact rootstock. The double powder-blue flowers cluster on the stem in the months of June and July.

Catananche

Catananche caerulea, Cupid's Dart, is quite a popular subject, with a very long season of papery blue cornflowers on wiry stems. It reaches 60 to 76 cm (2 to 2½ ft) and in well-drained soil will flower for three months from June onwards. Its faults are lack of longevity and a tendency to loll over so that flowers droop rather than stand up to face the sky, especially in damp weather. It comes from seed sown in May, or root cuttings taken during March.

Centaurea

This is another genus that includes coarse as well as choicer species with heights varying from 5 cm to 1.8 m (2 in to 6 ft) or more. *Centaurea dealbata*, as a species, is not to be recommended when the much brighter, deep pink-flowered *steenbergii* is an improvement. 'John Coutts' is another improved cultivar with even larger flowers of a lighter clearer pink shade. Both reach 76 cm (2½ ft) to flower freely in June to July, with ample greyish foliage. This is a vigorous, easy-growing type even in poor soil.

Centaurea macrocephala has yellow tufty flowers on plants to 1.5 m (5 ft) *C.*

hypoleuca is charming with a profusion of clear pink flowers on compact grey-foliaged plants. The stems are wiry, rising to 30 cm (1 ft) above and round the mounded foliage, to make a pleasing display from late May to July. *C. pulchra* 'Major', though sturdy in light well-drained soil, is a choice plant. It has jagged leaves of silvery grey unfurling to 30 cm (1 ft) or so in length, and then come ramrod spikes topped by handsome fluffy heads of a rosy hue in June and July to 90 cm (3 ft) tall.

Finally *Centaurea ruthenica*, which is distinctive for its shining deep green foliage, gracefully slender 1.2-m (4-ft) stems carrying very pretty canary-yellow, fluffy-headed flowers from June to August. The centaureas are easy but best divided in early spring.

Centaurea macrocephala

Centranthus

Many a garden would be the poorer without *Centranthus ruber*, Keys of Heaven, for it has the capacity for making good the neglectful use of a garden and can be seen naturalized on old walls as well as in old borders. If it seeds about, unwanted seedlings can be treated as weeds, leaving a group where it belongs to be self-replenishing. Flowering is profuse on 60- to 90-cm (2- to 3-ft) stems. The usual deep but rather dull pink heads are not especially attractive, a switch to the brighter red 'Coccineus' is advised, and if considered too common for a bed in which choicer plants are preferred, usually some odd dry corner exists where it can fill a need for colour.

Chrysanthemum

In the minds of many people, the name registers only as a florist's flower and though strictly the genus includes pyrethrums (p. 151), it also includes Marguerites or Shasta Daisies. The well-known *Chrysanthemum* 'Esther Read' was raised as a novelty when only single white-flowered varieties existed. Single white forms are still widely grown including the very large-flowered, lacy-petalled 'Thomas Killin'. 'Everest', large single white, 'Wirral Supreme', double white along with other doubles including the ineptly named 'Cobham Gold', as well as 'Esther Read' and 'Jennifer Read' still appeal. *C. corymbosum* grows stoutly to 1 m ($3\frac{1}{2}$ ft), carrying hundreds of 2.5-cm (1-in) wide white daisies, with greyish foliage, from June to August.

Cirsium

Cirsium rivularis 'Atropurpureum' is unmistakably a thistle, but it has no vices and is decidedly handsome. The long, not too prickly leaves hug the ground and the spikes topped by reddish-purple thistle blobs reach 1.2 m (4 ft), flowering from June to August, to give a good over-all appearance in any open situation.

Coreopsis

Coreopsis grandiflora is easily raised from seed in such cultivars as 'Sunray' and 'Mayfield Giant', but they deteriorate after one season's profligate show of deep yellow flowers, rather laxly carried on thin stems to about 60 cm (2 ft). The midget 'Goldfink' not only smothers itself in deep yellow, maroon-marked flowers on 20-cm (8-in) stems from June to September but mostly survives the winter as well. Hardiness is not in doubt, but if odd plants exhaust themselves, those remaining divide easily in spring to make replacements.

The most remarkable and distinctive coreopsis is *C. verticillata*, for it forms shapely 45-cm (18-in) bushes with an abundance of narrow foliage, decked with 2.5-cm (1-in) yellow-rayed flowers from June to late August. This sterling little plant is fully perennial with a slowly expanding rootstock and has a slightly deeper coloured edition in 'Grandiflora'.

Crambe

Crambe cordifolia is a decidedly ornamental species of sea kale, but too massive for a small mixed border. The leaf spread of a single fleshy rooted plant can exceed 90 cm (3 ft), and the much-branched spikes of white flowers even more, as well as reaching 1.5 m (5 ft) in height. The effect of such a profusion of flowers is quite startling during early summer but after that the space it has taken steadily becomes bare until another season.

Crepis

Though a member of the dandelion tribe, *Crepis incana* is a little charmer for a frontal position in full sun and very well-drained soil. The open flowers are mainly 2.5 cm (1 in) across and overall a soft pink shade, with silvery-grey mounded foliage that gives instant appeal, even if only about 25 to 30 cm (10 to 12 in) high, and flowers on and on from June to September.

Cynoglossum

These are long-lived, easy-to-grow members of the same family as anchusas. *Cynoglossum grande* is a trifle untidy but it makes a brave show of intensely blue flowers on 45- to 60-cm ($1\frac{1}{2}$- to 2-ft) stems in May and June. The sprays tend to become top heavy later on but cutting as flowering fades promotes more basal greenery and probably some more flowers as well. *C. nervosum* is a shorter and neater subject, inclined to be grey leaved on hummocky plants, above which come 25-cm (10-in) arching sprays of small but bright deep blue flowers from early June to August.

Delphinium

These majestic plants may be considered indispensable, but almost invariably they need staking in good time. They also need soil fertility for best results, and in some gardens slugs can be a menace. From seed sown under glass in spring it is possible for some plants to flower in late summer, otherwise sow out of doors to obtain stock to flower freely the following year after transplanting. Cultivars of flowering size are obtainable, but these will not flower true from seed, which mostly produces mixed shades of blue. A few strains come reasonably true especially in the shorter-lived Pacific Hybrids, having names taken from the Arthurian legends.

Belladonna delphiniums are less tall with more open spikes, and in their way are as attractive as the large-flowered forms. Such cultivars as 'Peace', 'Blue Bees' and 'Lamartine' are reliably good.

Diascia rigescens

A charming plant for mild districts, this has small rounded leaves and an almost endless succession of 45 cm (18 in) spikes of soft pink flowers. Easy to grow in any sunny position and worth protecting over winter in cold districts. Cuttings root readily.

Dianthus

The name covers both pinks and carnations. The latter are excluded but the former are garden favourites for both perfume and colour. There are a number of cultivars, mostly double, which include white, pink and red shades. These are increased by cuttings or divisions but from seed they throw singles as well as variable colours. All garden pinks are in the 15- to 30-cm (6- to 12-in) height range and much prefer an open position with well-drained soil, flowering from June to August.

Dicentra

The true Bleeding Heart, *Dicentra spectabilis*, has few faults as a hardy perennial, and it is worthy of a little extra fussing to give of its best. The lush foliage, the arching sprays dangling red and white lockets are a gladdening sight from April to June. The fangy but brittle roots should be planted carefully in well-drained soil, where some sun but not the worst of the winds can reach them. Division is tricky, but the vernal shoots, with a good base, will root in a cold frame.

Dicentra eximia (*D. formosa*) is a dwarfer plant which will spread below ground to give a mound of greenery and 30-cm (12-in) sprays of deep rosy-coloured flowers in early summer. There is a pretty, though less reliable, white form but the brightest and largest flowered is 'Adrian Bloom'. Flowers have twice the size of the type and much more colour as well as a longer flowering period. The white 'Pearl Drops' can also be well recommended. These are quite easy to divide and indeed are best divided and replanted after about three years in newly enriched soil. They will grow in sun or partial shade, and are less susceptible to gale damage than *D. spectabilis*.

Dictamnus

Dictamnus fraxinella, the Burning Bush, is a deeply rooting plant that likes full sun and perfect drainage where it will live for years to send up bush-forming spikes to 90 cm (3 ft) carrying a bright array of lilac-pink flowers from June to August. This is not a plant on which to attempt division, and from seed it is rather slow to reach maturity.

Doronicum

The leopard's banes are easy-to-grow subjects making a bright display of yellow in spring. The earliest to thrust up their widely rayed yellow daisies are the dwarfest. *Doronicum* 'Goldzwerg' reaches only 15 cm (6 in) from late March to May followed quickly by the 38-cm (15-in) 'Miss Mason'. This is the height of the fully double-flowered 'Spring Beauty', an outstanding form. 'Harpur Crewe' is the tallest, with wide-rayed flowers on 90-cm

Dicentra spectabilis

(3-ft) stems. Doronicums are easy to divide (preferably in early autumn) and respond to such replanting every few years.

Echinacea
Echinacea purpurea (syn. *Rudbeckia purpurea*), the purple cone-flower, has a special appeal with its somewhat drooping petals accentuating the cone from which they radiate, on stems up to 1 m (3½ ft). Cultivars as well as variable seedlings are offered but the best-known form 'The King' is not in my opinion the best garden plant. The colour is deep purple rose on stems apt to need supports. 'Robert Bloom' is a much warmer rosy-red shade, and it should not need staking. The strain from which this

was selected, 'Bressingham Hybrids', has only slight variations in colour. All give their best display from July to September. Echinaceas like good deep soil, well drained but not too dry, and can safely be divided in early spring.

Echinops
Without exception, the deep-rooting globe thistles are reliably hardy and perennial, but one or two are too massive for small gardens. All have greyish, jagged and slightly prickly leaves and branching stems to carry rounded flower heads of mainly light blue.

Echinops ritro grows erectly to 90 cm (3 ft), is a deeper blue, and is less troublesome than the taller, more massive kinds. *E. humilis* is amongst the larger ones and includes the 1.5-m (5-ft) 'Taplow Blue' and the 1.2-m (4-ft) 'Blue Cloud'. 'Veitch's Blue' is less robust at 90 cm to 1.2 m (3 to 4 ft), and has deeper blue flowers, but all these look somewhat shabby after flowering ends by late August, so that one is tempted to cut them hard back to encourage a tuft of new leaves instead. Old plants are easier to divide than to dig up, and roots left in the ground will mostly sprout again.

Epimedium

The barrenworts are valuable for pretty ground-cover foliage which lasts for most of the year and follows the dainty flower sprays in spring. Though adaptable, light shade is what they prefer, and quicker growth spread comes where not too dry. Roots are increased by dividing in autumn. Foliage effect is freshly green in all cultivars, but flower colour varies, from yellow in *Epimedium per-ralderianum*, orange in *E. × warleyense*, pink in *E. macranthum* and *E. rubrum*. The white *E. youngianum* 'Niveum' is the dwarfest at only 15 cm (6 in) tall. The stems support the foliage like a canopy, and though a new set of leaves is made every year, it is only during early spring, when flowering time comes, that foliage is absent.

Epimediums have a great potential in the modern way of gardening, which accounts for their steady rise in popularity. But although they are adaptable to some of the less hospitable shady places, they do respond to kindness with an occasional mulch with peat and added fertilizer.

Erigeron

The fleabanes are useful members of the daisy family, giving a good display from May to August, and some are excellent for cutting. They are happy in open positions, in any well-drained soil and are best increased by division in spring. The most reliable include the cultivars 'Schwarzesmear', which is single flowered, violet blue, 50 cm (20 in), and 'Foerster's Liebling', near double, bright pink, of similar height. 'Lilofee' and 'Adria' are lavender blue, 76 cm (2½ ft), 'Prosperity', light lavender blue, 50 cm

(20 m), almost double. 'Amity', lilac pink, 60 cm (2 ft), 'Gaiety', single, pink, and 'Sincerity', mauve blue, single, are long flowering and 'Dignity' is violet blue. The old cultivar 'Quakeress', pale lilac pink is still garden worthy, though not erect growing in a confined space.

Eryngium

By comparison with most flowers the sea hollies are freakish, as all have flowers without visible petals. In some the stems are as brightly coloured as the flower bracts and in others the flowers and leaves are both green. Such species as *Eryngium serra*, *E. bromeliifolium* and *E. pan-danifolium* grow from large green rosettes of vicious-looking, saw-edged leaves and send up stiffly branching spikes tipped by green spiny thimbles as flowers.

Eryngium alpinum is very handsome, with rounded green leaves and sturdy 76-cm (2½-ft) stems crowned with large, whiskery, silver-blue flowers. *E. bourgatii* is reliable. This is very silvery with a tinge of blue in the 50-cm (20-in) stems as well as in the terminal bract. *E. variifolium* has marbled evergreen foliage. This reaches 60 cm (2 ft) and *E. dichotomum* is also good on somewhat similar lines. *E. planum* is easy, green and leafy except for the blue flowering tips, but these are not so bright as in the widely branching *E. tripartitum* which is the best of this group growing 90 cm to 1 m (3 to 3½ ft). Some eryngiums will come from seed, but the usual method of increase is from root cuttings in spring.

Eryngium alpinum

Euphorbia

This vast and varied genus includes oddities, weeds and a few good garden plants. All have bracts or clustered flower heads and the characteristic white sap in the leaves and stems. *Euphorbia characias* and *E. wulfenii* are so much alike for garden purposes that they can be described together. They are sub-shrubs, with year-round, blue-grey foliage of a succulent nature, and slowly build up into imposing plants 90 cm (3 ft) high or more till they startlingly burst into almost a fountain of sulphur-yellow heads of flower in spring. These are scarcely plants for an ordinary border, but they look well with shrubs or on a wall. They prefer privation to richness, and though old plants may die out and severe winters may reduce them to pulp, there are usually sufficient self-sown seedlings around to refurnish the group. These are best transplanted when quite small.

One of the best of all spring-flowering herbaceous plants is *Euphorbia polychroma* (syn. *E. epithymoides*). It is very sturdy and hardy and remains compact, producing heads of bright sulphur-yellow bracts in April and early May. These reach 45 cm (1½ ft) by the time they begin to fade to green, and remain a neat bush of foliage until autumn.

Given an open site *Euphorbia griffithii* 'Fireglow' is a very good plant, with slow-spreading shoots from below ground that come through at first like asparagus to show the deep fiery heads in May and June. Afterwards these too fade into the greenery of a stiff shapely bush, 45 cm (2½ ft) high. *E. niciciana* makes a splendid show of sulphur yellow for many weeks of summer. Wiry stems with narrow leaves terminate in flattened heads to form a bush about 60 cm (2 ft) high from a compact rootstock. It is best in well-drained soil and full sun.

Euphorbia robbiae makes a wealth of deep green leaves and occasional flower heads with effective leaf cover at 25 to 30 cm (10 to 12 in) high. *E. amygdaloides* and *E. macrostegia* are on similar lines – deep green foliage and a reasonably rapid spread, but these are more suitable amongst shrubs than in a perennial border.

Gentiana

The name gentian has become so closely associated with alpines and rock gardens that many people are surprised when they learn that some species grow to 1.2 m (4 ft) high. In between the true alpine and these tall and not very special herbaceous species, there are a few first-class garden plants, of which one outstanding example is the willow gentian, *Gentiana asclepiadea*. This carries deep blue trumpets on slender stems about 60 cm (2 ft) high in late summer, but is much better in cool shade than in fully open or dry positions. It dies down in winter to a compact root

which dislikes being moved, much less divided. In just the right conditions it will naturalize.

Too little use is made in frontal border groups of the summer-flowering gentians of which *G. septemfida* is best known. Although none exceed 23 to 25 cm (9 to 10 in) in height they make such a wonderful show and are quite happy in ordinary soil, with or without lime. All have bright blue trumpets clustered on somewhat lax, leafy stems, and all much prefer to be left alone once planted.

Geranium

True geraniums, crane's bills, are hardy garden plants, and the majority are of the easiest culture with many adaptable for both sun and shade. *Geranium armenum* (a name preferable to *psilostemon*, now said to be correct) will grow up to 90 cm (3 ft) in a dense bush given ample moisture as against barely 60 cm (2 ft) where starved and dry. The flowers, over 2.5 cm (1 in) across on wide branching stems, are fiercely magenta from June to August, but 'Bressingham Flair' is less intense, with more pink showing in the flowers.

Geranium endressii forms dense mounds of light green, and sprays of light or bright pink make a good show in June and July, about 50 cm (20 in) high. 'A. T. Johnson', 'Rose Clair' and 'Wargrave Pink' are all pink with not much variation. *G. grandiflorum* spreads too quickly for what it gives in flowers, but 'Johnson's Blue' is very good indeed. It smothers itself in early summer in wide, blue, saucer-shaped flowers, and reaches a height of 45 cm (1½ ft). *G. ibericum* (syn. *macranthum*) *platypetalum* is taller at 60 cm (2 ft) or so, dark of leaf and a rich deep blue in flower.

Geranium renardii is a little charmer, in spite of its having a rather brief period in flower. The flowers are shallow cups of lightest mauve blue, marked with delicate crimson veins within. These disappear in June under a 25-cm (10-in) canopy of greyish leaves, downy and stippled and so remaining until autumn.

Geranium sanguineum spreads, though not to become a nuisance, and has a long succession of magenta-rose flowers in the solid twiggy-stemmed mound it makes, only 30 cm (1 ft) high, and there is a white form, *album*, also a good pink known as *lancastriense splendens* which makes a 30-cm (12-in) mound and keeps flowering for about ten weeks.

Geranium sylvaticum 'Mayflower' is among those that flower in May and June with light blue salver-shaped flowers nestling above the very pretty canopied foliage of buttercup shape, on 50-cm (20-in) stalks. Deeper blue flowers come for several weeks on the densely spreading mounds of the uncommon but easy *G. wlassovianum*. This covers the July to September period and is worth a place where space is not restricted though the root itself is compact. Deep and inhospitable shade will not prevent the 60-cm (2-ft) *G. phaeum* from flowering in May and June. It is best cut back after flowering but *G*. 'Claridge Druce' is longer flowering and evergreen with purple-rose flowers for several weeks, and will also grow in dry shade.

Geum

The best-known cultivars are the least reliable as perennials, but for reliability *Geum borisii* deserves a high rating with its intense orange single flowers on 30-cm (1-ft) stems above leafy plants in May and June and sometimes later. The shortest lived are the popular double red 'Mrs Bradshaw' and double yellow 'Lady Stratheden'. These flower very freely, but after a couple of years they lose vigour and die in most gardens.

Other hybrids of value, though all will need replanting and dividing every two or three years to retain vigour, are 'Fire Opal', orange red, and 'Rubin', deep red, which both grow to about 60 cm (2 ft). 'Georgenberg' is single yellow, long flowering and hummocky in growth, height 30 cm (1 ft), April to June, whilst 'Lionel Cox' is similar but soft yellow. *G. rossii* is a distinctive species, neat growing with somewhat carrotty foliage, and in May and June it sends up 23-cm (9-in) sprays of bright yellow.

Gillenia

Gillenia trifoliata is a subject for good moist soil, with or without shade, in which grace and charm compensate for lack of brilliance. Erect willowy leaved bushes grow to 90 cm (3 ft) to give open panicles of small white flowers from June to August. Its roots are tough, long lived and trouble free.

Gypsophila

The tallest but still popular Baby's Breath is not an ideal border subject because of its floppy habit. The double-flowered 'Bristol Fairy' has little advantage over the single, longer-lived type. Both are charming in their way, with clouds of tiny pure white flowers, but the fangy rooted plants need space, as well as free-drained soil, in which to make their expansive display in late June to September. There is a dwarfer neater double-flowered cultivar named *Gypsophila* 'Compacta Plena'. This makes a mound 45 cm (1½ ft) high and 60 cm (2 ft) across and is to be preferred in a mixed bed or border. Two dwarfer double pink forms exist. One is 'Pink Star', with small pale pink flowers on mounded growth to 45 cm (1½ ft) and the more prostrate 'Rosy Veil'.

Helenium

The sneezeweeds are quite indispensable for providing a rich display of colour, but neglect can cause some disappointment. As plants become old, starvation makes leaves wither to spoil the flowering effect, and this can only be corrected by dividing and replacing every three years or so in enriched soil. Heleniums are very easy to grow, but do best in fully open positions.

The tallest forms should be avoided and browny reds as 'Bruno' and 'Moerheim Gem' are in the 1.2-m (4-ft) range of heights, for July to September flowering, with 'Butterpat', a good yellow. Earlier sturdy forms are 'Bressingham Gold', 'Coppelia', 'Gold Fox' and 'Mahogany', all with orange and browny-flame shades. 'Golden Youth' is a fine clear colour, about 76 cm (2½ ft), and 'Wyndley' is also quite dwarf, parti-coloured. The dwarfest, under 60 cm (2 ft), is 'Crimson Beauty', but the colour is brownish red. Division of heleniums is safe in early autumn or spring.

Heliopsis

These have obvious family connections with heleniums, but they can be left alone for several years and relied upon to flower freely unsupported. All forms are basically yellow, tinged green in 'Goldgreenheart', to the rich buttery yellow of 'Golden Plume'. Both are semi-double flowered, and two good single cultivars are 'Ballerina' and 'Desert King'. The branching stems produce a long display of 8-cm (3-in) flowers from June to September, on a somewhat bush-forming habit of growth with ample greenery to about 90 cm (3 ft).

Helleborus

The true Christmas Rose has a never-failing appeal even though it seldom opens in time for Christmas. But January–February flowering is exciting enough to make this a very desirable plant, though it is best placed in shade, not where overhung or very dry, preferring a cool position. Old plants do not move or divide at all well, and young seedling plants do best.

Helleborus niger is followed in time of flowering by a complex range which includes the Lenten Rose, *H. orientalis*. This varies in colour from white to deep pink and even plum-purple shades. Flowering shoots appear long before winter is over and in March and April they can prove a real joy, with their up-turned, saucer-shaped, golden-stamened flowers, up to 8 cm (3 in) across, on 30- to 45-cm (1- to 1½-ft) stems. The annual change of leaf takes place as flowering fades, with the broadly fingered foliage, freshly green at first, making a 30-cm (1-ft) canopy for eleven months of the year. The *orientalis* hybrids – seldom available to name or colour – are most rewarding. A colony or just a few plants can permanently fill an odd corner of the garden even where it becomes quite dry in summer, so long as it is not sunbaked. *H. abschasicus* a very early plum-purple species and *H. viridis* has green flowers.

Helleborus corsicus makes quite a show of pale greenish-white flowers on 60-cm (2-ft) stems in spring. A somewhat more compact and reliable hybrid exists named *H. sternii* and this has the same saw-edged leaves, but of a darker green as well as whiter flowers than *H. corsicus*.

If hellebores in general are not altogether suitable for a summer border, they fit in well amongst shrubs, which can provide the shade they like, and the 60-cm (2-ft) tall *H. foetidus* can fill a really inhospitable place in dry shade to the extent of becoming naturalized, even though it is not long lived, after a full spring flowering of greenery has taken place.

Heuchera

Heucheras have that rare combination of compact well-foliaged evergreen growth and a show of brightly coloured flowers carried daintily on sprays or spikes for several weeks in early summer. Many have very pretty leaves, shaped much like the geraniums, in varying shades of green, sometimes with darker zonings.

The stems are thin and wiry, varying from 38 to 76 cm (1¼ to 2½ ft) high, and the number of individual flowers, small and bell shaped on a well-grown plant, run into hundreds. Colours range from white to every shade of pink, through to scarlet and red including coral, salmon and coppery crimson. Heucheras must firstly have good drainage, and are best in sun or only partial shade. They flower better for being enriched, yet they are drought resistant. Crowns become woody with age, and the remedy, often needed every three to four years, is to mulch deeply with soil or compost, or to dig up and replant deeply, using only the most vigorous shoots and discarding older woody growth.

Several cultivars are available, true to colour, but Bressingham Hybrids are a mixed strain giving a wide colour range. They do not come true from seed and division is best after flowering ceases in July. 'Scintillation', bright pink, tipped coral, 60 cm (2 ft); 'Sparkler', carmine and scarlet, 60 cm (2 ft); 'Splendour', salmon scarlet, 60 cm (2 ft); 'Red Spangles', 50 cm (20 in); 'Pretty Polly', soft pink, 38 cm (15 in); 'Hyperion', strong growing, coral rose, close-packed spike, 76 cm (2½ ft), and 'Greenfinch', greenish white, 76 cm (2½ ft), are all recommended.

A traditional
herbaceous border

A traditional herbaceous border

× Heucherella

× *Heucherella* 'Bridget Bloom' is a splendid little plant for fairly good light soil, preferring a little shade, and has been known to flower almost as freely in autumn as at its normal period of May and June, with a profusion of light pink sprays 38 cm (15 in) high. This and *H. tiarelloides* are hybrids between a heuchera and tiarella. The latter gives good ground cover with soft, slightly golden leaves and sends up in April and May a display of 30-cm (1-ft) foamy pink spikes. This is an easily grown plant for any but hot dry positions.

Hosta

The plantain lilies have indeed come into their own of recent years because all are such good garden plants, possessing hardiness, adaptability, reliable growth and good foliage, coupled with pleasing overall appearance. They will grow in shade or sun so long as their roots can find moisture and nutriment. In any but parched or starved conditions they can be left for years to develop into solid clumps. Ideally they are happiest in cool shade, especially those with variegated leaves. All lose their leaves at the onset of winter, and can be divided when dormant.

Hosta crispula has handsome creamy-buff marginal-edged leaves, with lavender-mauve flowers in June to August on 90-cm (3-ft) stems. This is the period when most hostas flower, but *H.*

Hosta sieboldiana

fortunei and its cultivars are earlier than others. The type has large pointed blue-green leaves and 60-cm (2-ft) stems carrying pale lavender flowers. *H. f.* 'Picta' comes through in spring with bright and very attractive variegations which last until flowering at mid-summer before turning green. 'Honeybells' is a green-leaved form, with 76-cm (2½-ft) spikes, freely produced, carrying sweetly scented lavender trumpets. *H. lancifolia* is a likeable plant, shapely of growth, with narrow, deep green leaves overlapping and having a fair show of 50-cm (20-in) spikes in late summer. *H. rectifolia* is a splendid free-flowering plant growing to a stately 1.2 m (4 ft), with lavender-mauve spikes.

The name *Hosta sieboldiana* is still to some extent in dispute because some consider *H. glauca* to be the correct name. There is a glaucous-leaved type which is less distinctive than the massive *H. sieboldiana* 'Elegans'. This also has pale mauve flowers but the spikes reach 90 cm (3 ft) and the leaves are up to 45 cm (1½ ft) across. Then there is what I call *H. s.* (or *glauca*) 'Coerulea'. This has large but more rounded leaves, and they have a more definite bluish hue, though the flowering is very similar.

'Thomas Hogg' – a form raised over a hundred years ago – is virtually identical with *H. albo-marginata*. The glaucous leaves are very large, inclined to be rounded and with a creamy-white edge – the 60-cm (2-ft) spikes carry mauve flowers. This is not very different from *H. crispula*, and they are certainly alike in preferring a place away from strong sun and wind to look their best.

Hosta undulata 'Medio Variegata' has brightly variegated leaves all summer. It is much smaller than most hostas and the deep mauve flowers are on 30- to 45-cm (1- to 1½-ft) spikes. *H. ventricosa* is easy and reliable. It flowers freely in July–August, with deep lavender trumpets on 90-cm (3-ft) stems. The leaves are deep green, but in *H. v.* 'Variegata' they have streaks of yellow which, with a free-flowering habit, make it one of the most attractive. The new cultivar 'Royal Standard' is green leaved with perfumed white flowers 76-cm (2½-ft) tall and is a welcome addition to the range.

A welter of interesting hybrids and species are now being offered from such miniatures as *H. venusta* and *H. tardiflora* to larger ones including the free flowering *H. rectifolia* 'Tallboy' and 'Frances Williams'.

Incarvillea

Once the deep fangy roots decide in early May to sprout, growth is rapid and startling. Within two or three weeks, the exotic-looking trumpet flowers of deep reddish pink begin to open. The deeply cut dark green leaves follow, and in the case of *Incarvillea delavayi* the stems reach 60 cm (2 ft) or more before the last flowers fade in early July. *I. mareli* begins flowering almost at ground level and seldom exceeds 30 cm (1 ft). Well-drained soil and sun is much preferred.

Inula

This is another genus of yellow daisy flowers, all of which have rayed petals. *Inula barbata* makes a fairly quick spread of soft leafy mounds on which 4-cm (1½-in) flowers nestle for many weeks after June, and *I. hookeri* is similar, but about twice as tall at 76 cm (2½ ft), with larger flowers. 'Golden Beauty' is neat growing and long flowering. It forms 60-cm (2-ft) upright bushes, and the yellow flowers keep coming from June to September.

Inula ensifolia 'Compacta' is a most useful little plant for frontal positions and is long lived and trouble free, and although *I. orientalis* grows only to 50 cm (20 in) or so, the flowers are 8 to 10 cm (3 to 4 in) across and very finely rayed. All inulas are easily increased by division and need no special treatment. *I. rayleana* has even larger flowers, whilst *I. magnifica* reaches an imposing 3 m (6 ft) in height.

Iris

The most popular section of iris is the *germanica* or June-flowering cultivars. There is a welter of cultivars in existence in a fascinating range of colours. Whilst agreeing that they make a glorious display, their period of glory is short. This is the chief fault also of so many kinds of iris, but there are some that help in spreading the flowering season. *Iris*

Planting the rhizomes of *Iris germanica*

pumila, for example, is at its best in April and May, in shades of yellow, blue and white, and all are under 30 cm (1 ft) in height.

Iris foetidissima is the wild Gladwyn Iris with deep evergreen foliage, and it will grow in quite deep shade. One seldom notices it flower, but cannot fail to notice the vermilion seedpods in autumn as they burst open. There is an excellent variegated form of this very useful plant, as there is of the old *I. pallida*, the Poor Man's Orchid of cottage gardens.

Iris missouriensis is easy and attractive and makes a bright display of light blue flowers on 60-cm (2-ft) stems, as does *I. beesiana*, and the deep blue *I. setosa* is also good value. All these flower for most of June and July.

Kirengeshoma

Kirengeshoma palmata is a native of Japan and it has waxy-looking flowers like small daylilies of soft yellow for many weeks in later summer, nodding over a mass of light greenery. The leaves are fingered and of nettle type but the whole plant has a distinctive appearance, at once bushy and graceful, reaching 90 cm (3 ft) high where moist. It likes a humus-rich soil, some light shade and no lack of moisture and though it makes no brilliant display, it is the type of plant one feels glad to have.

Knautia

Knautia macedonica (syn. *Scabiosa rumelica*) cannot be faulted on the score of distinction and long flowering, though it does not usually survive for more than about three seasons. It makes considerable mounded growth from a fairly small rootstock and gives a long display of deep red pincushion flowers from June to September. The habit is lax, and should be left that way for the best effect, because it will at least give ground cover at about 50 cm (20 in), and the short-stemmed flowers rise just above this.

Kniphofia

All red hot pokers like a sunny open position, and the range is now so wide that the six months from May to October can be covered, whilst heights range from 45 cm to 3 m ($1\frac{1}{2}$ to 6 ft) when in flower.

Many cultivars are no longer offered because of a virus disease and to make recommendations might be misleading. There are however hopes of some becoming immune. One of these is the charming dwarf 'Little Maid' only 60 cm (2 ft) tall with creamy yellow flowers. Also still available: 'Fiery Fred' a flame colour, 'Ada' a pure yellow, 'C. M. Prichard' a tall, late, deep orange and *K. caulescens*. The latter has large glaucous rosettes and a display of red and yellow pokers in September and October. The disease appears not to affect the hybrid strains raised from seed, but as they do not breed true to colour a mixture must be expected. Those with grassy foliage are likely to be dwarfer than those with broad leaves. Good drainage is essential for all.

Liatris

This is a showy, distinctive perennial. An unusual feature is that the bright lilac-purple furry flowers begin to open at the top of the 76- to 90-cm ($2\frac{1}{2}$- to 3-ft) stems, in contrast to nearly all other spiky plants. The species *Liatris callilepis* is most often listed, but those who order *L. spicata* or *L. pycnostachya* will be sent much the same plant though there is a dwarfer form in 'Kobold'. Flowering begins in June and lasts several weeks, especially on young plants. Old plants are best dug up in spring and rejuvenated by division into enriched soil.

Libertia

There are several species in existence, but even the best known *Libertia formosa* is not often seen. Plants make quite a packed mass of narrow evergreen iris-like fans but from a mainly fibrous root, and through this come 60-cm (2-ft) spikes of open-petalled white flowers in June–July. Hardiness is not a strong feature with libertias, and they thrive best in light soil and need a sunny place. *L. ixiodes* is shorter than *L. formosa*. Divide in spring.

Limonium

The most reliable is *Limonium latifolium* and it makes a large plant with a fair spread of shining leaves and wide branching 60- to 90-cm (2- to 3-ft) sprays of tiny blue flowers from July to September. For drying, cut stems before fading begins. Cultivars are offered in 'Blue Cloud' and the deeper blue 'Violetta'. These deep-rooting plants should be in a well-drained, open position.

Linum

The blue *Linum perenne* is not very perennial, seldom living beyond two summers. *L. narbonnense* is much longer lived, so long as the soil is very well drained and where happy it is one of the finest of dwarf border plants. The flowers are richly blue and 2 cm ($\frac{3}{4}$ in) across and are borne on narrow-leaved bushes about 50 cm (20 in) high, giving a brilliant show for ten weeks or more from June to September. The yellow linums also prefer sun and good drainage.

Linum dolomiticum makes a compact root and sends up erect stems to about 45 cm (18 in), crowned with a wide cluster of brightest yellow rounded flowers 2 cm ($\frac{3}{4}$ in) across from mid-June to late August. *L. campanulatum* and *L. flavum* are on similar lines but dwarfer.

Liriope

This name is seldom listed in hardy plant catalogues, but *Liriope muscari*, especially, is a first-rate plant. It forms a hefty tuft of narrow deeply evergreen leaves through which appear, from August till late October, little pokery 38- to 45-cm (15- to 18-in) spikes like grape hyacinths of a bright lilac-mauve shade. With small tubers amid the densely fibrous root system, it is fairly impervious to drought and is hardy and long lived.

Lupinus

Ranking as they do amongst the indispensables to be seen in practically every garden, little need be said about them here. The supply is now virtually confined to seed raised plants. Some are more or less to colour, under distinctive names, but the whole range is available as a mixture in the still popular Russell Lupins. Lupins prefer neutral or acid to alkaline soils, but do not revert, as some people imagine. Deterioration is due to self-sown seedlings taking the place of those originally planted.

Lychnis

Lychnis chalcedonica is a good perennial, making a compact plant and producing leafy stems capped with a head 60 to 90 cm (2 to 3 ft) tall of small but intense red flowers in the June–August period. *L. coronaria* is silver-grey leaved, and has loose sprays of pink or carmine flowers for a long period. This showy plant is best in a dry place, but will produce seedlings to make up for being rather short lived. *L. viscaria* in the double form 'Plena' has flowers on sticky 25-cm (10-in) stems of a very bright deep pink. Plants are neat growing with deep green narrow leaves, flowering June–July.

Macleaya

These easily grown plants make strong spikes up to 1.8 m (6 ft), with powdered stems and pretty leaves which are brownish beneath and bluish above, and sprays of tiny flowers in late summer. In the true *Macleaya cordata* the flowers are more definite – little ivory-white tubes 1.3 cm ($\frac{1}{2}$ in) long and as a background plant – by itself or against a dark background – it is very effective.

Macleaya microcarpa has a wider branching spike, but the flowers are of a brownish yellow, to be appreciated as a whole and not for individual florets. The name 'Coral Plume' was given to a slightly more colourful variation. The somewhat fleshy roots tend to wander and shoot up amongst neighbouring subjects unawares, though they are not difficult to check or eradicate. Both types will grow in quite dry soils.

Meconopsis

Few plants have achieved such an aura as the blue Himalayan Poppy and, as *Meconopsis baileyi*, common usage has stood firm against the more recently imposed name of *M. betonicifolia*. Like all meconopsis, this needs light leafy soil and some shade, and spikes attain 90 cm (3 ft) where suited. It is not long lived, but comes freely from seed. *M. chelidonifolia* is easy and fully perennial. The fingery light green leaves hang from wiry stems up to 76 cm ($2\frac{1}{2}$ ft) tall and from June to August, 5-cm (2-in) yellow flowers dangle above.

Monarda

These have both colour and curiosity appeal. All grow from mat-forming plants that may spread rather quickly in rich or moist soil, and make leafy bushes varying in height from 60 cm to 1.2 m (2 to 4 ft) accordingly. The terminal heads are of bract-like flowers, with arching lipped petals in red, pink and purple shades. Named forms are best. 'Adam' is cerise red; 'Melissa', bright pink; and there is 'Croftway Pink', and the old favourite 'Cambridge Scarlet'. 'Prairie Glow' is salmon red, not so tall, and both 'Prairie Night' and *Monarda magnifica* are purple. Monardas respond to the rejuvenating effects of replanting every two or three years, best divided in spring and young plants flower longer, are less tall and are altogether superior.

Moraea

For those who seek worthy but uncommon plants, *Moraea spathacea* is one which is not at all difficult to grow. It forms clumps of iris-like leaves, and above during May and June come 60-cm (2-ft) stems carrying bright yellow flowers, not closely resembling iris in shape, but quite open petalled. It is long lived and trouble free in well-drained soil.

Morina

Morina longifolia has long spiny leaves in bright green rosettes like a thistle, but they are shiny and hairless. It also has a thistly tap root but the spike of 60 cm (2 ft) or so develops to show the drooping-lipped pink flowers. In sun and any well-drained soil it will throw flowering stems on and off all summer, even into November.

Nepeta

The popular species of catmint is *Nepeta mussinii* which gives such a long succession of lavender-blue flowers from 30-cm (1-ft) spikes, from grey-leaved clumpy plants. Though adaptable to sun or partial shade, winter losses occur where drainage is poor. Division is best in spring. A larger edition exists in 'Six Hills Giant' which has sprays up to 60 cm (2 ft) tall over the same June–September period. 'Blue Beauty' differs in having erect spikes of larger violet-blue flowers, 50 cm (20 in) tall and plants expand by creeping shoots below ground. *N. nervosa* makes a bright display of small blue flowers at only 30 cm (1 ft) given a sunny place.

Oenothera

The name Evening Primrose applies to the short-lived *Oenothera biennis*, but there are several fully perennial kinds that make a bright display with their big yellow cup-shaped flowers. *O. cinaeus* comes through in spring with bright parti-coloured leaves – buff, pink, purple red, but these fade to deep green as the loose sprays of rich yellow cups open. 'Fireworks' is a deep yellow similar in habit but with purplish-green leaves, as is 'Yellow River' with green foliage, and the 60-cm (2-ft) tall 'Highlight' has a neat basal growth of clustered rosettes which when older increase easily from division in early spring.

Oenothera linearis has smaller flowers on 45-cm (1½-ft) twiggy branching sprays and *O. glaber* is erect at 38 cm (15 in) and bright yellow. Both are good plants of somewhat similar growth. The most distinctive oenothera is *O. missouriensis* but it is virtually prostrate in habit. It makes a quite wide spread of greenery which from July to October has saucers 10 cm (4 in) across of light canary yellow. This needs sun and good drainage.

Omphalodes

One species is worthy of inclusion for although it is of very lowly stature it has real carpeting value in shady places. *Omphalodes cappadocica* has crinkly greyish-green foliage of about 15 cm (6 in) and sprays of tiny but brilliant forget-me-not flowers in April and May. 'Anthea Bloom' is sky blue and very free flowering. They are long lived, trouble-free plants for cool positions.

Origanum

This genus includes some that have aromatic foliage and are of culinary value. The true Marjoram is *Origanum vulgare*, and the neater-growing *O. compactum* makes deep green bushes 25 cm (10 in) high covered in tiny blue flowers in late summer. The golden-leaved form *O. v.* 'Aureum' has no flowers worth mentioning though the aromatic foliage has almost year-round brightness. *O. laevigatum* makes a pretty show of tiny purple-blue flowers on wiry branching stems 38 cm (15 in) high.

Paeonia

These are amongst the longest lived of all perennials. They should be planted with permanence in mind, space in which to expand, and in an open situation. Peonies like rich deep soil, and respond to mulching after a time. Old plants can be divided, with the careful use of a knife with which to separate the liveliest chunks. This should always take place in the August–October period. Planting depth is important. The new buds should rest 2.5 cm (1 in) only below surface.

Cultivars of the popular June-flowering period are legion. Some have huge flowers, in shades of pink, red and white, mostly double. Some are more fragrant than others, but most specialist catalogues give details of this point as well as of colour and height. Cultivars under the specific name of *Paeonia sinensis* can be had to cover the whole of June – both double and single flowered. Doubles and singles occur, with a more limited colour range, in the earlier *P. officinalis*. *P. lobata* is single flowered, intense orange red in the form 'Sunshine', but the earliest is the charming single yellow *P. mlokosewitschii*, which often opens in April. Other worthy single-flowered species are *P. smouthii* and *P. arietina*, deep pink, and the white *P. obovata*.

A single-flowered form of *Paeonia officinalis*

Papaver

For size of flowers Oriental Poppies, *Papaver orientalis*, can easily compete with peonies. For brilliance of colour, they can excel them but they are not so permanent nor do they have the merit of pleasing foliage to carry on, as do peonies, after flowering. All flower from late May until late June, but not all are capable of standing without support which should be provided as unobtrusively as possible.

The most erect I know is the blood-red 'Goliath', standing nobly at 90 cm (3 ft) or more, a whole range of new cultivars is offered in a wide selection of colours including brownish red, various shades of pink, also white. Some of the double flowered are rather floppy. These poppies like a very well-drained soil, not too rich. Their fleshy roots are deeply penetrating. After flowering, growth should be cut back so as to encourage new leaves, without which an unsightly bare patch may occur.

Penstemon

The showiest kinds are the least reliable as hardy perennials. Some are used as bedding plants by taking cuttings in late summer or autumn and keeping them under glass until planting out time in spring, when they quickly fill out into bushy plants to flower from July to October. Flowers are of trumpet shape, coming on spikes up to 76 cm (2½ ft) tall, with ample base greenery. In milder localities, the deep crimson 'Garnet' and blood-red 'Firebird' will mostly survive for several years, along with the clear pink 'Endurance'. These have smaller flowers, but are colourful and long flowering.

Phlox

These rank very high amongst the brightest and most indispensable of border plants. They are happiest in light rather than heavy or alkaline soil. Phlox are offered in a bewildering range of varieties but the newest introductions do not necessarily supersede older varieties. Recommendations include older varieties which have stood the test of time.

The best dwarf white is still 'Mia Ruys',

and for a taller one there is 'White Admiral' at 90 cm (3 ft) 'Mother of Pearl' is a vigorous, weather-proof pink suffused white of similar height. 'Prospero' is soft pink and 'Dodo Hanbury Forbes' is somewhat deeper with 'Windsor', a carmine-rose shade. 'Endurance', salmon rose; 'Brigadier' and 'Spitfire', orange salmon, and the intensely bright 'Prince of Orange' should not be missed.

The most reliable deep red is 'Starfire', with 'Tenor', an early-flowering blood red while 'Aida', 'San Antonio' and 'Vintage Wine' are good representatives of the magenta-purple range. The 'King', 'Parma Violet' and 'Marlborough' are recommended violet purples. In lighter lavender-blue shades 'Skylight' and 'Hampton Court' are good whilst 'Balmoral' has a tinge of lilac.

A much neglected section of phlox is *Phlox maculata*. The pure pink 'Alpha' and the almost white purple-eyed 'Omega' are the only representatives of this distinctive range. Flowers come on column-type trusses, up to 90 cm (3 ft) tall, from a spreading mat-like rootstock, and make a long standing display from early July onwards.

Physostegia

The so-called obedient plants are good garden subjects, all having tapering spikes and subsidiaries from lower down and they remain in flower for several weeks. *Physostegia speciosa* 'Rose Bouquet' has a profusion of light rosy-lilac flowers on 60-cm (2-ft) spikes from July to September, but the dwarfer 'Vivid' flowers later, and is often at its best in October. The deep pink flowers make a bright display, but the shooting roots wander so widely that it pays to round them up every spring to replant back where they belong.

The others including the pretty white 'Summer Snow' and the deeper rose-pink 'Summer Spire' belong to *P. virginiana*, and have more slender spikes about 90 cm (3 ft) high. These flower from July to September, and have a vigorous rootstock consisting of spreading whitish crowns which tend to fall apart when lifting, and in moist or rich soil need curbing after two or three years. They are

reliably perennial and need no special treatment.

Platycodon

When the buds of *Platycodon grandiflorum* expand, the petals are joined together to form a hollow globe of about walnut size, changing into saucer-shaped campanula-type flowers. As garden plants the Balloon Flowers have real merit. They are long lived, having quite fleshy roots, and need only well-drained soil. Heights vary from the 30-cm (1-ft) *P. g. mariesii* in shades of light blue to 60 cm (2 ft) with the tallest clones of *P. grandiflorum* available in white, blue and very pale pink. Plants are slightly variable in colour, but old plants will divide. Dormancy extends till April, and newly emerging shoots can be damaged by winter and spring cultivations if the exact site of plants is not marked or seen.

Polemonium

Some of these are short lived and seed about to become a nuisance. More reliable and seldom setting seed, *Polemonium foliosissimum* is not only a good perennial but has a much longer flowering period, sometimes lasting from June until September, growing to 76 to 90 cm ($2\frac{1}{2}$ to 3 ft), with heads of lavender-blue, bird's-eye flowers.

Polemoniums are not fussy plants, and when old can be divided to promote rejuvenation. This applies especially to the dwarfer quite vigorous kinds, such as the light blue 'Sapphire', flowering in May and June at 38 cm (15 in) and the 25-cm (10-in) 'Blue Pearl' makes a clumpy growth and has slightly bronze-tinged foliage, but the flowers are well short of a true pink. The common name of polemonium is Jacob's Ladder.

Polygonum

Most knotweeds have pokery spikes made up of tiny flowers so closely set together that the spike itself is the colourful part. In the robust *Polygonum amplexicaule*, the spikes are thin, topping a rounded dense bush of pointed leaves, reaching 1.2 to 1.5 m (4 to 5 ft) high and at least 90 cm (3 ft) in diameter. The dull red form 'Atrosanguineum' and the lighter,

brighter red 'Firetail' can be recommended not only for reliability, but for a three-month flowering season.

Polygonum bistorta 'Superbum' is worthwhile. The stems run up to 90-cm (3-ft) or so, carrying 10-cm (4-in) stumpy pokers of a clear light pink in May and June. *P. carneum* grows more compactly, with smaller but deeper pink pokers during June and July.

From narrow-leaved tufts come bottle-brush heads for weeks of the startling red-flowered *Polygonum milettii*. *P. macrophyllum* has long wavy deep green leaves and branching stems 45 cm (18 in) high of clear pink pokers from July onwards. To make a trio of the choicest polygonums, *P. sphaerostachyum* must be included. Low dense bushes intricately branched show their bright rosy-pink pokery heads in late spring and where happy continue to make a bright show all summer. All three are slow growing as plants, all like good moistish soil, and much prefer shade to an exposed position. Some other polygonums are of a weedy nature and should not be used in gardens indiscriminately.

Potentilla

For rich colourings, long flowering and reliability many of the potentillas rank highly. They are mostly dwarf plants, easy to grow in any ordinary soil, and all have a good base of foliage, either green, grey or silvery, of strawberry shape.

Potentilla atrosanguinea has silvery leaves, vigorous growth and sprays of 2-cm ($\frac{3}{4}$-in), bright red flowers. 'Flamenco' is similar but larger flowered and green leaved, carrying sprays up to 60 cm (2 ft). Both flower from May to July, but it is from June to September that the more prostrate but equally brilliant 'Gibson's Scarlet' takes over. 'Firedance' is orange salmon, 'Miss Willmott' is pink, and good semi-double flowered cultivars are 'Glory of Nancy', orange and red; 'William Rollisson', flame orange, and 'Yellow Queen'. All grow about 45 cm ($1\frac{1}{2}$ ft). Potentillas are easy in open positions and can be divided in autumn or spring.

Prunella

These easy-to-grow plants, with the common name of self heal, are useful for frontal positions, and need only occasional replanting or curbing. Under the name 'Loveliness' can be obtained white, lilac and pink shades. From mat-forming plants come stumpy spikes 23 to 25 cm (9 to 10 in) high in June and July to make a bright if rather brief display. *Prunella × webbiana* is a little later with deep green mats and 23-cm (9-in) spikes of deep pink flowers.

Pulmonaria

These spring-flowering plants, the lungworts, are pretty adaptable, and can be effectively used in places one can more or less forget when summer comes. The brilliant blue little bell-shaped flowers of *Pulmonaria angustifolia* 'Azurea' come on 23-cm (9-in) sprays from March to May and 'Munstead Blue' is a little dwarfer and later to flower. *P. saccharata* is much more coarse, and even the red-flowered 'Bowles Red' takes up space with large rough leaves. Those with prettily white spotted leaves are effective even when flowering is over and 'Pink Dawn' is worthwhile, having flowers pink at first, on 30-cm (1-ft) sprays, which fade to blue, to give at times a two-colour effect without excessive growth.

Pulsatilla

Pulsatilla vulgaris is widely variable in both height and colour though basic features are constant. The Pasque Flowers are deeply rooting plants, which in early spring send up goblet-shaped flowers with silvery gossamer surroundings, followed by grey-green ferny leaves which last on through summer. Plants become larger with age but do not spread. Flowering ceases in May and is followed by prettily tufted seed heads. Colours range from pale lavender to purple, and include white and ruby red, with prominent golden stamens, reaching 23 to 30 cm (9 to 12 in) in height.

Pyrethrum

These brightly coloured daisy-type flowers are decorative from late May till July but unless planted with ample light and

OPPOSITE: *Campanula glomerata* (foreground) and *Polygonum bistorta* (pale pink)

shorter at 76 cm (2½ ft). Deeper shades are 'Rose Queen', 'Wensleydale' and 'Croftway Red', at 30 cm to 1.2 m (3 to 4 ft). All have small, mallow-type flowers and when finished spikes should be cut back to promote new basal growth which will carry them over winter.

Sisyrinchium

Sisyrinchium striatum is one of the most adaptable of plants. The growth is very much like that of *Iris germanica*, of a flattened fan of sword leaves, but without tubers. The flowers, unlike iris, are open petalled on 60-cm (2-ft) spikes from June to August. In spite of the small amount of fibrous root made by this plant it will grow in quite inhospitable soils and situations, as well as amongst fussier subjects and tends to naturalize itself from seed. There is a rarely seen and very pretty form with variegated leaves.

Solidago

Some species and named varieties too of golden rod are far too tall and invasive for good gardening, and one would do well to omit any that grow over 1.2 m (4 ft) tall, including 'Golden Wings'. 'Mimosa' will reach 1.2 m (4 ft), but the plants grow compactly and do not seed about, as do some, after the handsome yellow plumes have finished in September.

Those growing less than 1.2 m (4 ft) are worth having, though all have the fault of a rather short flowering season. The range of colour varies from the deep yellow of 'Golden Mosa', 'Golden Shower', or 'Golden Falls' to the lighter shades of 'Lemore' and 'Leslie'. All these grow about 76 to 90 cm (2½ to 3 ft) varying somewhat in the shape of the plume and flowering between July and September. 'Peter Pan' is earlier with distinctive lateral branches to the crested plume. 'Crown of Rays' is on similar lines, but very bushy in habit as well as being dwarfer at 60 cm (2 ft), whilst 'Cloth of Gold' is only 45 cm (1½ ft) tall, with a vigorous outward spread.

The neatest-growing dwarfs are the miniatures, 'Queenie' and 'Golden Thumb'. They do not differ much from each other and form bright almost golden-leaved bushes 23 to 30 cm (9 to

12 in) high, flowering from August to October. Although so easy to grow, these better solidagos are best planted or divided for replanting in early spring.

Stachys

The species *Stachys lanata*, with its felted silver leaves to which the Donkeys' Ears name has stuck, is an easy-growing, mat-forming plant seen in most gardens with its thin spikes of small pink flowers in June to July. It has ground-covering properties in quite dry positions, and for those who prefer a complete foliage backcloth, the non-flowering 'Silver Carpet' is available.

Stachys macrantha is a charming, easy-growing plant which produces bushy greenery topped with short spikes of rosy-purple lipped flowers in June to July, 60 to 76 cm (2 to 2½ ft) tall. *S. spicata* 'Rosea' has 30-cm (1-ft) spikes of deep pink and in the form 'Densiflorum' the flowers are closely packed on 38 cm (15 in) stems. This is a showy plant, as is the sturdier 50-cm (20-in) 'Robusta'. All these are long flowering and easy to grow and divide in autumn or spring.

Stokesia

Stokesia laevis has wide open semi-double blue flowers. Where happy, in deep light soil, the 5-cm (3-in) flowers come in long succession on 45-cm (1½-ft) branching stems from early July to September. The leaves are long and leathery, but the plant itself does not spread much, and old plants can be divided in spring. There are slight variations in shade from seed, but the cultivar 'Blue Star' has proved to be the most reliable.

Strobilanthes

Strobilanthes atropurpurea is a little known but trouble-free plant which has a stout long-lived rootstock. Twiggy branching stems carry small greyish leaves from a dense bush about 1 m (3½ ft) high on which appear small violet-purple lipped flowers from July to September. It makes no great show, but is interesting and distinctive. Old plants will divide in spring, and are best planted in fairly rich soil.

Stylophorum

Stylophorum diphyllum has rich yellow poppy-like flowers 3.8 cm ($1\frac{1}{2}$ in) across which nestle amongst a profusion of glaucous-green leaves in spring to make this an attractive subject for semi-shady situations, where not too dry. The somewhat fleshy roots have a fairly vigorous spread though not to become a nuisance for they can easily be curbed. Height 23 cm (9 in) when in flower with leaves fading in autumn.

Telekia

Telekia speciosa (syn. *Buphthalmum speciosum*) is a hefty, deep-rooting plant making a wide spread of broad leaves and demanding more space than the 90-cm to 1.2-m (3- to 4-ft) spikes of yellow daisy-type flowers deserve. It has a short season in flower, during June to July, and though easy to grow, there are other subjects, such as heliopsis, which will provide a longer better display in a smaller space.

Tellima

This is an unpretentious plant, grown mainly for its soft carpeting foliage rather than its 60-cm (2-ft) sprays of greenish-buff flowers in May to June. *Tellima grandiflora* 'Purpurea' has rounded, mounded leaves of a bronzy-purple tinge, and is to be recommended for its adaptability to shady positions where more colourful subjects will not grow. Plants divide readily and planting is safe in autumn or spring.

Thalictrum

Without exception, meadow rues respond to fertility and all dislike drought. The so-called Hardy Maidenhair, *Thalictrum minus adiantifolium*, is the easiest to grow, but it is by no means showy, having buff-green flowers on 76-cm ($2\frac{1}{2}$-ft) sprays. The tiny leaves are pretty, and this feature is shared, in varying forms, with all the species. The stately *T. angustifolium* has deep green deeply divided foliage beneath the fuzzy flower heads on strong 1.8-m (6-ft) stems. This flowers from June to August, as does the blue-grey *T. glaucum*, with fluffy heads of light yellow.

The earliest to flower is *Thalictrum aquilegifolium*. This is another easy-to-grow species, with bluish-green foliage, which comes into flower by early June. The strong stems are branched and they carry fluffy heads in shades of mauve and purple. There is also a pure white, and all grow to 90 cm to 1.2 m (3 to 4 ft). *T. dipterocarpum* makes a much smaller rootstock than the above, but sends up, where happy, a vast amount of rather lax top growth. This consists of small-leaved, much-branched stems which, if supported, will reach 1.8 m (6 ft). This species has individual flowers of mauve blue with orange stamens, and remains in flower from late June to September. 'Hewitt's Double' is not so tall and is less vigorous, and in greater need of rich moistish soil to give of its charming best.

Thalictrum rocquebrunianum is robust, with stems both strong and thick of a purplish glaucous hue. From the tip up to 1.2 m (4 ft) high, and from lateral branches, are borne the 1.3 cm ($\frac{1}{2}$-in) wide, lilac-coloured flowers with prominent yellow stamens from June to August. It needs rich soil to give of its splendid best. Most species will divide.

Thermopsis

With strong resemblance to its cousin the lupin, thermopsis is a long-lived plant for a sunny position and well-drained soil. The best known *Thermopsis montana* is, in my opinion, far from being the most worthy, for it runs underground and will not keep to its allotted space. The yellow-flowered spikes, on 60-cm (2-ft) stems, are less imposing than either *T. lanceolata* or *T. mollis*. Both these are light yellow with a compact bushy habit reaching 90 cm (3 ft) high, with the former flowering in May and June, and the latter in June and July. Old plants do not easily divide and roots are tough.

Tovara

Tovara virginiana makes a shapely bush up to 90 cm (3 ft) high, on which the flowering spikes are so thin that it makes a rather dull display. The form 'Painter's Palette' seldom flowers, but it is well worth growing for its foliage alone. The leaf shadings are subdued, but soft and pleasing and given a moist, sheltered position, it will grow to a shapely 76 cm

$(2\frac{1}{2}$ ft) retaining its effect till winter comes. Plants are slow growing but long lived and trouble free.

Tradescantia

There is nothing choice about the trinity flowers or spiderworts, but they flower for a long time. Rushy leaves and stems up to 60 cm (2 ft) carry clustered heads of three-petalled flowers 1.3 to 2 cm ($\frac{1}{2}$ to $\frac{3}{4}$ in) across in quite bright colours. Cultivars include white, light blue, mid and deep blue as well as purple and magenta, and smaller-flowered doubles exist as well. Flowering begins in June, but by August they may be looking tatty, and are best cut back to freshen them, and to prevent seeding which can be a nuisance. They have the merit of adaptability to varying soils and situations.

Tricyrtis

These are known also as toad lilies and in their way are quite charming given some shade and a not too dry and light humusy soil. They have lily-shaped flowers, often with curious inner markings. All grow from short creeping rhizomes just below the surface and have slender stems on which the pointed leaves are wrapped.

Tricyrtis macropoda is fairly vigorous with buff-white flowers which have purple markings, and soft light green leaves. *T. stolonifera* has shiny deep green leaves *T. hirta* and *T. flava* have flowers of a yellowish hue. The slender but erect stems reach 60 cm (2 ft) or more and one needs to pause to examine the intricate colour markings of mauve and purple. All the above flower in later summer and remain in flower for several weeks.

Trillium

These, too, are woodland plants for a light humus-rich soil, and a shady position. They have a unique charm but few nurserymen are able to offer them. The best known is *Trillium grandiflorum*, the North American Wake Robin, which in spring sends up smooth stems topped by a ruff of leaves on which sit pure white, three-petalled flowers 3.8 cm ($1\frac{1}{2}$ in) across which are effective from mid-April to mid-May.

Perhaps the most sought after of all double white flowers is the form 'Plenum', and no wonder. This rarity has perfection in form and lasts unspoiled for a longer period than the single – reminding one of a small pure white camellia *T. ovatum* is an early single white and *T. erectum* has reflexed white petals.

Trillium chloropetalum is spectacular with its mottled leaves and plum-red flowers in April on 45-cm (18-in) stems. *T. sessile* is of similar height and not far off the same colour, but the petals stand erectly and the leaves again just below the flowers are quite broad. *T. nervosum* is quite vigorous with a greater increase of crowns than those above. The flowers are pink on 30- to 38-cm (12- to 15-in) stems in April–May. Left alone in the right conditions, these trilliums will form quite large clumps, and produce more flowers as they expand.

Trollius

Though not for hot dry positions, the globe flower can add much to the garden scene in early summer. The vital period when plants need moisture for their tress-like fibrous roots is after flowering has ended, and for the rest of summer. Mulching with peat helps greatly and cuts down the need for watering. The lush green leaves emerge in early April and flower buds top them within two or three weeks. The globe effect appears just before the buds open.

Trollius europaeus 'Superbus' is a reliable light yellow, 60 cm (2 ft) tall, and 'Canary Bird' is paler and larger flowered. 'Goldquelle' has large mid-yellow flowers with 'Orange Princess' and 'Fireglobe' good representatives of the deeper shades. The dwarfest of the *europaeus* range is the very pale yellow 'Alabaster'. The distinctive *T. ledebouri* should not be missed. The petals open to reveal an upstanding crest of stamens of egg-yolk colour and stems reach 90 cm (3 ft), flowering in June to July. *T. pumilus* grows only 23 to 30 cm (9 to 12 in) in early summer, with shining yellow flowers.

Veratrum

Though the false hellebores cannot be regarded as colourful they always appeal. Broad-ribbed basal foliage and statues-

Trillium sessile

que pokery spikes up to 1.8 m (6 ft) have black, greenish or off-white flowers for a long time. They also live a long time without attention and though preferring cool deep soil are surprisingly adaptable, once safely established. The best-known species – and about the only one available from nurseries – is *Veratrum nigrum*, which is almost black, 1.2 to 1.5 m (4 to 5 ft) tall and at its best during June and July. *V. album*, greenish white, and *V. viride*, yellowish green, are also in cultivation.

Verbascum

Although some of the brightest of the mulleins are not fully perennial or long lived, a collection needs such spike-forming plants to break up uniformity. The most reliable have the stoutest root-stock, thick and fleshy or tap rooted and for a good yellow *Verbascum chaixii* (syn. *vernale*) can be recommended. From a base of large pointed dock-like leaves, strong spikes rise to 1.2 to 1.5 m (4 to 5 ft) and the open-petalled flowers on both

terminal and secondary spikes give a good show for several weeks from June onwards. A dwarfer yellow species growing to 1.2 m (4 ft) is *V. thapsiforme* (syn. *densiflorum*).

'Gainsborough' is 90 cm (3 ft), lighter yellow with woolly grey foliage, but it is rather allergic to winter wet. The hybrid 'Golden Bush' is distinctive, reliable and long flowering, though individual flowers are small. The habit is bushy with very twiggy laterals and it grows only 60 cm (2 ft) high. The deep rose 'Pink Domino' grows to 1 m (3½ ft).

Verbascums do not need rich soil and in fact prefer sandy or stony soil with perfect drainage to survive the winter. All are increased, true to name or colour, from root cuttings taken in early spring.

Vernonia

The iron weeds have the distinction of being even later to flower than Michaelmas Daisies, but only the species *Vernonia crinita* is listed in catalogues, though others exist. From a stout fibrous-rooted clump rise strong erect stems carrying narrow leaves to reach 1.5 m (5 ft) or so by the end of summer and then from mid-October till well into November, the broad head of small purple flowers can be seen. It is not a spectacular plant, but in its way it is quite attractive and has no fads or vices.

Veronica

A genus that provides several good garden subjects, few of which are difficult to grow. The varieities of *Veronica teucrium* are all blue and make a bright display in June–July, ranging in height from the 30-cm (12-in) 'Shirley Blue'; 38-cm (15-in) 'Crater Lake Blue'; 45-cm (18-in) 'Royal Blue', and 60-cm (24-in) 'Blue Fountain', all of mounded or bushy growth topped with short spikes.

V. gentianoides is early flowering, at its best in May. Spikes come from mat-forming, shiny-leaved plants, and heights are 15 to 30 cm (6 to 12 in) white or light blue. *V. spicata* is also mat forming, but the flower spikes open in June and July. Silver-grey leaves and violet-purple spikes to 38 cm (15 in) are seen in *V. incana* and though 'Saraband' is much freer to flower, the leaves are less silvery, as is the case with the taller and less tidy 'Wendy'.

A deep pink-flowered cultivar is 'Barcarolle', and 'Minuet' has greyish leaves and lighter pink spikes; both grow to about 45 cm (18 in) tall; 'Snow White' completes the colour range.

Veronica exaltata is late flowering with tall leafy spikes of light blue to 1.2 m (4 ft). It is quite attractive, though sometimes needs supports. This does not apply to *V. virginica* which also grows strongly to 1.2 m (4 ft) but both the blue flowered and the pale pink 'Rosea' are soon over, and by far the most attractive is 'Alba'. This reaches an imposing 1.5 m (5 ft), with whorled leaves at intervals along the stem, which branches to carry white-flowered spikes from August to September.

Zygadenus

One or two species of this little known genus are now coming in for attention. They have a demure charm, with a spray of green-tinged white flowers on 30- to 45-cm (12- to 18-in) stems from a slowly increasing rootstock. The leaves are deep green, pointed and leathery, and flowering continues from June to September. *Zygadenus elegans* and the slightly larger *Z. nutallii* both prefer a sandy soil and will adapt to conditions of sun or part shade.

Annuals and Biennials

FRANCES PERRY

Annuals are plants which complete their life cycle from small dormant seeds through germination, development, flowering and harvesting all within the space of a year. Although their life span is thus short, measured against herbaceous perennials, shrubs and trees, they make up for this with a prodigality of blossom unsurpassed by any other group of plants.

Their bright, long-blooming qualities render them invaluable wherever quick colour is desired. They are particularly useful for new gardens the first season, hiding the bare soil beneath a carpet of flowers. In later years or in established gardens the potentialities are even greater; their uses extending to window boxes, hanging baskets and containers, as well as beds and borders.

Biennials are plants which take two years to complete their life cycle. Seed sown one season develops a rosette of leaves that year and flowers and fruits the next. Usually the seed of such plants is sown outside – in shallow drills in late spring. Later the seedlings are pricked out in nursery beds prior to being bedded out in the autumn. While many biennials are mainly used for bedding purposes (for example wallflowers and forget-me-nots) others fit into the annual or mixed border if used during their second season. Canterbury Bells and Sweet William are frequently used in this way.

Again, a number of perennials often make better plants or are less subject to disease when treated as annuals or biennials. Antirrhinums, for instance, are almost invariably treated as annuals and polyanthus, hollyhocks and double daisies as biennials.

Another advantage of using annuals and biennials is economic. They are easy to grow and seed is cheaper to purchase than plants. The hardy annuals may be sown where they are to flower and some of them start to bloom within two months of sowing. Half-hardy annuals have to be raised under glass and planted outside when all risk of frost is past. Their use thus presupposes the possession of a frost-free – preferably heated – frame or greenhouse.

Preparing the ground

Although annuals have worldwide distribution, many of those which have become most popular with gardeners appear to be native to central and South America and South Africa. Their brilliant colourings seem in some way to be linked with the sunshine of their native lands. Background knowledge of indigenous conditions often provides clues as to treatment and generally speaking monocarpic plants do best in good soil and open sunny situations. With few exceptions flower beds solely devoted to annuals, window boxes, or groups of annuals in mixed borders should be sited in open positions and away from trees or hedges which can draw up the stems.

For best results the ground should be prepared in autumn; cleared of weeds and deeply dug. Organic material should be incorporated through the top 30 cm (12 in) to provide a reservoir of food and hold moisture in summer, but this must be well rotted. Farmyard manure, garden compost, leafmould and moist peat are all suitable. When this rots down to friable humus any type of soil, regardless of its original nature, will benefit in tilth and texture.

Because of their adaptability there is a common misconception that annuals do best in poor soil. This is not so. They will grow in a fashion on poor land, but there is no comparison between the resultant plants and those raised under more favourable conditions.

OPPOSITE: Annuals dorotheanthus (mesembryanthemum) and petunias with echeverias in a patio setting

If biennials are to be good, it is equally important that they too be grown in good soil. Stocks and Canterbury Bells particularly require fertile land. Others, such as foxgloves, honesty and meconopsis, need moist soil but prefer light shade in summer.

Once the border is adequately prepared hardy annuals will be sown in the positions where they are to flower and half-hardy kinds planted out from pots or boxes when weather conditions allow.

As with herbaceous border plantings, bold groups of the same plant create the biggest impact, so quantities of the same variety must be grown in order to make a show. Unlike permanent bedding, however, it is not essential that each group of plants should be the same shade. Very fine patchwork effects can be obtained by using mixed coloured eschscholzias – for instance – in one block, variously hued linarias in another – and so on.

Sowing hardy annuals out of doors
Ideal sowing conditions obtain when the soil is moist and the ground has been raked to a fine tilth beforehand. The smaller the seed – and annual seed is often very tiny – the more important this becomes. If soil particles are in contact with one another, the film of moisture surrounding each is readily available to the first, all-important plant roots. Large

particles and loose shifting soil make for air pockets and if seedlings fall into these they soon dry up and perish. Tread the ground beforehand therefore if it has been recently dug and then rake it down to a fine, smooth, even tilth.

Unless the plants are intended for cutting purposes avoid sowing annuals in straight lines. A good idea is to mark out individual areas beforehand, making these informal but running into each other like a jigsaw puzzle. Sometimes it is enough to draw lines with a hoe for this purpose or sand can be used to make a bolder outline. If each section is labelled with the name of the intended occupant it is easier to work methodically, sowing as one goes and also reserving spaces for the half-hardy annuals which cannot be planted out until later in the season.

Seed can either be scattered broadcast within the prescribed areas and then lightly raked in, or a pointed stick can be used to trace narrow drills. Sow thinly and later fill in the drills with the head of a rake – held in an upright position so that the teeth cannot dig into the ground and the seeds are only just covered. Water if necessary.

When the seeds germinate weed between the rows and then thin the seedlings to 2.5 cm (1 in) apart. If they are to develop to full size and maturity a second and more drastic thinning will be

Before sowing, mark out and label sections for each different kind of annual

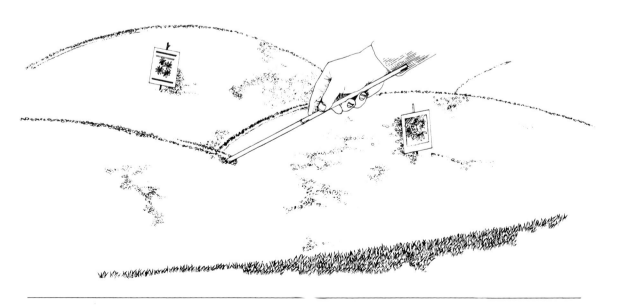

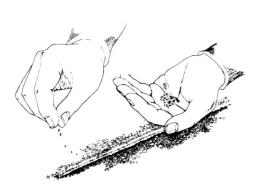

FAR LEFT: Seed can be sown in a shallow drill

LEFT: Weak-stemmed plants can be supported with peasticks. These will hardly be visible when the plants are fully grown

necessary. This final spacing will be determined by the type of plant and its spread and ultimate height, but as a rough guide, plants growing 30 cm (1 ft) in height under good conditions should be thinned to about 15 cm (6 in) apart; those of 45 cm (1½ ft) to 23 cm (9 in) and any 60 cm (2 ft) or thereabouts left 30 cm (1 ft) away from neighbours. Most annuals are self-supporting, but weak-stemmed varieties or plants in windy positions can be made secure with the aid of twiggy peasticks.

Keep the hoe going to eradicate weed seedlings and loosen the soil until the plants have grown sufficiently to render this unnecessary. Late germinating weeds will then be smothered at birth and any survivors can just be pulled out by hand.

The sowing of hardy annuals takes place out of doors in late spring (April to May in Britain). Typical of plants which can be treated in this manner are Shirley Poppies, Virginian and Night-scented Stocks and Nasturtiums. For details see under individual headings.

Autumn sowing

On well-drained soil and in favoured situations, hardy annuals are frequently sown out of doors the autumn prior to flowering. If all goes well – and it is a calculated risk, for winters are always unpredictable – they make stronger plants and bloom earlier than those raised in spring.

The beginning of September is the best time to sow in Britain; a little earlier in cooler climates and slightly later in warmer areas. The prospects of success are improved if cloches are placed over the seedlings in severe weather.

Although all annuals are not suitable for autumn sowing the following may be tried with reasonable success: calendulas, larkspurs, sweet peas, nigellas, eschscholzias, cornflowers, annual scabious, godetias, clarkias and linarias.

Sowing under glass

Half-hardy annuals are prone to frost damage, so to give them a good start they are first raised under glass, then potted separately or spaced out in boxes, and finally put outside in their flowering positions when the weather improves. In Britain it is usually safe to do this at the end of May or early in June – a week or two later in northern Europe or the north eastern states of northern America.

Growing temperatures will naturally vary according to the type of plant, but the hardier kinds for outdoor planting will do quite well in a frame or greenhouse from which frost can be excluded. Tender annuals will need temperatures of approximately 15 to 18°C (60 to 65°F) later.

In all cases the soil should be light and friable. Equal parts of coarse sand (or perlite), good sifted loam and peat moss or sphagnum moss provide the foundation of most home-mixed composts. Alternatively one can buy packaged composts, which have the advantage of added nutrients. John Innes Seed Compost is commonly used in Britain or General Purpose Soil in the United States.

Convenient, clean to touch and capable of excellent results are what are known as loamless, peat based composts. These are light to handle, but tend to dry out more rapidly than soil composts and once dry are difficult to remoisten unless the pots are stood in pans of water. Again, loamless composts should not be pressed down hard or the roots will not be able to penetrate them, nor should plants be left long in them without regular feeding. Another alternative is to sow seeds, or transfer seedlings to Jiffy 7s. These come as hard flat peat rings, but after soaking swell up to small flower pot-like receptacles. When the plants are ready to go outside they are planted just as they are, after loosening the net covering.

The containers, whether pans, pots or boxes, must be scrupulously clean and crocked if there is only one drainage hole, with a little peaty material above the crocks to prevent blockage. They should be filled with damp compost. Firm lightly and leave a smooth finish.

Now sow the seed thinly and cover it with silver sand or finely sieved compost. Label the pots and stand them in a shallow bath of water so that the liquid is just below the rims. Leave them there until the soil surface looks damp. This method does not dislodge the seed as much as top watering with a can.

Remove the containers to a frame or greenhouse and cover them with glass and a sheet of newspaper. The glass must be turned daily to prevent too much condensation and both coverings removed when germination takes place.

When large enough to handle prick out seedlings 60 to 90 cm (2 to 3 in) apart in boxes or pot them separately and grow on.

Biennials

Biennials are sown outside in shallow drills in spring or early summer (normally between April and June) for flowering the following season. Some, like meconopsis and primula, should be sown directly after harvesting as the seed deteriorates with keeping. The procedure is similar to that of hardy annuals except that the plants are raised in sheltered nursery beds and planted in their flowering positions in early autumn or the following spring. They are lined out 15 to 23 cm (6 to 9 in) apart in rows 30 cm (1 ft) apart.

Selected Annuals and Biennials

Annuals and biennials for containers

Annuals are ideal for containers of all kinds, but particularly window boxes, jardinières, strawberry jars, patio pots and tubs. Many remain in flower for weeks – even months – their bright colours cheering sombre spots and masking dull features.

Where window boxes are used they must always be securely fastened and ideally should be 2.5 cm (1 in) wider than the sill and have wedges pushed under the front edges so that they tip slightly backwards. Drainage holes are not essential if plenty of drainage material (crocks covered with rough peat) is placed in the bottom and they are carefully watered. Loose liners are the ideal for as each crop of flowers becomes shabby these can be lifted out and changed in minutes by previously prepared replacements.

Window boxes can also be fastened to brackets secured to boundary walls, which affords interest and provides more space and colour in very small gardens. Arrange them at different levels for a more artistic effect.

Hanging baskets have many uses. They can be hung from rafters in sun lounges, pergola arches and over doorways or the flat-backed kinds may be fixed to house walls. These again must be very secure and lined with moss or green plastic sheeting (with a few holes pierced round the sides about 2.5 cm (1 in) up from the base to avoid waterlogging after storms) to conserve moisture in dry weather.

Tubs full of annuals, urns and pots can be stood about in various situations or a strawberry pot used to mask an obvious and inconveniently sited drain cover.

A tub of annuals makes an attractive garden feature

Stand terracotta strawberry pots in large saucers and fill these with water daily. This is the best method of watering. The polyester and glassfibre types should not be filled too full as these have no drainage holes and being non-porous have to be watered from the top. Feed all container plants occasionally – foliar sprays are ideal in summer – and change the soil annually.

F_1 hybrids (first cross seeds) are preferable in some instances but not invariably, as the larger flowers produced can suffer in storms and windy situations.

Alyssum

Alyssum maritimum, now more correctly *Lobularia maritima*, is the familiar Sweet Alyssum so popular for edging window boxes, borders and beds or for growing in pavement crevices. Strictly a perennial, it is invariably grown as a hardy annual and flowers continuously from June until October. Growing 15 to 23 cm (6 to 9 in) high, it has tufts of small pointed leaves and racemes of white, honey-scented little flowers. Cultivars with pink and violet flowers are available. Seed can be sown where the plants are to flower in spring or raised earlier under glass and after

hardening off planted outside towards the end of May. Germination takes about five days.

Bellis

Bellis perennis is the English Daisy, a perennial which has produced a number of fine double forms. These come true from seed when treated as annuals or biennials. The flowers are large and showy on 13- to 15-cm (5- to 6-in) stems, the colours white, pink or red and the simple oval leaves ground hugging. Seed is sown in June, when they are treated as biennials, in a nursery plot outside and, after thinning and growing on, the young plants are set in their flowering positions in early autumn. They can also be raised under glass, by sowing seed in June or July and transferring the seedlings – by stages – to 10-cm (4-in) pots. Daisies like rich, moist soil and flower out of doors from May to July. They can be used in beds as well as containers, or as carpets in light shade beneath trees, or grown as cut flowers.

Dahlia

Dwarf bedding dahlias are often treated as annuals and make useful container plants with a flowering season extending from June until frosts cut them in early autumn. Seed production does away with the chore of overwintering the tubers and the results are reasonably predictable and true to type. Treat them as half-hardy annuals and pinch out the growing tips when the plants are 8 to 10 cm (3 to 4 in) high to induce a bushy habit. The seedlings should be separately potted and when weather conditions allow may be turned out and planted. They need full sun and rich soil, with plenty of water, and the occasional feed in the growing season. The most suitable races for container work are such kinds as the double Dwarf Early Bird Mixture or Unwin's Dwarf Hybrids; both in bright colours and about 30 cm (1 ft) tall. If singles are sought any of the Coltness types are ideal although they are taller (38 to 45 cm [15 to 18 in]).

Lathyrus

Lathyrus odoratus is the Sweet Pea, a

much-loved flower with a delightful colour range and exquisite scent. Whilst most sweet peas are more suitable for the cut flower bed or mixed border, there are dwarf strains well adapted for use in window boxes and other containers. They include the American 'Knee-Hi' which grows around 60 cm (2 ft) and needs no staking. Each flower stem carries five to seven blooms, the colours are as varied as their taller counterparts. 'Patio' and 'Snoopea' mixtures are excellent dwarf cultivars. For cultivation details see p. 170.

Limnanthes

Limnanthes douglasii is the Meadow Foam or Fried Egg Plant, a delightful little Californian, whose white, yellow-centered, saucer-shaped flowers seem irresistible to bees. Seed should be sown where the plants are to flower in autumn or spring. Germination takes about three weeks, when the young plants should be thinned to 8 to 10 cm (3 or 4 in). This is a beautiful little plant for early summer flowering, when it dies down and can be replaced if required. In the garden enough self-set seedlings come up each spring to maintain the stock. The height is 23 to 30 cm (9 to 12 in).

Matricaria

Chrysanthemum parthenium is more likely to be found in seed catalogues under *Matricaria eximia* than its proper name, for which reason it is included here. The type, a British perennial with small white daisy flowers and aromatic deeply cut foliage, is not worth growing, but the double-flowered kinds with branching stems and many ball-like heads are really arresting and stand well in containers. Typical sorts are 'Snow Dwarf', 'Golden Ball', and 'Lemon Ball', all 23 to 30 cm (9 to 12 in) high with 2-cm ($\frac{3}{4}$-in) blooms, and there is a golden-foliaged form 'Aureum'. These are best grown as half hardy annuals.

Matthiola

Stocks make good container plants if they can be sited away from strong winds which can snap the stems unless these are individually staked. They appreciate deep, rich, moist soil and given this thrive in full sun or partial shade. There are three main groups, all derived from *Matthiola incana*; the Brompton or Queen Stocks which are treated as biennials, seed being sown outside in June or July and then put out in their flowering positions the following September (or April in exposed areas); Ten Week Stocks, which are grown as half-hardy annuals and planted out in May from spring-sown seed under glass, and Intermediate or East Lothian Stocks, which can be grown as biennials or alternatively as annuals for autumn flowering.

In all cases the colour range is varied, from white and apricot to rose, lilac, carmine, mauve, purple and light blue. Since those with double flowers are the showiest always purchase seed from a reliable grower stocking good strains and check the seedlings before growing these on or pricking out. It is the light green foliaged seedlings with long leaves which produce double flowers – the dark green, short-foliaged ones are most likely to be single. Although seed deteriorates with keeping, the most persistent of life and able to survive are also doubles. Incidentally the germination of stocks takes about ten days.

In addition to their usefulness in containers, stocks merit a place against mixed bedding as well as for cut flowers or pot work indoors. Their rich scent, silvery foliage and long spikes of flowers commend them to most gardeners, so plant them in positions where these can be enjoyed, such as close to the house or near sitting out areas in the garden.

Petunia

Petunias are among the most desirable container plants for they are cheap and easy to raise and flower all summer. They have showy, trumpet-shaped flowers and entire, rough, rather stocky stems and leaves. If the stems become leggy, the flowering shoots can be cut back to young growths farther back along the stems. These soon take over and throw up fresh flowers. This operation can be repeated several times in a season if one feeds the plants in between times. The F_1 hybrids and doubles are more showy when grown as pot plants or in protected situations, but wind can damage the brittle stems, so that the smaller singles are often more useful in window boxes and hanging baskets.

A strawberry pot filled with pink, mauve and blue petunias makes a magnificent "all round" feature for summer and the leaves and flowers completely hide the pot in a few weeks.

Petunias should be treated as half-hardy annuals, the seed germinating in about fourteen days and, like stocks, the smaller seedlings are the ones which produce double or most brightly coloured flowers. A light rich soil suits them best, with plenty of water during the growing season. They are highly susceptible to frost and do not take kindly to drought.

For winter bloomers, seed can be sown in a cold frame in June or July, the seedlings potted on and stopped when about 10 cm (4 in) high to induce bushiness and brought under glass, temperature 13 to 16°C (55 to 60°F), in September or October.

Salvia

Salvia splendens is the Scarlet Sage, a beautiful Brazilian with spikes of fiery red, sage-like flowers and equally vivid bracts on branching 60- to 90-cm (2- to 3-ft) stems and smooth, oval, pointed leaves. For window boxes 'Dwarf Gems', 23 cm (9 in), or 'Fireball', 30 to 38 cm (12 to 15 in) are ideal. There are also white and dull purple varieties, but these are less arresting than the scarlets.

Although perennial the plants should be treated as half-hardy annuals. The seed germinates in eight days and seedlings should have the tops pinched out when 8 to 10 cm (3 to 4 in) high. They require light but rich soil with plenty of moisture and full sun.

Tropaeolum

Dwarf nasturtiums (*Tropaeolum majus*) make good container plants for sun or light shade as they bloom continuously all summer with variously coloured, helmet-shaped flowers and round silvery leaves. Seedsmen recognize and offer various races, particularly the cultivars

'Nanum', 'Tom Thumb', the lovely Gleam Hybrids and tall or climbing forms. These have double flowers of orange, primrose, scarlet, pink or salmon, some with dark foliage and another called 'Alaska' has cream-splashed variegated leaves.

The climbing nasturtiums can also be trained up trellises behind window boxes or in tubs to disguise dustbins and similar ugly features. Blackfly may attack the plants, but succumb to derris spray.

Nasturtium seed germinates in about ten days and can either be sown where it is to flower or grown under glass and put outside when there is no more risk of frost. The flowers are faintly scented and the crushed foliage has a pungent smell. Both flowers and leaves can be eaten in salads and the seeds used as a substitute for capers. See also p. 171.

Other plants to try in containers and dealt with on other pages are the trailing lobelia, silver-edged centaureas, wallflowers, polyanthus, forget-me-nots, poppies, ageratum, calendulas and calceolarias.

Fragrant annuals and biennials

Fragrance in flowers gives a bonus to beauty and most people would give extra points to a plant so favoured. A fair proportion should be grown in every garden and since the summer sorts (particularly) seem to smell most sweetly toward the evening, plant these close to the house and enjoy their fragrance at this quiet part of the day or by a garden seat where they may be appreciated at leisure.

Asperula

Asperula orientalis is a pretty little woodruff with 30-cm (1-ft) high slender stems carrying whorls of needle-like leaves and terminal heads of small, sky-blue, tubular flowers. It should be sown in early spring where it is to flower, selecting shady places in moist soil or damp pockets near water. It flowers about twelve weeks later.

Centaurea

Centaurea moschata is the Sweet Sultan, a

Pinch out the tips of young plants to promote bushy growth

A well-balanced
planting of annuals
which includes,
alyssum, petunias and
the grass *Briza maxima*

popular and sweetly fragrant plant much esteemed for cutting purposes. It has thistle-like heads of white, yellow, rose, red or purple on 60-cm (2-ft) stems and toothed leaves. Seed can be sown outside in spring and the seedlings thinned to 23 cm (9 in) apart, or in frames in September for flowering under glass in late winter. Germination takes place in about sixteen days.

Cheiranthus

The sweet scent and showy flowers of wallflowers (*Cheiranthus cheiri*) give them great appeal for spring bedding and cutting purposes. They are hardy, remain in character for weeks and, apart from mixed strains, seed can be bought to colour to conform with different bedding schemes. Although perennial they are treated as biennials; the seed being sown soon after harvesting. It germinates in about twelve days and then the seedlings should be pricked out in rows 15 cm (6 in) apart. In order to produce a fibrous root system and make them easier to transplant the tips of the tap roots should be broken at this stage. In early autumn they should be lifted again and planted in their flowering positions, in full sun and 30 cm (1 ft) apart. The usual height is around 45 cm (1½ ft), but dwarf types like 'Tom Thumb' only grow to half that height. The colour range includes reddish brown, blood red, crimson, salmon, ruby, rose, yellow and creamy white.

Dianthus

Dianthus are noted for fragrance and amongst those normally raised from seed are the popular sweet williams (*Dianthus barbatus*). Although perennial these are treated as biennial since they deteriorate after the first flowering, and self-set seedlings usually maintain the stock in future years. After germination the plants produce basal clumps of long narrow leaves and the following spring 45-cm (1½-in) leafy stems terminating in large flat heads of wide open flowers. Reds predominate but other colour combinations of shades occur, also varieties with double flowers. The species has been crossed with *D. × allwoodii* (itself a cross between an old English garden pink and

the border carnation) to produce the fragrant Sweet Wivelsfield pinks. These are also treated as biennials.

Exacum

Exacum affine is a delightful member of the gentian family with extraordinarily sweet-smelling flowers. These are small and mauve and the leaves smooth and oval in shape. The plant is bushy and low growing, 23 to 30 cm (9 to 12 in), but flowers for months and is especially fine for pot work in the home or conservatory. Treat as half-hardy; germination takes about fourteen days.

Heliotropium

Heliotropium × hybridum (heliotrope) is a half-hardy perennial from Peru with branching stems carrying dark green oblong leaves and clusters of richly scented violet-purple flowers. This fragrance is most marked towards evening. Heliotrope is often known as Cherry Pie and white, pink and rose-flowered forms can occur. The plants are popular for bedding and as pot subjects; particularly good forms being propagated from cuttings. Normally, however, they are grown from seed, as half-hardy annuals, since they flower freely the first year. They appreciate a rich, well-drained soil and full sun.

The seed germinates in about fourteen days and seedlings should be separately potted but not planted outside until there is no more risk of frost. To produce bushy plants pinch out the tops when they are 10 to 13 cm (4 to 5 in) high. For standards (which are best treated as biennial) leave the main stem and rub out all side shoots. Once the required height is reached remove the tip and let the side shoots develop.

Humea

Humea elegans is a striking plant for growing under glass or in a light window, although its powerful incense smell may not appeal to everyone. It has large, oval, sharply pointed leaves and loose pendent sprays of small crimson or reddish-brown flowers. Treat as biennial, sowing the seed in mid-summer.

Lathyrus

The Sweet Pea (*Lathyrus odoratus*) is a universal favourite, particularly for cutting. Almost every shade of colour is represented in the sweet-smelling flowers. To do well, however, the plants require rich well-prepared soil in an open sunny position. The ground should be deeply dug (approximately 60 cm [2 ft]) the previous autumn, or holes can be taken out to the same depth, and a good layer of well-rotted manure placed in the bottom before returning the soil.

The seed can be sown in late January or February (two or three seeds to a 8-cm [3-in] pot) in a cool greenhouse or frame and planted outside as the weather improves in early spring (March or April). The plants must be supported with peasticks or trained up netting or strings. They need plenty of water and feeding in summer. Keep the flowers picked to prevent seed formation (which checks further blooming) and remove tendrils and surplus foliage. For early flowering seed is sown in autumn or winter in a cold frame and exhibition flowers are grown on plants restricted to a single stem. See also p. 165–6.

Others with scented flowers include *Limnanthes douglasii, Alyssum maritimum*, hesperis, violas, antirrhinums and *Tropaeolum majus*.

Climbing Annuals

Climbing plants are useful to cover walls and sheds, mask old tree stumps and clamber over patio fences and loggias. Some can even be grown with perennial climbers like roses, so that they can take over and give colour when the roses have finished blooming. Most of those grown as annuals are only half hardy so have to be raised under glass and grown on in pots before it is safe to put them outside in early summer.

With the aid of climbers small gardens can be enclosed with "curtains" of flowers and leaves and a shady sitting out area is easily contrived by growing them up a light framework erected around three sides of a garden seat.

Ipomea cv.

Cobaea

Cobaea scandens is the Cup and Saucer Plant, a vigorous Mexican which can reach a height of 6 m (20 ft) or more in a season. It needs a sheltered position and full sun. The large 8-cm (3-in) flowers are greenish or creamy white at first, but the inner bell-like corolla becomes violet or purple with age. All the flowers are set off by green, saucer-like bracts.

Cucurbita

These non-edible members of the cucumber family are amusing to grow up trellises or fences, or the heavier-fruited types can be allowed to scramble over the ground. Treat as for marrows and give them full sun and deep rich soil. The fruits vary considerably – in size, shape and colour – and some are smooth skinned and others heavily warted.

Eccremocarpus

Eccremocarpus scaber, the Chilean Glory Flower, is best treated as a half-hardy annual, except where it is grown under glass or can be adequately protected in winter. Growing about 4.5 m (15 ft) high, it has slender spikes of tubular orange flowers and pinnate leaves with tendrils. It requires a sheltered sunny situation and makes an attractive drape for a south wall.

Humulus

Humulus scandens (*japonicus*), one of the hops, provides quick cover for unsightly fences and similar features during the summer months and soon forms a dense screen. The seed germinates in about ten days and can either be raised under glass for planting out later or sown outside in April. Either the cream-variegated leaf form called 'Variegatus' or the golden-foliaged 'Lutescens' are the most ornamental.

Ipomoea

These delightful ornamental climbers have large trumpet flowers in exquisite shades. The blues are particularly fine. *Ipomoea violacea* (*I. tricolor; I. rubro-coerulea*) is one of the loveliest, the deep blue, white-throated flowers 13 cm (5 in) in diameter. *I. purpurea* (*Convolvulus major*) is the Morning Glory, a beautiful half-hardy annual with violet flowers which become purple with age, but there are also white, dark and sky blue, and crimson forms. Plant ipomoeas outside in June, choosing a warm sunny sheltered situation.

Maurandya

Maurandya (now more correctly *Asarina*) *barclaiana*, a vigorous, free-flowering climber from Mexico, has violet-purple, foxglove-like flowers about 8 cm (3 in) long and smooth sharply pointed leaves. There are also white and rose-flowered forms. Treat as half-hardy annuals and grow in a warm sunny position.

Quamoclit

These half-hardy annuals can be grown outside in favourable localities if planted out when all risk of cold is past. Alternatively, they make beautiful climbers for a sun lounge or conservatory. *Quamoclit lobata* (syn. *Mina lobata*), from Mexico, grows to 1.8 to 2.4 m (6 or 8 ft) and has three-lobed leaves and showy bunches of scarlet and yellow flowers. *Q. pennata*, the Cypress Vine, is more delicate, with finely dissected leaves on 2.4- to 3-m (8- to 10-ft) twining stems and scarlet, star-like flowers.

Thunbergia

Thunbergia alata, the Black-eyed Susan, can be put out in summer in some localities but generally speaking is best grown under glass in pots and trained over hoops or sticks or up wire fixed to rafter beams. It flowers continuously all summer with vivid orange flowers which have almost black centres in 'Aurantiaca' or are white with dark centres in 'Alba'. Seed sown in February or March germinates in about fifteen days and needs growing on in a temperature of 13 to 18°C (55 to 65°F). The plants like moist, rich but well-drained soil and sun and should be fed occasionally if grown in pots.

Tropaeolum

Nasturtiums (*Tropaeolum majus* and cultivars are well-known plants, with vivid flowers and round glaucous leaves, which thrive in most soils. Both climbing

and bush cultivars are available, the former ideal for semi-shade in moist soil. They can be grown up trellises or pergolas and flower all through the summer.

A wide range of garden forms is now available, in many shades, from primrose, yellow and orange to rose, cherry red and scarlet. Seed should be sown where plants are to flower in April and covered with 2 cm ($\frac{3}{4}$ in) of soil. This takes ten days to germinate and seedlings should be thinned to the recommended distances and allowed to run up supports. See also p. 167.

Tropaeolum peregrinum (syn. *T. canariense*) is the Canary Creeper, a South American climber up to 2.4 m (8 ft), with small, five-fingered leaves and fringed golden-yellow flowers. It does well in a shady situation.

Annuals and biennials for drying

A number of monocarpic plants have flowers or attractive seedpods which can be dried for winter decoration. If these are picked just before they reach their peak they will be absolutely perfect for this purpose. Dry them in small bunches in an airy situation, protected from rain or strong sun – which might bleach the colours. Those with top-heavy flowers – like helichrysums – are usually mounted on wire 'stems'. The smaller kinds can be made into pictures, table mats, paperweights and other trifles.

Eryngium

Most species of eryngium (sea hollies) are perennials but *Eryngium giganteum* is a true biennial and also one of the loveliest. Growing 90 cm to 1.2 m (3 to 4 ft) high with branching silvery stems, it has toothed, arrow-shaped leaves and large silvery-blue flower heads backed by silver-veined, glaucous calyces. Once suited it colonizes freely and comes up every year.

Gomphrena

Gomphrenas or globe amaranths can be used as border edgings, pot plants, for bedding or the showy clover-like heads can be dried for winter decoration. They grow about 45 cm (1½ ft) tall and have globular heads of white, yellow, red or violet flowers. Treat as half-hardy annuals (the seed germinates in twelve days) and plant out 30 cm (1 ft) apart. *Gomphrena globosa* is the best (and most variable) species.

Gypsophila

Gypsophila elegans or Chalk Plant is a popular market flower with slender 30 to 45 cm (1 to 1½ ft) silvery stems, small lance-shaped leaves and masses of little white (occasionally pink or rose) simple flowers. These can be used fresh or dried for winter use. In gardens, the plants look pretty trailing down over steps or rocks. Treat as hardy annuals. See also p. 176.

Helichrysum

Helichrysum bracteatum is the Everlasting Flower or Immortelle, a hardy annual from Australia with lance-shaped leaves and large, papery-scaled flowers up to 5 cm (2 in) across. These can be white, yellow, orange, purple, rose or red on 76-cm (2½-ft) stems. They are half-hardy annuals, suitably for most soils if the situation is sunny.

Helipterum

These are pretty Australian composites, frequently catalogued under rhodanthe or acroclinium. *Helipterum* (*Rhodanthe*) *manglesii* makes a bushy 30 to 38 cm (1 to 1¼ ft) plant with many nodding, pink and white, papery-petalled flowers, something like daisies. Treat as half-hardy or hardy annuals – the latter giving later flowers. The very similar *H.* (*Acroclinium*) *roseum* can be sown outside in April and has white, pink or deep rose flowers with either gold or brown centres.

Limonium

Limonium sinuatum is one of the sea lavenders and is often listed as Statice. It is a biennial best treated as a half-hardy annual; the seedlings come through in eight days and the plants should be set out 30 cm (1 ft) apart when there is no more risk of frost. They have branching, flattened, rough, 30- to 60-cm (1- to 2-ft) stems with spikes of blue, mauve, lavender, rose, salmon-pink or white

Molucella laevis

flowers. These dry beautifully and are always very popular. The Candlewick Statice, *L. suworowii*, has long upright spikes packed with small rose flowers and lance-shaped basal leaves. It makes a good pot plant.

Lunaria

Lunaria annua, a biennial in spite of its name, is the Honesty, a good plant for odd corners, even in semi-shaded situations. Seed sown outside in April or May blooms the following spring, the flowers varying from white to deep purple or sometimes bicoloured. There is also a splendid variegated-leaved form called 'Variegatum' which comes true from seed. In autumn the seedpods should be rubbed between the fingers and thumb to remove the seeds and outer coverings, thus leaving the pearly, moon-like inner portions which are delightful for winter decoration.

Molucella

Molucella laevis or Bells of Ireland is grown for its calyces (the flowers are insignificant). These are borne on 76- to 90-cm (2½- to 3-ft) spikes and are pale green and shell shaped with delicate white traceries. They dry to a biscuit shade. The plant is a half-hardy annual which does well in light soil.

Nicandra

Nicandra physaloides, the Shoo-fly Plant (it is supposed to repel insects), is a vigorous half-hardy annual from Peru with 90-cm to 1.2-m (3- to 4-ft) branching stems, smooth oval leaves and bell-shaped blue and white flowers. These give place to swollen seedpods something like those of the Cape Gooseberry (physalis). It needs moist soil.

Nigella

Nigella damascena or Love-in-the-mist is attractive both in flower and fruit. The latter are used in dried arrangements. The flowers are 3 cm (1½ in) across, saucer shaped and usually blue – 'Miss Jekyll' is a particularly rich shade – but there are white and pale forms, also doubles. The seedpods are pale green, barred with brown and surrounded (as are the

Cotula

Cotula barbata is the Pincushion Plant, a compact half-hardy annual of 10 to 15 cm (4 to 6 in) with deeply-cut leaves spangled with golden flowers like daisies without the outer florets. It forms dense carpets of foliage, even in poor soil.

Dorotheanthus and Portulaca

Dorotheanthus bellidiformis (often sold as *Mesembryanthemum criniflorum*) makes dwarf mats of succulent linear foliage studded with vivid daisy flowers of cerise, crimson, buff, red, orange or apricot each more than 2.5 cm (1 in) across. On a bright sunny day (the flowers close in dull weather) the effect is brilliant. Treat as a half-hardy annual or sow outside in May for late flowers. Portulaca requires similar treatment and both do well in poor soil.

Portulaca grandiflora is the best species with round, succulent stems of 15 to 45 cm (6 to 8 in) carrying cup-shaped flowers of white, deep rose, rose and white, crimson or clear yellow. There are also double forms and the main flowering season is July and August.

Felicia

Felicia bergeriana is the Kingfisher Daisy, a dwarf half-hardy annual of 10 to 13 cm (4 to 5 in) with small but brilliant metallic-blue daisies which close in dull weather. Suitable for warm, sunny spots.

Gilia

Gilia hybrida (*Leptosiphon* hybrids) can be grown between flagstones or in small pockets. It does not mind poor soil and only grows about 15 cm (6 in) tall. It is a hardy annual with finely cut leaves and clusters of white, yellow, rose-pink, purple or violet flowers. All have yellow centres.

Gypsophila

Gypsophila repens is a dainty hardy annual having cobwebby stems and tiny leaves. It is smothered in summer with dense sprays of dainty little white flowers. These look very pretty trailing over rocks or stone steps. There are also pink and red forms. The usual height is 30 to 45 cm (1 to 1½ ft). Sow seed out of doors in autumn, or in cold districts in spring. See also p. 172.

Iberis

Iberis umbellata is the best of the annual candytufts with racemes of white, four-petalled, sweetly scented flowers in character all through the summer. Lilac and crimson forms are available and the normal height is around 30 to 45 cm (1 to 1½ ft). Treat as hardy annuals and grow in light, well-drained soil in open situations.

Ionopsidium

Ionopsidium acaule, the Violet Cress, can be sown directly on the rockery where it is to grow. In later seasons self-set seedlings usually maintain the stock. The violet-blue (sometimes white) flowers bloom from June to September on 5- to 8-cm (2- to 3-in) tufts of rounded leaves and stems. Hardy annual.

Layia

Layia elegans or Tidytips has yellow, 5-cm (2-in) daisies with prominent white petal tips. These occur on 30-cm (1-ft) stems and persist for weeks. Well-drained soil and sunshine suit this hardy annual.

Linaria

Linaria maroccana is a charming hardy annual with slender 25- to 45-cm (10- to 18-in) stems packed with small, snapdragon-like flowers. Normally these are violet with white blotches but white, mauve, crimson and yellow forms occur. The plants need full sun and well-drained soil and should be grouped for maximum effect. They also make good pot plants.

Lobelia

Among the smaller annuals no plant is more adaptable than *Lobelia erinus*, a charming, compact, half-hardy annual with smooth serrated leaves and pale blue, white-throated flowers. These bloom continuously all summer and may be grown in hanging baskets, pots and borders as well as in the rock garden. Selected forms, which come true from seed, include the deep blue, white-eyed 'Bluestone'; 'White Lady'; deep carmine-red and white-eyed 'Rosamund', and 'Mrs Clibran' which is brilliant blue with white eyes. The usual height is 15 cm (6 in) but there are also pendulous lobelias with lax, 45 cm (1½ ft) trailing stems, much used in hanging baskets. *L. tenuior* is a good blue for pot work.

Nemesia

Nemesia strumosa is grown as a half-hardy annual. Ideal for bedding in sunny annual borders, the plants also do well in rich, slightly acid soil in rock gardens. The stems grow 23 to 30 cm (9 to 12 in) tall with bunches of bright flowers in scarlet, orange, crimson, carmine, pink, purple, cream, white or yellow. The strain known as 'Suttonii' is particularly fine.

Nierembergia

Nierembergia caerulea (*N. hippomanica*) is a perennial usually treated as a half-hardy annual, although plants are occasionally lifted in autumn and over-wintered under glass. It blooms all summer, the 15- to 23-cm (6- to 9-in) stems spangled with cup-shaped flowers of lavender with yellow throats. It needs sun and shelter in moist but well-drained soil.

Phlox

Phlox drummondii does best in deep moist soil and should be treated as a half-hardy annual. The lightly scented flowers come in clusters and persist all summer in vivid shades of scarlet, violet, pink, white and yellow. There are large-flowered hybrids around 30 cm (1 ft) and dwarfs 15 cm (6 in). A warm sunny position is preferred.

Sedum

Sedum caeruleum is a lovely little annual with masses of pale blue starry flowers and needle-fine leaves on 5- to 8-cm (2- to 3-in) stems. Sow the seed in rock pockets out of doors in April.

Silene

Silene coeli-rosa, also known and sold under the names *Lychnis coeli-rosa* and *Viscaria oculata*, is a vivid, easy-to-grow annual which should be sown where it is to flower in March or April. Sometimes called Rose of Heaven, it has slender, 45-cm (1½-ft) stems with narrow leaves

and many rosy-red, white-centred flowers about 2.5 cm (1 in) across.

Annuals and biennials for cutting

Many annuals make excellent cut flowers and indeed constant picking – by preventing seeding – prolongs the life and vigour of some, such as sweet peas. For the rest, in order not to denude borders of bloom, it may be advisable to grow these in reserved beds away from general view. Make the beds long and narrow (not more than 90 cm (3 ft) wide), so that picking can take place in all weathers without treading all over the soil.

Agrostemma

Agrostemma githago is the Corn Cockle, a beautiful hardy annual with large, five-petalled magenta flowers (pale lilac in the cultivar 'Milas'), 5 to 8 cm (2 to 3 in) across on 60- to 90-cm (2- to 3-ft) stems. The long narrow leaves are greyish. The plant is also useful for pot culture or in borders.

Amaranthus

Amaranthus are esteemed for their foliage as well as their striking inflorescences. *Amaranthus caudatus* or Love-lies-bleeding takes its name from the long drooping spikes of flowers which may be blood red, white or green. When these are stripped of their leaves they make interesting cut flowers. The plants grow 60 cm to 1.5 m (2 to 5 ft) according to conditions, although rich soil tends to make them top heavy and coarse. *A. hybridus* (often listed in catalogues as *A. hypochondriacus*) is known as Prince's Feather on account of the colourful greenish-red leaves and spikes of blood-red flowers. The 45-cm (1½-ft) *A. tricolor* or Joseph's Coat is the best for foliage, however, this being strikingly patterned in scarlet, yellow and bronze green. All the family need sun and should be treated as half-hardy annuals.

Callistephus

Callistephus chinensis is the China Aster, a favourite for cutting but also useful in borders. There is a wide range of types, all of which should be grown in an open sunny position in good soil and treated as half-hardy annuals. Pompon Mixed has button-like daisies in shades of purple, blue, mauve, red, pink and white – also some bicolours, all 45 cm (1½ ft) high; 'Dwarf Queen' is a race of small, 23 cm (9 in), double bedding kinds; 'Totem Pole' has large shaggy flowers 15 to 18 cm (6 to 7 in) across, 60 cm (2 ft); the Single Flowered are naturally all singles, on 76-cm (2½-ft) stems, and 'Californian Giant' produces huge shaggy blooms on 60- to 90-cm (2- to 3-ft) stems in various colours. A virus disease (spotted wilt) sometimes attacks and kills aster plants. Buying seed from reliable sources and not too much warmth in the early stages of growth are the best preventatives.

Centaurea

Centaurea cyanus is the Cornflower, a pretty little blue-flowered annual with small thistle-like heads of flowers on branching, 45-cm (2½-ft) stems. There are also pinks and whites and dwarf forms. This is essentially a flower for cutting since dead blooms remain on the stems, which spoils them for border work. Sow the seed in autumn on light soil and in spring thin the plants to 30 to 45 cm (1 to 1½ ft) apart.

Chrysanthemum

Annual chrysanthemums make ideal cut flowers and come in self-colours of white, cream and yellow and also with contrasting bands around the petals or different centres. They are derived from such species as *Chrysanthemum coronarium*, *C. carinatum* and *C. segetum*. The usual height is between 30 and 60 cm (1 and 2 ft) and the plants should be treated as hardy annuals. Germination takes place in eight days. Grow them in an open sunny position and good but well-drained soil. *C. frutescens*, the white Marguerite, a popular long flowering bedding plant should be treated as half hardy. It has branching 60-cm (2-ft) stems with deeply cut leaves and many golden-centred, white flowers. There is also a yellow called 'Comtesse de Chambord' and a pink, 'Mary Wootton'.

Clarkia

Clarkia elegans (more correctly *C. unguiculata*) is a branching hardy annual from California which will grow 30 to 90 cm (1 to 3 ft) tall, according to when the seed is sown and the richness of the soil. The flowers are carried on long spikes and can be single or double in shades of pink, scarlet and purple – also white. The buds open up well in water.

Cleome

Cleome spinosa is the Spider Plant, an unusual half-hardy annual with strong, rather sticky, 90-cm to 1.5-m (3- to 5-ft) stems, spiny, palmate leaves (which smell unpleasant when bruised) and pink, rose, white or mauve flowers with 10- to 13-cm (4- to 5-in) protruding anthers.

Coreopsis

Coreopsis are North American annuals and perennials with daisy flowers mostly in yellow, gold and bronze shades. *Coreopsis basalis* (*C. drummondii*) and *C. tinctoria* are hardy annuals, the former 45 to 60 cm (1½ to 2 ft) tall with large yellow flowers; the latter embracing races and cultivars varying in height from 23 cm (9 in) to 60 or 90 cm (2 or 3 ft). The dwarfs make good border edging or pot plants; the taller kinds are excellent for cutting. 'Atrosanguinea' has dark red single flowers and there are also singles and doubles in various shades and mixtures of colours.

Cosmos

Cosmos bipinnatus is at its best in late summer and autumn. It is an elegant plant with pale green feathery leaves, tall branching 60- to 90-cm (2- to 3-ft) stems and long-stemmed white, pink, golden rose or crimson and striped daisies. There are also semi-doubles which come true from seed. All make excellent cut flowers. Treat as hardy annuals or half-hardy annuals (for stronger plants and earlier flowers). The soil should be on the poor side and the aspect sunny.

Delphinium

The ever-popular Larkspurs are derived from two species of delphiniums (*Delphinium ajacis* and *D. consolida*). They

Cosmos

OPPOSITE: Annuals provide colourful summer bedding

are reliable hardy annuals with dainty spikes of pink, mauve, blue or white flowers which blend pleasantly, dry for winter decoration and grace any border. Heights vary from 76 cm to 1.5 m ($2\frac{1}{2}$ ft to 5 ft), and apart from singles there are various doubles and a race of dwarfs at 45 cm ($1\frac{1}{2}$ ft). Although not fastidious they do best from autumn sowings in open sunny situations and well-drained soil. The seed germinates in about nineteen days and they flower from June over a period of eight to ten weeks. Spring sowing produces later blooms.

Gaillardia

Gaillardia aristata, although perennial, is usually grown as a biennial or half-hardy annual. It has showy daisy flowers up to 13 cm (5 in) across of bright yellow with zonings of other shades. There are also wine, copper, reds and tangerines in selected races like the Monarch strain. The height ranges up to 90 cm (3 ft) and the soil should be well drained and the aspect sunny.

Godetia

Godetias are valuable for summer bedding or pot work under glass, as well as cutting. For outdoor cultivation seed should be sown in a warm sunny position about March – or October, in gentle heat, for indoor work. *Godetia grandiflora* grows about 30 cm (1 ft) high with clusters of large flowers which, in the hybrids, range from white and various shades of pink to deep crimson. There are also doubles known as Azalea Flowered. *G. amoena* is taller and slenderer, up to 60 to 76 cm (2 to $2\frac{1}{2}$ ft), and has a similar colour range. The two species have been crossed to produce the very popular tall doubles.

Rudbeckia

Rudbeckia hirta is a splendid plant up to 90 cm (3 ft) in height with branching, hairy stems and large daisy heads of flowers 8 to 10 cm (3 to 4 in) across. These are golden yellow with dark centres. The 'Hirta Hybrida' race come in various autumnal shades of orange, bronze, scarlet and yellow.

Salpiglossis

Salpiglossis sinuata is a beautiful half-hardy annual from Chile with dainty 60- to 90-cm (2- to 3-ft) branching stems and many trumpet-shaped flowers of crimson, scarlet, violet, yellow, ivory to buff, usually patterned with gold. Grow in a sheltered sunny position in rich moist soil.

Scabiosa

Scabiosa atropurpurea or Sweet Scabious make delightful cut flowers with their long, stiff, 90-cm (3-ft) stems and round pincushion heads of white, pink, scarlet, mauve, blue or maroon. There are also doubles and dwarf strains. They can be treated as biennials or hardy annuals and also make striking border plants.

Zinnia

Zinnias (*Zinnia elegans*) need a rich moist soil and plenty of sun. Without these they invariably disappoint. They also resent transplanting so should be pricked out (from April sowings under glass) into small pots and from these to the garden in early June. Alternatively, seed can be sown outside in May. There are large-flowered strains of 60 to 90 cm (2 to 3 ft) in distinct colours like orange, pink, scarlet and purple. 'Giant Dahlia' is an example and among the smaller types come 'Pumila Pompon', doubles, 45 cm ($1\frac{1}{2}$ ft); 'Peter Pan' and 'Thumbelina', both 15 cm (6 in). 'Envy' is a curious chartreuse-green zinnia.

Other good cutting annuals include various grasses such as *Briza maxima* (Quaking Grass), *Pennisetum longistylum*, and *Lagurus ovatus* (Hare's Tail), annual lupins, nasturtiums, centaurea, dianthus, polyanthus, violas, calendulas, dahlias, lathyrus and stocks.

Long flowering plants

These plants remain in bloom for long periods so are particularly useful for container work and bedding; some also make good cut flowers.

Antirrhinum

Because rust disease is widespread and ruins their foliage, Snapdragons (*Anti-*

rrhinum majus) are usually grown as hardy or half-hardy annuals. Their varying heights, honey fragrance and showy flowers make them popular for summer bedding, window boxes and as cut flowers. Colours range from white and yellow through shades of pink to scarlet, blood red and near lavender. The F_1 hybrids are particularly good for cutting or forcing under glass. Heights vary from 90 cm (3 ft) in the 'Grandiflorum Spring Giant' range; 'Nanum Grandiflorum' is 38 cm (15 in) and 'Nanum Compactum' 15 to 20 cm (6 to 8 in). There are also double forms and 'Penstemon-flowered' types with flat-fronted tubular flowers.

Begonia

Begonia semperflorens are dependable, long-flowering bedding plants which can also be used in window boxes and other containers or rock garden pockets. They are neat and compact, on average 15 to 38 cm (6 to 15 in) high, with green or bronze foliage and masses of small, pink, red or white flowers. Treat as half-hardy annuals. Suitable for sun or shade.

Calendula

Calendula officinalis is the Pot Marigold, a splendid plant for bedding and cutting. The round daisy heads come in various shades of yellow and orange, the doubles being most popular. Pot Marigolds thrive in sun and most soils and can be raised from autumn or spring sowings out of doors.

Eschscholzia

Californian Poppies (*Eschscholzia californica*) are hardy annuals with deeply cut, glaucous foliage, fleshy tap roots and large yellow, orange, cream, pink and red single or double flowers on 30 to 45 cm (12- to 15-in) stems. Sow out of doors in spring or autumn in full sun.

Myosotis

Forget-me-nots (*Myosotis alpestris*) are best treated as biennials. These well-known, blue-flowered favourites are ideal for spring bedding, particularly between bulbs. The pink and white forms are less popular. They grow 10 to 30 cm (4 to 12 in) tall in sun or light shade. After flowering shake the old plants over a spare corner of ground, and enough seedlings will come up for the following season's use.

Papaver

Annual poppies should be grouped in borders, otherwise they make little impact. They are easy to grow in any open situation and reasonable soil and may be sown outside in autumn or spring. Shirley Poppies are derived from the scarlet, black-based Corn Poppy, *Papaver rhoeas*, and have larger and white-based flowers in a delightful range of pink and rose shades, also white. Double forms are also available. *P. nudicaule*, the Iceland Poppy, should be treated as a half-hardy annual. The long, 30- to 45-cm (1 to $1\frac{1}{2}$ ft) stems carry large flowers of glowing orange, yellow, white, pink or rose. *P. somniferum*, the Opium Poppy, has glaucous leaves and stems and very large single or double, white, salmon or scarlet flowers. Sow these out of doors in spring. See also p. 174.

Primula

Polyanthus, derived in the main from *Primula veris* and *P. vulgaris* crosses, are frequently raised from seed as biennials. They make excellent spring bedding plants with white, yellow, orange, pink, rose, red, blue, purple or violet flowers and after blooming can be lifted and divided and removed to a cool, moist, shady spot for the summer. In autumn they can be replanted in rich soil and a sunny spot. They grow to 30 cm (1 ft).

Tagetes

Although not natives of Africa or France, nor yet true marigolds, *Tagetes erecta*, the African Marigold, and *T. patula*, the French Marigold, are reliable half-hardy annuals which bloom right through the summer. The Africans are tall and vigorous with round and heavy, yellow or orange flowers up to 15 cm (6 in) across on branching stems and unpleasant smelling, cut-edged leaves. There are also dwarf types and 'Giant Crested' cultivars. Heights vary from 15 cm (6 in) to 90 cm (3 ft).

OPPOSITE: *Papaver nudicaule*, the Iceland Poppy, should be treated as a half hardy annual

Campanula medium

Helianthus annuus, the Common Sunflower

French marigolds are smaller and daintier with masses of single or double lemon, gold, orange or mahogany-red flowers, often striped or striated with other shades. The average height is 15 to 30 cm (6 to 12 in). Both kinds like sun but will also flower well in wet seasons.

Verbena

Verbenas (usually listed as *Verbena hybrida*) have flat heads of flowers in pink, red, mauve, blue and purple, also white. They make bushy plants 30 to 45 cm (12 to 15 in) high with simple serrated leaves and there are also dwarf forms. Grow as half-hardy annuals in full sun – although strictly speaking they are perennial and were once propagated from cuttings.

Other long season annuals include ageratum, alyssum, chrysanthemums, impatiens, matthiola and tropaeolums.

Other good annuals and biennials

Althaea

Because of rust disease the perennial Hollyhock (*Althaea rosea*) and the fig-leaved *A. ficifolia* are usually treated as hardy biennials. Their tall, 1.8 to 2.7 m (6 to 9 ft), stately spikes of single or double rosette flowers are ideal for backs of borders or as accent plants in key positions. They should be planted in full sun in heavy but rich and well-drained soil; stake the spikes if necessary. Colours range from pink, rose and maroon to white, apricot and yellow.

Arctotis

Arctotis or African Daisies are vigorous plants with hairy, silvery-grey stems and foliage and 8- to 10-cm (3- to 4-in) flowers of cream, yellow, orange, red, crimson or purple – frequently zoned with other shades – on 45-cm (1½-ft) stems. To encourage a bushy habit pinch out the tops when the seedlings are 13 to 15 cm (5 to 6 in) tall. Because of their mixed background African Daisies are usually catalogued as *Arctotis hybrida*. Treat them as half-hardy annuals and grow them in an open sunny position.

Argemone

Argemone mexicana is the Prickly Poppy and it likes a hot sunny situation. It grows about 60 cm (2 ft) with glaucous, prickly foliage and bright yellow, poppy-like flowers about 8 cm (3 in) across.

Atriplex

Atriplex hortensis cupreata is a wine-red-foliaged spinach, a useful foliage plant for borders and cutting. It grows up to 1.2 m (4 ft) and should be treated as a hardy annual.

Calceolaria

Calceolaria hybrids have honey-scented pouched flowers in shades of yellow, blotched red or rose, held on 30- to 45-cm (1- to 1½-ft) stems. The shrubby *C. integrifolia* (*C. rugosa*) can also be grown from seed; 'Sunshine' is a particularly fine flowering, 20-cm (8-in) form. Treat as half-hardy annuals and place in a warm, sunny situation.

Campanula

Canterbury Bells (*Campanula medium*) are delightful biennials for mixed borders, especially in rich soil with plenty of sun. In windy situations they may need staking. The bell-shaped flowers come with or without "saucers" in white, pink, blue and mauve and there are dwarf races such as the 45 cm (1½ ft) Musical Bells. *C. pyramidalis*, the Chimney Bellflower, is also grown as a biennial, but with protection in winter. The beautiful blue or white flowers are saucer shaped on 1.2 m (4 ft) (to 2.4 m [8-ft] under glass) spires.

Centaurea

Centaurea cineraria (*C. candidissima*) is grown for its fine silvery leaves which set off bright annuals and have many garden uses. It likes sun and well-drained soil, growing about 38 cm (15 in) high. *C. gymnocarpa* is similar but with wider leaves and taller at 60 cm (2 ft). Both plants are perennials but can be killed in cold winters so treat as half-hardy annuals.

Cladanthus

Cladanthus arabicus has deeply cut leaves

and bright yellow daisy flowers on 30- to 38-cm (12- to 15-in) stems. It appreciates sun and should be grown as a hardy annual.

Convolvulus

Convolvulus tricolor is a delightful hardy annual for full sun, growing 30 to 38 in (12 to 15 in) tall with brilliant blue, funnel-shaped flowers with white or pale yellow throats. There are also kinds with white, rose and dark blue flowers.

Echium

Echium lycopsis (*E. plantagineum*) or Viper's Bugloss is a hardy annual with spikes of bright blue flowers and rough leaves and stems. It grows 23 to 30 cm (9 to 12 in) tall and there are white, pink, purple and mauve-flowered forms.

Gazania

Gazanias are best treated as half-hardy annuals although named or selected varieties can be perpetuated from cuttings. They must be grown in full sun since the flowers fail to open in dull weather or shade. The long, narrow, ground-hugging leaves have a silver reverse and the brilliant daisy flowers come in cream, orange and pink, often with striking zonings such as green on pink and orange on silver.

Helianthus

Helianthus annuus is the Common Sunflower, a hardy annual with huge plate-like golden flower heads up to 30 cm (1 ft) in diameter on 1.2- to 3-m (4- to 10-ft) stems. Seedsmen also sell dwarf sunflowers on 90-cm to 1.2-m (3- to 4-ft) stems, with orange, yellow, cream and chestnut-brown flowers.

Lavatera

Lavatera trimestris rosea, one of the best of the taller hardy annuals, has large open, satiny-pink flowers like mallows on its branching stems. These are in character all summer and require full sun and good soil. Height 60 to 76 cm (2 to 2½ ft). Among the best are 'Loveliness', rose; 'Silver Cup', salmon-rose and 'Mont Blanc', white.

Linum

Linum grandiflorum 'Rubrum' is a red-flowered flax, very showy, with slender 30-cm (1-ft) stems carrying many saucer-shaped, deep red blooms. It likes sun and only shows to advantage in bright weather. Hardy annual.

Mentzelia

Mentzelia lindleyi (*Bartonia aurea*), an easy hardy annual, has large, golden, chalice-shaped flowers full of stamens on 45-cm (1½-ft) stems. It is also known as Blazing Star, likes sun and is sweetly scented.

Oenothera

Oenotheras may be annual, biennial or short-term perennials; many are night bloomers. The common Evening Primrose (*Oenothera biennis*) sows itself about after initial establishment, the 60-cm to 1.2-m (2- to 4-ft) stems carrying many 5-cm (2-in), lemon-yellow, sweetly scented flowers. Another night-scented biennial is the shorter 30 cm (1 ft) *O. trichocalyx* with white flowers. *O. acaulis*, although perennial, should be treated as a half-hardy annual and is worth the trouble as the 10 cm (4 in) flowers on trailing stems are very beautiful. They open white and develop to deep rose.

Silene

Silenes are showy plants for the border or rock garden with small white, pink or purple-pink flowers. The annual *Silene pendula*, growing 15 to 20 cm (6 to 8 in), makes compact plants covered with bloom in spring from autumn sowings. In cold soils, however, they may need winter protection. There are double forms as well as singles. *S. armeria* grows taller – 30 to 60 cm (1 to 2 ft) – and has sticky stems.

Verbascum

Verbascums (mulleins) carry their flowers on long straight spikes. They like sun and well-drained soil. Although perennial, some can be grown as hardy annuals. *Verbascum olympicum* is yellow and 1.5 to 1.8 m (5 to 6 ft); *V. phoeniceum*, red, purple, pink, white or mauve and 60 to 90 cm (2 to 3 ft) tall.

Flowering Bulbs

PERCY THROWER

The bulbous plants provide us with some of the loveliest of the garden flowers. Few other plants give such brilliance and profusion of colour for so little effort on the part of the grower. Many connect the word bulb with the spring-flowering kinds and especially the daffodils which hold such a special place in our affections but there are bulbous plants to give colour throughout the year even in the depths of winter and it is a pity that, with the exception of the gladioli, the lilies and the dahlias, the summer and autumn-flowering kinds are so often neglected.

A bulb is an underground storage organ and the term bulbous plants is a general one which embraces other similar structures known as tubers and corms, and sometimes plants with rhizomes are included in this classification. Although there are botanical differences between these structures, these are largely un-important from the gardener's point of view as their cultivation is very similar. They are all, with few exceptions, easy to grow and maintain and therefore can be relied upon by the busy gardener.

The function of a bulbous structure is twofold. It allows the plant to survive adverse weather conditions which may range from severe winter cold to drought and it stores food so that the plant grows rapidly when placed under suitable conditions. During the growing and flowering period of the bulbous plant, food is manufactured by the leaves. This is passed back down to the storage organ and the next year's leaves and flowers are formed. After flowering the leaves and roots of the present year's growth gradually die back to leave the swollen storage organ ready to produce the next year's growth.

Bulbous plants can be found to fit into any setting in the garden. There are kinds which look good in formal bedding schemes, others for mixed beds and borders while many look delightful when naturalized in grass. Some, too, adapt well to growing in window boxes, tubs and other ornamental containers on paved areas and patios.

Formal beds

The bulbous plants which are most suited for formal plantings are mainly spring-flowered subjects. They include the Early Single, Early Double, Cottage, Broken and Darwin tulips, hyacinths, some of the narcissi, snowdrops, crocuses, muscari, chionodoxas and scillas. Many of these look effective when planted on their own or they can be combined with other spring-bedding plants such as wall-flowers, pansies, violas, polyanthus, forget-me-nots, arabis and *Alyssum saxatile* in very many attractive combinations. For summer there are the tuberous-rooted begonias and dahlias. It is important when planning and planting formal beds to buy bulbs which are guaranteed to grow to a uniform height and colour and to flower at the same time.

Ensure that the drainage is adequate, then dig the bed over to the depth of a spade. The soil texture can be greatly improved by forking in a dressing of horticultural peat at the rate recommended by the supplier. The peat should be well soaked with water before it is worked into the soil. A dressing of bonemeal or hoof and horn, applied while wearing gardening gloves at the rate of 68 g per m² (2 oz to the sq yd) and forked in with the peat, will prove very beneficial. Never place fresh manure in direct contact with bulbs but it can be most profitably incorporated below planting level.

Planting depths and distances and the

Bulbs vary in shape and form:
(a) Daffodil,
(b) Lily,
(c) Hyacinth,
(d) Tulip

OPPOSITE: *Lilium auratum*, the Golden-rayed Lily of Japan

RIGHT: Cleaning
narcissus bulbs and
removing the dried
foliage before storing
them in trays
FAR RIGHT: In moist
soils, lily bulbs can be
planted on sand to
avoid rotting

RIGHT: Cleaning narcissus bulbs and removing the dried foliage before storing them in trays
FAR RIGHT: In moist soils, lily bulbs can be planted on sand to avoid rotting

times of planting too are dealt with in the list of plants which follows. It is best to plant the bedding plants first, if these are being used, and then to put in the bulbs using a trowel. After their display is over spring-bedded plants are removed to make way for the summer flowers. However, the bulbous plants must be allowed to complete their life cycle naturally. They should, therefore, be moved to a reserve bed in a secluded part of the garden where they can be lined out in shallow trenches and the soil well firmed around them. In dry weather, water the soil. By about late June the foliage should have withered and the bulbs can be lifted with care making sure that they are not damaged by the spade or fork. Dry in a cool airy shed or room and before storing in boxes, under similar conditions, remove old roots and other extraneous material and throw away any bulbs which appear diseased.

Mixed beds and borders

There are houses and gardens which, because of their style and layout, are most suited to a formal treatment of plants. Informal garden plants are, however, becoming increasingly popular and these allow for mixed beds and borders which are planted with a whole range of subjects – small trees, shrubs, herbaceous perennials, bulbs and even annuals and biennials. This type of planting is

especially economic where space is limited and with skilful planning it will give the garden year-round interest.

Soil preparation is similar to that described for formal beds though with a mixed border it is seldom necessary to prepare and plant the whole area at once. Plant with a trowel at the times and distances recommended in the following list. Gladioli and lilies are among the bulbs which should be bedded on sand as they will rot in moist soils.

Some subjects may need staking. Firmly secure one bamboo cane to each plant in the ground and tie the flower stem to this loosely with a soft material. The plant should be allowed some freedom of movement in the wind or it will look unnatural so take the tying material round the stake, knot it and then take it loosely round the stem, knotting it again.

Many of the summer-flowering bulbous plants are not reliably hardy. Some, like the dahlia, will have to be lifted and stored each winter, but the soil where others are growing can be covered with straw, bracken or a similar material as a protection against frost. It is better, if possible, to leave bulbs undisturbed for several years. Every third or fourth year they can then be lifted and sorted through and at this time offsets can be removed. Some protection can also be given to the less hardy kinds if they are planted in beds against warm south or south-west-facing walls.

Naturalized bulbs

Naturalized bulbs, as the term implies, are those grown under as near natural

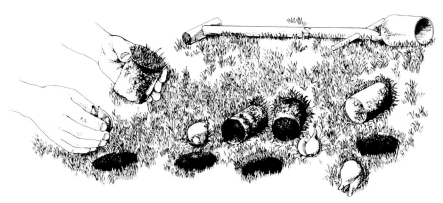

Naturalizing bulbs in grass is made easier with the aid of a bulb planter. This removes a core of soil, a bulb is then popped into the hole and the core replaced

conditions as possible. They can look very attractive indeed in an informal garden setting and once planted they demand very little attention from the grower. In fact this is the least troublesome way of all to grow bulbous plants. They can be planted around trees and shrubs, down banks, in small woodland areas or in drifts on the lawn. How about daffodils around forsythia to produce a brilliant splash of yellow in the spring; blue muscari round a flowering cherry; anemones down a bank; bluebells in a woodland setting, and crocuses on the lawn? The combinations are endless and all are equally lovely.

There is only one important point to remember when planting bulbs in a lawn and that is that the grass cannot be cut until the leaves of the bulbs have died down naturally for the plants must be allowed to complete their life cycle in order to build up food resources for the next year's growth. The grass when eventually cut may be an unattractive brown colour but watering and feeding with a lawn fertilizer will soon bring it round.

Naturalized bulbs should be planted in drifts, not in rows or rigid clumps. The best way of achieving a good effect is to scatter handfuls of bulbs and plant them where they fall. The easiest way of planting naturalized bulbs is with a special tool known as a bulb planter. This cuts out a core of turf and soil when it is pressed into the ground and removes it intact when it is given a twist and lift. The bulb can then be placed in the hole and the core of soil and turf replaced and firmed with the feet. Small quantities of bulbs can be planted with a trowel. Where only a small area is involved the turf can be lifted, the soil improved with a dressing of bonemeal at the rate of 68 g per m² (2 oz to the sq yd), the bulbs planted and the turf replaced.

Bulbs in containers

Patios are now very popular features in many gardens and they will be enhanced by tubs and other ornamental containers filled with bulbous and other subjects. This method of cultivation is especially suited to those slightly tender subjects – agapanthus, amaryllis, crinums, nerines and others – for the containers can be put in to the conservatory, greenhouse or a frostproof shed for the winter.

A most important point when growing bulbs in containers is to ensure that the drainage is good and there should be adequate holes to allow the surplus water to escape. These will either be at the bottoms of the sides of the container when the container may stand on the ground or they will be in the bottom of the container itself. In this case the container must be raised a little from the ground to allow the water to escape easily. Cover these holes with crocks and then a thick layer of roughage before the compost is added. If the provision of holes is impossible then a thick layer of drainage material must be laid in the bottom of the container before the compost is added.

I would recommend a good standard soil-based potting compost as the growing medium. If you do use ordinary garden soil, this must have a good texture and it is a good idea to add peat to it and a dressing of bonemeal. Plant at the same time and depth as stated in the plant lists. Watch the compost carefully during the growing season and water when it appears dry. Taller plants may require some unobtrusive staking.

A method of growing daffodils which I have found particularly rewarding is that of planting double layers of daffodil bulbs in tubs at least 30 cm (1 ft) deep. Place a layer of crocks over the drainage holes and cover this with roughage. Add a layer of compost and set the first layer of bulbs in position. Cover the bulbs with compost so that the tips are just showing and then position the second layer of bulbs between the tips of the first layer. Work in the compost among these bulbs and make this firm.

Selected Bulbs

Acidanthera

The lovely *Acidanthera bicolor murielae* comes from Ethiopia and grows 90 cm (3 ft) high. On each stem, during September and October, are borne five to six fragrant white flowers each marked with a maroon blotch at the centre. Of special interest to the flower arranger is that these flowers will last a long time if picked in bud.

The corms should be planted in April and May 8 cm (3 in) deep and 15 cm (6 in) apart in light, well-drained soil and in a sunny position which is sheltered from the wind. An ideal place is against a warm south or south-west-facing wall where it should be possible to leave the corms in the ground over winter if they are protected by a covering of straw or bracken.

Acidantheras can be increased by offsets or by seed sown under glass in the spring.

Agapanthus

Agapanthus orientalis (syn. *A. umbellatus*) is the African Lily or Lily of the Nile. It has large strap-shaped leaves and handsome funnel-shaped summer flowers which in the species are blue but there is

also a fine white form and one of a rich double blue. All grow 60 to 90 cm (2 to 3 ft) tall.

The creeping rootstock should be planted in March so that the crown is just below the surface in a sandy soil and a warm, sunny position. As it is inclined to be half hardy, it makes an excellent subject for flowering in pots which can be taken into the greenhouse or conservatory during the winter months. A single rhizome will give a good display in a 23- or 25-cm (9- or 10-in) pot. A hardier strain, the Headbourne Hybrids, has now been developed, however, with colours ranging from pale to deep violet blue. These can be left in situ during the winter with straw or bracken protection.

African Lilies can be increased by offsets, division or seed though from seed they may take five to six years to flower.

Allium

This is the family to which the onion belongs but it has many lovely ornamental relations which only give the characteristic onion smell if their leaves are bruised. Heights range from a few centimetres to over a metre and the colour range is from pure white through yellow and pink to deep purple. All produce ball-shaped flower heads freely from May to July, some being solid and others tasselled. They should be planted in a sunny, open position in the autumn and covered with two to three times their own depth of soil. The smaller-growing species can be planted 5 to 8 cm (2 to 3 in) apart, the larger ones 20 to 23 cm (8 to 9 in) apart. Increase by division of the bulb clusters in autumn or by seed sown in spring in a cool greenhouse or frame.

Allium aflatunense has the descriptive common name of the Powder Puff. It has dense rounded heads of lilac-purple flowers on 60- to 90-cm (2- to 3-ft) stems. The butterflies' haven, *A. albopilosum*, has heads of lilac starry flowers which can be as much as 25 to 30 cm (10 to 12 in) across on 60-cm (2-ft) stems. The globular heads of the 60-cm (2-ft) *A. caeruleum* are cornflower blue.

Allium moly is sometimes known as the Golden Garlic. It has bluish-green leaves and umbels of yellow flowers on 25- to 30-

cm (10- to 12-in) stems. Sweetly scented white flowers are the glory of the 38-cm (15-in) *A. neapolitanum*. And the last which I have room for here is *A. ostrowskianum*, at 15 cm (6 in) ideal for the rock garden, which it graces with its carmine-pink flowers.

Alstroemeria

The Peruvian Lilies are elegant, tuberous-rooted perennials and they make excellent cut flowers. The umbels of richly coloured, funnel-shaped flowers are in evidence from June onwards on 30-cm to 1.2-m (1- to 4-ft) leafy stems. They should be planted in April in a well-drained sheltered position and established plants will benefit from an annual mulch of well-decayed manure in the spring. This will also afford some protection from frosts.

I would strongly recommend the hybrids of *Alstroemeria ligtu* which can be had in beautiful shades of pink, orange, yellow and carmine. There is also *A. aurantiaca* 'Lutea' which has yellow flowers spotted carmine; *A. pelegrina* which is clear pink, and *A. haemantha* which is blood red.

Amaryllis

If you plant the Belladonna Lily, *Amaryllis belladonna*, under a south wall you will be richly rewarded during the late summer and early autumn with fragrant, rosy-red, trumpet flowers of which up to ten can be carried on the top of each 45-cm (18-in) stem. An August planting of bulbs 10 cm (4 in) deep and 30 cm (12 in) apart will flower within a few weeks. The dull green, strap-shaped leaves are produced after the flowers in the spring. Leave undisturbed but cover in severe winters with bracken or straw. Increase by offsets or by seed sown in heat in spring. This, however, is a very slow process as it can take seven years before flowers appear.

Anemone

Some of the members of this charming genus will have been written about elsewhere in this book but here we are concerned with the lovely tuberous-rooted species.

As its common name implies, the

Anemone nemorosa

Wood Anemone, *Anemone nemorosa*, is ideal for naturalizing and as ground cover beneath taller subjects in the mixed border which will give it some shade. The spring flowers of the species are white with pink tips on 15-cm (6-in) stems and there are several good varieties in the white to lavender-blue colour range. Plant 5 cm (2 in) deep in a leafy or peaty soil in September or October.

Anemone coronaria is the Poppy Anemone and two excellent strains – the St Brigid and the de Caen – have been bred from it. These have flowers of many colours and are, of course, well known as commercial cut flowers. The stems are up to 30 cm (1 ft) high. Plant the tubers 5 to 8 cm (2 to 3 in) deep and 15 cm (6 in) apart in November for spring flowering, in April or May for July flowering, and in June for September flowering.

There are numerous forms of *Anemone blanda* with flowers from white to blue. They prefer a sunny and sheltered site with good well-drained soil. *A. fulgens* has gay scarlet flowers in May and *A. apennina* is a charming plant for naturalizing in grass. It flowers in March.

All are increased by seed or by dividing the tubers.

Babiana

The beautiful forms of *Babiana stricta* can be grown out of doors in favoured areas given a light sandy soil and a well-drained sunny border. They will, however, need the winter protection of a covering of straw or bracken if the bulbs are not lifted and stored. The flowers appear in May and June and among the lovely colours available are blue, cream, rose pink and crimson. Plant 10 cm (4 in) deep and 5 cm and (2 in) apart in March or April and increase from seed or offsets.

Begonia

The tuberous-rooted begonias make splendid summer-bedding plants in their vivid colour range of red and pink through orange and yellow to white. The tubers should be started into growth in February, March or April in a green-house with a minimum temperature of 13°C (55°F). Plant them in boxes of moist peat or a moist peat and sand mixture and when growth begins pot into 13-cm (5-in) pots filled with a good standard soil-based compost. Harden off before plant-ing out. Lift and store the tubers in October. Increase from seed sown in January or February in a temperature of 18°C (65°F) or more.

Start begonia tubers off in a box of moist peat

Brodiaea

The genus now includes those flowers originally listed under *Milla* and *Tri-teleia*. As if to emphasize the surprising number of bulbous subjects which do flower during the summer and autumn months, these are in full bloom during June and July. They are ideal for the front of the border or rock garden and should be planted in a well-drained soil and a sunny position for the best display.

Californian Fire Cracker is the very vivid common name of *Brodiaea coccinea* (syn. *B. ida-maia*) which has lovely green-tipped, crimson flowers on 38-cm (15-in) stems. The 30-cm (12-in) *B. congesta* has lilac-blue flowers but the best of all is the free-flowering, fragrant *B. uniflora* (*Milla uniflora*) with pale lavender long-lasting flowers which have a thin violet stripe running down the centre of each petal. It grows to 15 cm (6 in) with lots of grassy foliage.

Bulbocodium

Bulbocodium vernum is especially suited to the rock garden for the crocus-like purple blooms appear on short stems during March and April. Plant in September 8 cm (3 in) deep and 10 to 15 cm (4 to 6 in) apart in a warm, sheltered place and well-drained soil. It can be left undisturbed for many years.

Calochortus

The butterfly tulips or mariposa lilies are not easy to grow and consequently they are not as widely known as their beauty suggests that they should be. However, the gardener with a warm, well-drained soil would do well to try them for they are like very delicately formed tulips on slender 15- to 60-cm (6-in to 2-ft) stems, the height depending on the species grown.

Plant in October or November in a warm, sunny position and a light, sandy soil to which leafmould or peat has been added for moisture retention during the summer. If protected with straw or bracken during the winter, or in severe weather with frame lights or cloches, they can be left undisturbed for several years.

Calochortus venustus is perhaps the most readily available with white, cream or yellow flowers with a blotch of dark red on each petal. It flowers in June and July and is 60-cm (2 ft) tall. *C. splendens* has lilac flowers on 30-cm (1-ft) stems in May and June.

Camassia

I like to see the amenable *Camassia esculenta* flowering in the summer border. It has spikes of star-shaped flowers which in variety have a colour range from white to deep blue. This species which grows to 60 cm (2 ft) and flowers in June and July can also be naturalized in light woodland. There is also *C. cusickii* which is 90 cm (3 ft) and *C. scilloides* (syn. *C. fraseri*) which is half that height. Both have pale blue flowers.

Plant camassias in the autumn 10 to 13 cm (4 to 5 in) deep and the same distance apart in sun or light shade and leave undisturbed for a number of years. Increase by seed or by division when the bulbs are lifted which some gardeners advocate should be every four years to keep the bulbs in a healthy condition.

Chionodoxa

The Glory of the Snow is native to the mountainous regions of Asia Minor and it is a delightful subject for the rock garden or window box. It should be planted in autumn 8 cm (3 in) deep and 2.5 cm (1 in) apart to flower from early March onwards. There are several good species. *Chionodoxa luciliae* is blue with a white centre; *C. sardensis* is a striking deep blue, and *C. gigantea* has large clear blue flowers with white centres although its cultivar 'Alba' is all white. They grow 15 to 18 cm (6 to 7 in) tall and need plenty of sun and good drainage. Propagation is by offsets or seeds.

Colchicum

There is a point of confusion to be cleared up here. Colchicums are often called autumn crocuses but this is misleading as they are totally unrelated to the true crocus species which flower in autumn. They are much better called by one of their other two common names which are Meadow Saffron and Naked Ladies. The name Naked Ladies arose because there is no foliage to be seen during the flowering season. The broad, lush leaves only appear after flowering is over in the spring.

Colchicums will grow in sun or semi-shade and like most bulbous plants prefer a light, well-drained soil. They should be planted 8 cm (3 in) deep and 15 cm (6 in) apart in July and August and can be increased by division of the clumps at this time or by seeds sown in a cold frame in late summer.

The crocus-like blooms are to be found in white and every shade of pink, mauve and purple and are 15 to 20 cm (6 to 8 in) high. Care must be taken in placing them in a planting scheme, however, as the spring foliage, often 38 to 45 cm (15 to 18 in) high, can smother neighbouring plants. They are perhaps better natural-ized though even here caution must be practised as the foliage is poisonous and they must not therefore be planted where there are grazing animals.

Colchicum speciosum comes into flower in September but *C. autumnale* and its cultivars flower a little earlier. There is also now a wide range of colchicum hybrids which flower from September to November and these are listed in cat-alogues under named varieties.

Commelina

The Blue Spiderwort is easy to grow in a warm sunny position. The best species is *Commelina tuberosa* which has lovely gentian-blue flowers on 38-cm (15-in) stems in the summer and long lance-shaped leaves. It should be planted in the spring.

Convallaria

The Lily-of-the-valley is not a true bulbous plant but it is usually included as such in any comprehensive list such as this. It likes a soil to which peat, leafmould or old manure has been added and a shady position. The crowns should be planted 8 to 10 cm (3 to 4 in) apart and they can be left undisturbed for many years for they only need lifting when they have become over-crowded. An annual topdressing of compost or decayed manure applied when the foliage has died down will ensure the continued pro-duction of large flowers in May. Re-member when picking the flowers to leave as many leaves as possible to manufac-ture the food which will be stored for next year.

Crinum

The beautiful South African crinums are superb plants for those sunny, sheltered sites which are backed by a south-facing wall. They like a rich, loamy, sandy soil containing leafmould or peat or they can be grown in tubs and other ornamental containers. Plant in March so that the tips of the bulbs are just below the surface of the soil and if grown in the border protect in winter with straw or bracken. Pro-pagation is by seed sown in spring in a warm greenhouse or by offsets.

Crinums have ornamental, evergreen, strap-shaped leaves and umbels of hand-some funnel-shaped flowers on sturdy stems from July to September. From the large bulbs of *Crinum macowanii* develop

60-cm (2-ft) stems crowned by fragrant white and purple flowers. The flowers of *C. moorei* are pink and those of *C. powellii*, the most widely grown species, are white veined red with white stamens.

Crocosmia

Crocosmia masonorum is a plant which teeters on the edge of hardiness and it, too, needs a warm, sunny border to be a success in our gardens with a light, sandy soil. The flowers, borne in arching sprays on 76-cm (2½-ft) stems, are an eye-catching orange-red shade and appear in August and September. The corms should be planted 15 cm (6 in) deep in spring and lifted and stored at the end of the season if there is any danger of them being damaged by frost. In warmer gardens it may be sufficient to protect with bracken or straw for the winter. Increase by offsets or by seed.

The name *Crocosmia crocosmiiflora* now covers the garden forms of the Montbretia and recently some very reliable hybrids have been introduced. Again they need a well-drained soil, a sunny position and winter protection. I would recommend planting them against a light-coloured wall to show off their bright yellow, orange or crimson flowers. Plant the corms 8 cm (3 in) deep in March or April and 15 cm (6 in) apart. Increase by division in March and April.

Crocus

A succession of crocus species and cultivars can be planted in the garden to give a wealth of beautiful jewel colours from September to April with a few breaks. They are perhaps at their best when naturalized in grass but they also look delightful when planted in borders, in the rock garden or as an edging to paths and borders. They prefer a well-drained soil and to be left undisturbed for several years.

The winter and spring-flowering kinds should be planted in September and October and the autumn-flowering ones in July. The planting depth of them all is 8 cm (3 in) with 5 to 8 cm (2 to 3 in) between them and propagation is by offsets or seeds.

The list of good species and cultivars is almost endless and reference to any good bulb catalogue will provide a plethora to choose from. Here is just a selection starting in the spring with *Crocus imperati*, scented violet flowers; *C. sieberi*, lavender blue; the cultivars of *C. biflorus*, with blue or purple feathering on a white or cream ground; *C. ancyrensis*, orange yellow, and cultivars of *C. chrysanthus*. The year continues with the Cloth of Gold Crocus, *C. susianus*, and *C. tomasinianus*, silver lavender.

Then there are the large-flowered Dutch crocuses which are so widely planted in parks and gardens. For a really bright display these can be planted in a mixture of named varieties.

For autumn flowering there is *Crocus zonatus* with large but dainty pinkish-mauve flowers with a gold base and orange-gold anthers. *C. speciosus* has bright blue flowers with violet veinings and orange stigmas and there is a pure white form 'Albus' with red stigmas. *C. pulchellus* has sky-blue flowers with white anthers.

Curtonus

Curtonus paniculatus was originally known as *Antholyza paniculata*. It flowers in late summer with handsome orange-red, tubular flowers on branched, arching stems to 1.2 m (4 ft). It likes a light, well-drained soil and sunny position preferably against a warm wall. Give a winter protection of straw or bracken. March or April is the time to plant the corms 10 cm (4 in) deep and 15 to 20 cm (6 to 8 in) apart. Increase by offsets or by seeds sown in a cool greenhouse.

Cyclamen

The gardener with a cool, shady corner to fill can do no better than plant some of these delightful little flowers. They should be planted during August and September in a peaty soil 4 cm (1½ in) deep and 8 cm (3 in) apart. They can then be left undisturbed for many years. Propagation is by seed sown in spring in a cool greenhouse or frame or by division of the old clumps in August or September.

Species can be found to flower from August to the following May and among my favourites is *Cyclamen coum* with dainty carmine blooms in February and March. *C. neapolitanum*, with rosy-pink flowers in August and September, *C. europaeum*, with carmine flowers in autumn, and *C. repandum*, with crimson flowers in spring, are species with beautifully marbled foliage. These make an extremely attractive ground cover which is with us for most of the year.

Dahlia

Here we are concerned with the growing of dahlias from tubers. These tubers are not fully hardy and so must be lifted carefully and stored each winter in a dry, airy, frostproof place. In late April and early May they should be planted out in a good, well-drained soil and sunny position. Insert stakes before planting and use a trowel or spade, depending on the size of the tubers, to make the hole. The tubers should be firmly covered with 8 to 10 cm (3 to 4 in) of soil. Taller-growing kinds should be planted at least 90 cm (3 ft) apart and the smaller bedding dahlias 45 cm (18 in) apart.

As the shoots start to develop thin these to leave about three strong shoots to each plant. When these reach about 20 to 23 cm (8 to 9 in) in height, it is a good idea to pinch out the main growing points. This will encourage the side shoots to grow and will result in a bushy plant with a larger number of flowers. Only the larger-flowered kinds and those grown for exhibition need disbudding to leave one bud at the apex of the shoot.

Dahlias need plenty of water and to conserve soil moisture the area around the plants can be mulched with a layer of peat, leafmould, garden compost or well-rotted manure. Feed regularly with a general fertilizer scraping away the mulch if you have applied one. As the taller-growing kinds develop they will require tying loosely to the stakes.

As the season reaches its climax, it may be necessary to thin out some of the surplus young shoots higher up the plant, otherwise it becomes a mass of foliage with poor quality flowers. This is done by snapping off all the side shoots for about 45 to 60 cm (1½ to 2 ft) from the tip of each stem.

After flowering and before any severe

frosty weather cut down the plants to within 23 to 30 cm (9 to 12 in) of the ground and label each with the name of its cultivar. Lift the tubers and store.

Dahlias are divided into groups according to the shape and formation of their flowers. Grow the small and medium-flowered forms for garden display reserving the large-flowered types for exhibition work. Dahlias are splendid mixed border subjects, they look striking when grown in a bed on their own and the dwarf cultivars are among my favourite bedding plants. The Cactus and Semi-cactus dahlias have spiky flowers and the flatter-petalled types are called Decoratives. Dahlias with globular flowers less than 5 cm (2 in) in diameter are called Pompons and above this size are called Ball dahlias. The dwarf dahlias, up to 60 cm (2 ft) in height, are the bedding dahlias. A good catalogue will offer you a wide choice of dahlias in a wide and beautiful colour range.

Dierama

Like so many other fine bulbous plants *Dierama pulcherrimum* comes from South Africa and as its native habitat suggests it needs a sunny, sheltered position and a well-drained but moist soil. The corms should be planted 8 to 10 cm (3 to 4 in) deep and 8 cm (3 in) apart in the autumn for flowering in July and August. The bell-like flowers of white or purple hang from long, arched stems and the leaves are grass like. Protect in winter and increase by seed sown in spring in a cool greenhouse or frame, or by division of the clusters of corms in March.

Eranthis

The winter aconites are very useful plants for they thrive in moist, shady conditions where little else will grow. They should be planted 5 cm (2 in) deep and 5 cm (2 in) apart in September or October and left undisturbed for as long as possible. They will provide excellent ground cover.

The most widely grown species is *Eranthis hyemalis* which flowers from January to March with a carpet of buttercup yellow against attractive, much divided leaves. *E. tubergeniana* has handsome deep yellow scented flowers, measuring 5 cm (2 in) across, and its cultivar 'Guinea Gold' which is somewhat later flowering has deep yellow fragrant flowers and bronzy foliage.

Increase by division of the tubers in September or October.

Eremurus

These are the foxtail lilies, tall, noble plants for the back of the border. They have strap-like leaves and long tail-like flower spikes which will need protection from the wind. Give them a deeply worked rich soil and plant the crowns from October to December. They may need some winter protection but can be left for three or four years before lifting and dividing.

The golden-yellow flowers of *Eremurus bungei* appear in July and are 1.5 to 1.8 m (5 to 6 ft) high. *E. himalaicus* is taller at 2.4 m (8 ft), flowering in May and June with white flowers which have orange anthers. The 3-m (10-ft) *E. robustus*

'Elwesianus' produces spikes of large delicate pink flowers in June.

Erythronium

The violets revel in a semi-shady place and moist but well-drained soil. Various forms of the Dog's Tooth Violet, *Erythronium dens-canis*, are available in white, purple, pink and mauve and in heights from 15 to 23 cm (6 to 9 in). The nodding flowers appear in March and April. Slightly later flowering is the handsome *E. revolutum* with delightfully mottled leaves. This species has rose-pink flowers and there is a white form, 'White Beauty', with brown markings at the base of the petals. *E. tuolumnense* is another fine species, with golden-yellow flowers and pale green leaves.

Plant in August or September 5 to 8 cm (2 to 3 in) deep and the same distance apart, in a soil which contains plenty of humus material. Increase by offsets removed in early autumn.

Erythronium dens-canis

Fritillaria

It is strange that the two most commonly grown members of this genus should be so very different from one another though they share the same month of flowering, April.

Fritillaria meleagris is the Snake's Head Fritillary and it grows about 30 cm (1 ft) high. The beautiful markings on the bell-shaped flowers are among the most unusual to be found for they are chequered in various shades of purple. There are fine named varieties available like the white 'Aphrodite', the purple 'Charon', and 'Saturnus', a pretty pinkish-purple shade. The Snake's Head Fritillary is a native of Britain and may be found growing wild in some districts. It likes a moist but well-drained soil and looks well in borders or naturalized in grass. The bulbs should be planted in September, 10 cm (4 in) deep and 15 cm (6 in) apart, and left undisturbed for as long as possible. Increase by offsets taken at the time of replanting.

Fritillaria imperialis, the Crown Imperial, is an impressive plant with a close-packed tuft of leaves encircling the tops of the 90-cm to 1.2-m (3- to 4-ft) stems above the nodding yellow, red or orange-red, bell-shaped flowers. It prefers a fairly rich soil which is on the heavy side and is best suited to a partly shaded border or a woodland setting. Plant as for *F. meleagris*, 15 cm (6 in) deep and 30 cm (12 in) apart.

Galanthus

Galanthus nivalis is the very popular Common Snowdrop which, at 15 cm (6 in) tall, flowers in January and February. It has two outstanding cultivars in 'S. Arnott', which has beautifully formed flowers, and 'Atkinsii'. Other species – *byzantinus*, *elwesii* and *plicatus*, all 23 to 30 cm (9 to 12 in) tall – extend the flowering season. Each has white flowers with green markings.

Fritillaria meleagris and the white cultivar 'Aphrodite'

Plant 8 cm (3 in) deep and 8 cm (3 in) apart in April. All three species can be propagated by offsets.

Lilium

There are two important points to remember when making a selection of lilies to grow in the garden. Some are lime haters and some are stem rooting i.e. they form roots on the lower part of the stem as well as basally from the bulb. This means that they have to be planted deeper – 20 to 23 cm (8 to 9 in) as opposed to 13 to 15 cm (5 or 6 in) for the others. To add confusion, however, there are exceptions to this rule notably *Lilium candidum* and *L. giganteum* (*Cardiocrinum giganteum*), both non stem rooters, which are covered with only 1 cm ($\frac{1}{2}$ in) of soil.

Lilies like a well-prepared, well-drained soil and a cool root run. They should therefore be planted with rather open-habited, low-growing shrubs and herbaceous plants in a mixed border as these will shade the lilies' roots. Plant during October and November and bed on sand as the bulbs have a tendency to rot. Once planted leave lilies undisturbed for as long as possible and mulch each spring with peat or leafmould. When deterioration is noticeable divide the clumps of bulbs and replant in autumn. Stake as necessary.

Lilies can be propagated vegetatively from an original single bulb, by means of scales, division or bulbils, or from seed.

Here is a brief description of some of the best garden lilies in alphabetical order starting with the Golden-rayed Lily of Japan, *Lilium auratum*. It has many highly scented white flowers with crimson spots, each petal marked with a golden ray in August and September. It is stem rooting and grows 1.5 to 2.1 m (5 to 7 ft) tall. *L. candidum* is the Madonna Lily with pure white, fragrant flowers on 1.8-m (6-ft) stems in July. Unlike many lilies, this one actually likes a limy soil. *L. davidii*, the handsome Chinese Lily, has red Turk's-cap flowers covered with black spots. It has two fine forms, 'Maxwill', a bright orange-red colour and about 30 cm (1 ft) taller than the type at 1.8 m (6 ft), and *willmottiae*, a very impressive deep orange. These are stem

rooting and lime tolerant.

For flowering in August and September, as well as in sun or shade, the lime-tolerant stem-rooting *Lilium henryi* is excellent with orange-yellow flowers marked with dark spots on 1.8- to 2.1-m (6- to 7-ft) stems. *L. speciosum* (*lancifolium*) thrives in sun or partial shade and flowers in August or September on 90-cm to 1.5-m (3- to 5-ft) stems. It is stem rooting and the form 'Roseum' is white, spotted pink; 'Rubrum' is white spotted red, and 'Album' is pure white. *L. longiflorum* has lovely, trumpet-shaped, waxy, white flowers on 90-cm (3-ft) stems in June and July.

Lilium martagon 'Album' is the white form of the Turk's-cap Lily. It does not mind limy soil and will grow 90 cm to 1.5 m (3 to 5 ft) high, flowering in June and July. *L. pardalinum*, the Panther Lily, has orange and crimson Turk's-cap flowers, heavily marked with crimson-brown spots. These are borne in July on 1.5- to 1.8-m (5- to 6-ft) stems. They like a damp soil and do not object to lime. *L. regale* has handsome trumpet flowers which are suffused with pinkish purple and maroon shades on the outside and white within, flushed yellow in the throat. It grows to 1.8 m (6 ft) tall, is stem rooting and lime tolerant. *L. tigrinum* 'Splendens' is a particularly fine form of the Tiger Lily with rich salmon-orange flowers in August. It is a stem rooter which does not like alkaline soils and it will grow 1.2 to 1.8 m (4 to 6 ft) high.

Apart from the species there are many excellent hybrid strains including the Mid-century Hybrids which grow 76 cm to 1.2 m ($2\frac{1}{2}$ to 4 ft) tall in a lime-free soil and flower in June and July with an excellent colour range. The African Queen strain of trumpet lilies has large flowers of apricot yellow suffused with reddish bronze. They are 1.5 m (5 ft) tall and flower in late June and July.

The Golden Clarion strain has trumpet flowers in varying shades of yellow, gold and orange, often marked with deep red. They flower in July on 1- to 1.2-m ($3\frac{1}{2}$- to 4-ft) stems. The strain of trumpet lilies called Golden Splendour includes only golden-coloured lilies. The Bellingham Hybrids have Turk's-cap flowers on 2.1-

OPPOSITE: *Leucojum aestivum*, the Summer Snowflake

frame or cool greenhouse. They like sunny, sheltered conditions.

The Double Turban ranunculus are obtainable in separate colours including scarlet, orange and yellow as well as mixed shades. There are also the Giant French varieties and the double Persian Mixed strain.

Salvia

Salvia patens is a tuberous-rooted perennial with large blue sage-like flowers on 60-cm (2-ft) stems from July to September. The tubers can be planted 10 to 13 cm (4 to 5 in) deep and 38 cm (15 in) apart in mid-April and they can be started into growth in a large flower pot under glass in early April and hardened off for planting out at the end of May.

The tubers should be lifted about the middle of October, dried and stored as for dahlias, for although the roots are hardy frost may kill the young shoots as they emerge in the spring.

Schizostylis

The Kaffir Lily is a handsome bulbous subject for the autumn border provided it is given warm, sunny conditions and a good loamy soil. Protection with straw or bracken is necessary in the winter. Plant between October and March and lift and divide the bulbous rhizomes every third year in March or April.

The species *Schizostylis coccinea* has crimson flowers on 30 to 45 cm (1- to 1½-ft) spikes. It has several good forms of which I would recommend the September–October flowering 'Mrs Hegarty' or the November-flowering 'Viscountess Byng'. Both have pink flowers.

Scilla

This is the genus to which the Bluebell belongs and the first species to bloom in the year is the February-flowering Siberian Squill, *Scilla sibirica*. The intensely blue blooms are borne in profusion on 10- to 15-cm (4- to 6-in) stems. Larger than the type is 'Atrocaerulea', or 'Spring Beauty', which also has flowers of a rich blue colouring. This is followed by *S. tubergeniana* with flowers of pale blue and white. It is very effective when grown in groups in borders on the rock garden or in grass in sunny positions.

A species for a warm, sunny position is *Scilla peruviana* with ball-shaped heads of flowers on 23-cm (9-in) stems in May and June.

The Spanish Bluebell is now *Endymion hispanicus* but it used to be *Scilla campanulata* (syn. *S. hispanica*). It looks good naturalized in light shade, among shrubs or under trees, and there are fine named varieties like the pale blue 'Myosotis', the tall 'Imperator', with pure white flower spikes, and 'Queen of the Pinks', a rosy-pink cultivar. The English Bluebell, now *E. non-scriptus*, is very well known. It has both white and pink forms, all being excellent for naturalizing.

Plant in ordinary soil at any time between August and November, 5 to 10 cm (2 to 4 in) deep and 10 cm (4 in) apart. *S. peruviana* should be planted 15 cm (6 in) deep and 15 cm (6 in) apart. Increase by offsets in autumn.

Sparaxis

These brilliantly coloured subjects live up to their common name of the harlequin flowers for the spring blooms come in colours like red, purple, black, white and yellow. The flowers are often up to 5 cm (2 in) across on stems 15 to 23 cm (6 to 9 in) high. The narrow foliage is also very attractive.

They need a warm, sunny position and a fairly dry soil, and protection from bracken or other material is necessary in very cold weather. Plant the corms in autumn, 10 cm (4 in) deep and 5 cm (2 in) apart. Increase by offsets.

Sternbergia

Sternbergia lutea is a charming little plant for autumn colour. The golden-yellow crocus-like flowers will look attractive in a border, in a rock garden, or when naturalized in grass. It grows to about 15 cm (6 in) in height and has strap-shaped leaves.

The bulbs should be planted 10 to 15 cm (4 to 6 in) deep and 15 cm (6 in) apart in July in a sunny, well-drained position. Protect in winter with straw or bracken. Propagation is by the new bulbs produced every year.

OPPOSITE: Daffodils, tulips and the blue Grape Hyacinth, *Muscari armeniacum*, brighten up the garden in spring

Tigridia pavonia

Tigridia

The unusual and exotic flowers of the Tiger Flower, *Tigridia pavonia*, are evocative of the country from which they come, Mexico. The orange-red, three-petalled flowers are spotted at the base with deeper colouring. There are also forms with pinkish, mauve, yellow and white colouring. Unfortunately each flower has only a brief day of glory in late summer and early autumn but each 60-cm (2-ft) stem produces several flowers to open in succession. This plant needs a sunny border and a moist but well-drained soil.

Plant the corms 8 cm (3 in) deep and 15 cm (6 in) apart in April and lift to store in October. Increase by offsets removed in April.

Trillium

The Wake Robin or American Wood Lily, *Trillium grandiflorum*, is a tuberous perennial. It is valuable because of its liking for rather damp, shady places and is an excellent plant for woodland conditions. Give it a peaty soil, topdress annually with decayed leaves and leave undisturbed for as long as possible, dividing when necessary in March. The white flowers, some 8-cm (3 in) across, are carried on 45-cm (1½-ft) stems above whorls of practically stemless broad leaves in May. There is a pink form, 'Roseum'.

Tulipa

Tulips run a close second to the daffodils for the title of most popular flowering bulb with their bright, dazzling range of colours and diversity of shape and form. They are happy growing in any reasonable garden soil provided it is well prepared and will thrive in sunshine and semi-shade. Tulips can be grown in a variety of situations but possibly look their best when interplanted with subjects which flower at the same time such as aubrietas, forget-me-nots, violas and wallflowers. Many combinations are possible, all of which give a lovely, long-flowering effect. They should all be planted about 10 cm (4 in) deep and 15 cm (6 in) apart in October and November and can be propagated by offsets or seeds.

Those used for bedding purposes should be lifted and replanted in a reserve bed until the foliage has withered when they can be lifted again and stored in a cool, airy room until replanting time comes round. In fact the bulbs of the garden cultivars benefit from an annual lifting whereas those of the species can be left undisturbed for several years.

I shall start this brief summary with the species tulips which are becoming increasingly popular. Many of them can be grown on the rock garden or as edgings to other plantings. A warm position with good drainage is needed for *Tulipa clusiana*, the Lady Tulip, but this elegant species is a joy in April when its red, white and purple flowers are in the full flush of their beauty. *T. eichleri* starts to flower at the end of March on 38-cm (15-in) stems. The scarlet blooms have petals marked with black, yellow-margined blotch.

Tulipa kaufmanniana is the Water Lily Tulip, a species which has given us a wonderful range of March–April flowering hybrids, all 15 to 20 cm (6 to 8 in) tall and suitable for rock gardens or borders. The small flowers of *T. orphanidea* are an attractive, unusual orange shade and those of *T. praestans* 'Fusilier' a spectacular orange scarlet on 23-cm (9-in) stems. *T. tarda* flowers in late April–early May and has yellow flowers with yellowish-green and white markings on 15-cm (6-in) stems.

The garden cultivars are so numerous that they have been classified into groups as follows. Early Singles which flower in mid-April and are about 30 cm (1 ft) tall; Early Doubles which are of a similar height and flower at the end of April. Darwin Tulips flower in May on 69-cm (2-ft) or longer stems and have well-shaped flowers in lovely colours: Cottage Tulips share the same height and flowering period but the flowers are of a less regimental shape. The elegant lily-flowered tulips have waisted flowers. Rembrandts resemble Darwins in all respects but colour having stripes and blotched flowers. Old English Tulips are very regular and refined in form whereas Parrot Tulips have flowers with curiously twisted and slashed petals, blotched and green. Then there are the Mendel and

Triumph Tulips, the late Doubles and the Fosteriana Hybrids. The Greigii Hybrids are especially notable for their lovely coloration and the handsome markings on the leaves. They are April flowering at 23 to 30 cm (9 to 12 in). The Multi-flowered Tulips have several flowers on each stem. The Viridiflora or green tulips flower in May on 23- to 60-cm (9- to 24-in) stems and they have distinctive green markings on the petals. In the Fringed Tulips, as the name implies, the edges of the petals are fringed or serrated. Broken varieties have lovely markings on the petals which are unusually attractive.

Zephyranthes

Zephyranthes candida is the Zephyr Flower of the west wind from America. The handsome star-like flowers appear on 15- to 30-cm (6- to 12-in) stems well above the grass-like foliage in September. It is another subject for a warm sunny border, preferably against a south wall and a light, sandy, well-drained soil. The bulbs should be planted between August and November 10 cm (4 in) deep and 10 cm (4 in) apart and given winter protection. It can be increased by offsets during the same period.

Rock Plants

ROYTON E. HEATH

Since Reginald Farrer's classic work, *The English Rock Garden*, was first published, there has been a steady but sure interest in the growing of rock plants in the United Kingdom and today two specialized societies of this form of gardening have a combined membership in excess of ten thousand.

With the ever-increasing cost of land, the number of large gardens are fast becoming a minority and the remainder are to be measured in square metres rather than hectares. Naturally with restricted garden space, the need for plants of a small stature, which will not readily outgrow their allotted space, is only too apparent and rock plants are well suited for this purpose.

There are a number of methods by which a site can be adapted to grow a worthwhile collection and these will be briefly dealt with here. It is normally quoted in books dealing with rock plants that the site must be open, away from all buildings, trees, shrubs and other growing plants. This idealistic advice would be easy to follow if all the necessary open space was available, but rarely is this so today. By all means choose an open site if possible, but to my knowledge many thousands of rock plants are thriving in alien situations, such as the heart of our industrial areas and even here the rarer plants are grown to perfection. There is only one type of site where this is not possible and that is adjacent to surface-rooting trees or those producing surface suckers, such as elms, limes, poplars and silver birches. In these circumstances reliance will have to be placed on troughs and other containers raised above the level of the ground and as far as possible from all trees.

If the available space is not large enough to incorporate a rock garden, although even a small one is better than none, it should be possible to build up border edges, or small walls, if the site is a sloping one, to grow a large number of plants. These can be planted with arabis, alyssum, aubrieta, phlox, campanulas and helianthemum cultivars which will, if intermixed, provide a carpet of colour from late March until July. An under-planting of dwarf bulbs will also enhance the display. They will add both colour and balance when used in conjunction with other garden features and where necessary provide a natural division between different parts of the garden.

Soils

The ideal soil for rock plants is a light open medium loam with faultless drainage. A lime-free soil is preferable, for lime can be added if required, whereas lime-hating plants will only grow in specially prepared pockets of lime-free soil. Even then they rarely succeed for long. A rich loamy soil can be lightened by the addition of coarse sand or gravel well worked into the top 15 cm (6 in). The amount to be used will depend on the texture of the loam, the heavier the loam the larger the quantity of sand.

A different approach will be needed if the soil is clay. No attempt should be made to lighten this medium, an almost impossible task, nor should pockets be dug and light mixtures used for filling in as in wet weather these will become just a series of pools, resulting in death traps for the plants. If there is a natural slope, it can be utilized and if possible a pit can be dug at the base and filled with rough drainage material topped with upturned turves or other roughage to prevent soil blocking the drainage. The rock garden is then built up above the ground level using a light well-drained compost. The minimum depth should be 23 cm (9 in), the height according to the type of rock

OPPOSITE: The author's garden

Right: Section through a rock garden on a clay slope.
(a) Original slope with irregularities removed and surface made firm.
(b) Stone or brick rubble to assist drainage.
(c) Infilling compost of equal parts loam, peat and sand.
(d) Rockwork.
(e) Reversed turves or brushwood to prevent clogging or silting.
(f) Drainage pit or trench, three-quarters filled with coarse rubble

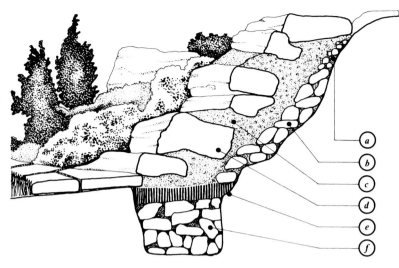

garden under construction. The line drawing gives comprehensive details of building on a flat surface over clay. At the base, adjacent to the drainage pit, leafmould or peat should be added in quantity to the compost, providing an ideal spot for growing the dwarf moisture-loving primulas and other kindred plants.

Instead of the drainage pit, a pool can be built and the line drawings show plans of such a pool using PVC sheeting which can be obtained either already formed to lay in situ or in sheet form to suit one's own taste.

Whatever type of soil is used, great care must be taken to ensure that this is free of all perennial weeds; a most important point because failure may result in many hours of tedious weeding after planting has been completed, or even having to dismantle and rebuild the rock garden. Nothing is worse than finding bindweed appearing in the middle of a treasured cushion plant.

Section through a rock garden on a flat clay site.
(a) Structure cut away to show drainage system.
(b) Low retaining wall placed over drainage trench covering.
(c) Reversed turves, brushwood bundles, or flat slabs over drainage trench to prevent clogging and silting.
(d) Drainage trench 90 cm (3 ft) deep and 60 cm (2 ft) wide, filled with coarse rubble.
(e) Drainage channels 23 cm (9 in) wide and 23 cm (9 in) deep formed to slope down to drainage trench at rear. Channels filled in with rubble for three-quarters of their depth and topped with brushwood.
(f) Channels approximately 1.2 m (4 ft) apart

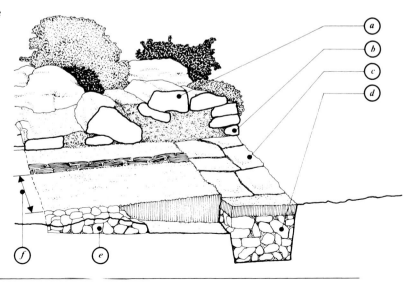

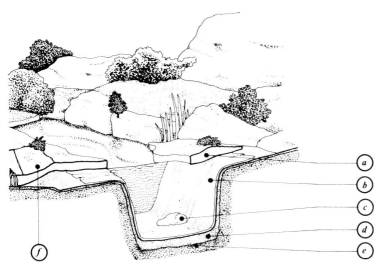

PVC-lined pool incorporated in a rock garden.
(a) Rockwork to overhang edge of pool by about 4 cm ($1\frac{1}{2}$ in).
(b) PVC sheet to overlap flattened edge not less than 23 cm (9 in) all round.
(c) Stones to hold sheeting in position.
(d) Bed of soft sand or sifted soil to prevent damage to PVC.
(e) Depth can be varied by contouring the soil.
(f) Paving slabs to overhang edge of pool by about 4 cm ($1\frac{1}{2}$ in)

Rocks

It is difficult to give precise instructions on building a rock garden, much depends on the available space and type of rock employed. The actual placing of the rocks must be left to the gardener's own choice and provided a few simple rules are adhered to a satisfactory result can be achieved. First, the rocks should have two exposed positions, one facing the sun, the other in shade or half shade to suit all types of plants. Second, if the rock has a natural strata, it should be almost parallel to the surface. Lastly, one or two simple outcrops are much better than a pile of stone placed higgledy-piggledy. The line drawings give a general idea of what is required.

There are a number of different types of stone available but for the rock garden they generally fall into three groups. Limestone is the easiest to use for it has a natural stratification which makes correct placing easy. The great disadvantage is cost for unless you live near to a source of supply it is very expensive. Sandstone

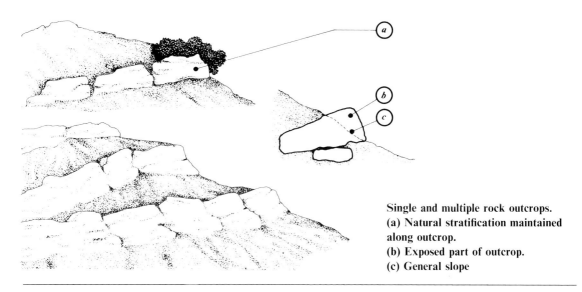

Single and multiple rock outcrops.
(a) Natural stratification maintained along outcrop.
(b) Exposed part of outcrop.
(c) General slope

Rock garden constructed from broken paving slabs.
(a) Tilted or dipping strata.
(b) Soil infilling.
(c) Cement.
(d) Paving abutting on to 8-cm (3-in) layer of hardcore.
(e) Upper layers of slabs should have a more pronounced backward tilt.
(f) Slabs laid in courses with soil between. Gaps left at intervals for crevice and trailing plants.
(g) Lowest course of slabs given a slight backward tilt and cemented to edge of paving.
(h) Crazy paving surround

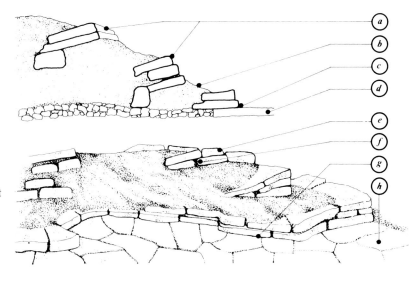

is normally less so and it is often possible to find a local source. It also blends in more naturally with the surroundings but a word of warning. If sandstone is used, make sure that it is not composed of soft material as this has a tendency to disintegrate after hard frosts. Tufa has several advantages; it is light to handle, extremely porous and it is easy to drill holes in which to plant cushion and saxitile plants. The disadvantages are cost and only a few sources of supply. A substitute, which can be used if cost has to be considered, is old cement blocks normally obtainable quite cheaply locally. No doubt for a year or so they would look raw, but a covering of plants and the resultant weathering would soon overcome this.

An ideal medium for constructing a rock garden is artificial broken paving slabs which are obtainable cheaply from local council yards. These are used to simulate a natural outcrop shown in the line drawing. Real walling stone is preferable, of course, but the difference in price is considerable.

When laying rock or other material a firm steady base is essential. Bury as little as possible, consistent with firmness, so that the roots of the plants have no difficulty in finding a cool moist root run. A dusting of HCH powder at the base of each rock will discourage most pests.

Rock borders and retaining walls
The retaining wall is a taller extension of the rock border and a study of the line drawings, which give all the relevant details for their construction, should make this easy. The soil required in these is the same as for the rock garden and the notes on drainage apply also.

Troughs
If the overall garden area is small and as often happens limited to a strip of communal grass and small patios, this method of growing rock plants is ideal. A large number can be successfully grown providing colour throughout the year, especially if some of the really dwarf conifers and berried shrubs are used as dot plants or a scenic backcloth. One of the great advantages of this type of gardening is that an ever-changing colourful landscape in miniature can be built or individual troughs used for collections of plants of specific genera or cultivars. For example saxifrages, sempervivums, sedums, miniature willows, crocuses, tulips, narcissi, and iris species are all better suited when grouped individually. Dwarf bulbous plants can be carpeted with prostrate plants such as antennarias, some asperulas, *Campanula arvatica*, *Gypsophila repens*, *Linum salsoloides nanum*, paronychia etc.

Diagram 1

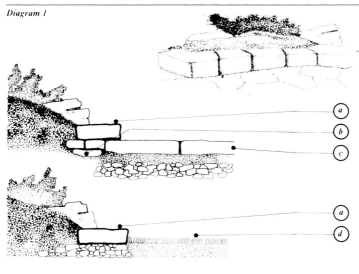

Diagram 1
Rock border using a single line of
walling stone.
(a) Single line edging.
(b) Bedding stones.
(c) Paving laid on bed of sand over
rammed hardcore.
(d) Grass surround or lawn edge as an
alternative to paving

Diagram 2
Rock border using a double line of
walling stone.
(a) Double line edging.
(b) Slight backward tilt.
(c) Paving or grass.
(d) Bedding stones

Diagram 3
Dry stone walling.
(a) "Headers" or "thro' stones" at
intervals in all courses.
(b) Note broken line of joints.
(c) Backward tilt or "batter",
approximately 10 degrees.
(d) Soil-filled gaps for planting up; insert
plants as wall is being built.
(e) Headers placed at vertical intervals
of four courses

Diagram 2

Diagram 3

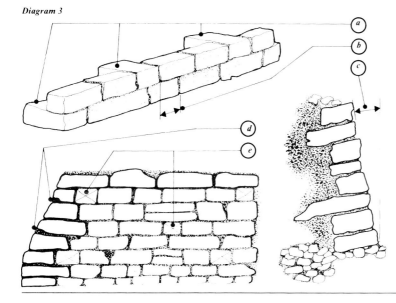

An attractive stone trough in a town garden

The natural stone trough is now a rarity and often difficult to find but there are a number of suitable stone substitutes on the market, the only restriction to their use is that they should not be less than 15 cm (6 in) deep. The line drawing is self-explanatory with all necessary details. One important point to remember is that the plants must not be allowed to suffer from drought in dry spells. The troughs should be raised off the ground to a height to suit the grower.

Planting

The vast majority of rock plants are pot grown so they can be planted at all times of the year with the exception of frosty weather. Small specimens should be chosen, these are seldom pot bound and acclimatize easier. They should not be allowed to dry out after planting especially during the summer months. The top 2.5 cm (1 in) round the collar of the plants should be left bare and when all planting is completed a top dressing of chippings is placed over the whole of the rock garden, troughs, walls or rock borders, including the necks of the plants.

Propagation

The various ways in which the plants can be propagated are mentioned in the A–Z list. A loam-based seed compost such as John Innes Seed Compost is a suitable medium for raising plants from seed. An ericaceous one without chalk should be used for the lime haters. After germination the plants should be potted on once they have formed their first true leaves.

Cuttings are best rooted in an equal mixture of peat and coarse sand either in a propagating frame or placed round the side of a pot and a plastic bag tied over the rim of the pot. They normally root in a matter of two weeks or so.

When dividing plants make sure that each piece has roots attached.

Pests and diseases

These can be kept to a minimum by spraying with a systemic insecticide and fungicide when growth commences in early spring, repeating approximately every eight weeks during the growing season. Slugs can be kept in check by spreading slug pellets where they are likely to congregate. Ants and woodlice are discouraged by using a dusting powder containing HCH.

Sink or trough garden.
(a) Stone.
(b) Compost (see below).
(c) Layer of leaf or peat roughage.
(d) Layer of broken crock.
(e) Surface layer of stone chips.
(f) Drainage hole

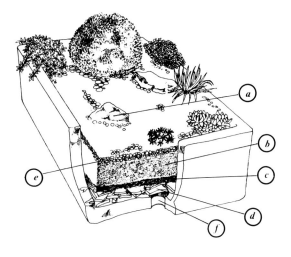

Composts suitable for trough gardens:
(a) Equal parts of loam, leafmould and sand. This is a suitable mixture for plants which require a light, open, porous soil with good drainage. A good mixture for troughs in a sheltered position in half shade. All bulbs and conifers do well in this medium.
(b) Equal parts of loam, leafmould, peat and sand.

Retentive of water but well drained. Suitable for plants which like full sun and also for woodland plants grown in half shade.
(c) Three parts Cornish silversand and one part flaked leafmould.
For all difficult and rare high alpines, including most of the cushion type. The trough containing this mixture is best sited in half shade

Selected Rock Plants

Acantholimon

This is a small genus, liking neutral or acid soil, which provides interest in winter with the persistent cup-like bracts. One of the easiest to grow is the Armenian *Acantholimon glumaceum* with loose cushions in rosette formation. This species has deep green needle-shaped, spine-tipped foliage and the rosy-pink flowers appear in June on 15-cm (6-in) stems. You can expect the Prickly Thrift to have a spread of 23 cm (9 in) in maturity. It is increased by cuttings in August.

Achillea

The milfoils or yarrows are mostly grown for their finely cut aromatic foliage. *Achillea ageratifolia* has a tufted habit and is only 5 cm (2 in) high with deeply toothed, narrow, intensely downy, white leaves and white daisy flowers. It comes from Greece. *A. × lewisii*, a garden hy-

brid, makes a mat of grey-green cut foliage and has light yellow flowers on 15-cm (6-in) stems. Both have a long flowering season from June to July and can be increased by cuttings in July.

Aethionema

This genus contains a number of easy rock plants known by the common name of the Persian candytufts. They are well represented by *Aethionema armenum*, which has narrow blue-grey leaves and neat heads of pink, veined flowers on 15-cm (6-in) stems from May to August; and 'Warley Rose', an improved garden form, with larger, deeper pink-coloured flowers. Both are 10 to 15 cm (4 to 6 in) high with a spread of 30 cm (12 in) and are suitable for a dry wall as well as the rock garden. Cut back after flowering and propagate by cuttings in June.

Allium

There are a number of ornamental onions which make an attractive display in the rock garden in August. They are all about 23 cm (9 in) high. *Allium cyaneum* is a Chinese species with grass-like leaves and semi-pendant blue flowers. *A. cyathophorum farreri* (syn. *A. farreri*), with pendant, bell-shaped, reddish-purple flowers, is from Kansu. *A. narcissiflorum* is a native of south eastern Europe and it bears semi-pendant bright rose flowers. Seed is an easy method of increase in March.

Alyssum

The madworts are evergreen plants from 8 to 23 cm (3 to 9 in) high with a spread of 60 cm (24 in). They are ideal for a wall and together with arabis and aubrieta will provide a riot of early spring colour. They should be cut back after flowering and can be propagated by cuttings in July.

Alyssum alpestre is a sub-shrub from the European Alps with grey oblong hairy leaves and pale yellow flowers in clusters. *A. saxatile*, with its descriptive common name of Gold Dust, is a sub-shrub with silver-grey leaves. The clustered flowers are golden yellow and named cultivars include 'Citrinum', lemon yellow; 'Compactum', smaller, bright yellow; 'Plenum', double yellow, and 'Variegatum', yellow and grey-green leaves.

Andromeda

These are evergreen plants for a shady lime-free rock garden and the edge of a pool. *Andromeda glaucophylla* is a dwarf shrub only 15 cm (6 in) high and 30 cm (12 in) wide with narrow grey-green leaves and pale pink urn-shaped flowers in May. *A. polifolia*, the Bog Rosemary, is a native of the northern hemisphere and has deep green leaves with pale pink flowers on 15-cm (6-in) stems in May. Its cultivars 'Compacta' and 'Minima' from Japan are both smaller with foliage variations. Cuttings are a ready means of increase in May.

Androsace

The rock jasmines are true alpine plants with a world-wide distribution. Their flowering period is April to May and they are from 5 to 10 cm (2 to 4 in) high and 10 to 35 cm (4 to 15 in) wide. All require faultless drainage and can be increased by seed in March or cuttings in June.

Androsace carnea, native to Europe, makes rosettes of narrow, evergreen foliage and the flowers are bright rose with a yellow eye. Good subspecies are *brigantiaca*, white; *halleri*, deep pink, from Switzerland, and *laggeri*, smaller rosettes with bright pink flowers from the Pyrenees.

Androsace sarmentosa is a native of the Himalayas and it forms rosettes of silver-grey hairy foliage. The large pale pink flowers are borne in clusters. The cultivar 'Brilliant', deep rose red, and subspecies *chumbyi* with compact clusters of deep pink flowers from the Chumbi Valley are recommended.

Anemone

There are a number of the charming, free-flowering windflowers suitable for the rock garden. *Anemone baldensis* is a herbaceous perennial with deeply cut leaves and starry white flowers, tinged blue on the reverse. Native of Europe, it blooms on 8-cm (3-in) stems in May and June. It requires a moist spot. Divide in July.

Anemone blanda is a bulbous plant with incurving segments of deeply cut green foliage and, during March and April, blue to purple-blue flowers on 10-cm (4-in) stems. The cultivar 'Atrocaerulea' is deep blue and 'Rosea' is bright pink. *A. obtusiloba patula*, the Blue Buttercup, comes from the Himalayas. It has rosettes of hairy three-lobed green leaves. The blue flowers are cup shaped and they appear in May and June at the end of prostrate shoots. Propagation is by seed in March.

Antennaria

The blue flowers are cup shaped and they provide covering for choice bulbs as well as being attractive plants. At home in the northern hemisphere, *Antennaria dioica* forms 5-cm (2-in) high mats of evergreen, grey-green leaves and in May and June clusters of pink flowers backed with green, pink-tipped bracts. The cultivar 'Minima' is less than 2.5 cm (1 in) high and 'Nyewood' has the attractive combination of silver leaves and crimson flowers. Division in August is an easy means of increase.

Anthyllis

There is one species and two forms of the kidney vetch which are very attractive. The European *Anthyllis montana* makes mats of silvery downy leaves 8 cm (3 in) high and 30 cm (12 in) wide with rose, clover-like flowers over a long period from June to September. 'Alba', white, and 'Rubra', deep rose red, are the good cultivars. Increase by cuttings in May.

Aquilegia

The columbine is a widely distributed genus of herbaceous perennials containing some delightful miniatures. *Aquilegia bertolonii* is about 10 cm (4 in) high and forms tufts of grey-green leaves with violet-blue spurred flowers in May. It comes from Italy. *A. canadensis*, from north west America, has tufts of green cut leaves and in May red flowers with yellow petals on 20-cm (8-in) stems.

Aquilegia flabellata 'Nana' is native to Japan and looks well planted in a trough. It has grey-blue cut leaves on 10-cm (4-in) stems and large blue and cream flowers in May. Propagation is by means of seed which should be sown in July.

Arabis

This is a family containing some gems which are all ideal for planting on a sunny wall together with aubrieta for an early spring display. The following species and cultivars of the rock cress are to be recommended.

Arabis alpina is a close compact plant with oval leaves and white flowers. It comes from Europe and is about 15 cm (6 in) high and 38 cm (15 in) wide. *A. caucasica* (syn. *A. albida*) makes a mat about 45 cm (18 in) wide with leaves in grey rosettes and fragrant white flowers clustered on 23-cm (9-in) stems. It, too, is a native of Europe. Its cultivar 'Billardieri' is rose and 'Flore Pleno' has double white flowers.

Arabis ferdinandi-coburgi 'Variegata' is a form with well-marked bright green foliage which has a marginal band of cream. The flowers are white on 15-cm (6-in) stems. They are all evergreen and

should be cut back after flowering. Increase by cuttings taken in July.

Armeria

The sea pinks or thrifts are all similar but the one listed here is possibly the best. *Armeria juniperifolia* 'Bevan's Variety' forms dense 5-cm (2-in) evergreen cushions of bright green soft spiny leaves about 15 cm (6 in) across. The flowers are rounded heads of deep cerise red on short stems in May and June. Increase by cuttings in June.

Artemisia

This is a family of aromatic silver-grey foliage plants useful as foils to other plants. Both the species mentioned are evergreen. *Artemisia glacialis* is a close sub-shrub about 5 cm (2 in) high and 15 cm (6 in) wide with narrow silver-downed leaves. The June flowers are yellow.

It comes from central Europe and is a good subject for trough culture. *A. schmidtiana* 'Nana' is Japanese in origin and makes a plant of 5 cm (2 in) high and 23 cm (9 in) wide with narrow deeply cut silver-grey leaves. The pendant, yellow flowers appear in September. Both can be propagated by cuttings in July.

Asperula

The woodruffs make good dwarf evergreen plants for the rock garden or trough and are easily increased by cuttings taken in July. *Asperula lilaciflora caespitosa* is a native of south east Europe and it makes a mat of bright green heath-like foliage only 5 cm (2 in) high with prostrate stems of lilac-pink flowers in June.

The Greek species *suberosa* forms a 10-cm (4-in) mat of down-covered grey leaves up to 20 cm (8 in) wide. The long tubular pink flowers which first appear in May continue over a long period.

Aster

The starworts are dainty wildlings providing colour during late spring. The species *Aster alpinus*, from Europe, has typical large daisy flowers of lilac-purple with a golden eye on 10- to 15-cm (4- to 6-in) stems during May and June. It is a variable species, however, with many

Aquilegia flabellata
'Nana'

colour forms which include 'Albus', white; 'Roseus', pink; 'Ruber', deep red and 'Speciosus', bright purple. Division in September is a ready means of increase.

Aubrieta

Along with arabis and alyssum, this is one of the widest grown rock plants providing colour in early spring. The forms of *Aubrieta deltoidea*, the Wall Cress, are 8 cm (3 in) high and 60 to 90 cm (2 to 3 ft) wide making good plants for a dry wall. The species makes a compact carpet of grey-green hairy leaves and four-petalled mauve flowers in April and May. Good cultivars include 'Barker's Double', double, red; 'Blue King', blue; 'Bonfire', red; 'Bressingham Pink', double, pink; 'Church Knowle', deep lavender; 'Dr Mules', purple; 'Fire King', red; 'Green-court Purple', double, purple; 'Joan Allen', double, crimson; 'Magician', crimson purple; 'Russel's Crimson', red; 'Variegata Argentea', pale mauve, leaves margined silver, and 'Wanda', double, red.

All should be cut back after flowering and propagation is by cuttings in June or division in September.

Berberis

The barberries are represented here by two cultivars of *Berberis × stenophylla* which are ideal evergreen rock garden shrubs both about 30 cm (12 in) high and 60 cm (24 in) across with flowers in May followed by berries in September. 'Coral-lina Compacta' has spine-tipped bright green foliage, coral buds, yellow flowers and purple, white-bloomed fruit. It is as attractive as it sounds.

'Gracilis Nana' is equally lovely with yellow-flecked holly leaves which are a brilliant orange when young. The flowers are orange yellow and the berries purple. Propagate both by cuttings taken in July.

Calceolaria

The slipperworts are charming, herbaceous plants for a cool moist spot near a pool. They can be increased by division in April. *Calceolaria acutifolia* hails from Patagonia and from a pair of hairy green leaves are borne the pouch-like, golden-yellow flowers, dotted red on the reverse, on 15-cm (6-in) stems during June to August. *C. tenella*, from Chile, is a prostrate plant with minute light green leaves and, during June to August, up to three flowers on thread-like 2.5 cm (1-in) stems. These are golden yellow with crimson spots on the tips.

Campanula

The bell flowers are a large family of mid-season plants and they extend the flowering period in the rock garden until late August.

Campanula arvatica, from Spain, forms a mat of minute bright green foliage. Its dainty flowers are like violet-blue stars and they appear on 2.5-cm (1-in) stems in June and July. It is excellent for planting in a trough garden.

Campanula carpatica is a Carpathian species with a large number of garden forms. All have open bell-shaped flowers over grey-green foliage and are about 15 to 30 cm (6 to 12 in) high with a spread of 38 cm (15 in). They flower from June to August and include 'Alba', white; 'Coelestina', china blue; 'Isabel', violet, and 'Turbinata', purple blue.

The Italian *Campanula garganica* forms rosettes of kidney-shaped leaves and its white-eyed, blue flowers are to be found in June on 15-cm (6-in) stems. It is a good wall plant with a spread of up to 38 cm (15 in) across.

Campanula portenschlagiana (syn. *C. muralis*) is a species from Dalmatia suitable for walls. It bears tufted rosettes of kidney-shaped green foliage. The star-shaped, light violet-blue flowers are around from June to August on 8 cm (3-in) stems.

All can be increased by cuttings in June or division in April.

Cerastium

The well-known Snow in Summer should be avoided like the plague in small rock gardens but *Cerastium alpinum* subsp. *lanatum*, the Mouse-ear Chickweed from the European Alps, is a small plant with silky oval leaves and shiny white flowers on 5-cm (2-in) stems during May and June.

It is a suitable subject for a trough as its ultimate spread is only 22 cm (9 in). Propagation is carried out by division in July.

Chamaecytisus

There is only one dwarf broom suitable for the rock garden and that is *Chamaecytisus pygmaeus* from Turkey. It is about 10 cm (4 in) high and 30 cm (12 in) wide with prostrate stems and much cut narrow leaves. The bright yellow pea-shaped flowers are to be seen in June and it makes a good plant for a wall. Cuttings can be taken in June.

Chamaespartium

Chamaespartium sagittale subsp. *delphinensis* from the Pyrenees is a must for even the smallest rock garden or trough. It is only 8 cm (3 in) high with zig-zagged branches and winged adpressed grey-green leaves. In June it is covered in a mass of golden-yellow, pea-shaped flowers. It prefers a lime-free soil and can be increased by cuttings in June.

Crocus

There are a large number of crocus species suitable for the rock garden or trough and the following will give a display over a long period. All are from 8 to 10 cm (3 to 4 in) high and can be increased by seed and division.

Among those that flower in autumn (August to October) are *Crocus byzantinus*, flowers bluish purple, eastern Europe; *C. kotschyanus*, large, rose lilac, throat yellow, Asia Minor; *C. speciosus*, lavender blue, veined, Asia Minor, Persia, and cultivars 'Artabir', lavender blue with deeper feathering, and 'Oxonian', bluish purple.

Those that flower in winter (November to February) include *Crocus chrysanthus*, flowers deep yellow, brownish-purple veining, Greece, Asia Minor, and cultivars 'Blue Bird', purplish blue, 'E. A. Bowles', rounded yellow goblets with bronze feathering, 'Moonlight', light sulphur yellow; *C. imperatii*, bluish-mauve flowers, veined deep purple, southern Italy; *C. laevigatus*, feathered blue-mauve flowers, Greece.

The show continues from February to April with the spring-flowering types.

Crocus balansae has goblets of bright orange with mahogany feathering, western Asia Minor; *C. candidus*, variable from white through cream to orange, Asia Minor; *C. fleischeri*, a snowy white species with orange-scarlet stigmata, Asia Minor; *C. susianus*, brilliant orange flowers with dark brown markings, Crimea.

Cytisus

There are some good prostrate species of the Common Broom for trailing over rocks and walls. *Cytisus ardoinii*, a native of France, is about 15 cm (6 in) high with bright green leaves in threes and pea-shaped, golden-yellow flowers in May. *C. procumbens* which comes from the same district is smaller at 8 cm (3 in) high but it has a spread of 60 cm (2 ft). The small oblong grey-green leaves provide a good foil to the bright yellow flowers of May and June. Both are increased by cuttings in June.

Daphne

The garland flowers are interesting dwarf shrubs with normally intensely fragrant flowers. Propagation of both the following species is by cuttings taken in June. *Daphne cneorum*, from Europe, is about 23 cm (9 in) high with a spread of 60 cm (2 ft). It has narrow oblong leaves and clusters of rich deep pink fragrant flowers in May and June.

Daphne collina is a native of Italy and Asia Minor. It grows up to 30 cm (1 ft) high and 45 cm ($1\frac{1}{2}$ ft) wide and has oblong leaves and terminal heads of fragrant reddish-purple flowers which appear in May.

Dianthus

The pinks are one of the backbones of the rock garden with many attractive flowering plants. *Dianthus deltoides*, the Maiden Pink, is from 10 to 15 cm (4 to 6 in) high and 38 cm (15 in) wide. It forms grey-green narrow foliage and deep pink flowers with a darker stripe in June and July. A native of Europe, it has produced a number of good colour forms. These include 'Albus', white with a crimson zone; 'Bowles' Variety', crimson-red flowers; 'Glaucus', grey leaves and rose

flowers, and the aptly named 'Huntsman' which is scarlet pink.

Dianthus gratianopolitanus (syn. *D. caesius*) is the British Cheddar Pink. It is about 15 cm (6 in) high and 30 cm (12 in) wide with blue-grey foliage and deeply fringed rose-pink, fragrant flowers in June and July. Good cultivars include 'Baker's Variety', rose red; 'Flore Pleno', double, rose pink and 'Icombe', smaller, rose pink. Both the foregoing species and forms are ideal wall plants.

Dianthus pavonius (syn. *D. neglectus*) from south-west Europe is only 8 cm (3 in) high with smooth tufts of narrow green foliage. The large fringed flowers are bright rose with a green central zone and they are out in June and July. It is a good plant for a trough in a lime-free soil.

There are many named hybrids in most nurserymen's catalogues including 'Grenadier', double scarlet maroon; 'Pike's Pink' with a crimson central zone, and 'La Bourbrille', a good cushion pink. All can be increased by cuttings in June.

Douglasia

Douglasia laevigata, from North America, is a good high alpine plant suitable for trough culture. It has tufted cushions of grey-green foliage in rosettes and rose-pink flowers with yellow eyes on 5-cm (2-in) stems in June. Propagate by cuttings in June.

Draba

This genus contains a number of high alpine cushion plants commonly known as the whitlow grasses and the following two from the Caucasus mountains are ideal plants for the trough. *Draba bryoides* subsp. *imbricata* makes a cushion of grey-green rosettes only 5 cm (2 in) high and 15 cm (6 in) wide with golden-yellow flowers in April and May. Flowering at the same time, *D. rigida* has a compact mat of minute green rosettes and large golden-yellow flowers on 8-cm (3-in) stems. Increase by sowing seed in March.

Dryas

The Mountain Aven, *Dryas octopetala*, is a fine British native dwarf shrub for walls while the cultivar 'Minor' is suitable for troughs. They are trailing plants from 2.5 cm (1 in) high and 15 cm (6 in) wide to 10 cm (4 in) high and 60 cm (2 ft) wide with oak-like green foliage. The white flowers are saucer shaped with golden stamens. Cuttings can be taken in June.

Erica

The dwarf forms of *Erica carnea* (syn. *E. herbacea*) are early peat-loving heaths for the rock garden. They come from Europe and range in height from 23 to 30 cm (9 to 12 in) with a spread of 45 cm (18 in). They flower from December to March and all can be increased by cuttings in June. The species is flesh coloured and the following cultivars are to be recommended: 'Alba', white tinged green; 'Ann Sparkes', yellow-bronze, reddish-tipped foliage, carmine-red flowers; 'Atrorubra', carmine red; 'James Backhouse', pale pink; 'Loughrigg', pale purple; 'Praecox Rubra', deep red, and 'Springwood White', white.

Erigeron

The fleabanes are charming dwarf compact plants with daisy-like flowers and they are small enough for a trough garden. *Erigeron simplex* from North America makes a tufted plant with ash-grey hairy foliage. The lavender flowers have golden centres and appear on 10-cm (4-in) stems over a long period from May. Increase by seed sown in March.

Erinus

Once introduced, *Erinus alpinus*, a European species, will seed itself in cracks and crevices, either in sun or shade. It forms small compact rosettes of glossy green foliage and has sprays of lilac-purple flowers on 8-cm (3-in) stems in May and June. Of the three good cultivars 'Albus' is pure white; 'Carmineus' is carmine, and 'Dr Hanele' is deep carmine.

Euryops

A small genus of shrubs, the one noted here being an extremely decorative evergreen from South Africa. *Euryops acraeus* is an erect-stemmed plant about 23 cm (9 in) high and 38 cm (15 in) wide with silver-grey foliage. The large golden-yellow flowers are prominent in June.

Cuttings in July are a ready means of increase.

Gaultheria

This is a genus of evergreen lime-hating shrubs of which the following are useful with charming flowers and brightly coloured fruits. They grow from 8 to 23 cm (3 to 9 in) high and can be propagated by cuttings in June. *Gaultheria adenothrix*, from Japan, is an excellent small shrub for a half shady position in a peaty medium. It has thick oval glossy green leaves and white-flushed-pink, urn-shaped flowers in June which are followed by red fruits in October.

The species *procumbens* makes a tufted shrub spreading to 76 cm ($2\frac{1}{2}$ ft) with oval glossy green leaves, pinkish-white flowers in May and scarlet fruits in October. It comes from North America.

Gaultheria trichophylla, from west China, grows 8 cm (3 in) tall with oval deep green foliage and bell-shaped, pinkish-white flowers in May and rounded lapis-lazuli fruit following in September.

Gentiana

Space only allows me to mention a few of this large race of gentians with a wide global distribution and the ones noted here should present little difficulty with regards to cultivation. *Gentiana acaulis*, a native of Europe, is about 8 cm (3 in) high with large tubular deep blue trumpets over tufts of bright green foliage in early spring. Although easy to grow, it can be temperamental in flowering.

Gentiana farreri, from west China, is 10 cm (4 in) high and bears radiating laterals with narrow green foliage. The August flowers are Cambridge-blue trumpets striped violet. It requires a lime-free leafy medium. *G. septemfida* is an easy species from south west Asia, about 23 cm (9 in) high, with straggling leafy stems and terminal clusters of bright blue trumpets in July and August.

Gentiana sino-ornata grows up to 15 cm (6 in) high with prostrate stems and narrow bright green foliage. The flowers are deep royal blue from September to December. A native of west China, it needs an acid soil composed mainly of leafmould. *G. verna*, the Spring Gentian from Europe and Asia, is about 5 cm (2 in) high with tufts of green leaves and erect flowers of deep azure blue in April and May. Seed sown in March is the best method of increase, division in March for *G. sino-ornata*. There are a number of named Asiatic cultivars which are suitable for autumn flowering.

Geranium

The crane's bills are good easy plants for the rock garden. They grow to 15 cm (6 in) high with a spread of 25 cm (10 in). They can be propagated by seed in March or division in April. *Geranium argenteum*, from the Alps, has large pink flowers with deeper veinings during June to August over much cut silver leaves. 'Ballerina' is a cultivar with lobed ash-grey leaves and large flowers of blue purple with reddish veinings and a basal blotch of red purple from June to September. *G. sanguineum* is a native of Europe including Britain with lobed green leaves and magenta-crimson flowers from May to October. The cultivar 'Lancastriense' is smaller with rose-pink flowers which have purple veinings.

Geum

Geum borisii is a natural hybrid from Bulgaria with roundish lobed, rough-textured, bright green leaves and large orange-scarlet flowers from May to September. It is about 23 to 30 cm (9 to 12 in) high. Divide in March.

Gypsophila

The gauze flowers are good plants to use as ground cover over bulbs in the rock garden. They can be propagated by division in April or seed in March. *Gypsophila cerastioides* is a native of the Himalayas and it makes a mat of tufted green leaves and has clusters of white red-veined flowers on 8-cm (3-in) stems in May and June. *G. repens* has narrow grey-green leaves and clusters of pink flowers on 23-cm (9-in) stems in June and July. It comes from south-east Europe.

Hebe

This is a wholly Australasian genus and there are a large number of dwarf evergreen shrubs for the rock garden but space forbids the mention of more than just a few.

Hebe buchananii is a compact much branched shrub from 8 to 15 cm (3 to 6 in) high with thick oval dull green leaves and spikes of white flowers in June and July. The cultivar 'Nana' is smaller in all its parts and is suitable for troughs. 'Carl Teschner' is a garden hybrid with procumbent purple stems, oval glossy leaves and 15-cm (6-in) spikes of violet flowers in June.

H. pinguifolia 'Pagei' is a garden form, up to 30 cm (1 ft) high and 60 cm (2 ft) wide, with oval leaves and clusters of white flowers with purple anthers in June. All propagate from cuttings taken during July.

Helianthemum

The following cultivars of the sun rose, *Helianthemum nummularium*, are all about 15 cm (6 in) high and have a spread of 60 cm (2 ft). They make good plants for walls after the spring-flowering plants have finished. They should be cut back hard after flowering and increased by cuttings in July. The species is a native of Europe and it has trailing stems with oval leaves and clusters of yellow flowers. Good cultivars include 'Amy Baring', bright orange; 'Apricot', apricot with a deeper eye; 'Ben Heckla', brick red; 'Ben Lawers', deep crimson; 'Coccineum', double, deep red; 'Golden Queen', golden yellow; 'Jock Scott', light rose; 'Rose of Leeswood', double, light pink, and 'The Bride', grey leaves, white flowers.

Hyacinthus

Hyacinthus azureus is a charming dwarf hyacinth from Asia Minor with azure-blue flowers in a tight cluster on 8-cm (3-in) stems in April. The cultivar 'Albus' is white. Propagate by seed in March or division in June.

Hypericum

There are a number of St John's worts suitable for the rock garden and all are extremely free flowering. *Hypericum empetrifolium* is an evergreen shrublet from Greece with slender stems and narrow,

A rock outcrop and pool

grey-green leaves. The pale yellow flowers are borne on 15-cm (6-in) stems during July and August. *H. nummularium* is a European species which grows about 15 cm (6 in) high with coppery-red young stems and rounded leaves. Like *empetrifolium*, it is summer flowering with golden-yellow flowers on 15-cm (6-in) stems. *H. reptans*, a sub-shrub from the Himalayas with oval green leaves, is only 8 cm (3 in) high but it spreads to 45 cm (18 in). The summer flowers are red in bud but they open to golden yellow. Propagation of all is by cuttings in June or by division in spring.

Iberis

Iberis sempervirens 'Little Gem' is characteristic of the candytufts with dwarf erect 10-cm (4-in) stems and crowded oblong dark green leaves. The white flowers in large tight heads appear during May and June. Increase by cuttings in June.

Ilex

Ilex crenata 'Golden Gem' is a miniature holly forming a low rounded bush with yellow-green leaves which turn deeper in the winter. After many years it will attain a height of only 30 cm (1 ft) and is therefore a good subject for trough culture. Propagation is by cuttings in June.

Iris

Of the bulbous irises, both *Iris reticulata* and its cultivars are suitable for the rock garden. *I. reticulata* has deep violet-purple flowers on 23-cm (9-in) stems during February and its cultivars include 'Cantab', 'Cambridge Blue'; 'Royal Blue', deep blue, and 'Hercules', purplish red.

Iris pumila, from Asia Minor, resembles a miniature flag iris with purple bearded flowers on 15- to 23-cm (6- to 9-in) stems during April. 'Amber Queen' is amber yellow; 'Azurea', pale blue; 'Cyanea', dwarf, purple; 'Gracilis', lavender pink, and 'The Bride', white. Divide in June.

Leontopodium

Leontopodium alpinum is the Eidelweiss with all its romantic associations. It has lance-shaped, grey-green leaves and the flowers are clustered and enveloped by a circle of thick strap-like woolly bracts. It grows 20 cm (8 in) tall and flowers in June and July. Sow seed in March.

Lewisia

The plants in this completely American genus are commonly known as the bitter roots. They are especially attractive when planted on walls. *Lewisia cotyledon* is distinguished by having large rosettes of thick strap-like pale green evergreen leaves with brown markings. The large flowers are salmon, veined pink and they are to be seen in June and July on 23-cm (9-in) stems. The subspecies *finchii* is pale pink with deeper veinings; *howellii* is deep rose veined salmon pink, and 'Weald Rose' is cherry pink with deeper veins.

Lewisia nevadensis is a herbaceous plant with narrow fleshy green leaves in rosettes. It has large white flowers on 5-cm (2-in) stems during May and is suitable for trough culture. Increase by seed in March.

Linaria

The Alpine Toadflax, *Linaria alpina*, is a close tufted plant only 5 cm (2 in) high with whorls of grey-green leaves. The summer flowers of the species are violet with an orange lip but the cultivar 'Alba' is all white, and 'Rosea' is pink with a golden-yellow lip. Sow seed in March or divide in June.

Lithodora

The garden forms of *Lithodora diffusa* are colourful late flowering plants for the lime-free rock garden. They grow about 15 cm (6 in) high and 50 cm (20 in) wide and should be cut back after flowering. 'Grace Ward' has mats of hairy green foliage and gentian-blue flowers, and 'Heavenly Blue' is a deep rich blue with a reddish tinge. Both these excellent cul-

tivars will flower from June to October. Cuttings can be struck in June.

Mimulus

The musks or monkey flowers prefer a cool moist root run and are good waterside plants for the rock pool. *Mimulus cupreus* is too rampant for most gardens but its cultivars are less invasive. Of these 'Bee's Dazzler' is deep red; 'Dainty', creamy yellow; 'Red Emperor', crimson scarlet, and 'Whitecroft's Scarlet', deep scarlet. All are 15 to 23 cm (6 to 9 in) high and they flower from June to August. *M. primuloides*, from west America, forms a carpet of rosettes of bright green leaves only 2.5 cm (1 in) high and the flowers which come from June to August are yellow with red-brown spots. Divide in April.

Morisia

Morisia monantha (syn. *M. hypogaea*), the Mediterranean Cress from Corsica, forms small rosettes of cut, deep green foliage only 2.5 cm (1 in) high. The flowers are stemless and golden yellow and come during May and June. Seed can be sown in March.

Narcissus

The dwarf species of the daffodil are ideal plants for both rock garden and troughs. *Narcissus asturiensis* (syn. *N. minimus*) is a miniature daffodil from Spain. It is only 8 cm (3 in) high with golden-yellow flowers in February and March. *N. bulbocodium* has the descriptive common name of the Hoop Petticoat Daffodil. It is a native of the South of France and Spain and has a narrow funnel trumpet and small petals on 15-cm (6-in) stems in March and April. The type is bright yellow and of the cultivars 'Citrinus' is lemon yellow; 'Conspicuus', deep yellow, tinged green on the reverse, and 'Nivalis', orange yellow. Sow seed in March or divide in August.

Omphalodes

Omphalodes luciliae is an evergreen sub-shrub from Asia Minor. It has tufts of light grey oval leaves and grows about 15 cm (6 in) high. The flowers, which are pink in bud, open to china blue during

May to September. *O. verna*, the Blue-eyed Mary, is a herbaceous perennial with tufts of light green leaves up to 15 cm (6 in) high. During the spring, it bears bright blue flowers which have a white eye. A native of southern Europe, it prefers shade. June is the month for taking cuttings.

Oxalis

Avoid *Oxalis corniculata* and *O. repens* for once these wood sorrels have been introduced they are impossible to eradicate. However, the following two species are both suitable for trough culture. *O. enneaphylla*, from the Falkland Islands, has fan-shaped, silver-grey, red-brown edged leaves. The flowers are white with a pale yellow-green throat on 2.5- to 8-cm (1- to 3-in) stems from May to August. The cultiver 'Minuta' is smaller with yellow-eyed pink flowers, and *rosea* has pink-flushed flowers. The Chilean *O. lobata* has lobed green leaves and golden-yellow flowers on 8-cm (3-in) stems in early autumn. Divide in June.

Papaver

A good poppy for the rock garden comes from the Pyrenees. It is *Papaver rhaeticum* which has divided light green leaves and bright orange flowers on 15-cm (6-in) stems in early summer. This poppy will seed itself in most gardens.

Paronychia

Paronychia argentea makes a mat of silver-grey evergreen leaves only 5 cm (2 in) high. Its minute July flowers have conspicuous white bracts. It provides an excellent ground cover for bulbs especially in troughs. The plants can be divided in March.

Penstemon

The beard tongues are all native to America and they are ideal evergreen sub-shrubs for the rock garden. All can be increased by cuttings in June. *Penstemon menziesii* 'Microphyllus' is a dwarf shrub, only 8 cm (3 in) high, with oval toothed green leaves and light purple, tubular flowers in June and July. *P. pinifolius* is a lax shrublet with needle-shaped leaves, about 15 cm (6 in) high. The clustered flowers, during the summer months, are tubular in shape and mandarin red in colour.

Penstemon rupicola will be found in most catalogues under the name *P. roezlii*. It is a prostrate plant, 10 cm (4 in) high, with grey-green leaves and large tubular crimson flowers in June.

Pernettya

Pernettya tasmanica is an evergreen sub-shrub with green oval leaves. As its name implies it hails from Tasmania and grows about 5 cm (2 in) high. It has white, urn-shaped flowers in May followed by red fruits in September. It reqires a lime-free leafy soil in some shade. Take cuttings in June.

Phlox

This genus from America provides a good follow on to the flowering season after the spring flowers are over. They make good wall plants and should be cut back after flowering. *Phlox douglasii* is a prostrate plant with narrow green leaves. It is about 5 cm (2 in) high with an expected spread of 38 cm (15 in) and the clustered, bright pink flowers appear in May and June. Good cultivars include 'Alba', white; 'Boothman's Variety', mauve, deeper at the base; 'Eva', bright pink, deeper at the base, and 'Violet Queen', violet. All prefer some shade in hot gardens.

The Moss Phlox, *P. subulata*, has narrow light to deep green foliage and grows from 10 to 15 (4 to 6 in) high and up to 45 cm (18 in) wide. The flowers of the species are lavender to purple with a darker central zone in late spring and early summer. In the cultivars 'Alba' is white; 'Aldboroughensis', deep red; 'Atropurpurea', deep red; 'Brightness', bright pink; 'Camlaensis', large, salmon; 'Lilacina', light blue; 'Temiscaming', glowing magenta crimson, and 'Vivid', salmon pink with a crimson eye. Take cuttings in June.

Pieris

Pieris japonica 'Variegata' is a slow-growing erect shrub about 38 cm (15 in) high and 45 cm (18 in) wide with oblong yellow-green margined white evergreen foliage. The white urn-shaped flowers are

Lewisia cotyledon
hybrid

abundant in April. It requires a lime-free shady spot and can be propagated by cuttings in June.

Polygala
Polygala chamaebuxus is a dwarf shrub with dull green foliage, about 15 cm (6 in) high and 30 cm (12 in) wide from Europe. This milkwort has pea-like fragrant flowers which have a white keel and bright yellow mouth in May. Take cuttings in June.

Potentilla
Among the cinquefoils which can be recommended for the rock garden is *Potentilla curviseta* from the Himalayas. It is a mat-forming plant, 5 cm (2 in) high, with palmate bright green leaves and golden-yellow flowers from June to September. *P.* 'Tonguei' is a hybrid with much cut palmate green leaves and orange-yellow summer flowers which become crimson at the base. It is 15 cm (6 in) high and 23 cm (9 in) wide and can be divided in April.

Primula
In such a vast family, it is difficult to choose only a few primulas but the following are representative. *Primula denticulata* from the Himalayas has round heads of deep lilac flowers before the leaves in March. It and the following cultivars grow to about 23 cm (9 in) tall. 'Alba' is white; 'Prichard's Variety' is deep ruby red, and 'Rosea' is rosy lavender.

Primula juliana is the collective name given to the hybrids of *P. juliae*. All are evergreen and about 15 cm (6 in) tall, flowering from March to May. 'Alba' is white; 'Betty Green', crimson; 'Blue Horizon', sky blue; 'Crispii', wine red;

'Dorothy', sulphur yellow; 'Gloria', crimson, golden eye; 'Jewel', crimson purple; 'Sunset Glow', tangerine red, and 'Wanda', claret coloured.

Primula marginata originates from the Maritime Alps. It has silvery-margined, much cut, leafy, evergreen rosettes and lavender fragrant flowers on 15-cm (6-in) stems during May and June. Good cultivars include 'Alba', yellow-green, silver-margined leaves, white flowers; 'Caerula', light blue; 'Drake's Form', deep lavender; 'Linda Pope', lavender blue; 'Prichard's Variety', bright lavender blue, and 'Rubra', ruby red.

The hybrids known by the collective name of *P. pubescens* have rosettes of toothed foliage. The flowers cover a colour range of pink to violet and crimson with a white eye and are borne on 15-cm (6-in) stems in May and June. 'Alba' is white; 'Christine', old rose; 'Faldonside', deep crimson; 'Jane', pale blue; 'Moonlight', pale yellow; 'Cardinal', rich velvety red, and 'The General', brick red.

Primula rosea is a species from the Himalayas. It is a good plant for a cool moist spot with rosettes of oval crinkled leaves. The flowers are dark rich rose with a yellow eye on 15-cm (6-in) stems during March and April. Most can be increased by cuttings in July or division in August.

Ptilotrichum

Ptilotrichum spinosum, from Spain, makes an erect rounded 15-cm (6-in) shrub with silver-grey leaves. The adult wood is very spiny. The crowded flowers of the species are white, those of the cultivar 'Roseum' are pink. Both appear in June and July and seed can be collected and sown in August.

Pulsatilla

Pulsatilla vernalis has the descriptive common name of the Lady of the Snows. It has much cut, bronzy-green foliage, about 10 cm (4 in) high. The flowers which unfold in April and May from furry bronze-violet buds are glistening white backed with violet and gold and crowned by a high central boss of yellow stamens.

Pulsatilla vulgaris is the Pasque Flower with much cut green leaves. The shaggy haired buds open to reveal rich purple flowers with golden-yellow stamens in April and May. It will grow to 15 to 30 cm (6 to 12 in), as do 'Alba', white; 'Rosea', rose pink, and 'Rubra', deep red purple. Increase by seed sown in July.

Ramonda

The Rosette Mullein, *Ramonda myconi*, hails from the Pyrenees. It is about 10 cm (4 in) high with rosettes of rough red-haired oval green foliage. The large rounded flowers are lavender blue with a yellow eye in May and June. Of the cultivars the inevitable 'Alba' is white, 'Rosea', deep pink. September is the month for sowing seed.

Ranunculus

This family contains the buttercups and *Ranunculus alpestris*, a native of Europe, has rosettes of grey-green, three-lobed leaves. The large flowers are white with golden stamens and are borne on 10-cm (4-in) stems in May and June. It likes a moist soil and is a good trough plant. Propagate by seed in March.

Raoulia

Raoulia hookeri (syn. *R. australis*), from New Zealand, is only 1 cm ($\frac{1}{2}$ in) in height. It has minute, silver-grey foliage and stemless yellow flowers during the summer. It will look most attractive when planted in a trough. Divide in July.

Rhodohypoxis

A South African species, *Rhodohypoxis baurii*, produces tufts of silky haired channelled green leaves and rose-red flowers in May on 8-cm (3-in) stems. Recommended cultivars include 'Eva', deep red; 'The Major', deep pink; 'Margaret Rose', bright pink, and 'Ruth', large, white. Divide after flowering.

Salix

The miniature willows are ideal deciduous shrubs for the rock garden in a moist spot. *Salix boydii* is an erect tree-like shrub with a bole which will reach up to 45 cm (18 in) in time. The grey-white leaves provide an effective background for the silky light yellow May catkins. It is a native of Scotland.

Salix reticulata is a dwarf shrublet of only 5 cm (2 in) high from Europe. It has deep green veined leaves and oval yellow catkins in April. Cuttings can be taken in June.

Saponaria

Saponaria 'Bressingham Hybrid' is a soapwort with reddish stems, narrow green leaves and deep pink flowers with a red calyx in May and June. It is about 5 cm (2 in) high and can be increased by cuttings after flowering. *S. ocymoides*, a species from the Alps and Jura mountains, forms a trailing carpet of bright green oval leaves and bright pink flowers with red-purple calyces in May. It has a white cultivar 'Alba'.

Saxifraga

From such a mighty family it is difficult to choose a few for inclusion here. To conserve space, therefore, I have placed the rockfoils in sections according to their cultural requirements. All can be increased by cuttings, best taken in June.

Mossy Section These require a cool, semi-shady position and they make loose carpets of light to deep green rosettes from 45 to 60 cm (1½ to 2 ft) across. The flowers appear in May and June on 10- to 15-cm (4- to 6-in) stems. 'Cambria Jewel', rich pink; 'Darlington Double', double, deep pink; 'Dubarry', crimson; 'Flowers of Sulphur', pale yellow; 'James Bremner', white; 'Peter Pan', crimson; *S. rosacea* (*decipiens*) 'Grandiflora', large, rose.

Encrusted Section A position in full sun suits these best and they make small to large rosettes of silver, lime-encrusted leaves. They flower in late spring and early summer. *Saxifraga aizoon* is white speckled red from Lombardy and its cultivar 'Lutea' is lemon yellow and 'Rosea' is pink. *S. cochlearis* is white from the Alps; *S. cotyledon* has huge rosettes and large spires of white flowers; *S. longifolia* 'Tumbling Waters' has a spire of white flowers 60 cm (2 ft) in length while *S. valdensis* is minute with white flowers on red stems.

Kabschia-Engleria Section These make spiny cushions or rosettes of silver-grey to green leaves 8 to 20 cm (3 to 8 in) wide and require shelter from hot sunshine in summer. They flower in spring on 2.5- to 8-cm (1- to 3-in) stems. *S. apiculata*, pale yellow; *burserana* 'Gloria', white, red stems; *S. b.* 'Sulphurea', pale yellow; 'Christine', cherry red; 'Cranborne', rose; 'Elizabethae', yellow; *S. grisebachii* 'Wisley Variety', the best Engleria, silver rosettes, crimson woolly spikes; *S. haagii*, golden yellow; 'Jenkinsae', deep pink; *S. prosenii*, reddish orange; 'Riverslea', purple rose; *S. stribrnyi*, pink, in woolly purple calyces.

Sedum

The following is a short list of the many stonecrops which make fleshy stems and leaves of varying colour and form. They range in height from 2.5 to 10 cm (1 to 4 in) and flower from May to July. All propagate easily by division in June.

Sedum album 'Coral Carpet' has reddish-purple leaves and pink star flowers; *S. anglicum* 'Minus', grey-green tipped red leaves and rose-coloured flowers; *S. caulicola*, rounded, fleshy, green margined, red leaves, deep purple flowers, from Japan; *S. dasyphyllum*, fleshy oval pinkish-grey leaves, white flowers; *S. ewersii*, oval glaucous-blue leaves with red margins and pink flowers, from the Himalayas; *S. lydium*, green turning scarlet leaves, white flowers; *S. spathulifolium* 'Cappa Blanca', greyish-white leaves and yellow flowers, from South Oregon, and *S. spurium* 'Atropurpureum', deep reddish-brown leaves and pink flowers.

Sempervivum

This is a large family and the houseleek owes its popularity to the different colours and forms of the rosettes varying in height from 8 to 15 cm (3 to 6 in) and flowering in June and July. The flowers are mostly indifferent. Increase is by division in May.

Sempervivum arachnoideum, from Europe, has green rosettes covered with spider-web hairs. Its cultivar, 'Stansfieldii', has rosettes which turn red. *S. arenarium* has green tipped red rosettes and yellow flowers. It comes from the eastern Alps. *S. ciliosum*, from Bulgaria, has grey-green, hair-covered rosettes and yellow flowers. In the species *giuseppii* the green rosettes are tipped brown and they are hairy in the centre. The flowers are rosy red and it comes from northern Spain.

Deep reddish-brown rosettes which turn red in winter and red flowers are the attributes of *Sempervivum marmoreum* from Bulgaria. *S. reginae-amaliae* has green rosettes tinged purple and red flowers. It comes from Greece.

Silene

The Catchfly or Campion, *Silene acaulis*, makes a cushion of small narrow leaves only 5 cm (2 in) high and 15 cm (6 in) wide. The flowers are pink with a reddish-purple calyx in May and June. It is a native of Europe whereas its subsp. *exscapa* comes from the Pyrenees and it is lighter green with similar flowers. Divide in March.

Thymus

The thymes are well represented by the many cultivars of *Thymus serpyllum*. The majority are intensely aromatic and are useful plants for planting in paving or in a dry wall. The species is a native of Europe and makes a rambling plant with narrow leaves from 2.5 to 8 cm (1 to 3 in) high and up to 60 cm (24 in) wide. It has semi-hemispheres of purple flowers throughout the summer months. Its cultivars include 'Albus', white; 'Anne Hall', clear pink; 'Aureus', golden-green leaves in winter, deep lilac flowers; 'Citriodorus', lemon-scented leaves, lilac flowers; 'Citriodorus Argenteus', leaves green and white; 'Carmineus', carmine; 'Coccineus', crimson, and 'Silver Queen', variegated leaves of silver and green. Take cuttings in June.

Trollius

Trollius pumilus, the Globe Flower, is a native of the Himalayas. It has five-lobed green leaves, up to 15 cm (6 in) high, and many petalled bright yellow flowers in June. It is a good plant for a cool moist spot and it is easily increased by seed sown in March.

Tulipa

The small tulip species are ideal for mass planting in troughs or other containers where they can be left undisturbed. They range from 10 to 20 cm (4 to 8 in) high and flower from April to June. The bulbs can be lifted and divided in August or seed can be sown in March. I would recommend the following species: *aucheriana*, pale rose, bronze basal blotch, Persia; *batalinii*, creamy yellow, greenish-yellow blotch, Turkestan; *biflora*, outer crimson and green, inner white, yellow base, Caucasus; *clusiana*, white, cherry-red bands, basal red blotch, Persia; *eichleri*, bright scarlet, black blotch, outside striped silver grey, Asia Minor; *kaufmanniana*, light creamy yellow flushed rose, central Asia. There are many cultivars of this tulip, all are good.

The list continues with *Tulipa linifolia*, bright scarlet, black blotch, central Asia; *pulchella*, crimson, black blotch, Asia Minor; *tarda*, bright yellow, white tipped, Turkestan, and *violacea*, crimson violet blue, bluish-green basal blotch, Persia.

Veronica

Veronica gentianoides is a compact tufted speedwell from the Caucasus with oval green leaves and spires of pale blue flowers on 15- to 30-cm (6- to 12-in) stems in May and June. Its cultivars include 'Variegata', leaves variegated and 'Nana', a reduced form.

Veronica spicata 'Nana' makes a compact plant only 15 cm (6 in) high with green rounded leaves and violet-blue flowers in June and July. Propagation is by division in April.

Pool and Waterside Plants

FRANCES PERRY

In countries with hot climates, water and shade are the most desirable appurtenances of comfortable living. For this reason homes are frequently built with their walls surrounding an inner court yard where fountains play, brightly coloured flowers are grouped and caged birds sing in the trees. This concept provides the basis for the modern patio.

In cooler climates, however, water features take on a different image. They then become an extension of gardening and are designed to keep fish and grow aquatic plants under formal or natural conditions. The fascination of the medium – its changing nature, the music of a gurgling stream or splashing fountain and its magnetism for birds – is another attraction.

Water is never the same two days together. As the weather changes so do its moods – its reflective powers and the pattern of its surface.

Siting and design

Garden pools should be built in an open position, possibly sheltered on the north or east by buildings, a hedge or a belt of shrubs, but never overshadowed by tall trees. Shade represses flowering, particularly with water lilies, and falling leaves build up the organic content and become the chief cause of water discolouration and infestations of algae.

The shape, size and nature of the pool will depend on the immediate surrounds. A formal pool must be of uniform outline, for example, round, square or rectangular, and situated in an open position amongst symmetrical lawns, flower beds or patios. Its edges can be raised or sunken as long as they are generously bordered by a broad coping or flat paving stones. Fountains are permissible and low plantings, but the symmetry should never be marred by irregular groups of emergent marginal aquatics.

Informal pools demand more natural treatment. They team well with rock gardens, when waterfalls and stream effects can be incorporated, or with bog gardens in a wild or woodland setting. These pools should always be sunken, their edges merging into the surrounding lawns, flower beds or rock garden and their shape irregular – as in nature.

The materials

Garden pools can be made of various materials and in fact any watertight container – even an old bath or water tank – can become a potential water garden.

Concrete entails the most initial labour but is strong and durable when properly made and can be constructed to any shape, depth or size. A formal pool with raised curbs must be fashioned of concrete. Use only good materials for its construction, otherwise it may leak (ready mixed concrete lightens the labour) and look upon 15 cm (6 in) as a minimum thickness for sides and bottom. Reinforcement may be necessary for large pools and all of them require maturing (to get rid of free lime) before plants and fish are introduced. Autumn-constructed pools which have been kept full of water all winter, then emptied, are usually safe for planting by the following spring. Alternatively the interior can be painted over with a protective sealing compound.

Prefabricated glassfibre pools, made in various shapes and sizes, are available from garden centres and shops. These are light to handle and quick to install. A hole is excavated slightly larger than the unit, the pool set in place and tested for levels and soil packed round to make it firm. Planting can take place immediately. Some of these pools can be linked to

OPPOSITE: An informal pool with variegated irises and hostas

precast cascade and stream sections for waterfall effects. An electrically powered pump of the submersible or centrifugal (surface) type will work these – or fountains – using the same water over and over again.

The easiest and most modern method of pool making is to excavate a hole and line it with a waterproof butyl liner. This is a flexible sheet of strong, heavy duty, PVC sheeting known as juralene which can withstand extremes of temperature and is resistant to pests and fungus infection, also sunlight and ultraviolet rays. It is harmless to plants and fish and can be used for any size of pool since it is possible to join the thicker fabrics (also patch accidental cuts) with a special adhesive.

Dig the pool to the size and depth, or

A pool can be linked to precast cascade sections to create a waterfall effect. Here a submersible pump recirculates the water

A prefabricated pool

Filling a pool made from PVC sheeting

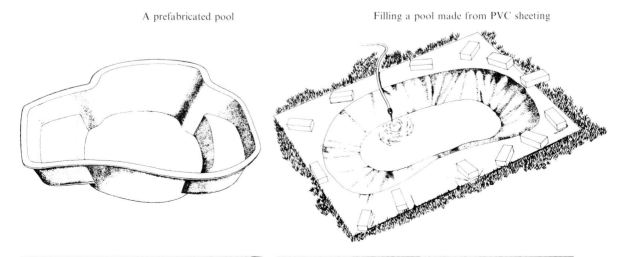

series of depths, required and if the sub-soil is stony spread 2.5 cm (1 in) of damp sand or ashes all over the interior. This helps to protect the fabric. Next stretch the material over the hole and weight its edges with rocks or bricks. Run in the water, pleating and tucking the liner into shape as filling goes on. When it is full cut off any surplus fabric, except for about 15 cm (6 in) all round the edges, and tuck this spare out of sight beneath turves, stone slabs, soil or plants.

Planting

The best time to plant deep water or marginal aquatics is in spring, between April and June, although the submerged kinds and floaters can go into the water at any season. Bog plants move successfully in spring or early autumn.

Water lilies should either be planted in special pockets, made during the construction of the pool, or in aquatic baskets. The latter are made of plastic with openwork sides. Water lily roots are sensitive to confinement and always thrive best where they can feel the influence of water, so that concrete pockets should have a few holes punched through their sides for the same reason.

After planting, about which more details are given in the section on water lilies on p. 234, lower the baskets into the water but prop them on bricks so that they are only just submerged. The lilies must now recover from the move but when new leaves appear they can be gradually lowered until – six or eight weeks later – the baskets are standing on the floor of the pool. Other deep water

aquatics such as nuphars and apono-getons can be treated similarly.

Emergent marginals need very little water above their crowns; their chief desideratum being soil which is always very wet. Some have to have their roots confined to keep them in check. Plant these in solid pockets or suitable containers where they are to grow.

Submerged aquatics have few if any roots so tend to float if they are simply thrown into the water. Anchor them by gently pressing a thin strip of lead around two or three stems and then throw them in. Floaters are simply placed on the pool surface and bog plants inserted – like land plants – with a trowel or handfork.

Pool depths

Garden pools should be deep enough not to freeze solid in winter, yet sufficiently shallow for the water to warm up quickly in spring. The last is essential for early flowers and in practice means 45 to 60 cm (18 to 24 in) of water above the floor level. Since fish feel the effects of heat they benefit from the greater depth in hot weather, although fountains and water-falls also help cool the water.

The marginal aquatics only require 8 to 10 cm (3 to 4 in) of soil and the same depth of water, so a shallow trough surround (with its inner edge 2.5 cm [1 in] lower than the outer) is sometimes built on to the deeper part during construction. When the pool is full of water this flows over to the outer contours and the trough does not show.

In the case of informal rock pools it is also expedient to build pockets for bog

Aquatic plants must be positioned at the correct depth. Marginals need shallow water so are planted on shelves around the edge of the pool, whereas water lilies rest on the bottom in deeper water

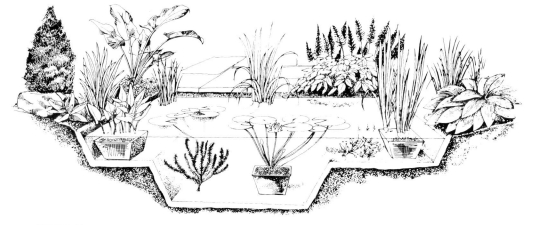

plants where they can be flooded over in dry weather. Alternatively, for large bog gardens, the soil can be taken out to a depth of 30 cm (12 in) and the area lined with thick PVC sheeting. Holes should be punched in the sides of this 15 cm (6 in) up from the base, so that although it holds a certain amount of liquid it never becomes completely waterlogged. A 8-cm (3-in) layer of stones or brick rubble is then laid for drainage and the soil returned.

Cultivation

Water plants rarely need feeding, except for water lilies which have been three or more years in their baskets. These can be helped by giving them nutrient pills. Mix equal quantities of wet clay and bonemeal (wear gloves when handling the latter) and mould into tennis ball-sized "pills". Push one or two down to the roots of each lily. After a further two years the baskets should be lifted and the lily roots washed, divided and replanted in fresh compost.

Remove old flowers and dead leaves regularly, also seedheads from aquatics likely to become too prolific.

Winter problems

Falling leaves from nearby trees should not be allowed to accumulate in ornamental pools. Dredge them out with a rake or else make a light framework of 2.5-cm (1-in) battens and plastic mesh netting. Lay this over the pool during leaf fall and most of them will be caught.

All pools should be kept full of water in winter and the shallow types protected against a complete freeze up. The installation of a pool heater will keep a small area free of ice and so safeguard fish and plants. Another idea is to float a

block of wood or a large ball on the surface and when ice forms take it out by pouring boiling water on top. Now bale out 2.5 cm (1 in) of water and cover the hole with plastic sheeting or hessian. The ice will then act like a greenhouse and protect the plants and fish underneath. Naturally, as soon as a thaw occurs, the pool must be topped up again with more water.

Selected Pool and Waterside Plants

There are five main groups among the plants of the water garden: deep water aquatics; floaters; marginal aquatics; submerged oxygenators, and bog plants – all with different functions and requirements.

Deep water aquatics

These have floating leaves and flowers and thick tuberous rootstocks anchored in mud at the base of the pool. The nymphaeas (water lilies) are the most important of these, with about seventy species and cultivars hardy in this country and suitable for pools of various depths. When making a selection it is important to bear the last in mind and to pick varieties from the right group.

All hardy water lilies need a stiff compost; fibre-free loam enriched with one sixth part well-decayed cow manure or a half pint (300 ml) measure of bonemeal to each bucketful of soil. The compost should be used in a moister condition than is usual for pot plants, otherwise it will not bind and the roots may float upwards. Covering the soil after planting with 2.5 cm (1 in) of washed shingle prevents fish from rooting in the mud and making the water cloudy.

There are two main groups of hardy water lilies; one with rhizomatous roots and the other with upright-growing tubers. The last, which includes the British native *Nymphaea alba*, should be planted perpendicularly, with its black

Remove leaves and other debris from the surface of the pool in autumn

Planting a waterlily:
(a) Always use very moist compost in the basket otherwise the plant may float upwards.
(b) Cover the compost with washed shingle to prevent fish rooting around

a

b

and white feeding roots well spread. It should be noted that any thick white roots present are old anchorage roots and useless to the new plant. These should be removed.

Rhizomatous lilies like the North American *Nymphaea tuberosa* and *N. odorata* should be planted horizontally – like bearded irises, which they somewhat resemble. Most members of this group have fragrant flowers.

The following water lilies will grow in water 50 to 75 cm (20 to 30 in) deep (less if there is room) and in time should each cover a surface area of approximately 1.5 to 1.8 m² (5 to 6 sq ft).

In this group the cultivar 'Gladstoniana' is superb, with large cup-shaped flowers of glistening white, the centres filled with rich golden stamens. The dark

Nymphaea 'Marliacea Chromatella'

green leaves are tough, with a polished texture. Other good whites are 'Gonnère', a semi-double, the squat blooms wrapped around with olive-green sepals and *N. tuberosa richardsonii* of globular habit. The only fully double water lily 'Gloire de Temple-sur-Lot' is suitable for 45 to 50 cm (18 to 20 in), but is not as free flowering as many others. The creamy-white petals of the flowers curve like those of an incurved chrysanthemum.

Among the pinks 'Colossea' is flesh coloured, *N. tuberosa rosea*, soft pink; 'Marguerite Laplace', deep rose, and 'Mrs Richmond', deep pink. 'Marliacea Carnea' and 'Marliacea Rosea' – soft and deeper pink respectively – were given his own patronymic by the great French breeder Latour Marliac – a sure indication of their worth.

There are several good reds in this group, particularly the prolific 'Escarboucle', a wine-red sort with flowers up to dinner-plate size and, excepting for 'William Falconer', the deepest in colour. 'Gloriosa' is a fine red for the shallower depths in this section, also the adaptable and free-flowering 'James Brydon' which produces masses of squat carmine-red blooms throughout the whole of the summer. 'Colonel Welch' is the most robust yellow, but less fine than those recommended in the next section.

The medium growers are suitable for 30 to 45 cm (12 to 18 in) of water and cover a surface area of approximately 1.2 m² (4 sq ft) in time. They are thus ideal for small pools and gardens.

Among the whites are 'Albatross', a very shapely sort; *N. caroliniana* 'Nivea', sweetly scented and very prolific, and 'Hermine', whose stellate flowers stand clear of the water.

'Fire Crest' is a fragrant pink sort with red-tipped stamens which look as if they have been touched by flame, but 'Laydekeri Lilacea', rosy lilac, and 'Laydekeri Purpurata', rosy crimson, are two of the most reliable with only medium-sized blooms but prolifically produced.

'Livingstone' is bright red flecked with white; 'Masaniello', deep rose, and 'Paul Hariot' changes colour with age – the new blooms being apricot yellow which gradually deepens to orange red. Two

good yellows in this section are 'Marliacea Chromatella', of a soft primrose shade with chocolate-blotched leaves, and 'Sunrise', which is semi-double with deep golden flowers.

There are also several miniatures for rock garden pools. These may need protection or lifting in winter and they can also be grown in small containers on a sunny windowsill indoors. *N. tetragona* (syn. *N. pygmaea alba*) is white with green leaves, and *N. pygmaea* 'Helvola', soft yellow with chocolate-blotched foliage.

Other deep water aquatics

Nuphars or pond lilies are strong-growing aquatics allied to but inferior to nymphaeas. Their only advantages over the latter lie in an ability to grow in shade, deep or running water – situations which are an anathema to the true water lilies. If used at all in ornamental pools, the roots must be confined and only the weaker sorts like *Nuphar pumila* (syn. *N. minima*), with pale yellow flowers; *N. japonica* 'Rubrotinctum', cup-shaped orange flowers with red-tipped stamens, or *N. japonica* 'Variegatum', which has cream-splashed foliage, should be grown. Plant them the same way as nymphaeas.

Nymphoides peltata (*Limnanthemum nymphoides*), the Water Fringe, has poppy-like, three-petalled flowers of golden yellow and crinkly edged, almost round, chocolate-blotched, floating leaves. It grows in long strands across the water surface, shading the depths beneath and so discouraging algae, but is easily pulled out if it becomes too rampant.

Aponogeton distachyus, the Water Hawthorn, takes its name from the vanilla-like scent of the black and white, forked flowers. These float, as do the long narrow leaves. It will grow in depths of 30 to 50 cm (12 to 20 in).

Floaters

This group takes its nourishment from dissolved salts in the water, and while some remain in character all the year round, others form winter buds or turons which sink to the bottom of the pool in autumn and reappear in spring. Floating plants shade water and so inhibit algae. They also provide nurseries for young fish and shelter for countless tiny creatures which later feed the fry. Some, however, can become a nuisance and the lemnas (duckweeds) should never be introduced to outdoor pools or, in warm climates, salvinas or water hyacinths (eichhornias).

Among the hardiest are the Frogbits (*Hydrocharis morsus-ranae*) with small, white, three-petalled flowers and tiny round leaves and the Water Soldier (*Stratiotes aloides*) which stays just under the surface and has prickly rosettes of leaves, something like pineapple tops. Male and female flowers – both white and three petalled – are on separate plants.

Azolla caroliniana, the Fairy Floating Moss, is closely related to the ferns and has mossy green fronds which turn red in autumn and then disappear for the winter. The lovely pale mauve flowers of the Water Hyacinth (*Eichhornia crassipes*) have gold and deeper blue "peacock" markings on their upper petals. The swollen leaf stalks support the plants which can be carried by wind right across the pool, but the first touch of frost kills them, so they are only suitable for indoor pools or summer effect out of doors.

Marginal aquatics

These plants have emergent flowers and foliage, with their roots always in shallow water. For best effect they should be grouped in threes, or more, of the same variety and, since many increase vegetatively and can become rampant, the soil should not be rich. Plain loam suits them admirably. Also, to prevent indiscriminate seeding, the spent flower heads should be removed regularly.

Among the best of the flowering marginals are the Kingcups or Marsh Marigolds (*Caltha palustris*). These are among the first to appear in early spring, the rich golden, buttercup-like flowers borne in great profusion on 23- to 30-cm (9- to 12-in) stems. The heart-shaped leaves are smooth and glossy and completely hidden at flowering time,

especially in the double form 'Flore Pleno'. The cultivar 'Alba' is white and there are also semi-double kinds and white species. *C. polypetala* is taller, up to 90 cm (3 ft) and comes later. It has branching stems, with many single blooms.

The British native *Iris pseudacorus*, or Yellow Flag, is particularly fine in its variegated form, for the gold and green suffusions on the young foliage are as colourful as flowers. Unfortunately this vivid colouring does not persist but disappears by mid-summer, but then the rich golden flowers appear and provide some compensation. *I. laevigata* thrives in 5 to 10 cm (2 to 4 in) of water and has flat grassy leaves and rich blue flowers in July. There are numerous cultivars including a white, 'Alba'; pink, 'Rose Queen'; variegated-leaved, 'Variegata', and two fine blue and whites called 'Colchesteri' and 'Benekiron'. The approximate height of all these irises is around 60 to 76 cm (2 to 2½ ft).

Another good flowering aquatic is the North American Pickerel Weed, *Pontederia cordata*. This flowers for weeks from mid-summer onwards, the spikes of soft blue florets set at the ends of 60-cm (2-ft) leafy stems. The foliage is long, heart shaped and glossy. This plant is very compact and rarely becomes a nuisance.

The Flowering Rush (*Butomus umbellatus*) has umbels of pink flowers on 60- to 90-cm (2- to 3-ft) stems and long narrow leaves which are bronze purple when young. Several aroids are also useful for shallow water, the most spectacular being *Lysichiton americanum*, which has large (up to 30 cm [12 in]) bright yellow arums before the leaves in early spring. The foliage which follows, however, is rather massive, so this is a plant which requires plenty of room. It is readily propagated from seed. A white-flowered species, *L. camtschatcense*, is smaller in habit, so more useful in some situations. *Orontium aquaticum*, the Golden Club, resembles an arum without the outer spathe. It is an adaptable plant, producing floating glaucous leaves and flowers in deep water, or large upright foliage in shallow.

Other flowering aquatics include *Saur-*

Nymphoides peltata

urus chinensis, the Lizard's Tail, a Japanese species around 30 cm (1 ft) in height, with oval leaves and white-bracted flowers which have long tail-like centres, and also various arrowheads of which the double *Sagittaria sagittifolia* 'Flore Pleno' (syn. *S. japonica*) is by far the best. This has white flowers in spikes, something like stocks, and arrow-shaped leaves. *Mimulus ringens* is a slender, 30- to 60-cm (1- to 2-ft), mauve-flowered musk and *Calla palustris* (Bog Arum) is of creeping habit with round rhizomes like thick pencils supporting small glossy, heart-shaped leaves and white arum flowers. Another scrambler is *Meny-anthes trifoliata* (Bog Bean) with trefoiled leaves – like giant clovers – and spikes of small, fringed, pink and white blooms.

Marginal aquatics with variegated foliage are invaluable when there are but few flowers in character. In addition to various irises there is the 60-cm (2-ft) *Acorus calamus* 'Variegatus' or Sweet Flag which looks something like a bearded iris but with brown spikes of flowers looking like bull's horns protruding from the tops of the stems. If the leaves of this plant are bruised, they have a pleasant aromatic smell.

Glyceria maxima variegata is the Manna Grass, with cream and green leaf patternings, also rosy pink when they are young. It grows around 60 cm (2 ft). There are also two variegated rushes; *Scirpus tabernaemontani* 'Zebrinus', the Porcupine Quill Rush, with fat round rushy stems, 60 to 80 cm (2 to 3 ft) tall, alternately barred in green and white, and the 1.5-m (5-ft) *S.* 'Albescens', which is striped longitudinally. *Juncus effusus* 'Spiralis' grows like a corkscrew, with each green stem spirally twisted.

Submerged aquatics

Although largely unseen these are some of the most important plants of the water garden. Their presence, in healthy growing condition, is usually the criterion of a well-balanced pool and their functions are many.

For one thing they are essential as oxygenators. Although plants, as well as animals, absorb a little oxygen during respiration, they alone in the living world can make food from a by-product of this

RIGHT: *Lysichitum americanum*

OPPOSITE: *Caltha palustris* 'Flore Pleno', the double form of the Kingcup or Marsh Marigold

operation. When living creatures breathe they take in oxygen and exhale carbon dioxide, but, certain parts of plants, given fuel for energy, take in carbon dioxide and build this, with water, into simple sugars. This is the basis of all plant foods. However, this chemical change produces a spare product – oxygen – and so this is released back to the air, or water.

The green chlorophyll in leaves is the essential agent which performs this operation and the motivating energy is supplied by sunlight. Fish, snails and other water creatures need oxygen and plants require carbon dioxide and so the aim is to create a balanced pool, so that each utilizes the others' waste products. Additionally, chemical salts in the water build up the food structure, so where there is plenty of underwater vegetation unicellular plants like algae are starved of light and nourishment. Where submerged oxygenators are growing well the water is usually crystal clear and there is little or no algae.

Other functions of these plants include providing depositories for fish eggs and nurseries for the young fry. The latter hide in the tangled masses and so escape from their cannibalistic parents. They also consume a little of the vegetation, as well as the small water creatures which find a haven amongst the foliage. There is also the aesthetic beauty of underwater plants to consider, for looking down on waving stems and leaves is much more pleasant than the appearance of bare soil or concrete. Some species also come to the surface to flower – an extra bonus!

When selecting oxygenators it is important to choose sorts which really are efficient in this respect and some are undoubtedly better than others. Among the most outstanding are the elodeas, particularly *Elodea callitrichoides* and *E. canadensis* (syn. *Anacharis canadensis*), the Canadian Pondweed. Both have small, deep green, narrow leaves on branching stems. *Elodea crispa* (more correctly *Lagarosiphon major*) resembles a giant elodea with curly leaves and it too is a splendid oxygenator.

The starworts take their name from the fact that the floating leaves of the spring starwort, *Callitriche palustris* (syn. *C.*

verna), form starry masses at the water surface. They are pale green in colour and help to provide shade early in the season. The Autumn Starwort, *C. hermaphroditica* (syn. *C. autumnalis*), with finer leaves, is more active in the fall and remains submerged.

Crassula (*Tillaea*) *recurva* is a succulent plant with needle-fine leaves and minute white flowers; all the milfoils (*Myriophyllum* sp.) are good; also certain of the pondweeds or potamogetons, particularly *Potamogeton crispus*, the Curled Pondweed, and *P. densus* or Frog's Lettuce. These are small plants with leafy, rather brittle stems. Caution should be exercised with certain other potamogetons and particularly with *P. natans*. This will rapidly take over a small pool and can become an obnoxious weed. For deep water both the Hornwort (*Ceratophyllum demersum*) and the Stonewort (*Chara hispida*) are useful; they have brittle stems with whorls of bristly needle-like leaves.

Among the prettiest of the flowering oxygenators is *Hottonia palustris*, the Water Violet. This has finely cut, fan-shaped foliage and, in spring, 15-cm (6-in) spikes of pale lilac, primrose-like flowers above the water. Later the plant forms winter buds and disappears until the following spring.

Ranunculus aquatilis, the Water Crowfoot, is another spring bloomer; its white, buttercup-like flowers starring the surface of lakes and ponds in March and April. It forms long trails and has two kinds of leaves; the submerged sorts, fan shaped and finely cut; the floating kinds, smooth and resembling small buttercup leaves. This species will also grow in running water.

Utricularia vulgaris is the Bladderwort and is a plant which does best in small shallow pools. The 10- to 15-cm (4- to 6-in) emergent spikes of antirrhinum-like flowers are rich yellow and in character in late summer. Utricularias have small bladder-type contraptions on the submerged stems which trap tiny insects for food.

Bog plants

These are plants which link pools, streams and other water features with the rest of the garden. They are moisture lovers which like to feel the influence of water without being in it all the time; so that the soil in which they grow must be always damp but never (except for occasional short periods) be waterlogged.

Since aerobic bacteria work where there are normal air conditions and because of the presence of oxygen in well-drained topsoil, bog plants can be given a richer diet than aquatics. For this reason plenty of humus should be dug into the soil initially or used as mulches in later years. Well-rotted garden compost, farmyard manure, peat or leafmould are all suitable – the aim being to produce a rich friable soil which allows for the easy penetration of plant roots.

Bog plants can be established in spring or autumn and for maximum effect should be grouped in blocks of the same sort of plant. Their numbers include trees and shrubs as well as ferns, grasses, bulbs and herbaceous plants.

Herbaceous bog plants

This is by far the most useful group and includes many which are frequently grown in other situations, such as the herbaceous border or wild garden. Being moisture lovers, however, they give a much better account of themselves when the soil is permanently damp.

The aconitums are good summer bloomers with mostly blue, but sometimes white, cream or bicoloured, helmet-shaped flowers on strong leafy stems. The roots are poisonous but since few people are likely to dig and eat them their cultivation should not be ignored on this account. Among the best are *Aconitum napellus*, the Common Monkshood, violet blue, and such forms as 'Bressingham Spire', deep violet and up to 90 cm (3 ft) and 'Newry Blue', 1.15 m (3½ ft). The rich blue *A. carmichaelii* (*A. fischeri*) grows to 76 cm (2½ ft) and the autumn-flowering *A. wilsonii* (by some authorities considered a form of the preceding) grows to 1.8 m (6 ft) with large violet-blue flowers. *A. vulparia* (*A. lycoctonum*) is a climber reaching to 1.8 or 2.1 m (6 or 7 ft) in moist soil. It has pale yellow flowers.

The actaeas grow well in damp ground and offer both flowers and berries as cultural inducements. *Actaea alba*, the White Baneberry, has racemes of white flowers on 30 to 45 cm (12- to 18-in) stems, also deeply cut leaves and white fruits. The Red Baneberry, *A. rubra*, is similar except for scarlet berries and the Cohosh, *A. spicata*, has purplish-black fruits.

Ajugas are adaptable and make good ground-cover plants in most situations – sun or shade, dry or damp – but nowhere do they give a better account of themselves than in soil which is constantly moist. The rich blue, nettle-shaped flowers come in short spikes and the leaves are smooth and entire. *Ajuga reptans*, the Common Bugle of British woodlands, has a number of forms with variegated foliage, such as 'Variegata', grey green and cream; 'Rainbow', bronze, buff, red and green, and 'Atropurpurea', dark purple. There is also a white-flowered form.

The Lady's Mantle, *Alchemilla mollis*, makes a delightful edging subject for a bog garden, particularly if it is planted where the frothy greenish flowers can be reflected in the water. The silvery cape-shaped leaves are also attractive, but since the plant tends to seed itself about rather too exuberantly, it is wise to remove the old flower heads.

Several anemones favour the rich moist soil of a bog garden, particularly *Anemone lesseri*, a garden hybrid of great charm with rounded, shining leaves and cup-shaped, rosy-purple flowers about 5 cm (2 in) across in early summer. It grows 45 to 60 cm (18 to 24 in) tall and can be propagated by root cuttings taken in early spring.

Aruncus dioicus (syn. *A. sylvester*) is a noble plant for key situations, with massive plumes of hay-scented, creamy-white flowers on sturdy 1.5- to 1.8-m (5- to 6-ft) stems in early summer. The large, deeply divided leaves accentuate their effect. Moist soil and light shade prolongs the flowering season.

Few bog plants are more rewarding than the astilbes, especially when they are associated with waterside irises, primulas and daylilies (hemerocallis). Both the pinnate leaves and plumes of variously coloured, feathery flowers are attractive and, given moist soil at all times, the plants persist for years.

For garden purposes any of the *Astilbe × arendsii* forms are the most reliable. These grow between 60 and 90 cm (2 and 3 ft) tall, with pink, red, lilac, crimson and white flowers. Representative cultivars are 'Deutschland', white; 'Cattleya', pink with a touch of mauve; 'Cologne', bright pink; 'Dusseldorf', cerise red; 'Fanal', deep garnet red; 'Federsee', bright red, and 'Amethyst', lilac purple.

Among the species *Astilbe rivularis* is outstanding for a key position in a damp spot. The stems grow 1.8 to 2.1 m (6 to 7 ft) with long arching sprays of greenish white flowers. The shiny green leaves are deeply divided. *A. chinensis* is a dwarf for a front row position. Usually less than 30 cm (1 ft) in height, it has fern-like leaves and deep purple-pink flowers. 'Perkeo' is a form of this with crinkled leaves and pink flowers. Astilbes are at their best in mid-summer and can be increased by division of the roots in spring.

Astrantias raised in ordinary borders never attain the quality of bog-grown plants. They need abundant moisture during the summer-flowering season and most borders fail them in this respect. Of erect growth, with lobed leaves and aromatic roots, they have quaint flower heads like tiny Victorian posies, set off by chaff-like bracts. Propagation is by seed or root division in spring or summer. *Astrantia maxima* is pink flowered and up to 60 cm (2 ft) tall but *A. major* with rose and green flowers, is the most vigorous and can attain a height of up to 90 cm (3 ft), its cultivar 'Rubra' has plum-red flowers.

Even lilies will grow in a bog garden; the best for this purpose is undoubtedly *Lilium canadense* which grows up to 1.5 m (5 ft) under ideal conditions, or 60 to 90 cm (2 to 3 ft) when less well situated. Plant the bulbs in autumn 15 to 25 cm (6 to 10 in) deep in moist peaty soil. They dislike lime so chalky ground is unsuitable. The pendant, yellow, bell-shaped flowers are spotted with maroon and purple, with up to twenty blooms on each stem. *L. canadense* can be raised from seed but normally takes three to four years to flower.

Lilium superbum, the Swamp Lily of the eastern states of America, is another for damp situations. In very wet soil plant each bulb on a mound so that its roots go down to the water and the bulbs remain free of standing water. The roots should be in semi-shade and the flower stems running up to the sun and light. *L. pardalinum*, the Panther or Leopard Lily, takes its name from the crimson-brown spots which speckle the reddish-orange, Turk's cap flowers. These are 8 to 10 cm (3 to 4 in) across, but variable both in size and colour. The stems can attain a height of 2.4 m (8 ft) and like all lilies they should be grouped for maximum effect. Treat as for *L. superbum* and divide the clumps every three or four years.

Camassias also belong to the lily family and make useful subjects for damp meadows and similar situations. They flower in early summer, with loose spikes of light to deep blue, funnel-shaped flowers, but white and cream forms are not uncommon. *Camassia leichtlinii* is the best species, but very variable. 'Plena' is a double sulphur-yellow cultivar.

The little milkmaids or "faint sweet cuckoo flowers" of Tennyson (*Cardamine pratensis*) can be allowed to seed and naturalize in damp meadows or the wilder parts of the bog garden. Growing 15 to 23 cm (6 to 9 in) high, they have cress-like leaves (once used for salads) and spikes of simple, pale mauve flowers. 'Plena', a form with double flowers, is more showy but has to be propagated by division.

The Snake's Heads are *Chelone glabra*, white flowered, and *C. obliqua*, reddish purple, and they flower in late summer with terminal heads of small foxglove-like blooms on 60-cm (2-ft) stems. These need deep moist soil at all times.

Cimicifugas bloom in late summer and are often seen in herbaceous borders. But they are even more effective in bog

gardens, either in sun or partial shade, with their graceful, feathery plumes of fragrant flowers on 1.5- to 2.1-m (5- to 7-ft) stems and smooth, doubly compound leaves. *Cimicifuga simplex* is one of the best, especially in the cultivars 'Elstead White' and 'White Pearl' but *C. dahurica* and *C. cordifolia* follow later in the season

and are useful on that account.

Eupatoriums are coarse perennials with large, flat, terminal clusters of white or dull purple flowers and nettle-like or slender pointed leaves in whorls. They are useful for late summer colour especially in the rougher parts of the garden. *Eupatorium cannabinum*, the Hemp

Candelabra primulas and *Rogersia aesculifolia* make an attractive waterside planting

Agrimony, grows to 1.2 m (4 ft) and is dull purple which becomes more effective in its double form; *E. purpureum*, Joe Pye Weed, is 90 cm to 1.2 m (3 to 4 ft) with 15- to 23-cm (6- to 9-in), purplish-pink flower heads and *E. ageratoides*, white flowered and 60 cm to 1.2 m (2 to 4 ft) tall, has nettle-like leaves.

Filipendula ulmaria is the Meadow Sweet, one of the most beautiful of British plants, frequently found alongside streams or in wet ditches. It is perennial with deeply cut leaves and spiraea-like plumes of small flowers. Under damp conditions it grows 60 to 90 cm (2 to 3 ft) tall, or shorter where there is less moisture. The double form 'Flore Pleno' is the most effective of any of the foliage variants with golden leaves or cream and green variegations.

Others for the bog garden are *F. camtschatica*, a species from Manchuria with 1.8 m (6 ft) or more of leafy stem terminating in loose panicles of white flowers; *F. purpurea* (*Spiraea palmata* of gardens) with palmate foliage and flat heads of carmine or deep rose florets and *F. rubra* (syn. *Spiraea lobata*) which has clusters of fragrant, pink flowers on 60- to 90-cm (2- to 3-ft) stems.

Massive-leaved plants are only suitable for large bog gardens, but given the space, nothing looks more impressive than a clump of *Gunnera manicata*. This noble plant produces giant, rhubarb-like leaves 1.5 to 1.8 m (5 to 6 ft) across and as much in length (even larger under good conditions) on thick, spiny, 3- to 4.5-m (10- to 15-ft) stems. The green-brown flowers come in 90-cm (3-ft) spikes and look like huge bottle brushes. Since the slightest touch of frost damages the leaves, protection is advisable in cool climates.

Others with large leaves are the ornamental rhubarbs. *Rheum palmatum* is a good waterside plant with creamy-white flowers on 1.5- to 1.8-m (5- to 6-ft) leafy stems and five-lobed leaves. There are also forms with red leaves and crimson flowers.

Among the most beautiful waterside perennials are the bog primulas, especially the candelabra types, which carry the flowers in whorls round their stems.

These must have moisture, ideal conditions being provided by a soil which is rich, cool and constantly moist without being waterlogged. For most telling effects they should be colonized in bold groups, possibly associated with blue poppies. If allowed to seed naturally, all sorts of interesting forms appear and in a wide colour range. Alternatively, collected seed can be sown as soon as ripe, in pans or boxes of peaty soil. Keep them cool and in a shady place to germinate, then prick out the young seedlings in boxes or pot them separately. They can then be planted in their flowering positions in spring or autumn.

Primula rosea is the earliest to bloom, often at the end of winter, the flowers brilliant deep pink on 15- to 23-cm (6- to 9-in) stems. Among the candelabra sorts are *P. japonica*, with pink, white or crimson flowers, often "eyed" in different colours and up to 60 cm (2 ft) in height, and *P. pulverulenta*, with mealy stems and rich crimson flowers in the type but variable in such strains as 'Bartley', when rose-pink, salmon, buff and apricot shades are common. The usual height is between 76 and 90 cm ($2\frac{1}{2}$ and 3 ft). *P. beesiana*, violet purple and 60 cm (2 ft); *P. bulleyana*, orange, 60 cm (2 ft), and *P. burmanica*, crimson purple, are others of this type. There are also a number of yellows of which *P. florindae* is one of the best. It is like a giant cowslip, with long, heart-shaped leaves and 90-cm (3-ft) spikes of pendant flowers. *P. sikkimensis* forms rosettes of long and narrow leaves with slender, 60-cm (2-ft) stems terminating in nodding, pale yellow flowers.

Moisture-loving irises are essential for the bog garden. Closely related to the aquatic *Iris laevigata* (see p. 237) is *I. kaempferi*, the Clematis-flowered Iris of Japan. This has large flat flowers, either in self blue, white, pink or red, but more often suffused, striated, centre eyed or banded in other shades. They are very striking with their unusual coloration and flat ribbon-like leaves. The species dislikes lime and needs to have the roots moist in summer but drier in winter. Named sorts (often with unpronounceable Japanese names) are available but mixed seedlings are usually very good and much more economical to buy. *I. kaempferi* can be distinguished from *I. laevigata* by the leaves; there is a prominent midrib down the centre of those of *I. kaempferi*, but none on *I. laevigata*. The usual height is around 60 cm (2 ft).

Iris sibirica, also with grassy foliage, has several dainty flowers poised on each 60-cm to 1.2-m (2- to 4-ft) stem. These make excellent cut blooms and are often grown in mixed or herbaceous borders. The flowers are mostly blue, but variable from pale sky blue to deep violet and mauve. There are also white varieties. Although the species and its forms will grow in dry borders and in sun or light shade, they give a better account of themselves in moist soil.

Iris delavayi, a native of the Yunnan marshes of China, grows 90 cm to 1.2 m (3 to 4 ft) under favourable moist conditions. The flowers are deep violet with some white spotting and *I. versicolor*, with claret-purple flowers on 60-cm (2-ft) stems, is another for moist soil.

Hemerocallis (daylilies) are indispensable plants for the garden since they seem to thrive in almost any soil, climate or situation; indeed they have even been grown in shallow water. I have seen daylilies in the arctic and others on the equator which gives some idea of their adaptability. Once established the clumps can be left undisturbed for years, the arching foliage attractive even when the flowers are not in character. The large, funnel-shaped, often fragrant blooms only live a day, but since modern hybrids produce countless buds the flowering season extends over several weeks. Besides such species as the tawny-orange *Hemerocallis fulva* and its double form 'Kwanso' and *H. citrina*, pale lemon, there are countless cultivars available, many of which are diploids. These come in a wide range of shades from palest lemon to canary yellow, tangerine, pinks (like 'Pink Damask' and 'Pink Prelude') and crimsons (like 'Stafford' and 'Black Falcon').

Good late summer perennials are the lythrums and ligularias. The purple loose-Strife (*Lythrum salicaria*) and cultivars have spikes of bright rosy-red or pink flowers on branching 60- to 90-cm (2- to 3-ft) stems. They should be massed for maximum effect and sited where the setting sun can shine on and through their petals, then they glow like fire. The best cultivars are 'Fire Candle', rosy red; 'Robert', clear pink; and 'Rose Queen', rosy red.

Ligularias belong to the daisy family and are linked – and are frequently confused – with senecios. Nearly all the waterside types have large handsome leaves, tall branching stems and showy daisy flowers. They require plenty of water during the growing season and should be given plenty of sun.

Ligularia dentata (syn. *Senecio clivorum*) has large kidney-shaped smooth leaves about 45 cm (18 in) across and lots of rich orange flowers on sturdy stems which may go up to 1.5 m (5 ft) when established. It is inclined to be coarse, however, and should not be planted near weaker plants which it can smother, although it makes an excellent subject to grow near a stand pipe, as it masks the latter in summer. Cultivars of the species are more popular for planting in water gardens, particularly 'Greynog Gold', which is more compact and around 90 cm (3 ft) high with bronze-centred gold flowers; 'Othello', rich orange, and 'Desdemona', also orange but with purplish foliage.

Ligularia hodgsonii has purplish overtones on the kidney-shaped serrated leaves and through these come clusters of rich orange flowers on 69-cm (2-ft) stems. *L. japonica* is the Giant Ragwort, a plant needing plenty of water when it will run up to 1.5 m (5 ft); it has orange-yellow flowers on branching stems.

The most arresting member of the group, however, is *Ligularia przewalskii* (syn. *Senecio przewalskii*), a very distinct plant with stately, wand-like, almost black stems. These grow 1.5 to 1.8 m (5 to 6 ft) high and are tightly packed along their upper lengths with bright yellow, raggle-taggle rosettes of flowers. The dark-stemmed, dark-veined, deeply jagged leaves are also handsome and as long as the roots are damp the plant thrives in sun or partial shade. All the ligularias can be divided in spring.

Lysimachia clethroides is a relative of the primrose and a Japanese species of 60 or 90 cm (2 or 3 ft) with long, pendant, buddleia-like sprays of small white blossoms and broadly lanceolate leaves. It is suitable for sun or semi-shade. The Great Yellow Loosestrife, *L. vulgaris*, is a British species, inclined to spread so best confined to wild garden settings. It has whorls of bright yellow flowers around the stems and tapering leaves. The Romans believed that the flowers put under the yokes of oxen kept them from quarreling, hence the popular name.

Ligularia punctata, also British and very similar but less rampant, grows around 45 to 60 cm (1½ to 2 ft). The golden-flowered, golden-leaved form of Creeping Jenny (*L. nummularia*) is often useful at the edge of a pool since it makes a compact ground cover and will even grow down to the water. It is suitable for sun or partial shade.

Mimulus hybrids are best treated as annuals, sowing the seed in spring under glass and then planting them out in moist soil and semi-shade. The large speckled and marbled flowers grow 15 to 23 cm (6 to 9 in) in height and come in a wide range of colour combinations, but chiefly red, yellow and orange. *Lobelia fulgens*, the Cardinal Flower, with wine-red leaves and scarlet flowers is a dependable summer bloomer if the roots are moist. It grows 60 to 90 cm (2 to 3 ft) tall and is best renewed frequently from cuttings and protected in winter.

Trollius and ranunculus are other moisture lovers, the former with round, globe-like flowers of yellow or orange. *Trollius europaeus* cultivars grow 60 to 76 cm (2 to 2½ ft) tall and associate well with irises and primulas. *Ranunculus acris* 'Flore Pleno' is a double yellow buttercup and *R. aconitifolius* 'Flore Pleno', the Fair Maids of France, has double white flowers. Both grow around 45 cm (1½ ft).

Rodgersias have handsome leaves and sprays of spiraea-like flowers. *Rodgersia aesculifolia* has horse chestnut-like foliage and white flowers; *R. pinnata*, also with deeply divided leaves, is rosy red and *R. tabularis*, now *Astilboides tabularis* has yellowish-white blooms and round umbrella-like leaves.

Finally Arum Lilies (*Zantedeschia aethiopica*) are often successful in bog gardens, particularly the form known as 'Crowborough'. The roots should receive plenty of water in summer but be kept on the dry side in winter; best effected by covering them with dry leaves and a polythene cover or laying pieces of glass propped on bricks over the crowns.

Rodgersia tabularis

Appendix
Trees and Shrubs for Selected Sites

Shrubs and Climbers

Climbers

Actinidia (all)
Campsis (all)
Clematis (all those listed)
Hedera (all except *H. helix* 'Aborescens')
Hydrangea petiolaris
Jasminium (all those listed)
Lonicera japonica (and cultivars)
L. periclymenum (and cultivars)
Parthenocissus (all)
Passiflora
Pileostegia
Polygonum baldschuanicum
Schizophragma (all)
Solanum (all those listed)
Wisteria (all)

For hot, dry places

Campsis (all)
Carpenteria
Caryopteris
Ceanothus (all)
Choisya
Cistus (all)
Colutea (all those listed)
Cotinus
Cytisus (all)
Genista (all)
Hibiscus syriacus
Lavatera olbia
Olearia gunniana
O. scilloniensis
Passiflora
Perovskia
Phlomis (all)
Rosmarinus (all)
Santolina (all)
Senecio 'Sunshine'
Solanum (all those listed)
Spartium
Tamarix (all)
Yucca (all)

For shade

Aucuba
Azalea (all)
Buxus
Camellia
Danae
Elaeagnus (all those listed)
Euonymus fortunei (and cultivars)
Fatsia
Hedera (all)
Hydrangea macrophylla
H. petiolaris
Hypericum calycinum
Leycesteria formosa
Ligustrum (all those listed)
Lonicera nitida
Mahonia aquifolium
Pileostegia
Prunus laurocerasus
P. lusitanica (and cultivars)
Rhododendron (all)
Rubus spectabilis
R. ulmifolius 'Bellidiflorus'
Sarcococca (all)
Schizophragma (all)
Skimmia (all)
Viburnum davidii

For damp places

Cornus alba 'Sibirica'
C. stolonifera 'Flaviramea'
Sambucus (all)
Sorbaria (all)
Spiraea × billardieri 'Triumphans'
S. × vanhouttei
S. veitchii
Symphoricarpos (all those listed)
Viburnum opulus (and cultivars)

Suitable for chalk

Aucuba
Berberis (all)
Buddleia alternifolia

B. davidii
Ceanothus (all)
Cistus (all)
Clematis (all those listed)
Colutea (all)
Cornus mas
Cotoneaster (all)
Deutzia (all)
Euonymus (all)
Genista cinerea
Hebe (all)
Hypericum (all)
Jasminum (all)
Lavandula (all)
Lonicera (all)
Mahonia aquifolium
Olearia (all)
Paeonia delavayi
P. lutea
Philadelphus (all)
Prunus (all)
Pyracantha (all)
Sambucus (all)
Schizophragma (all)
Senecio 'Sunshine'
Spartium
Symphoricarpos (all)
Syringa (all)
Vitis (all)
Wiegela (all)
Yucca (all)

Requiring acid soil (intolerant of chalk)

Azalea (all)
Camellia (all)
Enkianthus (all)
Kalmia (all)
Magnolia (all those listed)
Pernettya
Pieris (all)
Rhododendron (all)

For seaside gardens

Escallonia (all)
Euonymus japonicus (and cultivars)
Fuchsia (all)
Hebe × andersonii 'Variegata'
H. brachysiphon
H. hulkeana
H. 'Midsummer Beauty'
H. salicifolia
H. speciosa hybrids
Hydrangea macrophylla
Lavatera olbia
Olearia macrodonta
Senecio rotundifolius
Tamarix (all)
Yucca (all)

With coloured or variegated foliage

Actinidia kolomikta
Berberis thunbergii 'Atropurpurea'
B.t. 'Rose Glow'
Buxus sempervirens (cultivars)
Cornus alba 'Elegantissima'
C. a. 'Spaethii'
Cotinus coggygria (and cultivars)
Daphne odora 'Marginata'
Elaeagnus pungens 'Maculata'
Euonymus fortunei (and cultivars)
E. japonicus (and cultivars)
Fuchsia magellanica 'Variegata'
Hebe andersonii 'Variegata'
Hedera canariensis 'Variegata'
H. colchica 'Dentata Variegata'
H. helix 'Marginata'
Ligustrum ovalifolium 'Argenteum'
L. o. 'Aureum'
Lonicera japonica 'Aureo-reticulata'
L. nitida 'Baggessen's Gold'
Osmanthus heterophyllus 'Aureomarginatus'
O. h. 'Variegatus'
Parthenocissus henryana
Prunus 'Cistena'
Sambucus nigra 'Aurea'
Vitis vinifera 'Purpurea'

With autumn colour

Azalea (deciduous)
Berberis 'Buccaneer'
B. jamesiana
Callicarpa
Cotoneaster franchettii
    sternianum
C. horizontalis
Enkianthus campanulatus
Euonymus alatus
E. europaeus
E. latifolius
E. yedoensis
Hamamelis mollis
H.m. 'Pallida'
Hypericum × inodorum 'Elstead'
Parthenocissus (all)
Vitis coignetiae
V. vinifera 'Brandt'

Grown for berries or fruits

Berberis 'Buccaneer'
B. jamesiana
Callicarpa
Cotoneaster (all)
Daphne mezereum
Euonymus europaeus
E. latifolius
E. yedoensis
Hypericum × inodorum 'Elstead'
Leycesteria
Pernettya
Pyracantha (all)
Skimmia japonica 'Foremannii'
    (and other female
    cultivars)
S. reevesiana
Symphoricarpos (all)
Viburnum betulifolium
V. opulus 'Compactum'
V. o. 'Fructuluteo'
Vitis

Winter flowering

Chimonanthus
Garrya
Hamamelis mollis
H. m. 'Pallida'
Jasminum nudiflorum
Lonicera fragrantissima
L. standishii
Mahonia 'Charity'
M. japonica
Viburnum × bodnantense
V. fragrans
V. tinus

Trees

Trees of distinct shape or habit

WEEPING OR PENDULOUS
Betula pendula 'Dalecarlica'
B. p. 'Tristis'
B. p. 'Youngii'
Fraxinus excelsior 'Pendula'
Gleditsia triacanthos 'Bujoti'
Morus alba 'Pendula'
Populus tremula 'Pendula'
Prunus 'Kiku-shidare Sakura'
P. 'Shimidsu Sakura'
P. × yedoensis 'Perpendens'
Pyrus salicifolia 'Pendula'
Salix × chrysocoma
S. purpurea 'Pendula'
Sophora japonica 'Pendula'
Tilia petiolaris
Ulmus glabra 'Camperdownii'
U. g. 'Pendula'

OF NARROW, UPRIGHT
(FASTIGIATE) HABIT
Carpinus betulus 'Columnaris'
Fagus sylvatica 'Dawyck'
Malus tschonoskii
M. 'Van Eseltine'
Prunus 'Amanogawa'
P. × hillieri 'Spire'
P. 'Umineko'
Robinia fertilis 'Monument'
Sorbus aucuparia 'Sheerwater
    Seedling'
S. 'Joseph Rock'
Ulmus × vegeta 'Groeneveld'

OF WIDESPREADING OR
PICTURESQUE HABIT
Acer platanoides 'Globosum'
Arbutus andrachnoides
A. unedo
Catalpa bignonioides
Malus floribunda
Mespilus germanica
Morus nigra
Prunus 'Shirofugen'
P. 'Shirotae'
Sorbus scalaris
Trachycarpus fortunei

Notable for autumn colouring of leaf

Acer campestre
A. capillipes
A. davidii 'George Forrest'
A. griseum
A. japonicum 'Vitifolium'
A. nikoense
A. palmatum
A. p. 'Heptalobum Osakazuki'
Cornus florida (and cultivars)
Crataegus pinnatifida major
Liquidambar styraciflua
Malus tschonoskii

Nyssa sinensis
N. sylvatica
Prunus × hillieri
P. sargentii
Quercus coccinea 'Splendens'
Sorbus sargentiana

Notable for red or purple foliage, mainly persistent throughout growing season

Acer palmatum
    'Atropurpureum'
A. platanoides 'Crimson King'
Fagus sylvatica 'Purpurea
    Pendula'
F. s. 'Riversii'
F. s. 'Rohanii'
Prunus blireana
Prunus cerasifera 'Pissardii'
Quercus robur 'Fastigiata
    Purpurea'

Notable for yellow or golden foliage, mainly persistent throughout the growing season

Acer japonicum 'Aureum'
A. negundo 'Auratum'
Catalpa bignonioides 'Aurea'
Fagus sylvatica 'Aurea Pendula'
Gleditsia triacanthos 'Sunburst'
Populus 'Serotina Aurea'
Quercus robur 'Concordia'
Robinia pseudoacacia 'Frisia'
Ulmus × sarniensis 'Dicksonii'

Trees notable for grey or silver foliage

Eucalyptus species, particularly:
Eucalyptus gunnii
E. niphophila
Pyrus canescens
P. nivalis
P. salicifolia 'Pendula'
Salix alba 'Sericea'
Sorbus aria 'Lutescens'

Trees with conspicuously variegated leaves

Acer negundo 'Elegans'
A. n. 'Variegatum'
A. platanoides 'Drummondii'
Liriodendron tulipifera
    'Aureomarginatum'
Quercus cerris 'Variegata'

Trees with ornamental bark

Acer capillipes
A. davidii 'George Forrest'
A. griseum
A. palmatum 'Senkaki'
Arbutus andrachnoides
Betula costata
B. ermanii
B. jacquemontii
B. pendula 'Tristis'
Eucalyptus dalrympleana
E. niphophila
Fraxinus excelsior 'Aurea'
Prunus serrula
Salix alba 'Chermesina'
S. a. 'Vitellina'
S. daphnoides
Tilia platyphyllos 'Rubra'

A select list of trees with seasonal flowering or berrying qualities

WINTER/EARLY SPRING
FLOWERING
Arbutus andrachnoides
Prunus 'Accolade'
P. × blireana
P. cerasifera 'Pissardii'
P. dulcis and cultivars
P. 'Kursar'
P. mume and cultivars
P. sargentii
P. subhirtella 'Autumnalis'
Salix daphnoides 'Aglaia'

SPRING/EARLY SUMMER
FLOWERING
Aesculus × carnea 'Briotii'
A. pavia 'Atrosanguinea'
Amelanchier lamarckii
Cercis siliquastrum
Cornus florida (and cultivars)
C. kousa chinensis
C. nuttallii
Crataegus oxyacantha 'Paul's
    Scarlet'
C. o. 'Plena'
C. o. 'Rosea Flore Pleno'
Davidia involucrata
Fraxinus ornus
Laburnum × watereri 'Vossii'
Magnolia (most species and
    cultivars)
Malus (species and cultivars)
Paulownia fargesii
P. tomentosa
Prunus persica and cultivars

MID-SUMMER/AUTUMN
Arbutus unedo
Catalpa bignonioides
Crataegus lavallei (berry)
C. pinnatifida major (berry)
Eucryphia × nymansensis
    'Nymansay'
Koelreuteria paniculata
Ligustrum lucidum

Liriodendron tulipifera
Magnolia grandiflora
Malus (species and cultivars)
  (berry)
Robinia × hillieri
Sorbus (all species and
  cultivars) (berry)

Evergreen trees

Arbutus andrachnoides
A. unedo
Eucalyptus (species)
Eucryphia × nymansensis
  'Nymansay'
Ligustrum lucidum
Magnolia grandiflora
Metrosideros (species)
Myrtus apiculata
Quercus ilex

Trees for various soils

TREES PARTICULARLY
SUCCESSFUL ON HEAVY
CLAY SOILS
Acer negundo (cultivars)
A. platanoides (and cultivars)
Species and cultivars of:
Carpinus
Crataegus
Eucalyptus
Fraxinus
Laburnum
Malus
Prunus
Salix
Sorbus
Ulmus

TREES SUCCESSFUL ON SHALLOW
CHALK SOILS
Acer negundo (and cultivars)
A. platanoides (and cultivars)
Aesculus (most species and
  cultivars)
Arbutus
Catalpa
Cercis
Davidia
Fagus
Fraxinus
Ligustrum
Magnolia loebneri (and
  cultivars)
Malus
Prunus
Pyrus
Robinia
Sorbus aria
Tilia
Ulmus

TREES SUCCESSFUL ON DRY,
ACID, SANDY SOILS
Acer negundo (and cultivars)
Betula (species and cultivars)
Cercis siliquastrum
Gleditsia

Populus tremula
Robinia (species and cultivars)

TREES SUCCESSFUL IN MOIST
SOILS
Amelanchier (species and
  cultivars)
Betula
Crataegus
Mespilus
Quercus palustris
Salix
Sorbus aucuparia

Conifers

For windbreaks
Chamaecyparis lawsoniana (and
  medium-growing
  cultivars)
× Cupressocyparis leylandii
Picea omorika
Pinus nigra
P. sylvestris
Thuja plicata
Tsuga canadensis

For hedges

Chamaecyparis lawsoniana
× Cupressocyparis leylandii
Juniperus × media 'Hetzii'
Taxus baccata
T. × media 'Hicksii'
Thuja occidentalis 'Smaragd'
T. plicata
T. p. 'Atrovirens'
Tsuga canadensis

**For the small rock garden or
trough garden**

Abies balsamea 'Hudsonia'
Chamaecyparis lawsoniana
  'Minima Aurea'
C. obtusa 'Nana'
C. pisifera 'Nana'
Cryptomeria japonica
  'Vilmoriniana'
Juniperus communis 'Compressa'
J. squamata 'Blue Star'
Picea abies 'Gregoryana'
P. a. 'Nidiformis'
Pinus sylvestris 'Beuvronensis'
Thuja plicata 'Rogersii'
Tsuga canadensis 'Cole'

For seaside gardens

× Cupressocyparis leylandii
Cupressus
Juniperus
Pinus mugo (and forms)
P. nigra

For winter colour

Cedrus atlantica glauca
Chamaecyparis lawsoniana
  'Lanei'
C. l. 'Minima Aurea'
C. l. 'Pygmaea Argentea'
C. obtusa 'Nana Lutea'
C. pisifera 'Filifera Aurea'
C. p. 'Plumosa Aurea Nana'
× Cupressocyparis leylandii
  'Castlewellan Gold'
Juniperus chinensis 'Aurea'
Picea pungens (cultivars)
Pinus sylvestris 'Aurea'
Taxus baccata 'Fastigiata
  Aurea'
Thuja occidentalis 'Lutea Nana'
T. o. 'Rheingold'
T. plicata 'Rogersii'
T. p. 'Stoneham Gold'

For ground cover - prostrate

Juniperus communis 'Repanda'
J. horizontalis 'Glauca'

**For ground cover - semi-
prostrate**

Juniperus horizontalis 'Plumosa'
J. × media 'Pfitzeriana'
J. × m. 'Pfitzeriana Aurea'
J. sabina tamariscifolia
J. virginiana 'Grey Owl'
Taxus baccata 'Repandens'

For shade

Juniperus × media 'Pfitzeriana'
J. × m. 'Pfitzeriana Aurea'
J. sabina 'Tamariscifolia'
Taxus baccata and cultivars (no
  golden forms)

Biographical Notes

Adrian Bloom has made a name for himself as a specialist on dwarf and other conifers and the heaths and heathers which associate so superbly with them.

As visitors to Bressingham Gardens, near Diss in Norfolk will be well aware, Adrian Bloom has added to the famous collection of herbaceous perennial plants there a heather and conifer garden of the greatest interest and beauty. He sees these as very much plants of the future with their ease of maintenance and year-round visual appeal.

In a very real sense Adrian Bloom is attracting to this group of plants the kind of acclaim which his father, Alan Bloom, has brought to perennials. The collection in his own garden has been built up over nearly 20 years, during which time he has also been responsible for the commercial production of the huge range of hardy plants raised by the Bressingham establishement. Before that he worked in Europe and the United States of America.

In recent years he has often appeared on television gardening programmes, and he is the author of a number of books.

Alan Bloom, V.M.H., has had a lifelong association with plants being a son of a pioneer market flower grower in Cambridgeshire. Having gained experience in various nurseries after leaving school he decided to go in for the production of plants rather than market flowers. He began in business on his own account in 1931 at the age of 24 years, first at Oakington and later, at the end of the war, acquired Bressingham Hall near Diss in Norfolk with its 220 acres.

Today about 5000 species and cultivars of hardy herbaceous plants are grown, making up by far the most important collection of its kind in Europe. They include not only a wealth of uncommon species but new cultivars which have been bred at Bressingham. Many have received awards from The Royal Horticultural Society, and the island bed method of growing perennials, displayed so perfectly in the famous gardens at Bressingham, is widely accepted as the most effective and trouble free.

The farm and nursery now extend to 430 acres and although the business is still essentially wholesale there is a retail mail order catalogue of the greatest interest to discerning gardeners. The gardens are open to visitors on Thursday and Sunday afternoons between spring and autumn.

Mr Bloom was awarded the Victoria Medal of Honour by The Royal Horticultural Society in 1971, in recognition of his great services to horticulture.

Jack Harkness, one of the most respected and successful rosarians of the present time, is senior director of the famous rose nursery which bears his surname. The word successful is used advisedly for since he began breeding roses in 1962 – as distinct from growing them, which began much earlier – he has won 225 awards from the The Royal National Rose Society and from foreign trials. His best cultivars he would consider to include 'Escapade', 'Alexander', 'Elizabeth Harkness', 'Mountbatten', 'Southampton', 'Margaret Merril', 'Compassion' and 'Yesterday' – a galaxy of talent by any reckoning. In addition, he either assisted in, or directed, the staging of the exhibits which won for his company the R.N.R.S.'s Championship Trophy on no less than 23 occasions. (Harkness's have won it 40 times overall, nearly half the total number of times it has been awarded – a remarkable achievement considering the competition.)

Born in Shropshire and educated at Whitgift School, Croydon, he was apprenticed to the Slieve Donard Nursery Co., Newcastle, Co. Down, where he spent the years from 1934 to 1937. He then joined the family firm of R. Harkness and Co., of Hitchin, Hertfordshire.

Mr Harkness has served on numerous committees of the Royal National Rose Society. In 1969 he was elected a vice-president of the society, and in 1980 he received its highest honour, the Dean Hole Medal. He was editor of the society's publications from 1979–1983, and wrote their handbooks, *How to Grow Roses* and *The Rose Directory*. He has written three other books on roses, and is a frequent contributor to the gardening press. He is Secretary of the British Association of Rose Breeders.

Royton E. Heath, F.L.S., F.R.I.H. (N.Z.), an amateur gardener who is an acknowledged authority on rock and alpine plants, has been growing these fascinating members of the plant community for over fifty years. His books on the subject have been widely acclaimed in Britain and abroad.

He has studied alpines in their natural habitats on many European mountains, and has arranged displays of plants from his extensive collection at many horticultural shows.

For his exhibits of rock garden shrubs and other dwarf plants he has won several hundred prizes and awards, including the Lindley Medal of The Royal Horticultural Society for an exhibit of outstanding educational value.

Mr Heath is well known as a judge of alpine plants at provincial and national shows, and he has lectured all over Britain. He has also broadcast on the radio and appeared on television.

In 1958 Mr Heath was elected a Fellow of the Linnean Society and he is also a Fellow of The Royal New Zealand Institute of Horticulture.

Frances Perry, M.B.E., V.M.H., F.L.S., writer, journalist, lecturer and broadcaster, has achieved fame as a horticulturist and is the Royal Horticultural Society's first woman Vice-President. This singular honour was accorded her in 1979.

Her influence on gardening has been mainly through her work in the field of education – she was the first principal of Norwood Hall College of Agricultural Education and Horticultural Organizer for the County of Middlesex for many years – her various books on many aspects of gardening, her many writings which include a weekly article in The Observer newspaper, of which she is gardening correspondent, and appearances on radio and television.

Mrs Perry was trained at Swanley Horticultural College in Kent, and early on came under the influence of that great gardener and near neighbour, the late E. A. Bowles. With his guidance and that of her father-in-law, the late Amos Perry, a plantsman of great distinction, she had unique opportunities of which she made the most.

She has travelled in all five continents often lecturing and always looking for plants.

In 1972 The Royal Horticultural Society awarded Mrs Perry the coveted Victoria Medal of Honour, and, eight years prior to that, a Veitch Gold Medal. She was awarded the M.B.E. in 1962.

She is a 'Member at Large' of the Garden Club of America of which there are only two non-Americans and has received the Sarah Francis Chapman Medal from the Garden Club of America, for literary achievement.

Percy Thrower, V.M.H., N.D.H., has become a household name to millions of gardeners and non-gardeners alike through his appearances on televsion, radio broadcasts, his books and other writings and his many public lectures.

After leaving school he worked for four years with his father, the head gardener at Horwood House in Buckinghamshire. Then, at the age of 18, he became a journeyman gardener in the Royal Gardens at Windsor Castle.

A career in public parks followed. Two years at Leeds and nine at Derby preceded his appointment at Parks Superintendent at Shrewsbury, a post he held for 28 years until he retired in the spring of 1974.

Percy Thrower began his broadcasting career over 36 years ago and since those days has made hundreds of sound broadcasts and television appearances. He escorts many gardening tours abroad and is also joint owner of a leading rose nursery and general garden centre business in Shropshire.

His services to horticulture were recognized by The Royal Horticultural Society in 1974 when he was awarded the Victoria Medal of Honour.

Dennis Woodland could hardly have had a better grounding for his future career than student training at The Royal Botanic Gardens, Kew and The Royal Horticultural Society's Wisley Gardens in Surrey. After leaving Wisley he gained experience on several well-known nurseries before joining Hillier Nurseries of Winchester in 1950, the firm for which he has worked ever since.

As Hillier's horticultural consultant he spends his time visiting gardens all over Britain and overseas advising owners on such matters of design and planting problems.

He frequently leads botanical and plant hunting trips to the Mediterranean and mountain districts of Europe, and the Himalayas and lectures widely on his travels and on gardening and botanical subjects.

Index

Index

Morina 147
Morisia 224
Morning Glory, *see* Ipomoea
Morus 85, 248
Mountain Ash, *see* Sorbus
Mulberry 85
mulches 47, 72d
Mullein, *see* Verbascum
Muscari 72, 187, 202
  armeniacum 204
Myosotis (Forget-me-not)
  160, 181, 187
Myrtle 85
Myrtus 85, 249

Narcissus (incl. Daffodil) 187,
  202–3, *204*, 212, 224
  bulb 187d
Nasturtium 163, 167, 171
Nemesia 177
Nemophila 175
Nepeta 147
Nerine 203
Nicandra 172
Nierembergia 177
Nigella 163, 172–4
Nuphar 236
nurseries, commercial 8
Nymphaea (Water Lily) 233,
  234–6
  'Marliacea Chromatella' *235*
  planting 235d
Nymphoides 236
  peltata 237d
Nyssa 85, 248

Oak 89–90
Obedient Plant, *see* Physos-
  tegia
Oenothera 147, 185
Olearia 32–3, 247
Omphalodes 147, 224–5
Onion, ornamental, *see* Al-
  lium
orangeries 8
Origanum 147–8
  vulgare 'Aureum' *6*
Ornithogalum 203
  thyrsoides 203d
Orontium 237
Osmanthus 33–4, 247
Ostrya 85
Oxalis 203, 225
oxygenators 239–40

Paeonia 34, 148, 247
  lutea 'L'Espérance' *33*, 247
  officinalis 148d
Pansy 175, 187
Papaver (Poppy) 148, 163,
  174, 181, 225
  nudicaule 182
Paraquat 12
Paronychia 212, 225
Parthenocissus 34, 247, 248
  tricuspidata 'Veitchii' *10*
Pasque Flower, *see* Pulsatilla

Passiflora (Passion Flower)
  34, 247
  caerulea 34d
Paulownia 85, 248
Peach, flowering 89
Pear, ornamental 89
Peony, *see* Paeonia
Penstemon 148, 225
perennials *126*
  grouping 128
  height 128
  planning 128, 128d
  planting 129d
  preparations for 127
  selection 129–59
  spacing 128
  used as annuals or biennials
    160
Pernettya 35, 225, 247, 248
Perovskia 35, 247
Petunia 166–7, *179*
Philadelphus 14, 35, 247
Phlomis 35–6, 247
Phlox 148–9, 177, 209, 225
  maculata 154
Physostegia 149
Picea 107–8, 249
Pieris 36, 225–6, 247
  formosa forrestii 36
Pileostegia 36, 247
pinching out 167d
Pinks, *see* Dianthus
Pinus 108–9, 249
Plane, *see* Platanus
plans: for conifer and heather
  borders 116–17d
Plantain Lily, *see* Hosta
plant hunting 7–8, 9
Platanus 85–6
  orientalis 76
Platycodon 149
Plum, flowering 89
Podocarpus 109–10
Polemonium 149
Polyanthus 160, 181, 187
Polygala 226
Polygonum 36–7, 149–51, 247
  bistorta 150
Pontederia 237
pools *223*, *230*, 232d
  design 231
  materials 231–3
  planting 233–4, 233d
  plant selection for 234–46
  in rock garden 211d
  siting 231
  in winter 234
Poplar, *see* Populus
Poppy, *see* Papaver
  Californian 181
Populus 86, 248
Portulaca 176
Potamogeton 240
Potentilla 37, 151, 226
Primula (incl. Polyanthus)
  160, 181, 187, 226–7, 242,
  243, 244

Privet 14, 31, 82
propagation:
  grafting 8
  from seed 8, 162–4
Prunella 151
Prunus 37, 86–9, 247, 248, 249
  'Kiku-shidare Sakura' *88*
Pseudotsuga 110
Ptilotrichum 227
Pulmonaria 151
Pulsatilla 151, 227
Puschkinia 203
Pyracantha 37, 247, 248
Pyrethrum 151–2
Pyrus 89, 248, 249

Quamoclit 171
Quercus 89–90, 248, 249

Ramonda 227
Ranunculus 203–5, 227, 240,
  246
Raoulia 227
Red Hot Poker, *see* Kniphofia
red spider mite 48
Rheum 244
rhizomes 187
Rhododendron 13, 38, 247
Rhodohypoxis 227
Rhubarb, ornamental 244
Rhus 90
  cotinus, see Cotinus
Ribes 38
Robinia 90–1, 248, 249
  pseudoacacia 'Frisia' *92*
rock garden *223*
  annuals for 175–7
  construction 210–12d
  rocks for 211–12
rock plants:
  pests and diseases 214
  planting 214
  propagation 214
  selection 215–29
  siting 209
  soil for 209–10
Rodgersia 152
  aesculifolia 243
  tabularis 246d
Rosa (Rose) 45–67
  'Banksian Yellow' *65*
  classification 48
  climbing 59–61
  cultivation 47
  diseases 48
  'Double Delight' *50*
  feeding 47
  floribundas 53–6
  gallica 'Versicolor' *63*
  hybrid teas 48–53
  miniature 58–9
  'Mme Grégoire Staechelin'
    44
  modern shrub 57–8
  moyesii 65
  mulching 47
  old garden varieties 61–4